Strategies and Impact
of
Contemporary Radicalism

Studies of the Research Institute on
International Change, Columbia University
Zbigniew Brzezinski, series editor

Zbigniew Brzezinski is Herbert Lehman Professor of Government and director of the Research Institute on International Change at Columbia University, where he has taught since 1960. Dr. Brzezinski serves also in the Carter administration as assistant to the president for national security affairs.

Radicalism in the Contemporary Age
Seweryn Bialer and Sophia Sluzar, editors
*Vol. 3—Strategies and Impact
of Contemporary Radicalism*

To understand contemporary society, it has become more
and more essential to understand the phenomenon of radicalism—the aspirations of radical movements, the strategies and
tactics of radicalism, and the impact of radicalism on contemporary society. *Radicalism in the Contemporary Age*
grew out of the recognition of this need. A study in three
volumes, it is based on original papers that were prepared for
a series of workshops held in 1975 at the Research Institute
on International Change, Columbia University, and then revised in light of the workshop discussions.

This volume, *Strategies and Impact of Contemporary Radicalism,* deals principally with three themes: the models and
strategies of revolutionary change adopted by diverse radical
movements, the impact of radicalism on the societies where it
exists, and the prospects of radical success in the political
arena. Seweryn Bialer analyzes the reasons for the declining
appeal of the Soviet model for radical movements, the causes
for the upsurge in socialist influence in industrialized democracies, and the problems posed by the deradicalizing tendencies in West European communist movements. John Dunn's
chapter examines the conditions under which modern revolutions are possible and the dilemma in the relationship between goals and actual results achieved by the revolutionaries.
Alexander Dallin deals with the relevance of the traditional
communist models of revolution in the contemporary period.
Peter Lange and Massimo Teodori present and analyze the
strategies evolved by the French and the Italian communist
parties and by the New Left in Europe. Alfred Stepan addresses a specific aspect of response to pressures for change,
namely, that of the military in Latin America. He examines
in particular the "inclusionary" response in Peru as contrast-

ed with the "exclusionary" corporatism of the Brazilian or Chilean military. Charles S. Maier discusses the factors and conditions that limit the vulnerability of Western democracies to the appeals of radicalism, and Samuel P. Huntington closes with a reexamination of the concept of stability, its meaning and components, in the contemporary era.

Sources of Contemporary Radicalism, the first volume of this study, includes contributions on the definitional aspects and the sources and carriers of contemporary radicalism, the lack of socialism in the United States, the phenomenon of student radicalism in the U.S., differing radical responses in France and Italy after World War II, and peasant discontent in modern times. The closing chapter is a valuable interpretative survey of the literature on radicalism.

Radical Visions of the Future, the second volume of this study, treats the visionary component of radicalism, the component that encompasses an image of the "good society" and that provides inspiration and possibly even direction to a radical movement in its combat with the existing order.

* * *

Seweryn Bialer, an expert on comparative communism and revolutionary change, teaches in the Department of Political Science at Columbia University and is director of programs at the Research Institute on International Change.

Sophia Sluzar is assistant director of the Research Institute on International Change. A doctoral candidate in Columbia University's Department of History, she has taught modern European history at Pace College for four years.

Radicalism
in the
Contemporary Age

Seweryn Bialer, editor
Sophia Sluzar, associate editor

Volume 3

Strategies and Impact
of
Contemporary Radicalism

CONTRIBUTORS

SEWERYN BIALER	ALEXANDER DALLIN
JOHN DUNN	SAMUEL P. HUNTINGTON
PETER LANGE	CHARLES S. MAIER
ALFRED STEPAN	MASSIMO TEODORI

PREFACE BY ZBIGNIEW BRZEZINSKI

WESTVIEW PRESS
BOULDER, COLORADO

A Westview Special Study

Copyright © 1977 by the Research Institute on International Change, Columbia University

Published 1977 in the United States of America by
   Westview Press, Inc.
   1898 Flatiron Court
   Boulder, Colorado 80301
   Frederick A. Praeger, Publisher and Editorial Director

Library of Congress Cataloging in Publication Data
Main entry under title:
Radicalism in the contemporary age.
   (Studies of the Research Institute on International Change,
Columbia University)
   Papers from a series of workshops held at the Research Institute
on International Change, Columbia University, Feb.–May 1975.
   1. Radicalism—Collected works. I. Bialer, Seweryn. II. Sluzar,
Sophia. III. Series: Columbia University. Research Institute on
International Change. Studies of the Research Institute on International
Change, Columbia University.
HX15.R25   320.5'3   76-39890
ISBN 0-89158-129-4

Printed and bound in the United States of America

Contents

Preface

The three volumes composing *Radicalism in the Contemporary Age* are the outcome of a series of workshops held at the Research Institute on International Change between February and May 1975. Four workshops were organized to examine the sources of radicalism; the aspirations of radical movements; the strategies and tactics of radicalism; and the conditions of success and the impact of radicalism on contemporary societies.

The first workshop was designed to explore whether and to what extent the explanations given in past studies for the development of radicalism—explanations such as rapid changes in the stratification system, rising expectations, the characteristics of marginality in individuals, and so forth—still held true. It seemed possible that contemporary conditions required a different explanatory framework for radical behavior. The second workshop, dealing with the aspirations of radical movements, was organized because it seemed important to examine not only the much neglected "visionary" aspect of radical movements, but also the function of this vision in the formation, development, or decline of radical movements. By developing and linking new revolutionary theories with new forms of revolutionary warfare—for example, in the perception of the relation of forces underlying the revolutionary process, in the selection of methods, and in the expectations of success—radical movements since World War II have demonstrated distinctive characteristics.

Thus, the third workshop was devoted to a partial examination of these aspects of radicalism. The final workshop dealt not only with questions regarding the kinds of revolutions possible in the contemporary world, but also with conditions of stability in industrialized democracies in an era of rapid global change. It should be noted that the focus of the workshops was on radicalism in the United States and Western Europe; developing and communist societies entered only marginally into the discussions.

We attempted to assure continuity in the workshops by inviting to all four a core group of the same participants. We also tried to assure that the participants would be heterogeneous in terms of age as well as in their political and methodological orientations. The papers for the workshops were distributed to the participants in advance so that each session would be devoted entirely to discussion led off by a principal commentator.

It had been our original intention to publish not only the papers from each workshop, but also the remarks of the principal commentators as well as the discussions. The constraints of publication have necessitated the abandonment of this ambitious scheme and, we regret, the elimination of some papers. Nevertheless, complete transcripts of the discussions and the original papers, as well as summaries, are available and can be consulted at the institute's library.

An enterprise of this nature involves the efforts of many persons. First of all, I would like to thank the principal commentators and the authors of the papers for the workshops. Seymour Martin Lipset (then at Harvard University, now at Stanford University) spoke at the first workshop, Februrary 5, 1975, on "Sources of Radicalism in the United States"; Juan Linz (Yale University) wrote a paper on "The Sources of Radicalism in the Iberian Peninsula"; and Sidney Tarrow (Cornell University) wrote on "Sources of French Radicalism: Archaic Protest, Antibureaucratic Rebellion, and Anticapitalist Revolt." The principal commentator was Mark Kesselman (Columbia University). The paper by Stanley

Rothman (Smith College) et al., "Ethnic Variations in Student Radicalism: Some New Perspectives," was discussed by Dr. David Gutmann (Center of Psycho-Social Studies, Chicago). The principal commentator for Henry Landsberger's (University of North Carolina at Chapel Hill) paper, "The Sources of Rural Radicalism," was Donald Zagoria (Hunter College, City University of New York). William H. Overholt (Hudson Institute) contributed a paper on "Sources of Radicalism and Revolution: A Survey of Literature."

At the workshop on March 5, the discussion of a paper by Robert Nisbet (Columbia University), "The Function of the Vision of the Future in Radical Movements," was initiated by Leszek Kolakowski (Oxford University). William Griffith (Massachusetts Institute of Technology) and Ira Katznelson (University of Chicago) discussed papers by Bertell Ollman (New York University), "Marx's Vision of Communism: A Reconstruction"; Maurice Meisner (University of Wisconsin), "Utopian and Dystopian Elements in the Maoist Vision of the Future"; and Dick Howard (State University of New York, Stony Brook), "The Future as Present: Political and Theoretical Implications." Marcus Raskin (Institute of Policy Studies) spoke on "Futurology and Its Radical Critique."

At the April 2 workshop the principal commentator on Alexander Dallin's (Stanford University) paper, "Retreat from Optimism: On Marxian Models of Revolution," was Michel Oksenberg (University of Michigan). Bogdan Denitch (Queens College, City University of New York) introduced the discussion of Henry Bienen's (Princeton University) paper, "New Theories of Revolution," and Sidney Tarrow led off the discussion on Peter Lange's (Harvard University) paper, "The French and Italian Communist Parties: Postwar Strategy and Domestic Society." Klaus Mehnert (*Osteuropa*) gave the initial comments on Massimo Teodori's (Rome) paper, "The New Lefts in Europe."

At the fourth workshop the discussions were initiated by Lewis Coser (State University of New York, Stony Brook), on John Dunn's (Cambridge University) "The Success and

Failure of Modern Revolutions"; Douglas Chalmers (Columbia University), on Alfred Stepan's (Yale University) "Inclusionary and Exclusionary Military Responses to Radicalism with Special Attention to Peru"; and Seweryn Bialer (Columbia University), on Charles Maier's (Harvard University, now at Duke University) "Beyond Revolution? Resistance and Vulnerability to Radicalism in Advanced Western Societies." Samuel Huntington (Harvard University) spoke on "The Meanings of Stability in the Modern Era."

In addition to the authors of papers and the principal commentators, the participants in the discussions at the workshops were Isaac Balbus (York, City University of New York), Thomas Bernstein (Yale University, now at Columbia University), Bernard Brown (Graduate Center, City University of New York), Mauro Calamandrei (*L'Espresso*), Alexander Erlich (Columbia University), Stuart Fagan (Columbia University), Oleh Fedyshyn (Richmond, City University of New York), Clifford Geertz (Institute for Advanced Study, Princeton University), Charles Issawi (Columbia University, now at Princeton University), Joachim Kondziela (University of Lublin, Poland), Irving Kristol (Graduate Center, City University of New York, and *Public Interest*), Robbin Laird (Columbia University), Robert Lane (Yale University), S. Robert Lichter (Harvard University), Egon Neuberger (State University of New York, Stony Brook), William Odom (U.S. Military Academy, West Point), Harvey Picker (Columbia University), Carl Riskin (Columbia University), Joseph Rothschild (Columbia University), James Schmidt (Columbia University, now at University of Texas), Bhabani Sen Gupta (Nehru University, New Delhi), Allan Silver (Columbia University), Bruce Smith (Columbia University), Fritz Stern (Columbia University), and Ronald Tiersky (Amherst College).

It gives me pleasure to acknowledge the important contribution rendered by the staff of the institute. Mitchell Brody was helpful in the early planning stages of the workshops. Richard Royal helped not only with the organizational aspects but also in the preparation of summaries of the discussions. Richard Snyder and Robert Nurick were invaluable in contributing their technical and substantive expertise during the revision and preparation of the papers for publication. The institute owes a special debt to Reet Varnik, to whom the preparation of the transcripts was entrusted. Subsequently she prepared summaries of the discussions and had the responsibility of making many of the initial revisions on the papers. Her considerable editorial talents are deeply appreciated.

A central role in our efforts was played by the institute's director of programs, Seweryn Bialer, who designed the broad intellectual structure of the enterprise and provided the intellectual impetus for it, and by the assistant director of the institute, Sophia Sluzar, who contributed creatively to the intellectual format and also supplied the indispensable organizational leadership. Without them, this series would not have been realized.

The institute also wishes to acknowledge and to thank the National Endowment for the Humanities for providing partial funding for the workshops.

Zbigniew Brzezinski

Strategies and Impact
of
Contemporary Radicalism

Seweryn Bialer, an expert on comparative communism and revolutionary change, teaches in the Department of Political Science at Columbia University and is director of programs at the Research Institute on International Change. He is author of Stalin and His Generals, *which deals with Soviet World War II memoirs, as well as of numerous articles on Soviet and Eastern European affairs and on radicalism. His most recent publication is "The Soviet Political Elite and Internal Developments in the USSR," chapter 2 in* The Soviet Empire: Expansion and Detente, *edited by William E. Griffith (volume 9 of* Critical Choices for Americans, *published by Lexington Press). Professor Bialer is currently working on a monograph on Leninism and the peasantry in the Russian revolutions.*

1

The Resurgence and Changing Nature of the Left in Industrialized Democracies

Seweryn Bialer

The essays in this volume cover a very wide range of issues related to the strategies of contemporary radicalism in industrialized democracies and their impact on the social, cultural, and political life of those societies. This introductory chapter will address itself to four issues central to many of the essays in this volume and to the discussion in the workshops for which the essays were written. The four issues are—

1. the changes in the emulative standards which inform contemporary radical thinking and movements in industrialized democracies;
2. the growth of the influence of socialist ideas in the intellectual and political realm;
3. the connection between the growth of socialist influence and the crisis of liberal democracy;
4. the different types of strategic expressions of the radical impulse in industrialized democracies and their political prospects.

Radicalism and the Soviet Model

In chapter 2 of this book, Professor John Dunn shows
that the successes and failures of modern revolutions can
be evaluated in various ways, depending on the purpose of
the evaluation. My primary interest is the light an evaluation
may throw on the revolutionary prospects and the impact
of radicalism in contemporary industrialized democracies.
In this respect, three questions seem of special relevance:

1. To what extent do revolutions and the achievements
   of established revolutionary regimes provide a vision
   of the desired future, adopted and consciously emulated
   by radical movements and groups?
2. To what extent do the strategies, tactics, and methods
   by which the revolutionary regimes came to power
   (whether in reality or according to their "charter
   myth")[1] serve as standards to be emulated and followed
   by radical movements and groups?
3. To what extent does the material power and political
   influence of victorious revolutionary regimes further
   the international cause of radicalism?

The first question is absolutely essential for a number
of reasons. From a logical standpoint, the answer to this
question largely determines the answers to the other two.
Moreover, if politics is not entirely concerned with a quest
for power but also with ideas and values, the answer to this
question largely determines the answer to the other two
questions from a political standpoint, that is, from the
point of view of the political actors, both proradical and
antiradical. Finally, it can be said that the nature of the
answer largely determines the assessment by the analyst
himself of the most probable prospects and expected impact
not only of radicalism in general, but of different types of
radicalism in different contemporary industrialized societies[2].

In addressing the first question, I propose to concentrate
primarily on the Soviet-type model as the standard for
radical emulation. I do this not only because it is the most
advanced, durable, widespread, and historically influential

model of a successful radical transformation in the twentieth century, but also because—given that the level of socio-economic development in the Soviet Union and Eastern Europe is closest to that of the Western industrialized democracies—it is the most relevant model for discussing radicalism in industrialized societies.

The Soviet model of socialism, that is, the model on which both the Soviet Union and most East European regimes are based, is at present discredited among radical movements and groups of all shades and orientations. It is totally and convincingly discredited among virtually the entire spectrum of groups that constitute the New Left in industrialized democratic societies. It is discredited among most of the parties of the old left which constitute a vital and important force in the political life of their countries (i.e., the Italian, French, Spanish, Dutch, Swedish, British, and Japanese communist parties, which compose over 90 percent of the total membership of the communist parties out of power in developed societies).[3] In some cases, this discredit can be verified beyond question among both the membership and the leadership of those parties. In other cases the evidence is primarily based on the statements of the leaders of particular parties and radical groups which dissociate themselves verbally from attachment and commitment to the Soviet-type model.

The attachment and open support for the Soviet-type model is still strong among the numerous but marginal and sectarian communist parties; however, even there examples of estrangement from the Soviet model are easy to discern. There is, of course, a commitment to revolutionary change in the Third World. However, when it comes to a commitment to change along the lines of the Soviet model, let alone loyalty to Moscow, among the various "people's," "socialist," "liberationist," "revolutionary," and "Marxist-Leninist" organizations, groups, and parties, an anecdote about Michael Borodin is very apropos. Alexander Dallin recounted that upon his return from China to Moscow, Borodin remarked, "When somebody there comes to you shouting, 'Long live the revolution!', don't believe him, all he wants are guns.''[4]

The disrepute of the Soviet model among radicals extends in varying degrees to much of past Soviet history, in many cases including the October Revolution and the Leninist period. However, the disrepute is centered primarily on the basic principles of organization and of political process as existing and practiced in the Soviet Union and most East European communist countries today.[5] Probably a majority of radicals in the West, of whatever label, agree with the nonradicals that the Soviet-type system is among the most oppressive in existence among industrialized societies. (Where they disagree is on the questions of whether it is the *most* or the *only* oppressive system and why it is oppressive.) Radicals, nonradicals, and antiradicals alike point to its oppressive features in almost all dimensions of life—social, economic, political, and cultural. Most notable—and most important for radicals—is the oppressiveness in areas which were central to the traditional programmatic concerns of left radical movements from their inception in the nineteenth century, that is, social stratification, industrial democracy, and political participation. There is also basic agreement that in its external relations with other Soviet-type regimes, Soviet socialism displays behavior traditionally associated with imperialism, and that Stalin's old concept of "socialism in one country" has been replaced by "socialism in one empire."

It is no exaggeration to say that radicals and nonradicals alike recognize that today the Soviet Union is internally the most status-quo-oriented and conservative of the industrial societies—in economic and political organization, in cultural trends and mores, in moral standards and life styles, and in social theory. This by itself makes it less than surprising that the process of disesteem for the Soviet-type model among radicals is very far advanced, and that it will probably lead in this generation to the virtual rejection of the model as a standard for emulation.

Anything short of a very critical attitude towards the

Soviet-type model would not only demand an extraordinary degree of sophistry and blindness but would also reflect a great lack of political realism about its consequences for the radical appeal in the West.[6] The function of a segment of the "establishment" anticommunism in the West remains the defense of the internal and external status quo. This partially explains why criticism of the Soviet-type model by radicals opposed to it has been muted, treated as an internal affair, or totally rejected. Today, however, large numbers of radicals recognize that an open, specific, and extensive declaration of their own anti-Sovietism is absolutely essential to make the "establishment" anticommunism (and especially the obscurantist right-wing anticommunism) ineffective in its internal function.

The current rejection of the Soviet-type model by so many radical groups and organizations brings out the first seeming paradox of the situation. Little of the *internal* Soviet situation on the basis of which the Soviet-type model is discredited is unique to the present period. As a matter of fact, there is no doubt that the Soviet regime, let alone the East European ones, is less objectionable today by any objective standard than it was in the past. The demonic quality of the Soviet system which had permitted its comparison with nazism has largely disappeared. The Soviet political system is less repressive, the Soviet political leadership is more responsive to pressures and demands, and the Soviet government's progress in satisfying popular needs is more pronounced than it ever was in the past. Even with regard to its imperial policy, the commitment to a satellite empire seems a more benign form of imperialism than the straight annexation of entire nations or parts of their territories undertaken by the Soviet Union in the 1940s. Moreover, the international influence and prestige of the Soviet Union has increased immensely, as has its ability to provide material support to radical causes abroad. Yet it is today that scorn for the Soviet-type model among radicals is most pronounced and growing. If, as some see it, the end of the twentieth century will belong to the Soviets, it will be by the force of their arms and the strength of intimidation, and not at all by the force of their ideas or the emulative attractiveness of the system which they have built.

For many reasons, however, the paradox is in reality much less incomprehensible than formal logic would indicate. It is explicable in terms of political logic and of the logic of radical perception. Some of the reasons have to do with an increased visibility of past and present Soviet failures as well as with the "nonrevolutionary" nature of the accomplishments. Some represent the price of systemic success achieved by the Soviet Union. And some reasons have to do with developments in the West, both in the societies at large and within the radical movements, rather than with developments in the Soviet Union itself.

Among the most important reasons for the discreditation of the Soviet-type model and the decline of Soviet influence among radical groups and movements in the West are the following:

1. There has been a quantum jump in radicals' knowledge about past reality and the present state of the Soviet experience. This is due to the Soviets' own admissions in the Khrushchev era of past "errors" and crimes (particularly with respect to the party itself), to the Chinese communists' denunciation of the Soviet leadership, to Soviet and East European dissident writings, to the greater openness to outsiders, and to the enhanced visibility of the mechanisms of Soviet-type systems. Therefore, the desire by radical groups, parties, and individuals in the West not to believe what they previously denounced as "the big lie about the Soviet Union" is much more difficult to sustain than previously.

2. The deep and many-sided conflict between the Soviet Union and China, the two great revolutionary powers, has had an incalculable effect on radical movements—an impact that cannot be compared with the Stalin-Trotsky schism or the Tito-Stalin break. While the Chinese did not find major support within the organized communist movement,

the schism provided a mantle of revolutionary respectability for a critical attitude towards the Soviet Union and contributed to the undermining of Soviet legitimacy within the international radical community wherever this legitimacy still existed. These effects of the Sino-Soviet conflict on radical movements were reinforced by centrifugal tendencies within the Soviet bloc and by the invasion of Czechoslovakia in 1968.

3. The Soviet Union had been the main beneficiary of both the rise and breakup of the fascist phenomenon in Europe. In the 1930s, before the Stalin-Hitler pact, it benefited from what can be called the "Gletkin syndrome." In Joseph Koestler's *Darkness at Noon,* Gletkin, Rubashov's second interrogator, eloquently expresses the Soviets' and radicals' justification and rationalization of Soviet behavior in the 1930s: the fate of the world revolution depends on surviving the period of world reaction and keeping alive the only existing "bastion of socialism." Until then, says Gletkin, "we have only one duty: not to perish. . . . the bulwark must be held at any price, any sacrifice."

In the words of John Strachey:

> For a Communist in the nineteen-thirties who was seized of that argument, the local or temporary state of things in Russia seemed a matter of secondary importance. In front of everybody's eyes the Marxist prognosis of the development of a latter day capitalism was apparently fulfilling itself. Outside Russia, it *was* becoming more and more impossible to use anything like the whole of the productive apparatus; unemployment *was* consequently becoming endemic; the misery of the wage-earners and peasants *was* ever-increasing; the violence, hysteria, and general irrationality of the governing classes of the main capitalisms *was* mounting; attempts at gradualist reform by social democratic methods *had* failed; finally, Fascism was being established not only in such peripheral countries as Italy and Spain, but also, and decisively, in Germany, one of the major, advanced capitalisms. It was above all this apparition of evil incarnate in the form of Fascism which gave the

Communist argument power. For that argument taught that
Fascism was no accidental catastrophe but the logical and inevitable consequence of "capitalism-in-decay." . . . How much
did even the ugliest features of the new socialist society matter
if it gave even the possibility of the re-building of civilisation
upon a viable basis?[7]

In the first postwar decade the Soviet Union enjoyed
an enormous moral credit which it had accumulated as
the major force responsible for the defeat of Nazi power.
Yet, despite Soviet efforts, it became increasingly more
difficult in the postwar period to present its confrontation
with the industrialized democracies as a continuation of the
antifascist struggle. It did not look as though humanity's
choice was between going communist in the Soviet manner
or destroying civilization—sinking into perpetual barbarism.
The 1950s and 60s saw an extraordinary sustained growth
and revitalization of the Western democracies. With the
partial and very limited exception of the culminating period
of the Vietnamese War, it became virtually impossible to
infuse reality into the antifascist slogans used by the Soviets
in their confrontation with the West, and to build or sustain
any broad support in the West for the Soviet position in
this confrontation (especially when, at the height of the
bombing of North Vietnam, the Soviet leadership received
the American president in the Kremlin). In fact, the East-
West confrontation itself increasingly became one of the
determining obstacles to an acceptance of radicalism within
the Western countries.

4. The discrediting of the Soviet model within the Western
radical community is also due to a generational change among
the activists and the leadership of radical groups and organizations. The old militants and leaders were largely locked
into past issues, visions, and loyalties, and into a perception
of the present derived from the vantage point of the myth of
the October Revolution and of the heroic period of bolshevism. For the emerging younger generation of radicals, these
issues lack a similar saliency and depth of attachment.

5. All political movements and groups want not only to believe but also to win, or not only to win but also to believe. It may be suggested that in the past the fringe radical groups as well as the major radical parties of the West (primarily the communist parties) wanted more to believe than to win. Today for the first time these parties do not have to face so starkly the choice between believing and winning or at least advancing their political fortunes. They are increasingly in the happy situation where their political interests and their convictions coincide or can be reconciled. A main condition for such reconciliation rests in their attitudes towards the Soviet model and (what in my opinion is the subordinate question) their relations with the Soviet Union. In some respects, the conflict of interest and conviction which we posited with regard to the past is a false one. As long as the Soviet model of socialism was considered both authentic and emulative, it made the defense of the Soviet Union and of Soviet interests synonymous with the *main* interests of these parties, as was indeed postulated and is still desired by the Soviet leadership. But once the parties' belief in the authenticity and especially in the emulative value of the Soviet model has crumbled, the matter of self-interest in advancing towards power and pressing for far-reaching and realistically attainable changes within their own societies begins to acquire an overriding importance. A reinforcing process is generated when recognition of political self-interest promotes a further deterioration in the value attached to the Soviet model, which in turn (and in time) reinforces the recognition of the self-interest of these parties.[8] The connection between self-interest and the attitude towards the Soviet Union within these parties is based on two interrelated elements: the recognition that the advancement of radical movements in the West is subordinated by the Soviet Union to other aims that are more important from its point of view (such as Soviet foreign policy requirements, the Sino-Soviet conflict, the control of outside movements, internal economic needs, the control of the satellite empire); and the recognition by these parties

that they have very little chance of moving beyond the problems of permanent opposition and limited appeal without first shattering the image and the reality of subservience to the Soviet Union.

6. Studies on "true believers" very often note that insensitivity to violence, cruelty, and suffering on one level of consciousness co-exists in them with sensitivity to the same phenomena on another level. To put it differently, what is so striking about the radical way of thinking (among others) is the extreme politicization of morality and ethics, either in its crudest form which states that what is politically right is ethical, or in its more sophisticated and sophist form which divorces moral condemnation of an act or process from its political valuation.[9] Within this dual framework of perception and self-consciousness, the majority of radicals who took their beliefs seriously could and did excuse and accept (although not necessarily like) the cruelty, viciousness, and oppressiveness of the Soviet "construction of socialism" as long as they believed that this represented the extreme and unique birth pangs of a better world, of a genuinely "progressive" system. Today they cannot accept the much more limited cruelty and the dull oppressiveness of the Soviet system because very few can still believe that a birth of a better world is occurring in the Soviet Union or that the world which was born bears any relation to the vision of the good society that had inspired the revolutionaries of old. For the radical intellectual especially, the dilemma in the past was often expressed and rationalized as the value of intellectual freedom and the luxury of "formal" democracy for the relatively few versus the value for the many of abolishing hunger and exploitation.[10] Today, hunger in the Soviet Union has been abolished but intellectual freedom has not been restored even to the levels of the 1920s, when it co-existed with deprivation and economic hardships. The rationalization of a necessary exchange of one valued item for another no longer makes sense.[11] What does make sense is the conclusion of Edgar Morin that "if there is a loss of freedom that must be considered formal, there is no progress

in freedoms that can be considered real."[12]

7. An element of explanation closely related to the above, although growing from different roots, stems from the virtual helplessness of the Soviet-type systems in solving the problems of advanced industrialization besetting all industrial societies. The sociomaterial achievements of the Soviet-type societies are of the same category, if not magnitude, as those of industrialized democracies, as are also the socioeconomic consequences of those achievements. What is crucial here from the radical perspective is the fact that neither in its theory nor in practice did the Soviet-type system offer (any more than other systems do) convincing solutions to the ills, disproportions, and puzzles of advanced industrialism relevant to their own or to democratic societies. Of all the great issues and more mundane problems of advanced industrialism (for example, participation, bureaucratization, energy and resource conservation, environmental protection, consumer protection), the Soviet-type solutions are visibly more effective than their democratic counterparts in only one area, namely, in crime fighting and safety. One suspects that there are very few radicals of the left who are consciously attracted to the Soviet-type system because of its relative effectiveness in preserving law and order.

In my opinion, the above factors are most important in explaining why a decisive and growing number of left radicals in industrialized democracies today reject the Soviet-type model. They are saying, at the minimum, that what is good for the Soviet Union may not be (or is certainly not) good for Italy, France, Spain, international revolution, etc., or that it is not good for the Soviet Union either, or even that it was never good. At the same time, radical movements have a deeply felt need for an emulative model which exists not only in grand theory but also in reality. This need is partly reflected and expressed by their eagerness to accept less critically the "new" and "newest" revolutions such as, for example, the Chinese or the Cuban. Yet the older these new revolutionary regimes become, the narrower and less enthusiastic becomes the circle of their initial radical supporters in industrial societies.[13] What is more important from the point of view of our discussion, however, is that it seems slightly ridiculous to think that—let us say—the Chinese model with its cultural, political, and economic characteristics and problems might not only attract some groups of radicals in the West but also provide an emulative model which would acquire broad support in industrialized societies.

To sum up, what we see today is not only and simply the loss of control by Moscow over communist movements, or the lack of an organizational center around which many radical movements can coalesce, or a polarization of centers, or polycentrism. Equally important is that any structure which radicalism in industrialized societies possesses today is not oriented towards a single model or diverse emulative models of actual revolutions or revolutionary regimes, but is almost entirely based on concepts and programs that exist exclusively in the realm of ideas and social theory. In this respect, the situation today is not much different from that existing in the period preceding World War I. This leads to the second, even more striking and much more complex paradox, namely, the rise of the influence of socialist ideas and movements in industrialized democracies.

The Resurgence of Socialist Influence

The upsurge in the influence of socialist ideas and movements in industrialized democracies did occur, despite the experience of communist practice in power. It is commonly recognized that no single factor was as responsible for physical harm to the communist cadres as was the rule of Stalinism in the international communist movement. What Stalinism did to the communist movement, the past and present practice of socialism in the Soviet Union and Eastern Europe did on a comparable scale to the socialist idea in the West.

Yet today the idea of socialism in industrial societies is alive and its intellectual and political influence is again on the rise. Behind the present upsurge are in essence the assertions that the original socialist idea was right and only its form and place of implementation were wrong, or, going somewhat further in the reassessment, that the idea (or the Marxian methodology behind it) is basically right but in light of both past experience and the complexity of social reality, it needs to be adjusted, developed, complemented, and so forth.

Is it an accurate perception to see in industrialized democracies a resurgence of radical aspirations and militant actions in general, and an upsurge of socialist ideas and practical political influence in particular? As a rule, general statements of this kind should be suspect, not least because of their generality. However, it seems to me that there exists ample supporting evidence. Yet naturally such a proposition requires elaboration of its specific meanings and dimensions. In particular, amplification is required for the following questions:

1. To which "socialism" does this refer in its generalized meaning and its specific aspects?
2. To which countries is it especially applicable and, within those countries, to which social strata or groups?
3. What kind of influence does it imply and in what specific realms of social endeavor?
4. What time span does it encompass, and does it refer to a long-range secular trend or to a temporary or cyclical phenomenon?

The term "socialism" is used here primarily in its most general meaning. It refers to a complex of views, predilections, and preferences with regard to societal organization, expressed either in theory or in practical policies, which favor the socialization of the essential means of production, distribution, and exchange, their collective management, and a political organization of society which makes this possible. This can be defined as the primordial socialist message which still constitutes the basis of what can be loosely described as the socialist outlook in industrialized democracies.[14]

Naturally "socialism" both in its general meaning and in

its fundamental specific component concepts, such as "social control," "working class," "revolution," "ownership," and "equality," are used by different political groups in an infinite variety of ways. As a matter of fact, after an arid quarter-century, the questioning and the disputes about some core concepts (for example, about the central concept of the socialization of the means of production) and about the general meaning of socialism rival today the disputes at the other two turning points—the turn-of-the-century "revisionism" debates and the conflicts around Leninism and Stalinism of the 1920s.[15] Moreover, even the primordial socialist message in its original Marxian exposition is seen to contain major internal ambiguities and contradictions by a growing number of socialists. Despite all this, it is this message which still provides the point of departure and the framework for the socialist discussion and the road signs followed by socialist political and social programs.[16]

The distinction between various types of influence exercised by sociopolitical ideas is always somewhat artificial and arbitrary because the various kinds of influence are partly interdependent. Yet such distinctions are analytically helpful and politically significant. The distinction which differentiates the influence according to the social sphere in which it is mainly exercised—specifically between the intellectual and political sphere—will be discussed later. The distinction which I would like to stress first is that between the affirmative and critical aspects of socialist influence, that is, between the prevalence and intensity of commitment to socialist-type programs and solutions in industrialized democracies on the one hand, and the socialist critique of those democracies on the other.

Without any doubt, the socialist influence is strongest and most widespread in its negating dimension. In accordance with its own tradition, the major targets and most successful elements of the socialist critique are centered on, although not limited to, the economic organization and class system of the societies. In particular, the critique dwells on the inequities of the corporate business and market system, the inequalities in distribution of wealth and income, and the exploitative and dehumanizing effects of the work system. In addition to these traditional targets, the socialist critique has encompassed very successfully within its traditional attack on the coercive aspects of the state a vigorous and less traditional attack on the bias, inefficiency, and stifling nature of the bureaucratic state and its treatment of the issues which can be subsumed under the heading "quality of life."

There are major disagreements in the academic and political communities today over whether the economic or political institutions of industrialized democracies which are the targets of the socialist critique are more equitable and responsive in their performance and organization than they were in the past. What is beyond doubt is that within the last decade the positive societal perception and acceptance of these institutions has sharply declined almost everywhere.[17]

It would be foolish to attribute the decline in esteem for liberal democratic institutions, the market economy, and the business system to the growth of socialist influence and to socialist criticism. The main sources of the crisis of these institutions are, in my opinion, internal and independent of the socialist critique. In the past, this critique was at most a reinforcing causal factor (differing in degree of importance in various countries) contributing to the decline of those institutions. Under discussion here, however, are not the cause-effect relations between the socialist critique and the decline of liberal democratic institutions but their correlation and the effects of their coincidence.

A genuine decline of confidence in the economic and political institutions of industrialized democracies on the part of the general public and the elites provides a strong—or in such countries as the United States, a previously nonexistent —authoritative base for the socialist critique and its old and new anticapitalist and antiliberal arguments. Once the decline in confidence becomes a discernible trend, the socialist critique magnifies the effects of the trend on social and especially on intellectual consciousness, attacks the solutions proposed by nonsocialists for reversing the crises of liberal democracies, and channels the disaffection with the working of the system away from traditional liberal remedies toward a preference for different and more fundamental changes.

To some extent, all specific targets of the socialist critique are also objects of liberal critique within industrialized democracies. Moreover, as Leszek Kolakowski points out in his Introduction to *The Socialist Idea: A Reappraisal,* much of what has been achieved in the past by liberals to bring about "more justice, more security, more educational opportunities, more welfare and more state responsibility for the poor and helpless, could never have been achieved without the pressure of socialist ideologies and socialist movements, for all their naivete and illusions" (p. 16). Yet the liberal critique and liberal political action in the past were always based on a different perspective than that of the socialists even when their specific programs of reform partly coincided. The liberal perspective was that of far-reaching reform and improvement of the system without questioning its basic systemic assumptions.

At present, the coincidence of the social mood of disaffection and mistrust towards traditional institutions and of the negating dimension of the socialist critique leads to an intellectual and political polarization in industrialized democracies, the importance of which is difficult to exaggerate. Within the liberal camp three tendencies manifest themselves. The first tendency is a fundamental switch from liberal to socialist positions. It is the acceptance of the socialist dictum that liberal reform in industrialized democracies focuses on the manifestation of social ills and addresses their amelioration when what is needed is an attack on their sources, which reside in core system characteristics, particularly in the market and class system. This tendency and its polarizing consequences are lucidly expressed by Robert Lekachman, who recently embraced the label of radical and bade farewell to liberalism. Lekachman concluded: "It may be that the time has come to retire honorably the word liberal and continue the debate as a dialogue between radicals and conservatives."[18]

The second tendency is the phenomenon described by the

already notorious label "neoconservatism." A neoconservative is a liberal who opposes socialism, that is to say, is not
moving to the left; a liberal who has ceased to be doctrinaire
about liberal reforms which he had formerly accepted as effi-
cacious by definition, that is, because of their good intentions; a liberal who has moved from doctrinaire compassion
to pragmatic concerns, from the attitude which stresses that
"the system has to work better" to an attitude which asks,
"What will work better?"; a liberal who is more preoccupied
than formerly with the defense of libertarian values as compared to the quest for equality and faith in social engineering.
Such a stance is partly a response to the crisis of liberal
democracy, partly a response to the attack on its values, and
partly a reexamination of its past performance. This type of
liberal is now called a neoconservative because he is saying
that while the system may be in a crisis, he does not intend
to help in its destruction and finds its basic values worth preserving (whether one calls them democratic capitalist or
liberal bourgeois). His position has changed in comparison to
the typical liberal of the past, but only marginally. What *has*
changed radically is the spectrum of intellectual opinion in
which he acts, which has moved drastically to the left.[19]

The third tendency, although quite visible, consists of so
many shades of attitude and mood that it is very difficult to
describe. It includes a minority of "old-fashioned" and
"mainstream" liberals who, without doubts and with unflag-
ging optimism, restate their unchanging beliefs and set of attitudes carried over from the 1950s and the 1960s. But the
dominant spirit in this group is exemplified by disarray,
search for identity, doubts about the old creed, and fear
where its reexamination may lead; above all, it is exemplified
by the demise of the optimism of old.[20]

It is possible to speak about the negational dimension of
the socialist critique in a generalized way because if anything
provides a common denominator to socialist ideas and movements in industrialized societies, it is their main internal
targets and the complexion and contours of their critique.
When the question of affirmative socialist ideas arises, it is

not only much more difficult to establish the extent of their influence, but it is necessary also to distinguish between the various groups and shades of radicalism. Therefore, before evaluating the affirmative influence of various groups and shades of radicalism in the intellectual and political realm, I wish to identify their seven major groupings according to three indicators: key programmatic attitudes, organizational identity, and social base.

The first group would consist of orthodox communists who support entirely or with some critical reservations the Soviet-type model of socialism. They dominate the leadership and membership of various small communist parties (for example, in the United States, Portugal, West Germany, and Switzerland) and are very strongly represented in the French Communist Party. With the exception of France (and Portugal) it is difficult to speak about their social base, since their membership is so marginal. In the case of France, they have a strong working constituency and a solid base in the party bureaucracy.

The second group could be described as the critical communists. The degree and focus of their critical attitude towards the Soviet-type model of socialism varies from country to country and even within the parties themselves; what they have in common is their emphatic rejection of the Soviet-type model for their own countries and the acceptance of parliamentary and participatory forms of power and roads to power. They are represented primarily within the Italian, Spanish, Dutch, and Japanese communist parties and by a part of the leadership and membership of the French Communist Party. Their strongest base is among intelligentsia in the educational and state apparatus, the white-collar workers, and the municipal and parliamentary party bureaucracy.

In the third group I would put the Trotskyites and Maoists who, despite their many differences, are alike in their rejection of the bureaucratization and "revisionism" of the Soviet model and their acceptance of Leninism; in their middle- and upper-class student and intelligentsia base; and in their total marginality.

The fourth group consists of numerous "grouplets," remnants and offspring of the predominantly student-based New Left. With very few exceptions, their program and mood of revolutionary frivolity is best captured in the following description:

> The existing socialist states are all rubbish, but we are not interested in their history or in their actual conditions because we are going to do better. How? That is very simple. We just have to make the global revolution that will destroy alienation, exploitation, inequality, slavery, discomfort, pollution, overpopulation and traffic jams. The blueprint is ready, all we have to do is make the global revolution.[21]

The fifth group, very sizable and important beyond its size, consists of left socialists. The range of differences in basic outlook within this group is rather limited. But their social and organizational base is heterogeneous. Their basic outlook is democratic socialism—their democratic attachment real, their socialism militant not only in the sense of commitment to militant policies (for example, on redistribution), but in the genuine advocacy of structural changes. The proposed changes include both a much greater role for the state in the economic sphere and a much greater role for the worker in the productive unit. This group would typically include the German Jusos with their university and cultural-intelligentsia base, and the British Labour Party left wing which dominates that party's intellectual and, to a lesser degree, trade union establishment. At present, I would also include, although with some misgivings, the mainstream of the French Socialist Party within this group.[22]

The sixth group can be defined as the traditional mainstream Social Democrats. Its spokesmen are the leadership of the Swedish, Austrian, British, and German socialist parties. With a very strong working-class and middle-class constituency and a power base in the state and trade union bureaucracy, it is a group which can claim to have given birth spiritually and practically to the modern welfare state. Until recently

its commitment to socialism, apart from ritualistic pronouncements, was limited mainly to the area of policies of
redistribution through taxation and to indirect governmental
regulations. Of late, especially in the case of Sweden, it is
moving towards the formulation of proposals for more direct
state control in the economic sphere on the one hand, and
for restructuring and increasing the influence of communal
government as well as that of the employee at this work place
on the other.[23]

Finally, in the seventh group I would include the unat-
tached socialist intellectuals who represent nobody but themselves and whom I would call "moral socialists." They feel
totally alien to the millenial connotations of socialism and to
doctrinaire attachments. They see their key function not as
reformers but as outsiders of the movement who should and
may provide its moral conscience, its skeptical corrective.
Their view is best exemplified by Leszek Kolakowski and
Stuart Hampshire, who put it as follows:

> For me socialism is not so much a theory as a set of moral injunc-
> tions, which seem to me clearly right and rationally justifiable:
> first, that the elimination of poverty ought to be the first priority
> of government after defence; secondly, that as great inequalities
> in wealth between different social groups lead to inequalities in
> power and in freedom of action, they are generally unjust and
> need to be redressed by governmental action; thirdly, that demo-
> cratically elected governments ought to ensure that primary and
> basic human needs are given priority within the economic system,
> even if this involves some loss in the aggregate of goods and ser-
> vices which would otherwise be available. How these moral re-
> quirements are best realized, at particular times and places, and
> also both in general, are matters for the social sciences and also
> for a critical reading of history; after them also for personal ex-
> perience and for worldly insight. At present socialism needs
> a variety of evidence, open minds with moral conviction, and
> distrust of all unitary theories.[24]

The rise in the influence of socialism is most striking, visible, intense, and pervasive among the intellectuals of all industrialized democracies. This is not an entirely new phenomenon in Europe, although even there the intensity of the *gauchiste* trend, the degree of the swing to the left and its domination of the intellectual community, is new. In the United States, it is both new and less extensive—and all the more remarkable when compared to the rather recent past.[25]

Ironically though, the intellectual phenomenon which is most touted on the American scene is that of intellectual neoconservatism. The intellectual climate is further muddled by the blurring of divisions and test issues which separate the various streams of American intellectual opinion. On internal issues such blurring has occurred with regard to growth and "big government" but is especially pronounced in international affairs. This was illustrated by the spectacle of a Republican president praising Mao and refusing to see Solzhenitsyn so as not to offend Brezhnev; of the mainstream liberal expressing great doubts about the arms control agreements with the Soviet Union and expounding on the dangers of Soviet expansionism; of socialist journals becoming one of the most hospitable forums for Soviet non-Marxian dissident writings. The complexity of the trend in the United States is accentuated, moreover, by the absence of a mass socialist party, the dominance of the labor movement by nontheologized trade unionism, the demise of the organized student New Left and of militant black radicalism—in brief, by the dissonance between the politicizing intellectuals moving towards socialist positions and the lack of mainstream influence by political socialism.

The symptoms of a leftward trend in the United States are many and hardly contestable: the birth and enormous expansion of native and imported "Marxology" and the preponderance of Marxist, Marxist-oriented, and Marxist-derived studies and social science publications of a theoretical or theorizing nature; the growth in the popularity and influence of socialist periodicals of a general and academic nature (which, in my opinion, contests successfully the previous dominance of traditional liberalism in this area); the spread and, more importantly, the institutionalization of "new sociology," "new political science," and to some extent "new political economy," and of caucuses and committees calling themselves "Concerned Scholars for. . . ." This trend within the American intellectual community is a much more modest version of the situation in West European societies and—since it not only lacks an independent mass political organization but is also almost totally separated from either the organized or the amorphous groups at the bottom of the social ladder who express autonomously their own grievances against the existing order—the trend in America is much more abstract and less oriented towards practicable programs. The prevailing mood which it engenders is not a feeling about a social order under siege or endangered by revolutionary change, but rather a state of intellectual polarization and political uncertainty and drift.

Undoubtedly, today the radical left in industrialized societies shows—if one rightly discounts the fanatic "action at any price" fringe or the devout believers in Mao, Trotsky, Stalin, or Castro—both an intellectual vigor and balance that was largely absent before as a combination. The Arthur Koestler attitude of "withdrawal from political action after he had lost hope for revolutionary socialism, attempting, as George Orwell put it, to stay in an oasis 'within which you and your friends can remain sane'—in short, the attitude of Marxism in despair,"[26] is absent, and by and large the Marxian socialism of today's intellectual is not one of despair.

Muted and declining among the left is the color-blindness which showed an instinctive sympathy and a suspension of otherwise developed critical faculties with regard to anything that waved a red flag; which identified the "goodness" of a movement not on its own merits but by counterposing it to the "badness" of its opponents; which judged some oppressive regimes by what they are and other regimes by what they purported to be; and which forgot that a defeat for "imperialism" is not necessarily a victory for "revolution" but may be merely a revolutionary change of power. It is somewhat ironic that the socialist intellectual current today, both in the United States and in Europe, owes much of its vigor and its balance to the late New Left of the 1960s, which was noted neither for its intellectual depth nor for its equilibrium. One of the New Left's main intellectual functions, it seems in retrospect, was to stimulate and start a questioning, discussion, and reevaluation within the left as a whole, be it from sympathetic or unfriendly positions. In an introduction to a book published by the German Socialist Party in the series *Democratic Socialism in Theory and Practice*, it is stated:

> The members of the new left formulated their theoretical demands and provoked dialogue with the older and middle generations of social democratic and social liberal voters. To provide a good answer (to the new left) required from all participants (in the dialogue) a rethinking of their own fundamental theoretical formulations. Democracy ceased to consider itself anymore as self-evident, democracy became again a process of learning.[27]

Regarding its intellectual influence and quality, the greatest strength of the socialist upsurge, as noted previously, rests in its critical dimension. It has inspired some of the more profound and influential writings in the United States and Europe.[28] In critical academic theory it seems strongest and most original in historical analysis. One of its weaknesses is traditional—a preoccupation with the exegesis of Marxian texts and methodology.[29] Yet the major problem with critical socialist theory is a variant of an old malady of socialist and particularly Marxist thought which I would define as the "passkey syndrome." Problems and issues to do not seem to require separate keys to their understanding or possible solution, but are susceptible to a generalized approach that proposes the abolition of predictable and generalized root causes. The modern, creative Marxist may have avoided the first dimension of a twofold malady of academic social sciences, that of the empiricist who can say about his work, "I know that what I say is true, but is it significant?"—but they are susceptible with a vengeance to the second dimension, that of the theorist who can say about his work, "I know that what I say is significant, but is it true?" An interesting, and crucial, aspect of this malady is identified by Alvin Gouldner:

> Countercurrents, in the direction of "critical" theory or "radical" social science have thus far failed to resolve these dilemmas in their relation to the empirical. Largely united by their awareness of the limits of primary research, expressed partly in their critique of "positivism," they are often thrust back to a tacit newspaper sociology. Paradoxically, however, this does not emancipate critical theorists from the perspectives of the status quo, since these, of course, are built into the news (or other secondary research) on which they must now rely when they surrender primary researches of their own.
>
> Given a commitment to protect understanding of the social world from the biasing interests of dominant societal groups, there is a tendency to surrender and sneer at primary research. But this means to reduce the sociological enterprise to a dialectical exploration of the "implications" of what is said about the social world, either by newsmen or by technical social scientists.[30]

The range of issues to which socialists attempt to respond affirmatively on the intellectual plane and to find programmatic answers and prescriptive solutions is very broad and reads like a synopsis of the ills and troubles of advanced industrial societies and of the key controversies of our era. The major questions include the following: the concept of economic self-management and social control of production; the implications of modern technology for socialism; socialist planning and the market economy; socialism and ownership; socialism and the national question; socialism and the working class; the meaning of equality; socialism, revolution, and violence; socialism and the future of the state; socialism and the world outlook; education and the "socialist man"; socialism and the values of tradition.

What is typical and, to me, most attractive about the *main* currents of intellectual socialism, and what makes the criticism of it by Berger, Efron, Miller, and others partly unjust, is its honest *intellectual* commitment to seeking a socialist transformation within the framework of liberal democracy (which, if it is intellectually honest, must imply equal valuation of both)[31] and the consciousness of the false dichotomy of ends and means, that is, the belief which argues that "the revolutionary process itself has to be understood as something that is inseparable from the goals it wishes to achieve."[32]

Whether openly acknowledged or not, some of the commitments of the new socialist left are largely outside the proper Marxian tradition of all shades. In part, it is an attempt to achieve a synthesis of Proudhonian, Bakuninist, and general anarcho-communist and syndicalist accents with Marxism—a marriage which would not please Marx at all. (A separate question which will not be discussed concerns the attitudes of the main socialist intellectual currents today towards the scientific claims of Marxism, where the differences with traditional views are also considerable.)

With regard to the strength of the affirmative socialist influence, I would suggest that, once the crucial question of "faith" in socialism is discounted, it rests by and large on a spillover from the strength and attraction of its criticism of the status quo. Those radical currents which see the answers to the problems which besiege advanced industrial societies as being provided by an existing working societal organization, or see the problems only in terms of doing "better" what has already been done in communist societies, cannot claim any more to be intellectual currents. Other radical attempts to find the answers are to my mind no less and also no more intellectually convincing, let alone practically tested (or testable), than those solutions which are offered or suggested by the concerned nonradicals or nonsocialists.[33] The attempted solutions in countries where moderate socialist

programs have been tested in a democratic environment were
in some instances only marginally better and in others only
marginally worse than the solutions of countries where the
socialists were not in the government. The solutions proposed by groups out of power or totally divorced from the
possibility of attaining power, like those in the United States,
are either conceived on such a level of abstraction and
opacity, of generality and simplicity, or of both, that the
political revolution which they see as a prerequisite or as a
part of the proposed solutions amounts to a blank check. It
is a blank check for which past historical experience provides
only negative endorsement, and its theoretical underpinning
and intellectual force (if faith is excluded) no endorsement
at all.

In pointing out that in essence socialist solutions represent
social utopias, I cannot say whether they are sterile or creative utopias. In Gilles Martinet's view:

> In our time, which is in the true sense of the word a time of tran-
> sition (i.e. a time in which we can already do without private
> capital but not without the production relationships and the
> economic mechanisms created by capitalism), the self-government
> utopias, when they are not confined to the narrow framework of
> enterprise, and the egalitarian utopias, when they go beyond the
> single problem of remuneration, are creative utopias in so far as
> they open the way to an evolution which in the long run can
> really lead to the establishment of new relationships between
> men.[34]

What I do believe is that, as long as they consciously try to
avoid totalistic illusions and millenial hopes, they are preferable to the narcissistic pursuits which sweep America, and
which, in Christopher Lasch's words,

> elevated to a program and wrapped in the rhetoric of "authen-
> ticity" and "awareness," signify a retreat from the political
> turmoil of the recent past. Indeed Americans seem to wish to
> forget not only the Sixties, the riots, the New Left, the disrup-

tions on college campuses, Vietnam, Watergate, and the Nixon presidency, but their entire collective past, even in the antiseptic form of the Bicentennial.

To live for the moment is the prevailing passion—to live for yourself, not for your predecessors or posterity. We are fast losing the sense of historical continuity, the sense of belonging to a succession of generations originating in the past and stretching into the future.[35]

The growth of political socialist influence is both direct and indirect, uneven in different national settings and much less pervasive than in the intellectual sphere. Its major manifestations are as follows.

1. The period from 1955 to 1975 witnessed a very pronounced growth in the political role of socialist parties as major forces of political opposition, as members of parliamentary ruling coalitions, or as parties in power. The following table provides only one indication of this phenomenon in Europe, which is also reflected in the growth of the socialist vote, growth in control of local government, and growth of socialist membership.

West European Cabinet Members, 1955 and 1975[36]

	Social Democrats	Conservatives and Christian Democrats	Liberals	Others
1955	33.5%	33.0%	14.6%	18.9%
1975	54.1%	25.1%	12.6%	8.2%

2. Objections can be raised to identifying many of the social democratic parties as "socialist" in the strict sense of the word—that is, radical socialist, Marxist, committed to traditionally socialist transformations, etc. Such objections have merit; however, they miss what is most important, namely, the developments in the last two decades *within* the socialist parties. What has been happening in the majority of

cases is a growth of the left wing *within* those parties and a pronounced movement *of* those parties to the left. This phenomenon finds its expression in such indicators as increased militancy of the socialist trade unions, dominance by radical elements in the youth branches of these parties, the growing willingness of these parties to form local or national alliances with organized forces to their left, and the accelerated introduction of proposals in their programs and practical political demands or policies which are considerably to the left of what was typical in the 1940s and 1950s, proposals which are sometimes new or which sometimes constitute a return to the original socialist demands that had been toned down or even abandoned.[37]

3. The disintegration of the remaining authoritarian regimes in Western Europe, which left these societies with a "political hangover" and a power vacuum, pushed the leftist forces to the center of the stage, sometimes to commanding positions. In Portugal the socialists dominate the government, while the major opposition to their programs is to the left. In Greece a left alliance may form the government after the next national election. In Spain the socialist following among the urban middle class and intellectuals and the communist influence in the labor movement makes their possible future alliance the factor which would determine the fate of the present transitional regime. In all probability, the evolving Spanish system will be either a military dictatorship or a socialist-dominated coalition.

4. In the most visible and publicized gain for the left, the communist party became the strongest political force in Italy and will almost certainly in the near future share responsibility in the national government as it already does in the process of governance itself. The French socialist-communist alliance came very close to winning the national election and has very good prospects for succeeding next time.

5. One of the most startling political developments in Western industrialized societies is the appearance and growth of "mini-nationalism"—regional, ethnically based political movements (for example, the Scots, the Quebecois, the

Bretons, the Basques) demanding self-government or separation from the nation-states of which they are a part. For a number of reasons the nationalist movements are tilting to the left and adding thereby to the general leftward tendency. This seems to be due to their belief that they receive a more sympathetic response from the "metropolitan" left and will therefore have a better chance of accomplishing their goals. Also, the internal logic of opposition against heavy odds favors militancy, activism, and radicalization when the struggle becomes prolonged. The radicalization assumes a leftward direction because of the possibility of reconciling it with the democratic traditions of the nationalists' own societies, which a rightward radicalism cannot do—or, as in the case of Spain, because of the rightist nature of the regime itself.

6. The proliferation of independent small groups more radical in their immediate goals and more militant in their everyday methods than the established forces of the left reinforces the feeling of a movement to the left while adding little to its substance. Some of these groups I would call "televisionaries"—a hybrid achieved by giving the old revolutionary anarchists television exposure. Their membership often is not larger than the cast of a medium-sized spaghetti western; their words and rhetoric are, invariably, uncompromisingly revolutionary leftist, but in the Leninist meaning of infantile leftism; their actions are invariably dramatic and often staged primarily to be dramatic; and, most importantly, their visibility and seeming influence is basically dependent on the communications media's idea of revolution and thirst for dramatic news "happenings" and "scoops." The past of these groups is obscure, their future dim, and their present direct political influence has no relation whatsoever to their visibility and dramatics.

This does not mean, of course, that these groups do not influence indirectly the leftward trend which we are discussing. This influence is ambiguous and contradictory but nevertheless worthy of some attention. On the one hand, the existence and militancy of these groups puts restraints on the freedom of maneuver of the established left parties, especially the communists. It limits their tactical line and the moderation of their demands. The leftism and/or immediacy of the direct action tactics of these groups finds a sympathetic response among some elements of the membership and voting constituency of the established left parties, and creates therefore among the leadership an apprehension about the potential effect of this critique to their left. Such criticism, when expressed in language, concepts, and symbols used by the established parties themselves at a time when the latter's monolithic unity and discipline is waning, cannot be disregarded. On the other hand, the existence and militancy of these groups creates a powerful target on which the nonsocialist forces can take aim in their struggle with the left. The antisocialists can attempt to translate the fears which such groups evoke in the "average" citizen into a fear of the left in general. The established left finds itself therefore in a situation where it cannot afford either to tolerate these groups or to attack them with full force. Meanwhile, for the nonleft the existence and actions of these groups are on balance probably *politically* beneficial.

Clearly emerging from an analysis of the growth of political influence by the left is that it is primarily confined to the revitalized, refurbished, "old," "established" left. The "new" or "far" left's political strength, aside from the indirect influence previously discussed, manifests itself as a momentary or a localized phenomenon: either in moments of transition when the disintegration of an established regime leaves a vacuum of power, programs, and allegiances—the modern equivalent in West European societies of the post-February 1917 "dual power" period in Russia (e.g., Portugal in 1975); or when, in association with a specific grievance, it acquires momentarily a broader base and concentrates its attack on a vulnerable institution (e.g., the Vietnamese War and the university revolt in 1968 in the United States; the 1968 revolt in the French universities).

In countries such as the United States, where an established old left vehicle of political influence is absent, the gains of the left in the cultural and intellectual spheres are not translated into direct political influence, but they do result in a contribution to the undermining of legitimacy of the existing order and to a widespread feeling of cultural discontinuity and drift.

Maladies of Liberal Democracy

The trend to the left in the intellectual and political realms is distinctly uneven in different countries, both in intensity and in manifestation. Most definite is the growth of socialist influence in intellectual circles. Next in order of pervasiveness are the leftward tendencies *within* and *of* the socialist movements. Least clear and uneven is the growth of socialist influence on the general political arena. Yet the trend towards the left is not the only one which characterizes the present period. It is evident that even in the intellectual sphere one can speak not only about a movement to the left but also about a process of ideological polarization and weakening of the centrist, traditionally liberal positions. With regard to the leftward trend within and of the socialist movements, some signs of a countertendency are discernible, although they are often short-lived. The clearest reverse in the fortunes of the left wing occurred in the Socialist Party of Germany (SPD), where Chancellor Helmut Schmidt dealt rather harshly with the young socialists after Willy Brandt's retirement in 1974. Yet, even in this case, a comparison of the SPD of the late 1970s with that of the 1960s shows that the party as a whole has moved to the left; elements of the Jusos' demands and views became incorporated into the party's programs and outlook. In the other important socialist parties of Europe no signs are noticeable of even such a partial decline of the left wing.

The evidence of countertrends and parallel trends is most pronounced in the general political arena, especially in electoral politics. In the United States, naturally, one can hardly speak about any growth of socialist influence in mass politics and therefore about possible countercurrents. Yet contemporary voting-behavior studies show evidence "that the public has drifted significantly in a liberal direction on a number of social and economic issues over the past two decades."[38] There is insufficient evidence to state that this tendency has been reversed except in some very specific instances. And the alleged "conservative majority" whose emergence was proclaimed before every one of the last five national elections remains a myth. What can be seen, however, as an indirect manifestation of such a countertendency is an emerging split between the party activists and the party voters. For a very long period those active in the Republican Party were more conservative than the Republican rank and file; what is new, however, is that activists in the Democratic Party are more liberal than the Democratic rank and file. Yet the main tendency discernible on the American scene is neither a general turn to the right nor a general turn to the left, but a pronounced increase in the volatility of the electorate, the weakening or even disintegration of the orientation points which in the past provided an institutional structure to their vote.[39]

The major examples of a countertrend are to be found outside the North American continent—in the defeat of the socialists in Sweden, Denmark, Australia, and New Zealand, and, of course, in the inability of the SPD to retain the largest single share of the West German vote. I do not accept the argument that these defeats or near defeats are meaningless or irrelevant because the electoral opponents of the socialists will continue the welfare state on an undiminished scale and will not dismantle or reverse any of the established social programs and policies, or because the actual switch of votes in the elections was very marginal. (I also do not accept the argument that it signals a revolt against the welfare state as established under socialist auspices in Europe, let alone a reactionary conservative wave of the future.) If anything, those defeats are partly a countertrend to the growth of socialist influence that expresses fear not of what the socialists did but what they may plan to do if they retain power, and of which their leftward drift has provided some indication. In this narrow sense, the countertrend can be defined as conservative, although not in an ideological meaning. Many observers of the European political scene have suggested that the defeats are part of a broader tendency which is neither leftward nor rightward, prosocialist nor antisocialist. Rather, it is a tendency directed against entrenched parties and bureaucracies and expresses on an immediate level the blame understandably attached to those in government for the most difficult economic situation in the postwar era and, on a deeper level, a disaffection with government in general and a declining trust in politics.

In a way, I am suggesting that the recent political losses of the socialists in Europe are to a very large extent connected to socialist growth and achievement in European politics in the last decades, and to their more recent leftward movement. Most importantly, the setbacks are directly relevant to understanding the reasons why socialism gained almost everywhere in the political (and intellectual) arena in the last decades, and may continue to gain in countries where nonsocialists are in power.

What lies behind the growth of socialist intellectual and political influence in industrialized democracies today? What are the key contemporary factors which may explain it? Our discussion of *what* is happening provides many clues and indications of *why* it is happening, but the "whys" of the trend must be sorted out. As stated earlier, the political resilience of socialism and especially its influence in the intellectual realm is not a new phenomenon. Yet there are at least some new elements to it:

1. After a period of enormous expansion in the non-industrial world and decline or stabilization in advanced industrial societies, it has again become pronounced in the latter.
2. It has occurred despite and in opposition to the practice of communism in power.
3. For the first time since the period after World War I, socialism does not emulate any existing societal model but rather embodies an idea.
4. Even as an idea socialism has lost to a large degree its millenarian quality.

5. Finally, in the intellectual realm at least, this marks an
end to American exceptionalism also in this respect.[40]

The attraction of the intellectual stratum to socialist ideas
has been noted and its growth predicted by many social
theorists of the past, who provided a variety of explanations
for their observations and predictions. These explanations,
supplied primarily by Vilfredo Pareto, Robert Michels, and
Joseph Schumpeter, contain, despite their variations, some
basic repetitive elements and are by and large supplementary
to each other.[41] They apply to the present trend as well as
they applied at the time when they were written and are, in
my opinion, incisive about the roots of the phenomenon.

In a recent essay, Peter L. Berger aptly brings together the
various classic and contemporary strands of explanation of
the strength, pervasiveness, and staying power of the intellectual's attraction to socialism and of the phenomenon of
"adversary intellectuals" in industrialized democracies, and
adds a number of his own observations and conclusions,
which to me are quite convincing.[42] It seems true, for
example, that "intellectuals constitute a group particularly
vulnerable to the discontents of modernity." It seems true
that uniquely "the socialist myth promises the fulfillment of
both the rational dreams of the enlightenment and the mani-
fold aspirations of those to whom the enlightenment has
been an alienating experience." It seems true that "the socialist myth derives much of its power from its unique capacity to synthesize modernizing and counter-modernizing
themes."[43]

For all their relevance, these observations should be
complemented by a few simple, political rather than philosophical, explanations; secondly, and most importantly, they
do not elucidate sufficiently why these elements became
operative in the present period, particularly in the United
States where they were dormant for so long. The acceptance of
myths may be irrational, but the reason for their greater acceptance in particular periods usually has quite rational explanations. The stress on the structural societal changes
and on the growth of the "knowledge industry" which,

following Kristol and Bell,[44] Berger stresses, and on the cyclical nature of the fluctuations in the intellectual attraction to socialism, do not seem adequate as an explanation.

Among the additional elements which partly refer to the growth of socialist political influence and partly to the reasons for its present dominance in the intellectual realm, the following seem worth mentioning:

1. To quote Raymond Aron, "in the struggle against a certain form of complacency on the part of privileged persons who tend to put up with the poverty of the majority provided their formal freedoms are respected, the Marxist protest has lost none of its relevance and force."[45] To use Aron's genteel phrasing, "certain forms of complacency of the privileged" about poverty, injustice, and so forth, have far from disappeared in even the richest industrial societies. As a matter of fact, in most of the industrialized democracies and especially in the United States, after their pronounced decline in the postwar period inequalities have reached a plateau in the last ten or fifteen years or have increased—for example, with regard to inequalities in income. As was suggested earlier, the susceptibility to socialist ideas starts typically with an attraction to its critique of the status quo. It helps when the particulars of the critique, if not the designations of their root causes, are supported by convincing data or by the experience of everyday life.

2. A major factor that needs to be noted is both explanatory and paradoxical. It concerns the adoption of crucial elements from the "program minimum" of socialism by almost all nonsocialist parties after World War II. The results of this adoption are mixed economies and the welfare state in all industrialized economies. The co-optation did preempt for a prolonged period the social base of socialist support and the uniqueness of the socialist appeal. At the same time, however, it legitimized within and for bourgeois society, as never before in history, socialist programs and the underlying idea of equity as the supreme value. Once the mix in the economy and the saturation of social welfare programs reaches a point where further advance in the same direction

requires extensive structural changes—and especially once the rapid and solid economic growth, which had made the costs of equity politically relatively painless, becomes more difficult or even impossible to sustain—the socialist pressure for continuing the quest for equity grows and becomes again unique to the socialists. At this point the past legitimization of the program minimum of socialism makes opposition to such further progression very difficult to justify.

3. The example and impact of the practice of socialism in the Soviet Union and Eastern Europe, combined with the Soviet domination of the international communist movement in conditions of an East-West apocalyptic confrontation, drove the socialist parties in industrial societies to the right and the communist parties to a state of political paralysis—a dead-end situation in which they could survive as political entities but were condemned to a no-win policy. The decline of the East-West confrontation and the emergence of détente led to the abatement of the emergency or siege mentality in Western Europe and the United States which had restrained the leftward movement. At the same time, the growing dissociation of major communist parties from support of the Soviet model and their organizational independence and growing spiritual independence from Soviet tutelage is fulfilling a precondition for breaking out of the pattern of permanent opposition.

4. The political and ideological effects of poverty, injustice, and discrimination depend on the extent and intensity of their perception. As we all know well, the dynamics of social facts and their perception develop at best at different rates, and often are even moving in opposite directions. The last fifteen years saw an intensification of the perception of inequities which is in part a result of the communications revolution. In part the intensified perceptions stem from the very success of specific movements for redressing grievances, which has led to an increased awareness of their own grievances by less active and organized groups and has activated their movements (for example, the women's liberation movement).

It is generally recognized that in developing societies, particularly in the newly created states, the immense popularity of socialism as the vernacular of discourse, as an ideology, and as a political and economic orientation point is directly related to the absence in the social structure and in social allegiances of conditions and factors favorably relevant to modernization. This void, which cannot be filled by nationalism alone, is a result of past patterns of development. In the words of Charles Taylor, "socialism steps in to fill the breach."[46]

It was considered almost self-evident that in the industrialized societies of the West such a breach is absent. One of the implications of Huntington's proposition that modernization breeds instability while modernity equals stability was, when applied to industrialized democracies, synonymous with saying that no drift, let alone jump, towards socialism in those societies is to be anticipated.[47] (This view was supplemented and paralleled by Huntington's distinction between the Western and Eastern pattern of revolutionary change; in the first case such a change is possible only when a power vacuum occurs, while in the latter it can progress in the face of strong organized opposition.)[48] Here we come, in my opinion, to the single most salient and complex factor whose explanatory importance is crucial to understanding the trends under discussion. The key point is that such a breach has developed in industrialized democracies and socialism is trying to fill it, primarily ideologically but partly also politically. It is the breach expressed in the growing dissatisfaction with the status quo among a broad range of elite and nonelite social groups. This disaffection is not brought about by any single event or cause, it is not simply cyclical as at some periods in the past, but rather reflects a major discontinuity in the economic, social, and political developmental base of industrialized democracies. The latter are in a period of transition whose causes and directions are only starting to be perceived and whose possible, not to say probable, outcomes are even less clear.

The changing conditions which underlie the vulnerability

and crisis of industrialized democracies are becoming one of
the major motifs in social science writing, and constitute a
central theme in Charles Maier's and Samuel Huntington's
essays in this volume. I propose to elaborate on some of their
points which are most pertinent to the subject under discussion.

1. I agree with Maier's stress on the importance of growth
for democratic stability and would, in fact, go even further.
It is becoming clear that the social and class harmony that
accompanied and stimulated the unprecedented Western
prosperity in the last three decades is seriously threatened
and that the compact between classes, whereby unequal distribution of income, wealth, and power was accepted in
return for high employment, a flood of consumer goods, and
steady improvement in average standards of living, is coming
to an end. It is not only the present recession which creates
this reversal, but also the prospect of long-range slowing
down or perhaps a stagnation after unrivaled prosperity
which undermines the economic and political base for this
class compact. The political and social situation of the postwar period cannot be reproduced without steady and considerable economic growth, yet at the same time it is becoming very doubtful whether the internal and external
necessary conditions for such growth are at all replicable. The
real social and political impact of the changing and increasingly unfavorable conditions of growth will occur not at the
time when the recession is still in progress, or at the beginning of a recovery, but precisely afterwards. During the recession there is still hope of a return to the previous situation, but if such a return does not occur, if growth is hollow
even after recovery, then the time of trouble is at hand. The
recession is obviously a cyclical, passing phenomenon. Of
much more crucial long-term importance is the nature of
growth in the nonrecessionary periods. Here the prospects are
not for the kind of sustained, substantial growth that supported internally and internationally the social and political
structures in the postwar decades.

2. There is a general recognition that the role of the state

in industrialized democracies has expanded enormously, especially in economic life. But what needs stressing, as Huntington does, is the paradox of the expansion of the role of the state in economic life in tandem with a decline in the state's ability to control economic life. Most economists doubt whether the postrecession economic situation will return to a condition where Keynesianism will be again a fruitful, effective instrument of regulating the economy, of managing the economic cycle without a prohibitively high price of inflation or unemployment, or both. Very few believe that a withdrawal from regulation and the mythical free market play, even if politically possible, would make the economic price of growth less prohibitive, let alone socially more just. If this is true, then a paradoxical situation emerges: on the one hand, the increasing involvement of the state in the economy means the increasing politicization of confrontations over various aspects of economic life while, on the other hand, the instruments of the state to control, influence, or regulate the economy are limited or decreasing. So, while state intervention in economic life is growing, the state's ability to regulate the economy is effectively declining. This is a recipe for very basic systemic trouble. The proposition that the evolution of the state and its interpenetration with civil society reduces the chances for conflicts between the principles that govern politics and those of the economic order was challenged by a number of participants at the workshops, who suggested that the exact reverse was much more likely: the occasions for such conflicts were likely to increase in frequency as a result of the interpenetration of state with civil society and the increasing politicization of civil society.

3. That the parliamentary system of industrialized democracies is in a state of deep crisis is a truth accepted first of all by the parliamentarians themselves. What is even more important is the simultaneous crisis of the party systems. Political parties as important agents in aggregating and articulating interests, in representing effectively the major cleavages in society, and in mobilizing popular political participation

are losing their function and are becoming increasingly irrelevant to the political process. If an institution is not perform-
ing its assigned function, there is a crisis situation. If the
party system on the American national scene is increasingly
coming to resemble the one in New York City rather than the
patterns of its own past, this is just as much a crisis as the institutionalized chaos of the parliamentary system. If a new
political alignment is emerging in the United States from this
crisis, of which there are no indications, the alignment works
"not through but athwart the traditional major parties . . .
which cumulatively dissolves them as channels of collective
electoral action."[49]

The stress in Maier's paper (and in his book, *Recasting
Bourgeois Europe*)[50] is on the ability of industrialized democratic societies to resist radical change, to recast and adopt
their institutions to changing conditions and challenges. The
strength of this resistance did rest, in the past, as Gramsci eloquently formulated it, on the "sturdy structure of the civil
society." Counterposing the revolutionary tasks in Russia and
in the West and comparing them respectively to a frontal
attack and a state of siege, Gramsci wrote:

> In Russia the State was everything, civil society was primordial
> and gelatinous; in the West, there was a proper relation between
> State and civil society, and when the State trembled a sturdy
> structure of civil society was at once revealed. The State was only
> an outer ditch, behind which there stood a powerful system of
> fortresses and earthworks: more or less numerous from one State
> to the next, it goes without saying—but this precisely necessitated
> an accurate reconnaissance of each individual country.[51]

The bulwark of the sturdy structure was an all-pervasive
and intense commitment to the basic values and founding
assumptions of the bourgeois social order within the
society at large and particularly among the societal elites—
in other words, not simply the strength of the government
and the stability of the state but the pervasiveness and
strength of authority within and throughout society. It is

exactly this bulwark which is giving way.

The present decline in the strength and pervasiveness of authority amounts to nothing less than the process of delegitimization of authority in industrialized countries. The list of elements of this delegitimization as perceived by one influential report is very long indeed:

> In the past decade there has been a decline in the confidence and trust which the people have in government, in their leaders, and less clearly but most importantly, in each other. Authority has been challenged not only in government, but in trade unions, business enterprises, schools and universities, professional associations, churches and civic groups. In the past, those institutions which have played the major role in the indoctrination of the young in their rights and obligations as members of society have been the family, the church, the school, and the army. The effectiveness of all these institutions as a means of socialization has declined severely. The stress has been increasingly on individuals and their rights, interests, and needs, and not on the community and its rights, interests and needs. These attitudes have been particularly prevalent in the young, but they have also appeared in other age groups, especially among those who have achieved professional, white-collar, and middle-class status. The success of the existing structures of authority in incorporating large elements of the population into the middle class, paradoxically, strengthens precisely those groups which are disposed to challenge the existing structures of authority.
>
> Leadership is in disrepute in democratic societies. Without confidence in its leadership, no group functions effectively. When the fabric of leadership weakens among other groups in society, it is also weakened at the top political levels of government. The governability of a society at the national level depends upon the extent to which it is effectively governed at the subnational, regional, local, functional, and industrial levels. . . .
>
> This weakening of authority throughout society thus contributes to the weakening of the authority of government.[52]

Yet during a discussion of the Trilateral Commission's

report on the governability of democracies, Ralf Dahrendorf
summed up brilliantly how even the discussion on the crisis
of democracy and the ways of overcoming it was explicitly or
tacitly pervaded by a questioning of the "charter" assumptions on the ideas of progress, growth, market economy,
public interest, the work ethic, the separation of the political
and public structure, etc. In the study of the Trilateral Commission, notes Dahrendorf,

> you find a number of remarkable statements about the relation-
> ship between democracy and economic growth. . . . It is clearly
> desirable, at least that is my view, that economic growth should
> continue. Yet there may be a point in asking a number of ques-
> tions in relation to these statements. And there may be a point in
> discussing them at some length. Why should it be so that democ-
> racy is to some extent dependent on economic growth? Is there
> anything in the concept of democracy that relates it to economic
> growth? Is democracy unthinkable without it? Is it actually true
> that those countries in which economic growth was least effective
> were also the countries in which democratic institutions were
> least effective? Could it not be said that it is the one-party social-
> ist states above all which are in trouble without economic
> growth? . . . Is growth presumably growth of a gross national
> product? Is this the only kind of expansion of human life chances
> which we can think of in free societies? Are there not perhaps
> other forms of growth and improvement of human lives? Is it
> really necessary to assume that we have to continue along the
> lines which have been characteristic for the last twenty-five years
> in order to maintain democratic institutions? The important and
> prima facie plausible statements about democracy and economic
> growth would warrant and perhaps require a rather more elab-
> orate reasoning.[53]

The elite dimension of the decline in legitimacy in industrialized democracies is particularly pertinent to our discussion of the trend towards an increase in socialist influence.
The disaffection of the mass strata of society—of people as
producers, consumers, city-dwellers, members of the political

community—is not sufficient for evaluating the degree of the crisis of stability in democracies. To evaluate the conditions for radical change, it is important to look also at what is happening among the upper social strata, among the elites; that is, to address two aspects of legitimacy: popular legitimacy and legitimacy within the elite. I would not dismiss lightly the insights of the elite theorists on the problem of elite legitimacy, which should not be reduced to the question of corruption—it is a question of will and ability to govern, of faith in the justness of the system, of dynamism and belief in the future. One of the most crucial aspects of the present crisis and the possibilities of radical change is precisely the very great decline of legitimacy within elites. Some splits and divisions within the Western elites today are not simply divisions of interest but of beliefs and sometimes of basic values. Just as it has been remarked that societies do not come apart by a majority vote, so it can also be said that elites do not fall apart by majority vote. The views and behavior of small minorities within the elites, located in strategic positions, may make a crucial difference for the stability of the system.

This brings us back to the question of the growth of socialist influence among the intellectuals, to "Why particularly socialism?" and "Why socialism particularly now?" In answer, I would like to summarize and to expand on what has already been said:

1. In the face of the crisis of industrialized democracies, a socialist with the knowledge of tradition cannot help but feel that "this is where we came in."[54]

2. The socialist idea is there, it is available and ready to fill the breach, while other systems of ideas are in disarray, not because socialism has better answers, but because it believes it has answers while liberalism at present has mostly questions.

3. Socialism is attuned to the criticism of the status quo, which is in real need of such criticism, and is often more profound in this criticism than its ideological opponents.

4. "The apparent cyclical human lust for philosophical monism,"[55] especially among intellectuals, is particularly pronounced in times of transition when the old has not yet died and the new is not yet born.

5. Despite the unenviable past experience of "philosophers" who tried to change the world, the urge to subordinate the task of understanding and interpreting the world to the urge to change it is still irresistible to men of ideas at a time when both understanding and change are clearly needed.

In the past, the expectations and predictions of social scientists, politicians, and journalists (with a few exceptions, such as the marvelous quotation from Schumpeter given at the beginning of Maier's chapter 7 in this volume) tended to err in the direction of exaggerating the probable systemic impact of the problems faced by industrialized democracies and underestimating their built-in stabilizing elements and ability to adjust to changing conditions. It could be that the present expectations and predictions tend to err in the same direction. It may well be that the cumulative impact of a decade of political shocks and social and cultural upheavals, combined with the powerful effects of the energy crisis and of the deepest recession and the highest inflation in postwar history, leads to a temporary exaggeration of the nature and depth of the crises of the advanced industrialized democracies; and that after the cycle of troubles and gloom, a cycle of recovery and stabilization will set in, providing a basis for a more balanced and optimistic view of the future of these societies.[56]

In my opinion, however, the trends which we discussed are not simply cyclical in nature, although their intensity might well be cyclical. Neither do they seem to constitute the tail end of a trend which future historians would confine to the 1960s and 70s. It seems to me that Maier puts too much faith in the resiliency of the industrially advanced democratic systems and in their historically developed and proven ability for self-adjustment, and that he underestimates the probable impact of present-day challenges and the seriousness of the new problems faced by these societies. It seems true that revolution in the classical sense, that is revolution understood as a single act, an uprising, no longer seems possible, if it ever was, or has a very low level of probability in industrially developed societies. I am also inclined to accept, although to a lesser extent, the conclusion that fascism, again in the classical sense, is no longer highly probable. If, however, instead of looking at the revolution as a political act of departure from legal procedures in the quest for power, or as an act of violence, one looks at it from a less confining perspective as a process that may occur through legitimate or semi-legitimate channels (which are difficult to define, just as it is difficult to determine to what extent the transfer of power was illegitimate in the case of the Nazi revolution), then I would see the prospects as quite different. Revolution as a process is not only possible, but probable. There is a probability of radical change through such a process to the left or a change in the right authoritarian direction, which would also denote a qualitative departure from the democratic system. The level of probability for such changes taking place is, of course, different for different societies. For the United States, a development in a right authoritarian direction seems more likely than one towards the left.[57] For West European societies, such as France and Italy, a left radical change is clearly a distinct probability. For Great Britain, Gramsci's half-facetious view that for some countries no working system is possible may very well be less facetiously appropriate.[58]

The outcome of the trends depicted here, their persistence and direction, is neither clear nor preordained. It depends enormously on the impact of international factors, especially on the evolution of the developing world—a prime causal dimension for the dynamics in industrialized democracies which we have not discussed at all. It depends on the political, social, and intellectual leadership of those who want to preserve the liberal democratic system and who can achieve it only by an ability "to implement and effect change without revolution—the ability to rethink assumptions—the ability to react to new problems in new ways—the ability to develop institutions rather than change them all the time—the ability to keep the lines of communication open between the leaders and the led—the ability to make individuals count above all."[59] Last, but not least, it depends to a large extent on the evolution, the strategies, and the nature of the primarily socialist-oriented radical movements within the industrialized societies themselves.

New Revolutionary Theories and Strategies

Three chapters in this volume—Alexander Dallin's, Peter Lange's, and Massimo Teodori's—deal directly with models and strategies of revolutionary change and the evolution of radical movements in industrially advanced democracies. If they point to any common theme, it is that if the radical impulse is to make gains, let alone succeed, in industrially advanced democracies, it must be expressed in an evolutionary strategy and has to abandon old-fashioned revolutionary rhetoric, theory, and action.

Two topics directly related to this theme on which I shall concentrate are (1) the new theories and models of revolution and their new left inspiration, and (2) the reformist and revolutionary tendencies in the European old left in general and the question of their deradicalization in particular.

The new theories and models of revolution which concern us are not academic theories but the distinct sets of views advanced by the revolutionaries themselves. Their approach is quite different from that of academic theories. The academic theories—"theories of revolution"—primarily ask why revolutions occur, under what circumstances they could occur and succeed or fail; the theories developed by revolutionaries—"revolutionry theories"—primarily expound why revolutions should occur, and what should be done in order for them to occur and succeed.

After decades of drought, the 1960s and early 1970s saw a proliferation of revolutionary theories (or in most cases, rather what Robert Merton in another context called "theoritas") probably unequalled in all modern history.[60]

Were the fate of world revolutionary progress dependent on the number of revolutionary theories, very little would remain to occupy revolutionaries except perhaps "a revolution against the revolution." But what occurred, according to the apt title of Regis Debray's book, is only a revolution within the revolution, if by revolution one understands revolutionary theory.[61]

The revolutionary theories which surfaced in recent decades are undoubtedly new in the sense that they explicitly and consciously depart from the dominant Leninist (or Trotskyist and even Maoist) model. Their relation to Marxism is much more ambiguous. If, as Bertell Ollman suggested very perceptively, there is no such thing as a "Marxist theory of revolution other than all the works of Marx which are directed at understanding how capitalism functions,"[62] the intellectual roots, the general orientation, and the language and symbolism of the revolutionary theories is very largely Marxian. Moreover, it is certainly not the derivative vulgarized and emasculated Marxism of today's orthodox Leninists. Yet, at the same time, it is hardly the Marxism of the founders in any of its original versions and especially not in its aggregate completeness. Marxism can be seen here as only one of the inputs, one of the major orientation points of their critique and affirmation. What is striking is rather the heterogeneity of their intellectual and practical orientation points.[63] This heterogeneity shows itself not simply in the diversity of the revolutionary theories and the differentiation among various groups that form the new revolutionary movement, but is discernible within each theory and within almost every group. Undoubtedly, the other major input, often as important as Marxism, is the anarcho-syndicalist and especially anarcho-communist tradition. Therefore, the heterogeneity of orientations and the dissolution of the previously hermetic divisions in the international revolutionary movement represent one aspect of the newness in the current theories and movements.[64]

Naturally the question arises immediately, "Why new theories?" From among the many elements in the explanation I would stress the following: First, these theories (and the movements which brought them about or loosely followed them) are a sign of the failure of the twentieth century revolutionary effort in industrially advanced liberal democracies. As a matter of fact, one may suggest a "law" of inverse relationship between actual revolutionary progress and the proliferation of revolutionary theories—in countries in which one advances, the other atrophies. It is the atrophy of revolution in industrialized democracies which pushes the revolutionaries to reevaluate and reexamine reasons of failure and to look for new remedies in theory as they seek them in practice.

Second, the new theories and the new movements can be seen in part as a reaction to the disillusionment—sometimes even revulsion—with the end results brought about by the old Leninist revolutionary model in the Soviet Union and its East European dominions. How a "good" revolution could bring about an outcome so demonstrably undesirable is a question no longer easily dismissed by stressing and blaming the outcome on the peculiarities of the Russian revolution (such as underdevelopment or capitalist encirclement) while exonerating the revolutionary model itself. The question calls for and often leads to a reexamination of the relations between the means and ends of revolutionary struggle, especially as they pertain to the forms of association by the revolutionaries, and to the whole complex of problems that can be summed up by the slogan of the new revolutionaries, "One should not only make the revolution, but live the revolution."[65]

Third, one may view the proliferation of revolutionary theories and movements as a response to the perceived deradicalization of the old left, and particularly of the communist movements. These movements, when they embraced the Soviet-type model of socialism and adhered to the principle of Soviet international leadership, became basically conservative, pursuing Soviet interest in the international arena rather than revolutionary change in their own societies; and when they began to condemn the Soviet model to a greater or lesser degree and to declare sincerely their independence from Soviet tutelage, they embraced a gradualist approach to change that to the new revolutionaries is too reminiscent of tactics of the "renegade" and certainly nonrevolutionary Second International.

Fourth, the proliferation of revolutionary theories is in part a reflection of the successful spread of revolutionary regimes in economically underdeveloped societies and a generalization and rationalization of their revolutionary success. As a matter of fact, most of these theories deal directly with developing societies or are explicitly inspired by the revolutions in such societies. (There is to my knowledge only one extensive and well-developed theory that is revolutionary and derives from, and is entirely oriented towards, advanced industrialized democracies. It is most extensively developed in the writings of André Gorz.[66]) The main emphasis of these theories, when contemplated or actually applied by their supporters in industrial democracies, is to adapt the strategic and tactical experience gained in successful revolutions in developing and nondemocratic societies. In this sense, the process of proliferation of new revolutionary theories can be viewed as a continuation of the trend started with the victory of bolshevism in Russia. It was a trend of transplantation of a revolutionary theory, Leninism, from a developing society to industrial democratic societies; it was ultimately unsuccessful in its aims although very successful in its influence. To a large degree, the new revolutionary theories constitute the second round of such transplantation, this time not necessarily limited to *ex oriente.*

When looking at the New Left activity in industrialized societies, and counterposing it to the great revolutionary activities of the past, some writers cannot resist the temptation to use the Marxian aphorism from the *Eighteenth Brumaire:* history repeats itself, but what was drama the first time becomes a farce the second time around. More just is P. H. Partridge's comment that with repetition the initial drama becomes melodrama.[67] The same can be said about the second round of transplantation of revolutionary theories.

The new revolutionary theories are melodramatic in the truest meaning of the term—they stress the sensational in situation and in action. Melodramatic is the search for the magic wand, for the special approach which will accomplish what decades of efforts failed to do. Melodramatic is the predilection to seek shortcuts to revolutionary accomplishments and the desire to believe that one can somewhat short-circuit the complicated mechanism of power in contemporary industrial societies. Melodramatic is the predisposition to envisage the creation of situations propitious to a sudden revolutionary breakthrough rather than the old-fashioned old left predilection to exploit propitious situations when they arise.

The source, support, adaptation, and application of these new theories and attitudes are entirely associated with the revolutionary conglomerate that is designated as the New Left. As a matter of fact, their association with these new theories and attitudes forms a component core part of their "newness." (I am using the term New Left in only one, most inclusive meaning: those groups and "groupuscules" which are neither part of nor organizationally dependent on the old left—socialist and communist—and which reject the "old" strategies, tactics, policies, and, in most cases, principles of internal association.) Moreover, in every instance that I can think of, a part of the newness is that invariably the groups subsumed under the label New Left are farther to the left— more militant, more immediate and far-reaching in their demands, more extreme in rhetoric and actions—than the old left. Their leftism is so complete as to invite the kind of response which the famous Mayakovsky poem, "Left March," evoked from the Polish writer Slonimski: "He who marches continuously to the left, marches in circles." Yet one should note that in many respects and to an increasing degree the old left is also quite new (although in a different way than the New Left), as the examples of the French Socialist Party and of the Spanish and Italian Communist Parties increasingly show. On the other hand, I would suggest that

the New Left is in many respects much older than it sometimes appears to be on the surface.

Among the tendencies and views which dominate the New
Left and are expressed in its new revolutionary theories, concepts, and attitudes, I would mention the following.

1. It is within the New Left where the only remaining
groups of the left in industrialized democracies will be found
which still explicitly adhere to the view of the necessity of
revolution as an *act* of overthrow by force of the bourgeois
government and state and which reject gradualism as an effi-
cacious revolutionary strategy.

2. These groups reject the social and political arrangements
of their societies to the extent of refusing in their own political actions to abide by the rules which prevail in these societies. In practice this attitude is expressed by the emphasis on
extraparliamentary activity, direct action, and, in some cases,
by the stress on violence and—in the lunatic fringes of the
movement—even on terror. This stress has to do not only
with their belief in the greater efficacy of these types of
actions—that is, their disruptive effect on the system of bourgeois domination and their mobilizing potential—but also and
sometimes even primarily with their belief that only by such
actions can individuals become revolutionary and the revolutionaries themselves remain revolutionaries, and that they can
thus prevent their own degeneration and cooptation into
their corrupt environment.

3. For all practical purposes most of these groups subscribe
to the view that liberal democracy—that is, the "dictatorship
of the bourgeoisie, camouflaged by the fig leaf of formal
democracy"—is less propitious for revolutionary change than
a "naked dictatorship" which exposes the inner workings of
the system in its stark reality, destroys illusions, and forces
the exploited to revolutionary activity or to sympathy for
such activity. In this sense, they are not averse to the view
"the worse the better" and are resistant to criticism of their
actions by the other left, which argues that their behavior
strengthens the forces, or creates the danger, of right reaction
in industrial democratic societies.

4. In its views about the social base of the revolution, the New Left is no longer wedded exclusively to the myth of the proletariat. In some cases, in the light of experience and of the changing social structure of "monopoly capitalism," it doubts the revolutionary potential of the industrial working class. In other cases, it generalizes the societal base of revolutionary transformation to be all-inclusive and simply dichotomizes between the exploiters and the exploited.

5. One way of portraying the New Left is to stress its almost total preoccupation with the present, with the actual making of the revolution and "living the revolution," that is to say, with immediate experience and tactics. The end goals, the vision of the new "good society" in which the revolutionary effort is to find its ultimate justification, are dimly perceived or dismissed entirely. It is as if revolution finds its actual legitimacy and justification in the perception of the evil of what exists rather than in the goodness of what can be. But the weakest and most disastrous void in the theoretical and tactical program of the New Left is to be found in the intermediary link between the experiential and the tactical present and the programmatic and theoretical ultimate future, that is to say, in the area of broadly conceived strategy and of intermediate-range affirmative programs. The New Left groups seem to have "no consecutive coherent views about the points at which established society is to be attacked: they seem to move from issue to issue."[68] This trait and weakness is well caught by the famous Mexican essayist and poet, Octavio Paz, in his "Thinking Back to the Student Revolt":

In 1968 the Mexican political system was plunged into crisis. Five years have since gone by, and we still have not succeeded in creating an independent democratic movement that can offer any real solutions for the enormous problems confronting our country. The spontaneous and healthy negation of 1968 has not been followed by any kind of affirmation. We have proved incapable of drawing up a coherent and viable program of reforms and of creating a national organization. The truth of the matter is that the primary

beneficiary of the events of 1968, and very nearly the only beneficiary has been the regime itself, which in the last few years has
embarked upon a program of reforms aimed at liberalizing it.[69]

The antiauthoritarian orientation with regard to its own
internal organization, and its extraordinarily strong stress
on the participatory principle, is often noted about the
theoretical outlook and practice of the New Left in
comparison to the old left, particularly the communists.
One discussant at the workshop perceptively suggested:

> In the pretty untidy situation we find now as we look around the
> world, there are, it seems to me, two distinctly separate impulses,
> the authoritarian and antiauthoritarian, within the radical fold.
> . . . Now it is certainly true that in particular instances we find
> transmutations from this antiauthoritarian to the old left, com-
> munist type, let's say in West Berlin or in other instances, and
> there are ambiguities in the appeal, the Peronista appeal and to
> some extent the Maoist appeal perhaps to both the authoritarian
> and to the other. But perhaps if we go on further, especially in
> the context of Western Europe, one might ask then whether the
> antiauthoritarian left, the New Left, if you will, is not essentially
> an ineffective replacement precisely because of its antiinstitu-
> tional, antiorganizational impulses. In a sense it seems to validate
> that old saying—the only trilingual pun I can think of—that the
> left is more gauche than sinister.[70]

The stress on the antiauthoritarian impulse which underlines the differences betweeen the orientation of the majority
of the New Left and traditional Leninism is without doubt
valid. Similarly, it is valid to say that organizational weaknesses are a major reason for the ineffectuality of the New
Left. This characteristic reflects the conscious or instinctive
proclivity of most New Left groups to anarchism and anar-
cho-communism, and, more interestingly, to Luxemburgism.
Yet their distance and remoteness from Leninism, especially
from both Leninist dilemmas and solutions, can be and is
vastly overstated, it seems to me.

The newness of the New Left as compared to Leninism is most pronounced in the realm of ideas or, to be more precise, in the counterposition of the Leninist *myth* of the Russian revolution with New Left ideas. Where the counterposition of Leninism and the New Left holds less, if at all, is in the comparison of *actual* Leninist attitudes and actions with those of the New Left. What has the New Left, in the deepest sense, in common with Leninism, despite all the apparent and very real differences?

First, the New Left is a response to basically the same dilemma which faced Leninism—the dilemma of revolutionaries in a nonrevolutionary situation and in a nonrevolutionary society (that is, nonrevolutionary in a socialist sense). This was the dilemma which underlay the "terrible impatience" and frustration of Lenin that struck so many students of the Russian revolution and which also underlies the impatience of the New Left.[71] This dilemma is only magnified in the case of the New Left. While Lenin's Russia was not, and could not be, revolutionary in the socialist sense, it was a society in deep turmoil, suffering from an ultimate crisis of traditional authority with rebellious rural and partly urbanized working classes and a profound mood of antifeudal, antitraditional, and antiauthoritarian revolutionism. The industrially advanced liberal democracies of today are revolutionary neither in the socialist sense nor in the sense that Russia was. (Their only revolutionism is that of the prosystemic techno-scientific and organizational revolution, and their basic antisystemic revolutionary potential is of a different nature: that of disintegrative privatization of concerns and politics and not of the unification of streams of diverse disaffection into a single revolutionary channel.)

Second, the answer to the dilemma implicit or explicit in the New Left's prescriptions, especially on the part of its most extreme components, is fundamentally similar to that of Leninism. The difference with Leninism is not a new direction for solving the dilemma, but rather the New Left's willingness and determination to move further than Leninism on the same path. Lenin's answer to the dilemma was essentially, "You make the revolution with what you have—you seize the opportunity, however slight, whenever it presents itself." It was in fact Lenin and not Che Guevara who first proclaimed, "The duty of every revolutionary is to *make* the revolution." The key to understanding Lenin in the pre-October Revolution period is not so much *organization* as *determination*.[72] This determination is pushed by the New Left a giant step farther by pressing not "simply" for the exploitation of a revolutionary situation, which in Lenin's case was not of his making, but by proposing that through establishing "revolutionary points of action," revolutionary situations can be *created*. To quote the well-known saying by Che Guevara, "It is not always necessary to wait for all the conditions of a revolution to exist; the insurrectional focal point can create them."

Third, a fundamental attitude pervading Leninism and forming the true kernel of his *What is To Be Done* (rather than the overstated question of organization) has also taken hold of the New Left despite all the rhetoric about "people," "participation," and "insertions": it is the attitude of disdain for the worker, the "common man," for his good sense, his everyday aspirations, and his dreams. It is the attitude of knowing better what his "real" interests are than he may ever know by himself and through his own experience. (Whenever the term "real" is used, almost invariably its actual meaning is "ideal," by the standards of those who profess to know what those interests are.) It is the attitude which underlies the Leninist idea of "bringing in" the revolutionary consciousness, and which informs, in fact if not in theory, the practice of the New Left—and it fails both in the case of Leninism and the New Left.

It seems to me that the importance and efficacy of revolutionary theory and guiding models of revolution for the revolutionaries themselves is very dubious, except for their usefulness as unifying myths. An argument can be made that on balance their value is on the negative side. Revolutions are analytically comparable, but despite the similarities of some of their discrete patterns, at the level of action itself, in their irreplicable combination of macro and micro factors, in their unique individuality, they are one of the most inimitable sociopolitical phenomena. One may suggest that, as a rule, if a revolutionary theory (or a guiding model) generalizes the actual experience of an accomplished recent or past revolution, it is already obsolete. If the theory or model generalizes not the actual experience but the *myth* of a past or recent successful revolution, the mystification and harm are only multiplied. It was indeed the good fortune of Castro and his comrades, as Regis Debray remarks, that none of them had read the works of Mao Tse-tung.[73]

For generations the Leninist model of revolution as distilled from Lenin's (and Trotsky's) writings held sway among the radical left. But by its stress on organization, on unification of diverse oppositional streams, on the unevenness of development, on the weak-link thesis, and so forth, it generalized not from the actual successful experience of the revolution in Russia but from the myth of the Russian revolution. The Leninist model was a failure in industrialized democratic societies not only because they were and remain so different from the Russia of the revolution but also because it presented and generalized from a mystified picture of the revolution, glossing over what was unique and decisive for the success of the Russian revolution: a combination of the disintegration of traditional authority, the war, the spontaneous peasant war, the determination and flexibility of Lenin and his followers, and the appalling weaknesses of his opponents.

The New Left's models of revolution in industrialized liberal democracies, born partly from frustration with the Leninist model, also generalize either from the actual successful revolutionary experience in vastly different societies or from a mystified picture of revolutions, already once removed from the reality of their societies. Whether the first or the second is the case, the success of the New Left's models would require an even more exceptional congruence of circumstances, practically beyond the realm of the possible, than those which led the Bolsheviks to victory in Russia.

Prospects for Deradicalization of Communist Movements

The achievements of the left in industrially advanced democracies described previously, and the prospects of further left advances or even of possible major breakthroughs, are almost totally associated with the revitalized and refurbished old left. The future of left radicalism in advanced industrialized societies is being decided in our generation in noncommunist Europe, more specifically in its southern tier, primarily in Italy, France, and Spain. The particular form of the present surge of the old left is coming to be known by the neologism "Eurocommunism," which exemplifies the parliamentary quest for power of center-left or left-of-center party alliances, including the communist parties. These alliances have a better than fair chance of succeeding in their immediate electoral objectives and could signify the beginning of a major transformation of the societies in which they occur.

Why and how the present situation came about in France and Italy, how it differs in the two countries, and the most likely prospects for its resolution are treated admirably in the essays by Sidney Tarrow in volume 1 of this work and Peter Lange in this volume. I would like to concentrate on evaluating the nature of this phenomenon and, more specifically, on examining the question of whether Eurocommunism signifies a beginning or even an advanced stage of deradicalization of the major communist parties of Europe.

The phenomenon of Eurocommunism involves three discrete processes: the revitalization and movement to the left of some socialist parties, most notably the French; the deep crisis of the center parties, most notably the Italian; and the adoption by a number of communist parties—the French, Spanish, Belgian, British, and especially the Italian—of a new, long-range political strategy. This strategy commits the parties explicitly and programmatically to gradualism in their effort for structural change of their societies, to adherence to the rules and procedures of democratic and parliamentary politics, and to electoral alliances and governmental coalitions with less radical or nonradical political partners. I shall deal here with the third element, communist strategy.

One may argue that in two major respects the communist strategy and behavior are not very new or striking but a continuation, in the countries in question and in other European countries, of a well-established pattern of political behavior. In the first place, the revolutionism of the communist party in industrially advanced European liberal democracies, or even in the not-so-democratic European states, has been questionable since the time that Stalin established domination over the international communist movement. The communists' programmatic and tactical phraseology, their propaganda and internal party education, their adherence to the vision of a "last battle" was very revolutionary indeed, but their actual policies and the tools of their political trade were rather conventional even if predominantly negative. In this sense the communist parties of Europe ceased to be revolutionary in practice. However, they remained parties with revolutionary *potential* because of their internal organization; the weight of the "true believers" among their militants, the insularity of their membership and organization and the nature of the parties as separate "communities," "subcultures" within the nation rather than traditional political associations;[74] the loyalty of their leadership to the Soviet super-domination; their negativism and their voluntary or involuntary isolation from the mainstream of the political life of their countries.

Second, the explicit strategy which stressed gradualism and a desire for alliances in coalitions with "nonbelievers" emerged periodically in the European communist movement and in the past had very often been considered a major, even secular, change of its basic attitudes, only to prove later to have been a stratagem.[75] This stratagem was sometimes defensive in nature, like the united-front and popular-front policies of the 1930s, directed against the onslaught of an overwhelming danger to the communist parties and to the Soviet Union. Sometimes it was offensive in nature, as in Eastern Europe in the 1940s, when it was a calculated design to take advantage, at lowest possible cost, of situations propitious to the expansion of influence or domination by the communist parties and the Soviet Union.

Indeed, it is largely because of these past memories that some argue very ardently for the probability that the present strategy, despite the presence of many new and different elements, may turn out to be basically a repetition of the past and, if accepted at face value by those committed to democratic changes, will have incalculable negative consequences for the future. The developments within the European communist parties, writes Walter Laqueur, "are very interesting. They would be even more reassuring if they were not repeat performances. . . . There is no denying that the West European communist parties have learned from past mistakes and that they have become more modern and more pragmatic in their approach. But they have not become more democratic, and it is difficult to imagine that parties which are still strictly authoritarian in their own internal structure could become guardians of liberty in the sphere of national politics."[76]

Naturally, more is involved than past experience. The Leninist-type party organization, the traditions and connections of the majority of the leadership, and the heavy blocs of not only pro-Soviet but also pro-Stalinist supporters among the party activists make the fears and doubts about the authenticity of the European communist commitment to democracy legitimate, to say the least. These characteristics and doubts are naturally much more pronounced with regard to the French than to the Italian party. In the French case, in addition, one discerns a major resemblance between the present strategy, with its claim to communist monopoly on representing industrial workers and its stress on political rather than social alliances, and the French Communist Party's strategy in the 1930s.[77]

Yet it is equally legitimate and necessary to point out some of the major differences which make the present European communist strategy different from the past pattern, and therefore to consider the possibility of its being a part of a process not only of the advanced *disintegration* of communism as a world movement, which very few observers doubt, but the beginning of a *transformation* of some of its component parts away from its Leninist tradition—a process comparable to the transformation of components of the revolutionary Marxian socialist movement at the beginning of the twentieth century.

The most obvious and most important difference is the ideological crisis that underlies the European communist strategy. The main expression of this crisis is the loss of faith in the Soviet model, the loosening of ties with the Soviet party, and the end of Soviet domination of those parties. In the past, the strategies of apparent gradualism were not only accepted but engineered by Moscow. Today, for a number of reasons, including the dangers to Soviet imperial legitimacy in Eastern Europe and to its investment in and potential benefits from détente, the Soviet Union is far from happy with its West European comrades.[78] The Soviet Union is conducting what amounts to a holding operation—on the one hand attempting to minimize the potential losses inherent in the drive for independence of the West European parties, on the other hand trying to determine what can be gained if the West European parties succeed in their strategies *and* do hold to their electoral promises.[79]

Another major difference is the nature and extent of *programmatic* changes proclaimed by some of the West European communist parties. In the past, whatever the change in the West European parties' strategic line and tactics, whether in the 1930s or in the immediate postwar period, the basic programmatic declarations remained untouched. Moreover, the parties toned down but never really concealed the fact that they considered the gradualist and coalitionist strategic line to be applicable to a phase in their effort. It was a phase that was described as transitional, as being the "lower stage" preceding the "pure," socialist, higher stage of their struggle. Today, the ideological, programmatic changes in the West European communist parties are, at least on the face of it, both much farther reaching and of a different kind.[80]

Still another difference, the least researched and least known as well as certainly the least pronounced and the most ambiguous, rests in the nature of the West European communist parties themselves—with the profile of their leadership and membership, with their internal structure and activity. (Here again the Italian example represents the most extreme case of change away from the Leninst "ideal" model.) With regard to this dimension of a developing difference between the present and the past of the West European communist parties, one would have to stress the diversity of their memberships, the divergent tendencies within their leaderships, the contradictory basis of their outside support, and the development of competing and semiautonomous bases of internal power; in other words, the ambivalence and heterogeneity of the internal power and policy dynamics.[81] The term ambivalence is usually used to describe situations which do not display a clear trend, a clear-cut tendency of development. Such ambivalence is precisely a change in comparison with the past and represents the greatest divergence from the "ideal" Leninist model. It is an ambiguity which does not square well with any idea of a monolithic and extremely rigid organization. I am not suggesting that this makes the parties non-Leninist, but only that it makes their Leninism in internal party affairs diluted and more open to pressures from different directions than ever before.

One more additional point: I do not wish to minimize the importance of the centralistic, undemocratic internal structures and procedures of the communist parties, originally imposed by the Comintern on all its sections, for evaluating the prospects of the West European communist parties and the meaningfulness of their changing strategies. The process of change in this respect, however slow and uneven, is proceeding within these parties. This is the most difficult of all the processes of change through which the Western communist parties have been going in the last decade and, of course, in the words of Richard Lowenthal,

> we must expect resistance against organizational change to be tougher than any other issue. Here, not only the vested interests of the party machines are at stake, but ultimately the distinctive character of the Communist parties itself—their "being" as dis-

tinct from their "consciousness." If they renounced that, they would turn into some kind of militant democratic-socialist parties, and might well find that their only remaining reasons for separate existence are of a historical, not to say sentimental kind.[82]

Yet, if this process continues even without reaching the relative openness of other parties and political associations in the West, is it not legitimate to question the attempts to impose a too-stringent correlation between the degree of democratization in the *internal* organization and procedures of these parties and their commitment to adhere to the basic *external* democratic "rules of the game" within the society at large? After all, Michels' "Iron Law of Oligarchy" was derived not from the experience of the communist parties but from that of the German social democracy and trade unions.[83] It may be well to remember that American trade unions, let alone business corporations, are internally not exactly models of democracy and can nevertheless be committed to the larger political democratic system. The problem with respect to the communist parties is not of any utopian democratization but of the departure from the distinctive stringent "Eastern" characteristics of their internal life, of their becoming undemocratic according to the "Western" rather than the "Eastern" pattern—and this process, if not very advanced, has already started.

Like every transition, the present situation in European communism is ambiguous: the old is far from being over, the new is far from being firmly established. It is a situation where the evidence is contradictory, the lines of division murky, and the trends balanced in such a way that they can still go in either direction. That is not to say that the situation in European communism may return to the pre-1970s conditions, but rather that it can remain frozen for a prolonged period.

Under such conditions an attempt to make generalizations demands a degree of clarity about a number of pertinent terms and concepts. Three such central concepts which will have to be examined briefly are revolutionism, reformism (or opportunism), and deradicalization. Revolutionism and reformism are paired concepts. Each separately makes little sense without the other. To know what one is not, one has to know what the other is. Their contrapuntal unity is both logical and historical. The concepts of revolutionism and reformism denote a state, a mode of behavior, a cluster of attitudes, predispositions, and policy orientations; and the concept of deradicalization denotes the dynamics by which revolutionism becomes transformed into reformism.

It is easier to define revolutionism and reformism by what they are *not* with regard to goals, strategies, and tactics rather than by what they are. Revolutionism does not mean a denial of partial reforms and of the struggle for specific demands which are consistent with the preservation of the capitalist system; it does not mean a refusal to employ traditional forms of political struggle and pressure; it does not mean a commitment to the constant employment of the most militant measures of mobilization against the existing system. Reformism, by the same token, cannot be identified only by its devotion to policies which tinker with the system and by its participation in the traditional game of politics. In the opening lines of the preface to her best-known pamphlet, *Social Reform or Revolution,* Rosa Luxemburg makes this point with utmost clarity (a point, incidentally, later repeated endlessly by other antireformists, especially Leninists):

> At first view, the title of this work may be surprising. Social reform *or* revolution? Can Social Democracy be *against* social reforms? Can it *oppose* social revolution, the transformation of the existing order, its final goal, to social reforms? Certainly not. The practical daily struggle for reforms, for the amelioration of the condition of the workers within the framework of the existing social order, and for democratic institutions, offers Social Democracy the only means of engaging in the proletarian class struggle and working in the direction of the final goal—the conquest of political power and the suppression of wage labor. For

Social Democracy there exists an indissoluble tie between social
reforms and revolution. The struggle for reforms is its *means;* the
social revolution its *goal.*[84]

Revolutionism is, above anything else, a belief that reforming efforts make sense and are acceptable only to the extent
that they prepare for the social revolution and help to bring
it about. Reformism, then, is above anything else a belief that
social revolution is impossible, or unnecessary, or both.

While in theory reform and revolution are unified by the
logic, or if one prefers, dialectic, of their mutual relationship,
and while Rosa Luxemburg rhetorically asks how one can
consider separating them, in the practice of radical movements there is always a built-in tension between the two. Reform and revolution are the two poles that push and sometimes even tear apart radical movements from within. The
conscious energy needed to keep them together within a
movement is in the long run much greater than the spontaneous centrifugal energy that pushes apart parts of the movement, into revolutionism or reformism.

The clear-cut conceptual distinction between revolutionism and reformism is complicated by a number of factors,
both in the general application and particularly in specific
cases. Some of these factors are old and apply as well to the
past as to the present; some are new and reflect the complexity of the present state of the left movements in Europe and
of their sociopolitical and international environment. As with
all paired social concepts or phenomena, it is not at all difficult to identify the extremes which fall squarely within one
of the two poles, and it is also easy to discern and contrast
their extreme identifying characteristics. Such a clear-cut
situation occurs when reformist tendencies within the radical
movement find their way into the movement's programs and
begin to be expressed in explicit ideological terms. This is
what happened within German social democracy at the beginning of the century, when groups with pronounced reformist
tendencies openly embraced Bernstein's revisionism.[85] European social democracy ceased to be a revolutionary move-

ment with the formalizing of internal divisions within the socialist parties into organizational separateness during and directly after World War I.

It is also possible to make more or less clear-cut distinctions even when the reformist tendencies are not expressed in programmatic and ideological terms but are so strong in practical politics as to be unmistakable. Thus at each party congress before World War I the German Social Democratic Party under the centrist leadership of Kautsky and Bebel reaffirmed its devotion to the Erfurt program, whose explicit goal was social revolution, and presented its reformist activity as steps on the road to such revolution. Yet this was clearly a case of a very evident, pronounced split between theory and practice; a case of *ritualization* of the revolutionary theory and program to the point where they lost all vestiges of their operational meaning.[86]

The situation that concerns us here, however, does not involve such clear-cut departures in both theory and practice or a practice which leaves little doubt that the ideological invocations of social revolution are nothing more than incantations. When neither is true, one has to treat reformism and revolutionism as competing tendencies within a radical movement and especially within its leadership. These tendencies are not necessarily vested in separate groups or leaders but co-exist in the movement as a whole and in the actions and thoughts of individual leaders and activists which compose it. One has to look for a dominant trend, if there is one.

Revolutionary leaders and theoreticians of the past, especially Lenin, Trotsky, and Rosa Luxemburg (as well as many social scientists), have suggested a great number of telling intermediary indicators (that is, indicators that show a tendency which has not yet been expressed and sanctified in theory) of reformist tendencies and behavior in revolutionary movements. These indicators are related to the nature and range of the demands being advanced, to the focus of organizational activity, to the tactical forms of action adopted, and to the organizational structure of the movement.[87] All these indicators can be summarized as the lack of effort to build bridges, ties between the "program minimum"—the program which according to the movement can be accomplished *before* the revolution—and the "program maximum," which can only be accomplished *through* the revolution. This comes very close to stressing the importance of what Michael Parenti, in the context of radical politics in today's United States, defines as "transitional revolutionary demands"— and, one may add, forms of action. In Parenti's view, such demands

> are essentially reformist and non-revolutionary in appearance *yet they are impossible to effect within the present system if that system is to maintain itself.* Students demand, for instance, that the university cease performing indispensable services for the corporate-military economy, including various kinds of vital research and personnel training, and that it withdraw its investments in giant corporations and devote a substantial portion of its resources to the needs of the impoverished, many of whom live within a stone's throw of its ivy-covered walls. And they demand that the multibillion dollar system of domestic and international service and armed protection given to the corporate elites be ceased on behalf of a multibillion dollar public investment against domestic and international poverty (one that would preempt some important private producer interests at home and abroad). While sounding enough like the reformist, peaceful-change-within-the-system policies of the gradualist, these demands are essentially revolutionary in their effect in that they presuppose a dedication to interests which deny the essential interests and power of the prevailing elites.[88]

In his book *The Marxian Revolutionary Idea*, Robert Tucker devotes a chapter to deradicalization of Marxist movements. His focus is on the deradicalization of communist parties *in power*, most notably that of the Soviet Union. He devotes some attention to deradicalization of Marxist movements out of power, specifically to social democracy before World War I, and on this subject he summarizes and develops Michels' arguments. His major propositions are at least partially applicable to Marxian movements in general.

The consequences of the process of deradicalization are summed up by Tucker as follows:

> It appears to be the fate of radical movements that survive and flourish for long *without* remaking the world that they undergo eventually a process of deradicalization. A loss of *élan* is not necessarily involved, for this process can go on in a movement at a time of significant growth and advance. Deradicalization signifies a subtle change in the movement's relation to the social milieu. Essentially, it settles down and adjusts itself to existence within the very order that it officially desires to overthrow and transform. That is not to say that the movement turns into a conservative social force opposed to social change. Rather, it becomes "reformist" in the sense that it accepts the established system and its institutionalized procedures as the framework for further efforts in the direction of social change. . . . The phrase *"coming to terms with the existing order"* best indicates what deradicalization means. In the stage of deradicalization, the movement loses its revolutionary otherworldliness, the alienation from existing conditions arising out of its commitment to a future perfect order, and makes an accommodation to the world as it stands.[89]

Among the numerous causal factors that account for deradicalization, Tucker stresses especially the following two: *leadership change,* because the new generation tends to concentrate its energies on the organization as such and on its social constituency, while the old radical founders have mellowed with age; and *worldly success,* when the growth of the organization and its constituency, and its recognition and acceptance as a force in the society, dilutes its radicalism and fosters deradicalization.[90]

Is deradicalization and eventual reformism the dominant trend and the fate of the West European communist parties?

The answer is not yet in, and for a number of reasons cannot yet be in, even with regard to the Italian Communist Party. This is so primarily because the answer, while vitally dependent on what is happening in Europe today, is even more dependent on what will happen in the next decade. In considering the question of deradicalization as applied to the present situation in West European communism, it is my contention that: (1) The past standards applied by the left, and largely adopted by the academic community, to distinguish between revolutionism and reformism are now of limited applicability. (2) The dimension of the problem which has to do with the relationship of a European communist party to the Soviet Union has to be separated from other dimensions. (3) Some questions about the present and future behavior of the European communist parties are often formulated imprecisely, or are simply the wrong questions.

In analyzing the process which we are witnessing today in West European communism one deals with a transitional situation in which clear-cut answers are impossible and in which the most important characteristics of the phenomenon are not the extreme ones but those in the middle range, where shades and subtle distinctions predominate and are very difficult to pinpoint. Equally important, a number of factors enter into the equation which make past standards of evaluation very questionable. The main complication hinges on the understanding of the terms "revolution" and "revolutionary transformation." The complication is far from being merely terminological; it concerns the meaning and substance of revolutionary transformation, goes to the heart of the present strategies of the European communist parties, and is crucial for their evaluation.

From Marx and Engels to Lenin and Trotsky through Luxemburg and Gramsci, the crucial meaning of socialist revolution in an industrial society in its most direct and specific sense, and the mark distinguishing revolutionism from reformism, concerned the act of attaining political power. Naturally, how one envisaged the *act* of taking power "of the working class, by the working class, for the working class" differed significantly through time for the various strands of the Marxian revolutionary movement. Some, like Lenin, put greater stress on the formula "for the working class," seeing in the party and its elite the instrument of workers' interests; some, like Rosa Luxemburg and Gramsci, followed the more traditional Marxian view by putting greater stress on the participatory and partly spontaneous formula "of the working class and by the working class." But in all cases in the past the revolution referred primarily to an act of taking power, an act of force and of violence, carried out against determined opposition.

Rosa Luxemburg's interpretation—directed against the German reformists—of Engels' famous preface to *Class Struggles in France* is a typical example.

> In a word, democracy is indispensable not because it renders *superfluous* the conquest of political power by the proletariat but, on the contrary, because it renders this conquest of power both necessary as well as *possible*. When Engels, in his Preface to *Class Struggles in France,* revised the tactics of the modern labor movement and opposed the legal struggle to the barricades, he did not have in mind—*this comes out in every line of the Preface*—the question of the final conquest of political power, but the modern daily struggle: not the attitude of the proletariat *opposed to* the capitalist state at the moment of the seizure of state power, but its attitude within the *bounds* of the capitalist state. In a word, Engels gave directions to the *oppressed* proletariat, not to the victorious proletariat.
>
> On the other hand, Marx's well-known declaration concerning the agrarian question in England, on which Bernstein leans heavily— "We would probably succeed more easily by buying out the landlords"—does not refer to the attitude of the proletariat *before* but *after* its victory. For, obviously, it can only be a question of buying out the old dominant class when the working class is in power. The possibility envisaged by Marx is that of the *peaceful exercise of the dictatorship of the proletariat* and not the replacement of the dictatorship by capitalist social reforms.
>
> The necessity of the proletariat's seizing power was always un-

questionable for Marx and Engels. It is left to Bernstein to consider the henhouse of bourgeois parliamentarianism as the correct
organ by means of which the most formidable social transformation in history, the passage of society from the *capitalist* to the
socialist form, is to be completed.[91]

To expunge the understanding of socialist revolution as an
act of assuming state power is contrary to the very letter and
spirit of Marxism. Once the idea of socialists taking power as
the *supreme revolutionary act* and as the *initial act of socialist transformation* is abandoned, the entire past distinction
between reformism and revolutionism does not make sense
any more. The distinction becomes so tied to the intentions
and goodwill of the movement's leaders, so lacking in any
material, objective distinguishing standards, as to be meaningless and totally subjective.[92]

In my opinion the old standards of Marxian movements
for distinguishing between revolutionism and reformism have
lost their validity insofar as the dividing line between the two
had been the attitude towards revolution as an act of taking
power. No party of the old left in industrialized democracies
subscribes any longer to the view that a socialist revolution
thus understood is possible. It seems that this evaluation is
very realistic. Unless the Western military-political alliance
breaks down and an active intervention of Soviet forces is
contemplated, and unless the internal disintegration of
authority reaches a level where it encompasses the police
and military forces, a successful old-fashioned revolution in
industrially developed societies is unimaginable. But once this
dividing line which had separated reformists from revolutionaries has disappeared, the only possible reply to the question
"Who is reformist and who is revolutionary?" is that of the
New Left, which, applying the old standards, considers all
groups except itself reformist; or of the doctrinaire anticommunist who judges the communists not by their behavior
but by their dark intentions and traditions; or of those hopeful souls who consider everything that is not New Left and
does not subscribe to terrorism, urban guerrilla struggle, and

other histrionics, to be reformist. In my opinion, all three attitudes do not reflect reality because they are based on outmoded and invalid standards.[93]

Nevertheless, another traditional standard, although much less clear-cut and satisfactory, may have retained its validity in distinguishing between reformism and revolutionism. It is the standard which assigns a much broader and far-reaching meaning to the term revolution than merely the acquisition of power. Revolution in this case is understood as a revolutionary political and social transformation of the system. According to the old Marxian truths, accepted by all revolutionaries in the past, such a transformation would require a revolutionary takeover as its precondition. Once this precondition is dispensed with, however, the attitudes and practical steps directed towards a revolutionary transformation can still be considered as the dividing line between contemporary reformism and revolutionism.[94] The question is whether the West European communist parties have a commitment to such a transformation. The difficulty with the question is that it is impossible to deduce from the present-day strategies of these parties whether they have such a commitment.

That such a commitment is contained in their programmatic statements and long-range slogans is quite evident. What is not so clearly evident is the presence in their everyday policies of demands which Parenti characterizes as "transitional" and of the determination to press for the fulfillment of these demands. Some see a departure in fact if not in word from a commitment to revolutionary transformation in the adoption by the communist parties of the strategy of "peaceful transition to socialism." This viewpoint considers the question of *what*—the goals of the transition, transformation —to be subordinate to and crucially dependent on the *how*— the commitment to a peaceful process. Others still see the communist parties as committed to revolutionary transformation even if the emphasis of their strategies is on "peaceful transition." The question of *how* is seen as subordinate to and crucially dependent on the *what*.

Those who are impressed (or distressed) by the Italian or

French Communist Party's accent on the peaceful strategy of socialist transformation should consider whether there is not a resemblance between the attitudes of those parties towards revolution and socialist transformation and the Bismarckian position on the relationship between German national goals and war. It is said that when Bismarck was asked whether he wanted war, he replied: "Certainly not. What I want is victory." (The crux of the matter, of course, is whether victory or socialist transformation is attainable without external war in the first case and internal war in the second case.)

Those who dismiss a European communist party's stress on the peaceful strategy of socialist transformation or consider it of very limited importance should remember that in the past deradicalization always began with changes in the means by which programmatic goals were to be attained; if, for one reason or another, such changes in the means persist over long periods of time, they become institutionalized; they influence vitally the formulation and perception of desired and attainable goals and the order of priorities attached to those goals. Regardless of which point of view one prefers, the question whether reformism or revolutionism is dominant in the strategy of peaceful transformation cannot be answered, since the crucial factors pertain not to the present but to the future behavior of the European communist parties.

The West European communist parties of the past were characterized by three distinguishing traits. First, their own interests and the acquisition of power were subordinated to Soviet international interests. In the past forty years the European communist parties were nonrevolutionary by standards other than those applied by the Soviet Union. The Soviet standards of revolutionism, similar to their standards of internationalism, were and remain very simple: what is good for the Soviet Union is good for the world revolution. That is to say, revolutionaries and internationalists are those who support Soviet defensive and offensive intentions and policies, whatever they may be.[95] For the European communist parties, revolutions in their own countries were a secondary priority to this overwhelming pro-Soviet international duty. Whenever a conflict between the two arose the Soviet interests were dominant.

Second, despite their influence within their societies, the West European communist parties remained largely a subculture within their polities, reduced to the status of permanent opposition, a condition in which they neither disappeared nor attained governance. The European communist parties remained revolutionary in the sense that they kept alive among their leadership, activists, and members the vision of a final battle to come; that they on the whole successfully cultivated the attitude of basic rejection of the existing social, political, and especially economic system; and that they preserved a tight, separate, and insular organization and a distinct identity of separateness and divergence from other political associations.

Third, the vision of the good society to which the West European communist parties aspired and towards which they oriented their membership was that of the Soviet type of socialism. Regardless of the tactics of the moment and the stress on the validity of "different roads to socialism," there was never any doubt in the minds of their opponents and, more importantly, of their followers, that the model of socialist transformation towards which they ultimately wanted to lead their societies was that which existed in the Soviet Union.

These three characteristics did not point to a deradicalization of the type described by Michels, a deradicalization symptomatic of the social democracies before World War I as well as of the communist parties after their attainment of power, described by Tucker. All of these characteristics stressed the causal importance of the factors that deal with the *internal* dimension of the process of deradicalization. With regard to the West European parties of the past it was a process where the *international* dimension was crucial and could be defined as deradicalization only in two limited and very distinct meanings—first, in their subordination to an external power, the Soviet Union, which had ceased to be revolutionary in its internal goals and behavior; and second, in their adherence to the Soviet model of a "good society," which departed radically from the original Marxian idea.

The West European communist parties of today have in varying degrees discarded or are discarding all three characteristics described above. The moving away of the West European communist parties from subordination to international Soviet interests can make them more revolutionary rather than less, by orienting them to revolutionary opportunities in their own countries. The moving away of the West European communist parties from their isolation, negativism, and permanent oppositionism may lead to an "old-fashioned" deradicalization primarily, or perhaps only, when their integration into the mainstream of political life in their countries will not lead to their rapid acquisition of dominance within their polities. The moving away of the West European communist parties from their subscription to Soviet socialism as the model of revolutionary transformation does not have to mean that they are becoming or will become less revolutionary; it may indicate now and in the future a reorientation to a different model and type of revolutionary transformation. George Lichtheim once said, "The West European communist parties show signs of reviving the Marxist inheritance. In doing this they are, after all, simply reverting to a tradition older than the Russian revolution—a tradition, moreover, which grew on European soil and does not have to be laboriously retranslated into English, German, French, Spanish or Italian."[96]

It is in this context that questions about the present and the future of Eurocommunism have to be answered, to the extent that they can be answered at all.

The question that is being asked about the "new" communist parties of Western Europe is "Do they really mean it?" —that is, is the change in their beliefs, attitudes, policies, and commitments real or transitory? It is my contention that one form of phrasing this question is very imprecise and provides a built-in answer; in another form, the question is unanswerable; and in every form in which it is phrased it is somewhat misleading and fallacious.

When the question is formulated as "Will the communists, after they come to power in Italy or France, adhere to the rules of democratic behavior as they promise now?," the question is imprecise and misleading. It should be pointed out, first of all, that if the communist parties succeed in their electoral and coalitionist strategy, they will become a part of the national government; they will, in other words, share in the national power and not "gain power" in the sense in which the term was applied to communist parties previously. Once an assumption is made about a communist party *taking power*, the question is answered. If the communist parties attempt to take power, that is to say, try to disentangle themselves from their confining alliances and become *the* ruling party in their countries, they have already broken their solemn promises and are on their way to traditional communist rule. The present balance of social and political forces within West European countries as well as the international balance of power makes it virtually inconceivable for the foreseeable future that from a platform of *participation* in a national government the communist parties can become the absolutely dominant force or even the sole occupant of the seat of national government, let alone national power, by electoral, traditional parliamentary means. This is not to say, of course, that such an eventuality is impossible, just as it does not mean that if and when it does occur, it will be resolved without a full-fledged civil war. One of the most possible developments of this kind is pictured realistically by Irving Howe:

> The biggest danger one can foresee is not a revolutionary coup but a situation something like this: a Communist-Socialist bloc wins an election by a narrow margin, it enacts a portion of its joint program, sections of the middle class grow fearful, a crisis verging on civil war follows, and in the ensuing social chaos the hard-line Communists, grown stronger within the party and entrenched in government offices, try to grab power.[97]

In any case, once the question of communist parties acquiring power enters into the equation, the whole question "Do they really mean it?" does not make sense. It should be reworded rather to ask not what they will do after they attain national power but "Are they determined to gain national power and by what means can they achieve it?"

When the question is phrased more precisely and realistically to inquire about the behavior of the communist parties as members of a center-left or left-of-center government, it becomes in my opinion partly unanswerable and partly fallacious. It is unanswerable because the answer depends only to a very limited degree on the party's behavior today and decisively on the party's behavior in the future, if and when it attains its immediate goal of becoming part of a ruling national coalition. It is unanswerable because, prior to such an electoral success, it hinges completely on reading the intentions of the communist leadership. For this reason it is fallacious, because of its underlying assumption that the intentions of the communists today, *before* they are a co-governing party, are crucial rather than the restraints and processes which will be unleashed or will develop slowly *after* the immediate goal of reaching a place in the governing coalition is attained. It is fallacious because it assumes that such intentions do not change, do not depend on situational factors, and, most importantly, because it does not consider the fact that both the intentions and the actual behavior of the communist parties in the coalitions will depend crucially on a number of restraining and confining conditions.

One confining condition is internal to the communist parties themselves and concerns the limitations in their ability to manipulate their mass members and their activists. Remarks McInnes:

> The nightmare that haunts skeptics who argue that the communist parties have not "really" changed—the vision of a party that has won a following counted in millions by practising peaceful, electoralist tactics suddenly reversing to a posture of violent revolutionism while *retaining its millions of followers*—that nightmare, that vision presupposes a faith in Leninism that

should be reserved to communists. A change in policy or in constitution that could not be reversed without crippling the party might nevertheless be reversed, that is, a party can commit political suicide, as the communist parties did in 1939 by approving the Hitler-Stalin pact; but it is, all the same, a change that cannot be dismissed as a mere tactical sham.[98]

Another confining condition is imposed by the very fact that if the communist parties succeed in their strategic goals they will enter the national government as partners in a center-left or left-of-center coalition and in all probability as the junior partners. Aside from the fact that the coalition itself imposes constraints on their freedom of action, it poses also the dilemma of their co-responsibility for coping effectively with the difficult problems of their society and retaining at the same time the electoral support which their oppositional policies outside of the government had made possible. According to Alexander Dallin, "In the case of Finland, minority participation by communists led to a decline in the vote for the communists because they shared the onus for the failures of the government in which they participated; they began gaining after pulling back out again. So this is an issue on which they themselves are split, and which I think makes some difficulties for them."[99]

A major question with regard to the communist parties of Western Europe is the degree of political and organizational *autonomy* and *hegemony* which these parties possess in their self-selected central sociopolitical environments (e.g., among industrial workers, trade unions, local government centers). The possible dangers and trade-offs which successful electoral or governmental alliances pose with regard to their position becomes an important constraint on their policies.

It is also my opinion that in the study of Eurocommunism a tendency to one-sidedness exists which expresses itself in putting too much emphasis on the questions concerning the strategies and tactics of the communist parties and taking too little account of the actual and potential responses, views, and developmental tendencies of other political elements in these societies. We have to examine much more closely how strong and how resolute the actual and potential allies of the communist parties are, what the context of the decisions among the allies will be in various situations, and the response of the rest of the society to these situations.[100]

This brings me finally to a recent experience outside Europe which exerts a tremendous influence on the thinking of European communist parties. I am speaking here about the Chilean experience and the potential of the establishment of an authoritarian rightist regime as a way out of a serious national crisis.

"The communists are fully aware of this and have drawn the logical conclusion. If they get into power, they must do everything they can to prevent a crisis, they must be ready to be ejected from the government by normal constitutional means. To pursue any other course, given the assumptions on which they are operating, would be to invite a violent fascist counter-revolution. This is precisely the lesson the Western European communist parties have drawn from the Chilean experience."[101]

In describing the dilemmas, and the tragedy, of the developments in German social democracy towards the end of World War I, Carl Schorske concluded: "The frustrating experience of yesterday had blinded the revolutionary leaders of tomorrow."[102] To paraphrase Schorske's conclusion as applied to today's leadership of the West European communist parties, it can be suggested that the heady atmosphere of today's achievements and of the expected successes in the near future may in all probability hide tomorrow's frustrations.

* * *

The communist parties in power and the social democratic parties in parliaments and governments have failed to accomplish the "socialism of the great vision."[103] The resurgence of the vision of "the great, just society" implicit in the explosion of the New Left in the industrialized West bequeathed important radical residuals in the cultural field but was short-lived.

The upsurge of the new old left in Western Europe, despite the gradualism and pragmatism on which it is based, rekindles again hopes, and fears, of major transformations, of revolutionary breakthroughs. One does not know how much those hopes and fears are justified. What one does know is that any system which evolves from the present transition will have no ready-made prescriptions for the multiplicity of problems faced by industrially advanced societies, any more than liberalism has. Neither will it have much in common with the socialist millennium.

John M. Dunn is university lecturer in political science at King's College, Cambridge University. Included in his numerous publications on the dynamics of political change and revolution are Dependence and Opportunity: Political Change in Ahafo *(co-author), and* Modern Revolutions: An Introduction to the Analysis of a Political Phenomenon.

2

The Success and Failure
of Modern Revolutions

John Dunn

Success for Whom? Failure of What?

Ever since there have been politics, there have been political upheavals. As soon as systematic reflection about politics began in the Western world, it was recognized that political upheavals could mean not merely an alteration in the ruling personnel of a particular polity but also a change in the form of its political regime. The core of modern ideas of revolution remains the conception of transforming political regimes by means of or as a result of political upheaval. The main difference between ancient and modern ideas of the connection between political upheaval and regime transformation lies in the directional character of modern conceptions of regime transformation. Such ancient theories of regime transformation as were directional in character at all were explicitly cyclical.[1] Modern analysis of regime transformation need not accept a directional view of historical process; but if it accepts any view of historical process at all[2] it can hardly, except at the most abstract level, suppose its direction to be circular. Elites may circulate, individual rulers or groups of rulers may come and go; but regimes themselves can hardly now be supposed to follow a cyclical path. Modern revolutionaries are historical actors who aspire to transform political regimes in an intended direction by promoting political upheaval. The promotion of political upheaval is a regrettable necessity for (or an invigorating prelude to) regime transformation. It is an instrument which some clearly cherish more tenderly than others; but few revolutionaries would be prepared to admit, were it in some case to prove dispensable, to loving it for its own sake.

The role of revolutionary is central to modern revolutionary processes. It is also unique to modern revolutionary processes. The birth of the role can be fixed with some precision as lying between 1789 and 1796: between the first meeting of the Estates General and the abortive *Conjuration des Egaux* of "Gracchus" Babeuf, as mythically transmitted to the revolutionaries of the nineteenth century by Filippo Buonarroti.[3] At the beginning of 1789, as George Taylor neatly indicates,[4] no significant political force in France expected or advocated a revolution, partly at least because no one in France knew that a revolution was a possible type of historical occurrence.[5] Before 1789 there were classical utopians who set themselves to imagine a better moral world —Rousseau, for example, or Morelly.[6] But classical utopians were above all else men who knew that there was *nothing* to be *done*. As Morelly himself put it: "It is, sadly, only too true that it would be impossible in our day to form any such Republic. . . . I do not have the temerity to claim to be able to reform the human race—only the courage to tell the truth, without troubling myself over the bleating of those who fear it."[7] Since 1789 temerity has increased greatly (partly no doubt at the expense of veracity and the courage this demands) and professional revolutionaries have come to display this temerity in action. Until the French revolution, revolutionary practice was linked to overtly sacred theories. There were religious prophets before 1789 who had taken or aspired to take state power: Müntzer, possibly Savonarola, certainly the Fifth Monarchists.[8] There were agitators, too, who had struggled more or less self-consciously to alter government and society by direct political action, most notably among the Levellers of the Great Rebellion, like John Lilburne.[9] But there were no examples of men who saw their life in strictly secular terms and devoted the whole of it to the project of transforming the political and social order of their country by an attempt to seize power within it. Shortly after the fall of Robespierre in Thermidor of the Year II such men came into existence, and they have existed ever since, living in closed or open conspiracy or in the solitude of their own fantasies,[10] in the hope and with the purpose of changing the political and social world by their acts.

To look at political upheavals through the eyes of these men is to see at once not just a single definition but two very different definitions of success and failure. If their aspiration is to use political upheaval to take state power, they fail if they do not contrive to take state power. There is very much more to revolutionary success than the taking and keeping of state power, but there certainly cannot well be *less*. Revolutionaries, like any other rebels, risk military defeat by incumbent state power, and they also risk defeat by other contenders for the state power which they seek. But even if they contrive to take state power they do not necessarily succeed in realizing their ambitions. Post-revolutionary regimes are seldom wholly unmodified by the political vicissitudes which precede their inception; but they are also seldom or never modified solely in the directions intended or proclaimed by the victorious revolutionaries.

It is not difficult, if one takes the more inflated statements of revolutionary intention *au pied de la lettre,* to mount a strong case for the view that no revolutionaries *ever* succeed. At the other extreme, where political upheaval is perceived by at least some participants or bystanders as purely reactive violence, without clearly conceived goals or even hopes of desired consequences, the issue of success or failure scarcely arises. Most participants in revolutionary processes in practice fall somewhere in between those who have literally no hopes at all and those for whom a more or less coherently conceived utopia is not merely the limit of their ambitions but actually no great distance from their expectations. Insofar as revolutions are constituted of mass processes of social change with ill-defined chronological,[11] geographical, and demographic boundaries, it is apparent that the concepts of success and failure fit them poorly indeed. Social process, one might be tempted to say, does not succeed or fail. It merely occurs. It is men who succeed or fail[12]—or perhaps, more reductively still, it is particular human actions or projects that do so. It only makes sense to speak of success or failure in relation to intended actions or assemblages of actions. To the question of precisely what it is or who it is that succeeds or fails in modern revolutions, the natural answer is that professional revolutionaries and their careers as a whole or particular actions they undertake are the subjects of success and failure. Such a judgment is likely to be common ground between those who sympathize with modern revolutionary enterprises and those who abhor them. The breadth of audience to which it appeals, however, is not a trustworthy measure of its analytical merit. Its crucial weakness is the status which it gives within the revolutionary process to the beliefs of professional revolutionaries themselves. Acceptance of this status suggests that revolutionaries are obliged, if they wish to vindicate the rationality of the revolutionary process, to establish the logical coherence and the grounding in social reality of their whole system of beliefs. It also suggests, conversely, that anyone who can expose major incoherences within the belief systems of revolutionaries, or gross disparities between their beliefs and special or political fact, has established the substantive irrationality of the revolutionary process, at least in this instance. To establish the logical coherence and the grounding in social reality of one's whole system of beliefs may possibly be thought to be an obligation incumbent on all who occupy the professional role of a social scientist. But it is not a light endeavor, and there is some doubt whether it is a task at which it is in principle possible to succeed.[13] If the criterion for historically rational action is made as strong as this, the effect may well be to denude the historical process of rationality altogether. And, whether we appreciate the historical opportunities for doing so or not (and whether or not we grasp the fact that we *are* doing so), act we must.

It may help at this stage to distinguish the rationality of action from the rationality of belief. What is rational for an agent to do in a particular context depends logically upon what the agent believes. His beliefs may turn out to be factually false; but although that may make it more likely that his action will prove unsuccessful, it does not suffice to make his action any less rational. But, if the rationality of action is tied directly to an agent's belief, what is rational for an agent to believe does not rest, unfortunately, in any such neat logical niche. If act-rationality is taken on its own, the individual acts of revolutionaries considered seriatim are probably as rational as the acts of any other miscellaneously sampled group of social actors. There would certainly be no reason, for example, to suppose that the acts of revolutionaries are any less simply related to their clearly identified beliefs than are those of policemen, a grouping seldom selected by social scientists for axiomatic epistemological disdain. Edmund Burke, searching, as counterrevolutionaries will, for a firm epistemological put-down for the French enthusiasts, took his stand on the axiomatic sanity of the British House of Commons: "Madmen are not our lawgivers."[14] As social scientists have been badgered into acknowledging the large measure of not merely act-rationality but even rational belief which subsists among those who have lapsed or been forced into the moral career of the insane, such epistemological put-downs have become far harder to maintain.[15]

To note that it has become much harder to challenge the belief-rationality of revolutionary practice is not, however, necessarily to admit that it has become impossible to do so. It may be tempting, for example, to suspect that the lives of revolutionaries taken as wholes are in some way less rational than the lives of most other men; but to suppose this is probably to adopt a rather credulous view of the coherence of the lives of the majority of human beings. The more important point is to grasp the extent to which the lives of revolutionaries demand to be taken as wholes. Professional revolutionaries, as Macintyre argues,[16] are obliged (along perhaps with some sorts of social scientists) to claim to transcend that agitated precariousness which he identifies as the epistemological situation of the ordinary agent and which, rethought in tranquillity, he commends as the proper self-image for those engaged in intellectual practice in the human sciences. It is an easy matter to defend the act-rationality of revolutionaries against the external charge that they in fact know worse than other men what they are doing, act by act. What is far more difficult and may well be quite impossible is to defend professional revolutionaries against the charge that they are obliged to *claim* to know what they are doing better than it can in fact be *known*. The most distinctive feature of professional revolutionaries is the degree to which their beliefs put them permanently epistemologically on the line. The lives of professional revolutionaries are necessarily teleological to a degree that ordinary agents have no ground for emulating; and, even if the telos can be tacitly or explicitly reconsidered in the light of experience, there is always a real possibility that such a modification will imperil its essential identity as a goal. More even than most political careers, the careers of professional revolutionaries are an exercise less in learning how to get what they want than in learning to like what they can get. The teleological logic of the career and its adaptive content are necessarily very much at odds. In the doctrine of the unity of theory and practice, theory usually proves easier to adjust than does practice. Even if one fails to change the world quite as one intended, one can always hit upon a more attractive redescription for the consequences which one's actions prove to have. The limiting case of the unity of theory and practice is complete capitulation to *la force des choses.*

Revolutionaries can certainly fail: when Robespierre lay in

the former Hotel de Ville as the troops of the Convention entered on the tenth of Thermidor, his jaw smashed by a pistol shot in an ineffective attempt at suicide, or later stretched out in agony on a table in the antechamber of the Committee of Public Safety, taunted by curious passers-by, he was fully justified in supposing that success had eluded him.[17] But it is a very nice question indeed whether any professional revolutionaries ever really succeed—not because there are no projects in which any of them ever really succeed (a clearly preposterous claim), but because what they do succeed in bringing about may be very different from what they had hoped. The greatest dead revolutionary of the twentieth century is by common consent Lenin. Even sympathetic analysts have wondered just in what sense Lenin had succeeded at the end of his life, and there is good reason to believe that Lenin himself was at least ambivalent about the question.[18] Revolutionaries who never take state power fail. But even those who do take state power and keep it as long as they live do not necessarily succeed. No man can keep state power forever. Lenin, it is widely agreed, should have died hereafter. But if his death was Russia's tragedy, it may well have been (as Trotsky's political defeat almost certainly was for Trotsky himself) his own moral salvation. One revolutionary who cannot very aptly be said simply to have failed is Josef Stalin; but then few professional revolutionaries would be happy in prospect to adopt such a drastic interpretation of what the unity of theory and practice requires as emerged from Stalin's later years. It would hardly be an apter judgment from the perspective of 1975 to claim that Stalin had in fact succeeded. Succeeded in what precisely?

The careers of professional revolutionaries, like the careers of all professional politicians, stand in a somewhat uncomfortable relation to the beliefs which they (at least publicly) hold. But some beliefs are much less embarrassing to discard for instrumental reasons than are others. It may be no more unlikely for a professional revolutionary to be a careerist than it is for any other professional politician; but it is more damaging for him to be identified as such in the course of his career. The logic of revolutionary belief systems requires that the career of the revolutionary be taken, as good radicals were supposed to take the French revolution, en bloc. Considered en bloc, their careers and the consequences of their careers have always been in uncomfortable tension with aspects of their belief systems, and there are strong (if in the end inconclusive) reasons for expecting them to continue to be in such tension in the future.

But all this holds good, if it holds good at all, only of professional revolutionaries. It does not hold good of the vast preponderance of their followers or colleagues in the wars which they judge just. Amateur revolutionaries, those whose actions *give* power to professional revolutionaries, do not have revolutionary careers. Rather, they take part in revolutionary episodes. They neither live *for* nor *off* revolution, as their professional prompters often must. Consequently they cannot properly be said to undertake revolutionary careers which require to be assessed en bloc though they certainly perform revolutionary acts; and the sense in which they succeed or fail is more contextual and less teleological than the sense in which professional revolutionaries do so. The Paris artisans who made the great revolutionary *journées* of the first five years of the revolution, or even the peasant infantry whose gun barrels carried Mao to power, may not have known quite what they were bringing about; but they undeniably achieved something. On balance it requires an excess of skepticism to believe that they were unhappy with their handiwork in retrospect: the breaking of the *ancien régime*, the founding of the People's Republic. Both as particular acts and as completed episodes, there is no reason to suppose these performances any less well adjusted to beliefs, or adjusted to less well justified beliefs, about their situation than any other segments of their lives. Amateur revolutionaries need not make (and in practice seldom would wish to make) the least pretense to transcend the epistemological situation of ordinary agents. Robespierre and Babeuf, Lenin and Mao, may all have been epistemologically hopelessly overcommitted. But the great majority of actors in revolution are amateurs and not professionals. They do not make revolutions because they suppose themselves to know better than men can in principle know. Rather, they act as they do because these actions seem preferable in each instance to any identified alternative. They make revolutions *faute de mieux*.

In considering the careers of professional revolutionaries it makes good sense to begin by conceiving the making of revolutions as the performance of bounded rational acts, since the making of revolutions is the goal to which revolutionaries address themselves. Revolutionaries who do not contrive to make a revolution fail both in their own understanding and in ours. The positive judgments, however, define themselves much less deftly. Do revolutionaries who contrive to make a revolution necessarily succeed either in their own understanding or in ours; and if they are thought to succeed, what exactly is it that they are thought to have succeeded in doing? The doctrine of the unity of theory and practice readily celebrates accommodation to the practicable, to what it turns out to be possible to do. Revolutionaries who have made a revolution in this understanding have succeeded in doing what could be done, and this in itself constitutes the theoretical sanction for their practice: a providentialist theory of the divine right of postrevolutionary state power.[19] A less bleakly tautologous version of this line of thought would be the ascriptive classification of postrevolutionary state power as socialist by virtue (and solely by virtue) of its having shifted a territorial area from the perimeter of the capitalist mode of production to that of its historically designated, if blearily described, successor.[20]

But if success is not permitted in this fashion to be wholly self-defining, the question of what criteria ought to be employed in defining it presents severe difficulties. The unity of theory and practice does offer a formidable resource for moral evasive action; but it does so precisely because of the real force of its emphasis on the conceptual instability of the revolutionary process. It seems worth insisting on three valid aspects of this emphasis in particular.

1. Revolution is a learning process, both social and

individual, not simply an exploration of technically efficient means for moving towards precisely specified ends. Conservative interpreters of the revolutionary process were very quick to stress that what revolutionaries learn is rational despondency in place of moral willfulness, by virtue of their complete practical subordination to the logic of the revolutionary situation.[21] More sympathetic accounts would stress the extent to which what is learned in the revolutionary process is not the fact of moral impotence nor the attitude of moral passivity, but a deep moral realism which grasps at last how it is indeed possible to transpose the values of utopia into values which are no longer too good for this world: the education of the educators. A more detached view would underline the extreme heterogeneity of what is learned both individually and collectively in revolutions, its discomfitingly wide moral scatter and necessary unpredictability. It would also, since what is learned may always be learned by counter-revolutionaries as well as by revolutionaries, stress the symmetry in this perspective between the success or failure of revolutions and that of other national political ventures. What succeeded in the Russian revolution may well have been the certainty or at least the probability of Stalinism. What succeeded in the failure of the German revolution was perhaps the probability and certainly the possibility of nazism. In considering precisely what succeeded in the Russian or North Vietnamese revolutions it is essential to bear in mind what succeeded in the partition of Ireland or in the prolongation of the life of the government of South Vietnam or in the establishment of the present government of Chile. Much of what is learned in revolutions stands in a most disagreeable relationship to the proclaimed values of revolutionaries (or, for that matter, of their opponents): electric drills through the kneecap as a disciplinary expedient in the oldest war of national liberation in Western Europe, the application of electrodes to the genitals in defense of the *mission civilisatrice* in Vietnam and Algeria. Such increments of practical learning have a way of turning out to be more permanent possessions than many of the more edifying novelties of social organization. If initially unintended desirable consequences can be counted to the credit of revolutionaries, they cannot expect wholly to escape blame for initially unintended consequences of a less inviting character. Modern revolutionary history begins with the storming of a prison, but in the subsequent century and three-quarters it has given ample and evenhanded sustenance to the jailing trades.

2. A consistently consequentialist assessment of revolutions establishes some definite dimensions of success (not always of a very attractive kind) and some dimensions of claimed success which are more contested either factually or conceptually. If the minimal condition for revolutionary success is the taking and keeping of state power, the least factually disputed attainments of revolutionaries are likely to be those most nearly related to the proven capacity to retain state power. The most enticing political hypotheses can get slain by the ugly little fact of defenselessness.[22] Military power is the best demonstrated idiom of revolutionary success precisely because it is a (causal) necessary condition for any such success. Stalin may not have left a country culturally ripe for the transition to communism; but he did (with assistance) win the Great Fatherland Patriotic War. A comparison between the economic base and social organization of the United States and that of Russia late in 1917 and of their comparative military power today, even ignoring the German invasion of Russia during World War II, establishes an astonishing measure of success in generating military power. Whether or not it is true that capitalist societies need to spend a large proportion of their national income on armaments, it seems most unlikely that those societies which remain democracies have proven (or will prove in the future) politically capable of devoting such a large proportion of their wealth to increasing their military capability as has the Soviet regime. However prudent an investment it may be, this mode of achievement is not the most ingratiating of revolutionary performances, but a success it undoubtedly is —and so, *mutatis mutandis*, for China and North Vietnam and perhaps also for Yugoslavia.

A second idiom of achievement, more dependably ingratiating and hence more factually disputed, is that of
economic development. Sympathetic assessments of the
performance of the Soviet economy would emphasize its
rate of expansion over decades in heavy industrial production, the rapidity of its educational, scientific, and technological development from the appallingly low level at the
end of the civil war, and perhaps, once again, the formidable
military apparatus which it has contrived to sustain. Less
sympathetic assessments would concentrate on the problems
of agricultural organization and output, the inefficient utili-
zation of factors of production, the unimpressive volume and
quality of products offered to individual consumers, and the
distortions of official statistics as a basis for comparison with
the economies of predominantly capitalist countries.[23]
Similar but more acute difficulties of assessment arise in the
case of the Chinese economy. Travelers' tales and sympathetic rapportage stress the striking improvements in urban
diet and rural economic comfort and security since the early
1950s. They tend to contrast a picture of rural China as a
society which has fundamentally solved the problem of how
to improve steadily the economic welfare of its population
with a picture, in particular, of rural India as a society
moving relentlessly towards famine and ruin (the *terminus ad
quem* of the capitalist road). But, as in the case of Russia,
other analysts think differently.[24]

Far more complex and puzzling to assess than the sowing
of dragon's teeth or the production of economic goods are
questions of social organization and cultural change. Here
what is learned in revolution may quite often be not simply
how to do something which others have already discovered
ways to do, but how to do something which no one had
previously envisaged doing at all. Yugoslavia, for example,
more by ideological impulsion than by good judgment and
not at all by initial intention, stumbled upon a form of
productive organization which is unique in the modern
world.[25] There is ample doubt as to its merits or durability;
but there are also grounds for viewing it as the sole vital

reflection of a whole moral tradition or even, in extremis, as the sole embodiment of that tradition.[26] In the case of China, more formidably, there have been extraordinarily elaborate and persistent attempts to establish novel and much more egalitarian styles of organization within the units in which men and women reside and work.[27] Furthermore, the development of these organizational novelties has been genuinely a product of (among other factors) collective social learning, not simply a matter of brushing in the initially imagined characters onto blank paper, as Mao incautiously suggested. But to say that it has been a product of social learning is not to imply that it has necessarily been at all a pleasant trip. One people's labor discipline is another people's brainwashing, and it is hard to tell for sure (at least without personal comparative experience) whether working for the east wind to prevail is really more consistently agreeable than working for Ford.[28] From the outside, the way other cultures learn seems like collective religious trance—to cite an old English adage, subjects for social anthropology begin at Calais. If we were they, we probably would not wish to learn that. But the proof of the learning is in the experience; and, while the Cuban New Man no doubt has elements of risibility, it requires great assurance to be certain that the Chinese are not learning something to their own advantage. Nor is the ritual expression of egalitarian social values by any means the only field in which the Chinese revolutionary experience has generated the learning of novel social strategies which, if they do in fact work, might represent major world historical achievements. In particular, the Chinese response in practice to the problems of relating city and countryside in a largely preindustrial society in ways which promote the benefit of both is something of a tonic in the face of the spreading panic at the economic parasitism and culturally blighting impact of the Third World city upon its rural hinterland. Mao's orientation towards industrial society has, as Maurice Meisner has well insisted, more in common with the utopian socialist phase of European political thought than it has with Marx's own bracing commitment in the medium-term future to the "urbanization of the country-side."[29] But there is no reason in principle to believe that utopian socialists with state power at their disposal (a facility denied to Fourier or Cabet) might not hit upon some new advantages of backwardness[30]—at least in comparison with those whose conception of the demands of progress is more rigid. Even though their performance may as yet be more clearly delineated as ideological project than as concrete achievement, there seems good reason to believe that what the Chinese are now attempting in the relationship between their countryside and their cities, in economic complementarity, in education and in health provision, is a major advance on what other comparably poor countries have had the social insight or the political capacity to essay.[31]

3. The third point can be made with merciful brevity. Professional revolutionaries may be necessarily in some degree utopians. They may set themselves to achieve what cannot in practice (or perhaps even in principle[32]) be brought about. But this does not license those who are not themselves revolutionaries to adopt utopian standards of assessment when considering the achievements of revolutionaries. Those who are not utopians must deploy nonutopian standards, and for them the criterion of revolutionary success is not some form of social transcendence but simply doing better: a plain improvement on how matters were before.[33] Yugoslavia has national problems and persisting regional economic inequalities (as has Great Britain). It bullies its intellectuals. A large section of its labor force works as migrants abroad and its domestic economy is heavily penetrated by foreign capital. Even the rate of growth of its economy is becoming a little sluggish. But even when all due allowance has been made for the frailties of real social history, a comparison between Yugoslavia in 1942 or 1930 and Yugoslavia today does *not* suggest failure in the interim. Even if its more distinctive social innovations prove to be something of a historical dead end (which is as yet far from self-evident), there are ample ways in which its title to have done better than could reasonably be expected has already been established. As the Cuba

of the Soviet periphery, it has made friends along with its initial enemies. But in the end both the credit and the blame for its social balance sheet rest with the leadership of the country itself, and the net balance is clearly positive. In the same sense, there is much about modern China which is not endearing to most inhabitants of the West: its grim Puritanism, its sometimes demented political simplicity of mind. But what it was readily open for China to become in 1911 or 1919 or 1945 was not the United States of America or Sweden or Switzerland. In the end professional revolutionaries, like amateurs, make such history as they can, make revolution *faute de mieux*. In the universe of real possibilities, if not in the universe of fantasy which they have at times invoked, the Chinese revolutionaries too have to their credit towering achievements of social betterment. It is not a somehow logically or scientifically guaranteed truth that revolutionaries who can take and keep state power learn how to improve on the objective consequences of their predecessors' rule. But it does seem to be a fairly frequent conjunction.

When Is State Power Likely To Founder?

Whatever else they may constitute, all revolutions necessarily represent the debacle of existing state power within a more or less distinct territorial perimeter. But while the debacle of existing state power is plainly a necessary condition (and one of evident causal significance) for revolutionary success, it is some way from being a sufficient condition. A plausible minimum criterion for revolutionary success would be the destruction of existing state power and the effective establishment and maintenance of a new state power. Such a criterion has the advantage of providing a reasonably firm set of boundaries for the concept which it specifies and of edging the set of cases considered away from simple changes in governing personnel or transfers between different segments of the state apparatus, particularly from barracks to presidential palace. Any specification of the concept must be in some measure arbitrary and politically tendentious. This criterion for success at least avoids violence to ordinary linguistic usage, and such broad *tendance* as it does clearly imply can, on the whole, be deserted only at the cost of abandoning historical reality. Criteria of greater moral stringency do offer firmer obstacles to the temptations of euphemism. But the time to consider them more seriously in the context of practice will be after men have shown that the social world *can* be changed to that attractive a degree by revolutionary action. If we define revolutionary success in these terms—as the historical experiences of very many real men and women, living and dead—two points are immediately apparent. The first and probably the more important is that, even in the twentieth century, the century of revolutionary *success* par excellence, not very many states have in fact succumbed to the assaults of revolutionaries. The second is that even when revolutionaries have succeeded in destroying incumbent state power they have often not contrived to build a stable alternative with which to replace it, and even where revolutionaries have succeeded in establishing a new state power they have not always been substantially responsible for the demise of its predecessor. The lexical paradigm for revolution is a political analogue of domestic murder by overt assault. But, as they occur, revolutions are seldom purely domestic in their causation, and in many cases the destruction of the regimes which they eventually replace is in fact a service performed by other historical actors with little intrinsic interest in domestic animosities.

The great bulk of revolutionary success in the twentieth century has been very intimately related to one or the other of two very undomestic processes: world war and decolonization. The most striking anomalies in this pattern—the Mexican revolution (the most domestic of twentieth-century revolutions) and the Cuban revolution—serve on closer inspection to strengthen rather than to weaken the force of this observation. The Mexican revolution eludes the pattern by having commenced before the pattern was set. But after October 1917 the most domestic of revolutions will hardly escape international entanglements. After October 1917 residual revolutionary features of Mexican history on the whole have been contributions of the state power itself.[34] The Cuban revolution breaks the pattern more recklessly by delaying the making of its major external enemy and its indispensable external friend until it was too late for the former to act effectively against it without immediately encountering the latter. This is scarcely a tightrope which one could expect to see walked to the end twice. Even in retrospect the completion of the transition retains a distinct air of fluke; and it may be doubted whether it could have been walked to the end even once by an agent who was clear throughout what he was doing. It is not wholly inappropriate that the strategic lesson learned from the Cuban experience has been a form of ultravoluntarism.[35] If the damndest things *can* happen, reasons for not trying to make them happen can hardly be presented as conclusive.

It is not obscure how involvement in a major war (and above all crushing military defeat), let alone effective foreign military occupation, could wreck the control of an incumbent government. The connection between the revolutions of 1917–19 in Central and Eastern Europe and in Russia and the impact of World War I scarcely requires emphasis. The disproportion between the damage inflicted by foreign armies on the effective political standing and repressive capacity of incumbent governments and the additional harm which the revolutionaries themselves were able to (or needed to) inflict can be left to speak for itself.[36] The survival of the Soviet revolution and the dramatic military recovery of the Red Army in the face of the Nazi invasion meant that revolutionary energies in the aftermath of World War II in Europe had to work themselves out in a considerably more effectively interventionist environment than that of 1918–21. But as in 1917–19, the closing years of World War II and the period which immediately followed saw a clear revolutionary advance: the successful establishment of one new revolutionary power in Yugoslavia, the attempt to establish at least one other (Greece), and levels of revolutionary mobilization in two of the Western European nations (France and Italy) which had not been attained before in the present century and have not recurred since. The same years also, of course, saw massive territorial conquest by the armies of the Soviet Union. Whatever the scope of its social and economic consequences, it does not serve the cause of either conceptual clarity or political honesty to consider the Russian occupation of Eastern Europe as any sort of revolution. But it is perhaps worth indicating one continuity between the Soviet-established governments in Eastern Europe and the self-established government of Yugoslavia: in both cases they owed the effective destruction of incumbent state power in the countries which they came to rule largely to the military efforts of others. The Yugoslavs managed, for the most part, to dispose of the instruments of this destruction (the German invaders) for themselves, while the other East European successor regimes did little but gratefully accept the gift of their foreign friends. But even in the Yugoslav case it is hard to imagine how they could have succeeded without the intervention of these initially unwelcome external aids.[37]

The drastic weakening of incumbent state power through heavy military defeat, and still more through foreign military occupation, is naturally a far more frequent occurrence during world wars than at any other time. But the insight that world wars provide ecologically favorable conditions for revolutionary mobilization (precisely because they provide ecologically threatening conditions for the survival of even the less unfit powers) does less to illuminate the future than it does to summarize the past. A third world war, if it occurs, will undoubtedly be unpropitious for many incumbent state powers. But, despite Chairman Mao, it seems not only in lamentable taste but also arithmetically baffling to attempt to calculate how far it is likely to be propitious for any revolutionary triumph. To turn instead to the second major geopolitical process which has plainly favored revolution in this century is certainly less depressing and may well also prove more instructive.

The largest single ebb of incumbent state power in the twentieth century has been the rolling back of the map of European empire in the last three decades. The beginnings of this process (except perhaps in the case of the Indian subcontinent) are plainly very much involved with World War II, the collapse of the French Third Republic, the German conquests in North Africa, and the Japanese triumph in the Far East. Even in noncolonial territories in the Far East this aspect of World War II was clearly of great importance in the changing balance between revolutionary and counterrevolutionary power, though the precise significance of the relationship is still in some dispute.[38] In colonial territories, Vietnam, Indonesia, even Burma and Malaysia, the meaning of the impact is more unequivocal. Despite its impressive global scope the maintenance of colonial empire always depended upon a narrow balance of cost and advantage, repressive force and military liability. World War II tipped the balance decisively. Since 1947 the map of Western empire has rolled back apace, leaving only a last few feet, the imperial status of which is for the most part worse than ambiguous—the colonies lack an imperial overlord or the colonists no longer possess a metropolis to which they can, even resentfully, return: South Africa, Ulster, perhaps Israel. The only nineteenth-century empires which have lasted are either themselves now postrevolutionary states like the Soviet Union (the only European dynastic empire to survive the aftermath of World War I with its territorial limits intact), or else they belong to a distinctive set of white colonies of settlement, like the United States, Canada, and Australia. Both of these categories teach a lesson of sorts about the viability of empire, in neither case a wholly agreeable one. Both, of course, emphasize the advantage of a single territorial unit. But both also hint broadly that if you are an imperial power and you wish to avoid revolution within your own territory the best course is to pick a thinly peopled territory in the first place, one with its indigenes at a very low level of technology, and to kill off substantial numbers of them as you go along. The paradigm of imperial counterrevolutionary insurance is, in short, the commonwealth of Australia (most spectacularly the state of Tasmania); and the distinguished nineteenth-century American performance in continental clearance has been marred in retrospect solely by the fecklessness of its eighteenth- and early nineteenth-century importation of what was to become at least in part a domestic racial enemy. In the politics of empire comprehensive massacre is the only dependably final solution.

These somewhat strident considerations serve to make plain that what is precarious in imperial rule is not a relation between alien rulers and indigenes ruled, but essentially a demographic ratio of very few rulers to very many ruled, where these groups are differentiated along essentially ethnic lines. In the immediate aftermath of World War II, it was easy for British or French colonial authorities to confuse the suddenly apparent frailty in imperial authority with the disagreeable conjunctures of the war itself—above all the Japanese invasions. The Fourth Republic subjected this conjunctural theory to the most rigorous practical tests, first in Vietnam and then in Algeria, and in due course paid for the privilege of doing so with its own life. The British, the French, the Belgian, and now the Portuguese empires have all been duly liquidated, though not because the Vietnamese experiment proved that colonial rebels in the postwar geopolitical context could thrash the armies of their colonial masters (an incorrect report of the result of the experiment in even the Vietnamese case). The empires have certainly been liquidated because they were structurally unviable; but the unviability was more political and economic than it was purely military. What Vietnam did show up to 1954 (and what all subsequent repeats of the experiment have essentially served to confirm) was that almost any colony, Guinea-Bissau as much as Algeria and Kenya, could be made to cost its masters, in the blood and domestic disaffiliation of conscript armies and in strictly economic terms as well, exorbitantly more than it could possibly be worth to them to retain it. The shift in the geopolitical context of colonial power was plainly important at the margin. Foreign arms and training and treasure and indeed political friendship were of some importance in Vietnam even at the beginning, and they have certainly retained their importance there as well as in later cases like Algeria or Mozambique. But it is important to insist that the differences have come at the margin and that what they reveal is how narrow the balance of repressive capacity had always been. Just as success proved incremental in colonial expansion, so failure naturally proved to be incremental in colonial contraction, until in the end colonial rule came to seem even to the imperial powers to be an *economically* superannuated mode of promoting the foreign economic relations of the metropolis. The collaborative equation, as Robinson and Gallagher like to put it,[39] evidently required reworking. The shift in the external ecological context of colonial rule may have been crucial, but what it showed was that the frailty in colonial authority was not superficial but fundamental.

The Changing International Context and the Restrictions on Inductive Generalization

Revolution is far from being the only or even the most frequent manner in which the practical commitments of the state apparatus within a given territory can alter drastically and rapidly. More sharp and politically significant change probably occurs in the twentieth century as a result of shifts in the loyalty of the apparatus of coercion than as a direct consequence of any other political factor. Egypt, Libya, Ethiopia, Indonesia, Brazil, Iraq, Chile, Greece, Argentina, Peru, France, Portugal, and very many other countries have had their political history changed drastically in the last quarter of a century by the desertion of their incumbent regimes by the armed forces. The social consequences of such regime changes have been extremely varied, as have their immediate precipitants. In one or two cases it still seems possible that the longer-term consequences of the regime change may be aptly describable as revolutionary. But even in these cases it would be the process of constituting the new political order which might be reasonably thought to merit the epithet "revolutionary," while to apply this epithet in the majority of cases would be to debase the language of political analysis and to deplete its meaning. To insist that there have been few modern revolutions, even at the minimal criterion of revolutionary success, is not to deny that in recent years as in the more distant past many regimes have foundered. But to widen the scope for the analysis of revolution to take in all cases in recent years in which the janissaries have turned on the palace would mean taking in such historical heterogeneity as to preclude any but the most bleary analytical definition of the conditions for success or failure. Definitionally, revolution implies the debacle of existing state power and the constitution of a new state power. In 1789 the symbolic homogeneity and historical depth of the European *ancien régime* was such that its demise at the hands of its own armies might have coined the modern conception of revolution even if no popular assault had taken place. But after 14 July 1789, the medium of the dynasty's fall had become part of its message, and the popular *journée* came to be considered as essential to the revolutionary process as the debacle of the dynasty itself. The forms of popular action in the twentieth century in most cases do not much resemble those of the Sansculottes' *foules révolutionnaires*.[40] The long march has perforce a less hasty rhythm than the *journée,* and organization through time is well understood as an instrumental precondition for its success. Modern revolution is a professional venture, and its professional exponents are very clear that it is better to arrive than to travel hopefully.

Very many regimes, then, may have foundered in the twentieth century, but rather few of them have foundered as a result of revolutionary action by significant sections of their civilian populations. Military coups have been successful by the score, but very few revolutionary attempts have attained even the minimal success of displacing the incumbent regime and replacing it with what proved to be a viable successor. Even among these, much the greater part have depended on two very drastic geopolitical processes, one of which (the collapse of colonial rule) appears to have very nearly run its course and the other of which (world war), although it may not be nearly improbable enough, is excessively difficult to assess clearly in the form in which it may occur in the future. Looking inductively at the twentieth-century record, it is thus tempting initially to conclude either that future revolutions closely resembling those of the first three-quarters of the twentieth century are most unlikely to occur, or that if revolutions do occur in the future they are likely to follow the path of the Cuban revolution—a model the main theoretical property of which is thus in effect identified as its merciful improbability[41] and the ultra-voluntarism to which this improbability lends a slender license. For a number of reasons, however, thinking inductively about revolutions is a very poor basis for predicting the probability of their future occurrence and the forms which they are most likely to take.[42] Whatever it is likely to be like, the revolutionary future is least likely to be an exact replica of the past. In studies of voting, the fallacy of induction may be more often a philosophical error than empirical misguidance. In the study of revolution it is almost certain to prove to be both. Under the revolutionary sun new things happen almost all the time. The Cuban revolution may have had elements of a fluke; but it did, after all, occur.

Improving Our Understanding of Revolutions and What We Might Hope to Learn from Doing So

There is good reason to believe that we cannot *know* about the prospects for future revolutionary success. We may certainly, however, attempt to tune up our sensibilities. It seems worth attempting to do so in at least two ways, first by examining briefly such augmentation of theoretical understanding as has come out of recent analysis of the revolutionary process,[43] and second by considering in an even more ad hoc fashion what sorts of regimes appear especially prone to revolutionary accident or what sorts of social relations seem to nurture the most vigorous and socially persuasive revolutionary entrepreneurship.

The most striking theoretical shift in the analysis of the revolutionary process has been the progressive abandonment of strictly reductionist ambitions by both sociologists and political scientists. The incessant oscillation between determinism and voluntarism characteristic of the theory of revolutionary action ever since the mid-nineteenth century, and perhaps even logically implied by the union of theory and practice, has been transposed into the academic analysis of revolution. Even such a dogged reductionist as Chalmers Johnson has come to believe that the role of conscious action in revolutions needs greater emphasis.[44] In some measure we are all, it seems, voluntarists now. The awesome spectacle of the collapse of the French and later of the European *ancien régime* served to shape the imaginative responses of both revolutionaries and counterrevolutionaries and to impose upon their understandings of revolution an image of ineluctable process, an image which was to be of enormous practical importance in subsequent historical action.[45] Recently these hypnotic effects have begun to wear off, leaving a less providential and far more dangerously contingent world for revolutionaries and counterrevolutionaries alike. An understanding of revolution in terms of profound systemic crisis can only appear adequate where observers are reasonably confident of their ability to discriminate societies which exhibit profound systemic crisis pospectively from those which do not. In retrospect any postrevolutionary society exhibits the symptoms of prerevolutionary systemic crisis, even to the most casual historical analyst. But the ready identifiability of the symptoms, and the possibility of discriminating them with assurance from the superficial difficulties to which all regimes are liable, have come with the privilege of hindsight. If it had been clear that Cuba was in a state of so much profounder systemic crisis than the rest of Latin America, if foresight had been so easy, it is not improbable that the Cuban revolution would not have been permitted to occur at all, and it is virtually certain that the process of its occurrence would have been markedly different. The category of stable polity, once so prevalent in American political science, and so intelligibly extracted from American domestic political experience, never had much theoretical merit.[46] Exposing its practical limitations has enabled revolutionaries to provide not merely an index of how much more voluntarist real revolutionary political history has been in recent decades than it used to be in the bad old nineteenth century, but also an incentive to make it distinctly more voluntarist still. The Napoleonic zest for engaging and seeing what happens is highly infectious when something does happen, though it frequently ebbs fast in the face of effective repression.[47] In retrospect the objective probabilities for the success of any revolutionary enterprise are always low when evaluated in the context of all other revolutionary enterprises contemporary with it: revolutionaries lose far more battles than they win.[48] But sometimes revolutionary enterprises do succeed; and because it is as hard (if not harder) for revolutionaries as it is for political scientists to discriminate a stable polity from an unstable one when they confront it, it is not irrational for them to commit their forces if they attach a high enough value to their (highly improbable) success. The revolutionary wager may have more in common with that commended by Pascal than with most of those placed at Las Vegas. But, unlike Pascal's, it does sometimes pay off in this world.

The central focus of any analysis of the modern revolutionary process must be on the rising net reproduction rate and spreading geographical scatter of professional or semi-professional revolutionaries in the modern world (seen essentially as rational actors, at least in their contention for state power), and on the environmental conditions which appear to militate for or against their accumulating committed popular support in this quest.[49] Analytical explanations of revolutionary allegiance have for the most part centered on the consciousness of individuals, seen as rational actors whose conduct is determined by perceived balances of prospective reward and risk, resentment and protection. Such accounts, whether cast in terms of relative deprivation[50] or of more explicit individual calculation,[51] can in principle have great explanatory power, but they require inordinate quantities of information if they are to be at all illuminating prospectively. Moreover, they require *types* of information which, although they may well be available to the intelligence services of a few major nations, political scientists in their private capacity are unlikely to be able to accumulate in time. A historian considering such theoretical explanations is apt to be struck by their descriptive viscosity, and to suspect that they have much in common with the retrospectively imputed rationality which any plausible and careful storyteller can always fictively impose upon known past behavior.[52] A more promising line of thought is that sketched out by Charles Tilly in a series of interesting papers. Tilly's inquiries began with an examination of the changing nature of collective violence in mid-nineteenth century France from an idiom of localist and communally defensive behavior to an idiom predicated upon the expected responses of the central state apparatus.[53] From this, Tilly proceeded to consider, *inter alia,* the relationship between economic and social modernization and the tendency of alternative polities to begin to build themselves within the territorial authority of legally sovereign states and to compete with their incumbent governments for dominion.[54] It is certainly helpful to think of the voluntarist contribution of professional revolutionaries at least since 1917 (and in some measure in the creation of secret societies and putatively revolutionary political parties for a century beforehand[55]) in terms of the attempt to create competing polities within sovereign states. The shift from legally recognized political organization to illegal and armed political organization may have depended more on the intolerance of incumbent power than on the initiative of revolutionaries themselves. But even conditions in which legitimate political activity was precluded from leading towards socialism—or indeed wholly forbidden—by no means always furnished environments in which such competing polities were successfully created *ex nihilo* or sustained at all handsomely. Both instrumental political calculation, and structural change in the society at large which permits the creation of novel competing polities, plainly require emphasis. But it is most helpful to concentrate rather more attention on a middle term: the capacity of a distinctive type of social organization, the potentially revolutionary party or the party already in arms, to build itself in varying social, political, and geographical environments.[56]

This focus escapes from nineteenth-century conceptions of revolutionary process without committing the analyst to any facile reductionist credo of more recent vintage. It cannot well hinder us and may well assist us to move from a fetishism of geography, tenurial relations, communal animosities, foreign sustenance, or counterinsurgent striking power towards the development of a more inflected sociological sensibility as to just what sorts of regimes and social relations are most likely to generate revolution. The predictive contribution of such a sensibility would be much less than that of an effective predicting machine, an invention which in this case there are good reasons neither to ancipate nor much to welcome. But we may reasonably expect our sensibilities to contribute to other ends than that of increasing our predictive skills; and we might at least hope in this instance that they might edify our social purposes and improve our taste in which polities we choose to succor and which we attempt to erase.

Guessing and Refusing To Guess the Future

At this point prudence probably requires an analyst to throw in his hand. The more sensitive the analytical touch developed in the analysis of the revolutionary process, the more acute the feeling for all political order as an intricate balance of multifarious forces which are almost as difficult to identify with assurance as they are to calibrate with any accuracy, and the stronger the grounds for supposing that an adequate discussion of the potentiality for revolution must inevitably be a discussion of the concrete particularity of individual societies at particular points in time. To offer cheap wisdom in this context is almost necessarily asinine. The appeal of a global strategic vantage point from which it would be possible to inspect the susceptibility of entire societies to revolution in terms of an essentially external ecology is plain enough for academic analysts, as it is for professional revolutionaries themselves. Virtually the only body of writing which seriously undertakes to attempt such a treatment arises out of Marxist analysis of the operations of capitalism as an integrated system functioning on a world scale: the law of uneven development (*plus c'est la même chose plus ça change*), or more generally the theory of imperialism.[57] This body of writing has been of practical importance ever since 1917[58] because of its impact on the political strategies of the governments of the Soviet Union and later of China. But its theoretical importance lies rather in its attempt to take account of the geopolitical context of domestic politics,[59] one of the two aspects of the revolutionary process (the other being the dynamics of state power[60]) for which classical Marxism's focus on revolution as a product of endogenous socioeconomic struggle[61] has proved singularly ill equipped. Unfortunately, the merits of Marxist understanding of imperialism as a metaphysical gloss on the character of international power relations fail more or less completely to extend to an ability to generate particular concrete implications for the prospective experience of particular societies. Marxist analysts of imperialism proclaim the potential significance of the world market and the geopolitical context for revolutionary prospects in all societies with resonance and plausibility. But they scarcely contribute much as yet to telling us just where to look next and when. That geopolitical factors are of crucial importance to revolutionary prospects is evident enough; and there is no a priori reason why geopolitical factors should prove less predictable than the course of domestic social development. But the amateur eye is likely to be caught by how often geopolitical developments which in retrospect were so glaringly predictable as to seem almost inevitable come as a great surprise to those most deeply concerned. Macintyre's insistence on the epistemological significance of the fact that we are all being surprised a great deal of the time[62] has obvious applications in international relations. What could have been more totally predictable in international affairs than the eventual formation of the OPEC cartel?[63] It is hard to imagine that there is often as much conjunctural necessity in major shifts in the world context of revolution as there was in the OPEC case; and the less the conjunctural necessity the less real the prospect for warding off surprises merely by more sustained study and reflection.

Further generalities are likely to be worth stating here only in the very crudest of terms. In the revolutions of the twentieth century there have been essentially two very different models: revolutions, as Tilly puts it,[64] from the center outwards and revolutions from the periphery inwards. The classical nineteenth-century model of revolution moved politically from upheaval in the metropolis to political reconstruction throughout the society. Even in the case of the great exemplar, from 1789 onwards, the role of the metropolis as political cynosure does not adequately disclose where exactly the regime was broken;[65] and, in its pettier recapitulations, three glorious Parisian days might have very little provincial impact by the time their ripples had reached out into the more distant *départements*.[66] But the political image of the capital imposing its will on the countryside epitomized a type of political project which stretched from the Terror and its bedraggled *armées révolutionnaires*[67] through the careers of Buonarroti and Blanqui and the experience of the Commune to the reconsolidation of political control over Russia by the militarized working classes of Petrograd and Moscow (with their more or less reluctant allies), working their way out down the railway lines with firearms in their hands.[68] Even Engels judged that military technology and urban planning had rendered the tactics of mass urban uprising anachronistic in Western Europe by the late nineteenth century.[69] History has yet to prove him wrong. But, even if the experience of May 1968 was more of a cultural fete than a real threat to the viability of the French state (a contentious verdict in itself),[70] the capacity of such a fete to present itself even evanescently as a real political menace is plainly a reflection on the enduring strength of a particular cultural tradition. If in the future there are going to be any centrally engendered political revolutions in industrialized capitalist societies, it will be considerably less surprising if they prove to take place in societies where large sections of the industrial work force are ritually instructed in the merits of revolutionary practice than if they do so in, for example, the United States of America.[71]

The alternative paradigm for revolutionary process (pioneered in China—or perhaps even in Mexico), encircling the cities from the rural periphery, has been more widely emulated in recent decades. Countries plainly vary greatly in their susceptibility to this type of assault. Among the more susceptible groups of countries might be the few surviving colonial societies or societies perceived as colonies by a large proportion (not necessarily a majority) of their indigenes or current inhabitants: South Africa, Israel. In the case of Ulster, even urban guerrilla tactics[72] have proved sufficient to pose a serious threat to the continuity of a regime in a war of national liberation which has not merely lasted intermittently for three centuries but which is now confined to a periphery in which the self-identified indigenes are in a demographic minority. The potential for ethnic mobilization in any society which is seen to be governed by a group drawn from a minority is plain enough. But more careful consideration tends to emphasize the distinction between the now almost wholly abandoned colonial systems of the Western European countries or the United States, and these rumps of the colonial process. Mass popular challenge to the state power is more likely in a territorially extended Israel, in South Africa, or in Ulster over decades than in perhaps the commonwealth of Australia; but such popular challenge is not only sustained by assistance from outside the units in question, it is also plainly largely dependent for its prospects of success on the possibility of external pressure on the existing state power. The political situation of long-lasting immigrant communities which for a variety of reasons no longer perceive themselves as having a metropolis to return to is decisively different from the situation of those colonies from which France, Britain, Belgium, Holland, and now Portugal have elected to withdraw in such haste. The rhythms of decolonization proved so hasty in substantial measure because colonies turned out to be economically such ready targets for revolutionary pressure. It was the colonial metropolis which could be politically priced out of the market. "Colonial" societies which no longer possess a metropolis are less accessible targets, and the rhythms in which they could become "decolonized" should prove rather less hasty—if indeed it turns out to be possible for them to be "decolonized" at all. In these societies mass ethnic mobilization will not be enough: some means of rendering the repressive purpose or capacity of the incumbent state infirm is also required.

A further group of societies in which peripherally initiated revolutionary efforts might prove effective in due course are those which combine a potentially sympathetic neighboring power with a substantial section of their own peasant population trapped in distinctive tenurial relations (outlined by Donald Zagoria[73]) in family-size tenancy systems in areas with high literacy rates. Much has been written recently about the relationship between the degree and type of economic discontent and the capacity for political initiative among peasant populations.[74] Where endogenous peasant discontent is high and the social preconditions for peasant political initiative are widely satisfied, and where geographical circumstances facilitate external military and economic assistance, there are likely to be at least some prospects of building a revolutionary polity from the ground up. But even then the prospects for that polity to succeed in wresting state power from an incumbent regime will continue to depend to a great extent on the political and military capabilities of the regime itself. In the revolutionary process nothing succeeds nearly as well as success and nothing fails like failure.

One final point requires underlining. Unexpected major upheavals in the world economic,[75] political, and perhaps even military environment will continue to occur. The role of professional revolutionary will continue to draw more than ample recruits in many places because there will continue to be many regimes which invite enmity more intensely and more dependably than they are capable of punishing its expression. Armies will continue to shift their allegiance from the regimes which have created and nurtured them, sometimes with consequences far more drastic than their generals or colonels intend. It may be impossible (and it is certainly excessively difficult) to predict with assurance exactly where and when future revolutions will take place. But it is child's play to predict that *some* revolutions are going to take place at some time somewhere. And which revolutions *do* take place will subsequently have very sharp effects on which further revolutions take place after them. A revolution which was permitted to survive in Italy or France would change the politics of Western Europe. Even a revolutionary outcome in Portugal or Spain (perhaps a less improbable eventuality) would have its consequences. A revolution in Brazil or even Argentina would change the politics of Latin America. Nor is it self-evident that there will never be successful revolutionary enterprises within what is now the Soviet bloc. The collaborative equation in the present American "empire" (the imperialism of semi-open economics) or the present Russian "empire" (a neater geographical perimeter) is not a wholly stable balance; and even if it were wholly stable now, there could be no guarantee that it would still be so in ten years' time. We cannot tell which revolutions will happen: only that *some* undesignated revolutions are very likely indeed to occur and that some designated places are less likely to experience them than others. The close ties between geopolitical factors and internal revolutionary processes within a society, and the extent to which revolutionary practice involves mimesis and conceptual invention, taken together, imply one very clear conclusion. What we may be *certain* lies ahead for us in future decades of revolutionary experience is surprises.

Alexander Dallin, formerly Adlai E. Stevenson Professor of International Relations at Columbia University, is currently a professor of history and political science at Stanford University. Primarily interested in foreign and cross-national political institutions and political behavior, revolution, and violence, Professor Dallin has published, among other works, German Rule in Russia *and* Political Terror in Communist Systems *(co-author).*

3

Retreat from Optimism:
On Marxian Models of Revolution
Alexander Dallin

This chapter is concerned with the meaning of "revolution" for different schools and generations of Marxists and Leninists. It seeks to examine their views of and their operating assumptions about the conditions of "revolutionary situations," the actors in such situations, the stages of revolution, the possibilities of success or failure, the likely loci of revolutions, and their relation to levels of socioeconomic development. It is, of necessity, a somewhat selective and impressionistic survey and does not pretend to exhaust either the varieties of Marxism or even the views and behavior of those chosen for discussion below.[1]

We can usefully think of the crystallization of Marxist views over time as the outcome of beliefs confronting reality—an encounter apt to lead to cognitive dissonance and, in turn, adaptations and rationalizations.

I have benefited greatly from the comments on an earlier draft by a number of colleagues. I am particularly indebted to Seweryn Bialer, Zbigniew Brzezinski, Alexander Erlich, Michel Oksenberg, Stanley Rothman, and Donald Zagoria.

Marx and Engels on Revolution

Marxism may be thought of as the last flourishing of bourgeois rationalism. With its belief in an orderly universe and
the goodness of man, with its inherent optimism born of a
faith in progress, Marx's world view stands in closer relation
to the Enlightenment than to the world of Freud and
Einstein, Hitler and Stalin, television and nuclear bombs.

Karl Marx, much like his mentors, saw history as a universal and unilinear process. There is an organic connection
between his perception of social forces in history, his formulation of "scientific socialism," and his conviction that the
good society can be brought about only by revolution.[2]
Given the familiar Marxist scheme of the five successive
stages of socioeconomic development, each determined by a
distinct mode of production, it follows that to Marx a social
revolution is a change in the mode of production. For Marx
and Engels it was precisely the organic, fundamental process
of socioeconomic change—and the contradictions between
the mode of production and the so-called forces, or means, of
production—that constitutes the essential precondition for
the political revolution, which is but the outward and momentary climax, much as the process of birth completes and
makes manifest the process of gestation that precedes it. The
inherent contradiction finds its expression in the class
struggle, which in turn culminates in revolution.

Marx and Engels focused on the dialectic under capitalism,
when the state is an instrument of the ruling bourgeoisie.
The latter, itself (in the words of the Communist Manifesto)
"the product of a long course of development, of a series of
revolutions in the modes of production and exchange,"
plays a "most revolutionary role in history," fighting and
ultimately replacing feudalism. "It has been the first to show
what man's activity can bring about." In time, its constructive role is exhausted; "the weapons with which the bourgeoisie felled feudalism to the ground are now turned
against the bourgeoisie itself." Marx sees in capitalist society
the "laws" of capitalist accumulation, concentration of
capital, and increasing misery in operation. In the age of the

machine. Ultimately (to oversimplify the argument) "centralization of the means of production and socialization of labor reach a point where they become incompatible with the capitalist integument. This integument is burst asunder. The knell of capitalist private property sounds. The expropriators are expropriated."[3]

The rescue from the crisis of capitalism must come through the forcible action of the proletariat—the chosen people (a notion Edmund Wilson called the Hebrew element in Marx)—once its situation becomes a paradigm for the human condition, in Shlomo Avineri's phrase.

If the thrust of the argument in Marx (and even more in Engels) is the inexorable operation of historical "laws" and impersonal "forces," there is here an undeniable element of humanism and human concern as well. Putting it in "modern" terms, Robert C. Tucker has persuasively argued that in Marx's vision "'the source of revolutionary energy in a class is the frustration of man. . . . The goal of all social revolutions, according to Marx, is . . . the liberation of human creativity," and the obstacle to this liberation is the division of labor. If in Marx's optimistic, Promethean image of man, it is man's nature to strive to become a "totally developed individual," then the division of labor is an unnatural impediment to self-fulfillment, alienating man from his "true" self. One need not question the moral impulse or the sincerity of such an approach merely because of the naiveté of the vision that the division of labor in an advanced society would wither once class conflict and profit disappear in the wake of a socialist revolution.[4] The quality of compassion is scarcely surprising against the background of the Marxists' own bitter but realistic depiction of working and living conditions in mid-nineteenth-century Britain.

Both base and superstructure—the material conditions and the "revolutionary consciousness" of the proletariat—are, for Marx, prerequisites of successful revolution at this stage. The economic reality is a necessary but not a sufficient prerequisite, for if "the proletariat is still unaware of its historical position . . . the objective conditions by themselves will not create the revolution until and unless the proletariat grasps that by shaping its own view of the world it also changes it."[5]

This points to the centrality of "understanding" in the original Marxian view: the task of the philosopher is not merely to comprehend but to change reality. "Revolutionizing the world depends on an adequate understanding of it."[6] Here is the point of departure of the "unity of theory and practice." Somehow true science and reason are expected to merge with the irrational ideology of a class, to put an end to the "prehistory" of mankind.

If class consciousness is a necessary precondition, no less important in the original Marxian scheme is the objective attainment of an economy of abundance as a prerequisite for successful communist revolution. In a remarkably utopian view of industrial society, Marx (and Engels even more) saw material progress no longer as the cause of alienation but as the warrant of liberation from the discontents of civilization. Abundance is the sine qua non of humanity's leap "from the realm of necessity into the realm of freedom." It follows that a socialist revolution can succeed (i.e., a true "revolutionary situation" can arise) only in the most highly developed, best-off capitalist societies.[7]

While the etiology of revolution is economic, the climactic event is political. Withal, Marx's notion of the political revolution is strangely unsatisfactory.

> Neither [Marx] nor Engels was very specific in outlining the features and consequences of this revolution. Essentially, they thought of it as a brief period of political violence in the course of which power is seized by the industrial proletariat, followed by a thorough transformation of economic relationships.[8]

We cannot here dwell on Marx's assumptions of the effects of revolution, other than to underline the vagueness in Marx's own thought. There is little precision in the notion of the dictatorship of the proletariat, which (Marx at times suggested) would, if only briefly, accompany the overthrow of the old order; there is the vision of the abolition of classes, property, profit, and the division of labor; the withering of differences between mental and physical toil, between urban and rural labor. And there are occasional glimpses of the ultimate future in which man will strive to be universal.

Whatever the disagreements among interpreters of Marx, there was no evident conflict between the elements of historical determinism and the assertions of inevitability of revolution, on the one hand, and the contingent view of the need for conscious human action, based on a correct understanding of a revolutionary situation, and the application of will, on the other hand. As Avineri puts it, for Marx, "the question of the inevitability of the revolution is a tautology. . . . The dilemma of determinism vs. voluntarism is transcended by the dialectical nature of this revolutionary consciousness. Never does Marx guarantee the success of the revolution in advance or take it for granted. He only indicates its possibilities historically."9

Yet, if not in doctrine, then in their view of political reality, there was a distinct element of simple hope in something resembling the automatism of history, an optimism which—for instance, in 1847–48—led Marx and Engels to read the signals so as to maximize the seeming chances of looming revolution (ignoring what must have been their realization that capitalism could not yet have exhausted itself). The "specter of communism," Marx seemed to believe in 1848, was a real threat to Europe. But before long his hopes were dashed. The revolutions failed, and so did the proletariat. As George Lichtheim remarks on the Marxist view that European capitalism was ready for socialization, "This was to mistake the birthpangs of the new order for its death throes."10

Thus, in the years following 1848, Marx and Engels themselves were to be the first in the long sequence of revolutionaries who began to retreat from the pure and elegant optimism of their youth, from faith in the automatic and unalterable laws of history to a series of improvisations, rationalizations, explanations, and complications, intended to reconcile observation with prior formulae without jettisoning the essentials of their belief. They began, more specifically, to move from contemplation to manipulation, from analysis to strategy, from observation to intervention, with an orientation that would ultimately give rise to new concepts of organization, party, vanguard, and elite, and would lead to new semantic and conceptual amplifications intended to account for a new reality that did not square with the sophisticated simplicities of the early Marx.[11]

As Alfred Meyer remarks,

> From a mere theory of revolution the emphasis was shifted to the strategy of actually working toward revolution. . . . The optimistic belief in spontaneous progress was shattered. Increasing misery and class consciousness, capital accumulation and crisis, do not develop in step with each other; hence the idea of the unity of theory and practice is transformed from a belief or assumption into . . . a wish. . . . Theory now anticipated practice and seeks to promote it. . . . Idea and reality, aim and movement, freedom and necessity have come in conflict with each other.[12]

After 1848, then, the Marxian vision is inherently ambiguous and fluid. Momentarily, in March 1850, Marx and Engels (in their draft "Address of the Central Committee to the Communist League") espoused a new activist, manipulative, and elitist approach, apparently sparked by the expectation of a new revolution. Here were references to "permanent revolution," to the "dictatorship of the proletariat," to united front tactics, and more. Small wonder communist theorists were later to focus on this document, while many other Marxologists have dismissed it as a "brief Jacobin-Blanquist aberration."[13]

In fact, time and again in the following years, Marx would warn against illusions about imminent or easy revolutions, stressing political education and organization rather than conspiracy.[14] More than anything else, prosperity under capitalism prevented revolution. True, at times Marx again succumbed to visions of new revolutionary upheavals—in

1858, 1868, 1871, and 1877: always in vain. As one astute student of Marx assesses his political acumen,

> Every crisis that seems to shock the stability of the established order he projects into a portent and prelude to revolution. His philosophical system is quite unable to help him to greater discrimination about the precise location of the next revolutionary outburst. . . . The more concrete predictions Marx attempted he could not relate to his philosophical premises. They grew out of his ordinary sociopolitical intuition, which did not prove to be much superior to that of his contemporaries.[15]

The growing concern with revolutionary strategy led Marx and Engels to pay greater attention to organization. The need to satisfy both objective and subjective preconditions for revolution is central to Marx's polemic with Bakunin, including his argument in favor of a Workingmen's International Association. Yet one must agree with the view that "nothing could be more different from Lenin's concept of a revolutionary party than Marx's view of the League and the International."[16] Shlomo Avineri once said,

> Marx concludes that any merely political insurrection of the proletariat trying to create politically conditions not yet immanently developed in the socio-economic sphere is doomed to fail. Hence Marx's stubborn opposition, throughout his life, to a political *émeute* of the working class. The political sphere, according to Marx, cannot impose itself on civil society unless civil society has already developed within itself the elements that make this *tour de force* unnecessary. Marx's general view that political arrangements have their root in the conditions of civil society has been projected onto the strategy of revolution; politics by itself is impotent.[17]

It is well to recall Marx's condemnation of the Blanquists, whom he labeled the alchemists of revolution.[18]

While Marx and Engels remained inconsistent in their expectations of violence in the revolutionary process, they inched towards a more gradualist approach, at least in regard to the Western democracies. They took cognizance of the spread of universal suffrage and political liberties, as well as the changes in the labor movement itself. One result was the familiar references in their pronouncements to the possibility of socialist victory by the ballot box, implying what was later to be called the possiblity of "peaceful transition" in England, the United States, and perhaps other Western European countries. Bourgeois democracy was now seen to offer new and welcome opportunities for the socialists, too.[19] But there remained areas of ambiguity that were to bedevil the disciples. The promotion and support of bourgeois democracy could not be easily reconciled with the vision of the revolutionary overthrow of that very system (except at some abstract level invoking the dialectic or justifying any strategy that was assumed ultimately to serve the ends). Some students of Marx have gone so far as to argue (as George Lichtheim did) that Marx came to abandon the notion of a vanguard and of a dictatorship of the proletariat; that "Marx in the end evolved a political outlook which fitted the requirements of the modern age. In this mature conception, labor's conquest of power represents an aspect of the struggle for democracy. . . . The pragmatic theorist . . . had finally outgrown the man of 1848."[20] Perhaps that is too sharp an image of what remained an ambiguous legacy, but a legitimate image it surely became.[21]

What about the scope and locus of the proletarian revolution? As Marx and Engels envisaged it, the process was essentially intranational in each instance, but it was replicated throughout the "civilized" world. The thought is expressed in Engels' draft for the Communist Manifesto (1847):

> The communist revolution will therefore not be merely a national event, but will take place simultaneously in all civilized countries, i.e., at least in England, America, France and Germany. In each of these countries it will develop more rapidly or slowly depending on whether a given country possesses a more highly developed industry, greater wealth, or a more significant amount of

productive forces. Hence it will be carried out with slower speed and greater difficulties in Germany, and more rapidly and easily in England. It will also exercise significant influence on the remaining countries of the world; their previous mode of development will be entirely changed and very much accelerated. It is a universal revolution and therefore will have a world-wide arena.[22]

Just as the feudal and bourgeois takeovers were worldwide, so was the proletarian revolution bound to be. Yet this article of faith did not prevent the emergence of different expectations in regard to various societies. England was generally accepted to be the most likely locus of the first successful revolution. And yet, the revolution failed to occur. In time Marx was to remark that England lacked the subjective requirements:

The English possess all the necessary material preconditions of the social revolution. What they lack is the spirit of generalization and revolutionary passion. Only the General Council [of the International] is able to inculcate them and thus speed up a truly international movement in this country and consequently everywhere.[23]

Meanwhile his attention had shifted to other, less industrialized countries as the possible loci of revolution, however unlikely in terms of his own beliefs. In fact, he toyed with an intellectual construct that was to be central to Lenin's argumentation half a century later—what has been called the "dialectics of backwardness." If Germany was deemed to be lagging, Marx came to see this as an asset for revolution. What was irrational (and Germany was) was unreal and could not last. Given the gap between potential and reality, the dialectic was brought into play so that the last should be first. Once again wishful thinking prefigured the later Leninist notion of two stages of revolution. The Communist Manifesto asserted that "the bourgeois revolution in Germany will be but the prelude to an immediately following proletarian revolution" (a forecast hard to justify in terms of Marx's own view of historical stages). But all the handy and heady intellectual manipulation could not alter the course of events. Marx had to recognize that the weak German bourgeoisie was prone to compromise with absolutism and feudalism.

As time and again revolutionary prospects in the West proved to be chimeras, Marx and Engels found comfort in going farther afield. Now they seemed to go after targets of opportunity, juggling categories and rationalizing exceptions as they went along. In the 1880s even Russia became *revolutionsfähig*: after all, industrialization there was proceeding apace, the state was moribund, the bourgeoisie was weak; revolution in Russia might become "a signal for a proletarian revolution in the West."[24] Even further they went. Because of the universality of capitalism the colonial world might have a crucial say. "England having brought about the revolution in China, the question is how that revolution will in time react on England and through England on Europe."[25] In 1877 Marx wrote: "This time the revolution begins in the East, hitherto the unbroken bulwark and reserve army of the counterrevolution."[26]

If there seems to be some disjunction between the universal criteria for proletarian revolution and the specifics of historical circumstances in Marx, one may posit a psychological, rather than logical, explanation. We find a restless mind at work, seeking answers, formulae, and successful solutions: a search inspired by an abiding optimism not borne out by reality. The tension between belief and perception is resolved by a sophisticated and unconscious escape from reality into wishful thinking. When prophecy fails, the faith may falter, or the forecast may be updated and revised, or else the target date of fulfillment may be placed further into the future.

Marx and Engels were, after all, themselves the first revisionists of Marxism. The ambiguity of their legacy was rooted in the problem which has remained with international communism to this day—what Eric Hobsbawm has described as the dilemma of a revolutionary party in a nonrevolutionary situation.[27]

Lenin and Revolution

While Marxism was gradually to be revised and divided into a multiplicity of variants (especially in the West), Lenin evolved a new doctrine and strategy based on his reading of Marx but in some essentials at variance with "orthodox" Marxism.

Russia lacked the socioeconomic prerequisites for proletarian revolution. Even bourgeois democracy seemed frustratingly far away. By the turn of the century Russia had a backward, albeit developing, economy; its bourgeoisie was weak; its working class was small, untutored, and unorganized. The vast majority consisted of the peasant mass, which, Lenin had been taught, was doomed to disappear as a class. Orthodox Marxism counseled patience: after decades of development and the growth of capitalism, Russia too was bound to experience what Marxists saw as the common destiny of mankind. For Lenin this was not good enough; he would not spend a lifetime waiting for "maturity" (even though, as in 1915–16, there sometimes seemed little else for him to look forward to).

If Lenin was not prepared to wait for preconditions to ripen, his task was to find surrogates or substitutes for the lacking ingredients. He could not manipulate the *objective* criteria until he came to power: only after political victory could he undertake to create the economic foundation that should have been the prerequisite for success—the superstructure building its own base after the fact. Abundance, too, was tacitly abandoned as a precondition: instead it became—and remains—a goal, to be attained long after the achievement of the revolution.

What remained for Lenin to act upon were the *subjective* elements. In Lenin's reading revolution is defined as a political seizure of power. "In effect Lenin substituted the conquest of political power, the destruction of the existing state and all its works, for socialism as the goal or end-in-view of the socialist movement. Socialism as a form of social organization and as an ideal of fraternity can only become an end-in-view after political power has been won."[28] If, in his two-stage view of revolution, the first or minimum objective was a democratic bourgeois republic, Lenin thought the Russian bourgeoisie too inept even to act in its own interest: the proletariat had to act as the spark that would touch off the bourgeois revolution. Political events became the products of human will and action.[29] In 1917 Lennin appropriately recalled the formula, "On s'engage—et puis on voit. . . . "

His suspicion of spontaneity reinforced Lenin's stress on organization. It is this concern with the "organizational weapon" that has led some observers to credit Lenin with introducing a "modern" approach to politics. Effectiveness demands secretiveness and elitism: it was easy for Lenin to rationalize the view that the vanguard—in the presence of an inert mass—becomes the repository of proletarian conscious- ness, entitled to act (self-appointed though it was) on behalf of the proletariat. Lenin's view of the Party also prefigured the future willingness to embark on "revolutions from above."

Given this shift of emphasis, the proletariat—the real, live working men and women—was reduced to a "force," to be taken into account in the Leninist calculus of revolutionary behavior. To be sure, the Party acted in their name and on their behalf. But, in contrast to the idealistic nineteenth- century vision that took for granted massive, or even majority, support before a revolution could be attempted (let alone won), the active involvement of the masses—though obviously desirable—was no longer deemed essential.[30]

Curious and characteristic in this connection was the wan- ton use and abuse of labels. The games people played with names served a political purpose. The Party was equated with the proletariat. When Lenin spoke of "proletarian hegemony," he meant Bolshevik control. When he spoke of the class interest of the proletariat, he referred to his own point of view. This was not simply a matter of deception (or self- deception). "After 1905 . . . the term 'proletariat' was more and more neglected; in its stead Lenin began to speak of the masses, the poor, the have-nots, or the toilers."[31] The cate- gories of class analysis were to become increasingly instru- mental and meaningless with the passage of time.

Yet classes were precisely the actors Lenin saw on the stage of revolution. Who were they and what could they be expected to do? Orthodox Marxism would have posited that in Russia only a bourgeois-democratic revolution was possible. Lenin in fact shared this view until about 1905. But this was not good enough. First, the proletariat (read: the Bolsheviks) must set off the bourgeois revolution and whenever possible play the leading part in it. Second, Lenin was not content to witness the realization of the first—bourgeois—stage and merely the expectation of the second—socialist—at some future point. He sought a formula, a strategy, and a device to move on from the first to the second, at all times with his own organization in command.

Lenin found an intellectual, ideological justification in his notion of *pererastanie*—the bourgeois revolution "growing into" the proletarian stage.[32] How could such a smooth and prompt transition across historical stages be contemplated in Marxist terms? As a later Soviet commentator sums it up, "The cornerstone of the theory of this 'growing over' is the Leninist concepts of the hegemony of the proletariat, the alliance of the proletariat with the peasantry, and the leading role of the Marxist-Leninist party in the revolution."[33] The hegemony of the proletariat becomes tantamount to the third condition, the leading role of the Party. No effort was made to justify this demand: if in Leninist (and later, Stalinist) terms power is the crucial problem, the claim to the hegemony exercised by the communist party becomes a practical, self-serving goal that requires no defense or excuse. Lenin was to make it a general rule even when advising communists in colonial areas: "There is practically no industrial proletariat in these countries. Nevertheless, we have assumed [and] we must assume the role of leadership even there."[34]

No less important an innovation than the political, voluntarist, and elitist orientation of the Leninists was their discovery of the peasantry. Marx and Engels had viewed the peasantry as the main reserves of the reactionary forces. It was a dying class whose poorer, exploited members would join the proletariat once the class struggle polarized society.[35]

Until 1905 Lenin too had argued that the workers had no interest in strengthening the class of landowners. But as he looked about for allies—and suspected the Russian bourgeoisie of selling out—he focused on the opportunities that were inherent in the prospect of agrarian revolution. In Russia—unlike England—the peasantry was indeed a potentially revolutionary force (as the Revolution of 1905 had shown), and the agrarian problem remained one of the plagues of the old regime. Lenin was obviously perceptive in grasping the revolutionary potential of the peasantry. The movement's aim, as he formulated it between the 1905 and 1917 revolutions, was a bourgeois republic to be achieved by an "alliance of the proletariat with the peasantry." This must be juxtaposed to the injunction that "the proletariat should lead the peasantry." Translating "proletariat" into "Bolshevik Party," Lenin demanded, in essence, that the communists use the peasants in the pursuit of their immediate objective. Unlike Marx, his awareness of the peasantry was immensely enhanced; unlike Mao, his sympathies were not with the peasantry: they were a means and not an end, but a vital means nonetheless.[36]

Lenin thus launched the characteristic (until 1917) slogan calling for a "revolutionary democratic dictatorship of the proletariat and peasantry" as the first target of the revolution (the dictatorship of the proletariat alone was to follow later). While each element of this formula had its ideological and tactical *raison d'être,* the whole nonetheless smacked again of the verbal gymnastics that increasingly accompanied Leninism.

Lenin's theory of the uneven development of capitalism opened the door to other new departures. Since capitalism was developing at an uneven pace in different countries, Lenin proposed, it was entirely possible for proletarian revolution to occur in some countries (or even in a single country) before it occurred in others. The recurring image used to illustrate and explain this phenomenon was that the worldwide chain of capitalism breaks at its weakest link (essentially, a tautology). "The victorious proletariat of that country [where the revolution has occurred] . . . will arise against the rest of the world, the capitalist world, attracting to its cause the oppressed classes of other countries, stirring uprisings in those countries against the capitalists, and in the event of need using even armed force against the exploiting classes and their states."[37] Here also is the basis and authority for the concept of "socialism in one country," as it was to be developed (and distorted) under Stalin in the following decades.

The "law of uneven development" was part of Lenin's theory of imperialism, which saw the colonial world as the victim of exploitation and the great powers as parasites using imperialism to postpone their downfall. Imperialism, Lenin wrote, is dying capitalism; the age of imperialism is the "eve of socialist revolution." But where would the chain break first? Lenin pointed to three criteria: the presence of a certain mass of industrial labor in a given country (just how much, he failed to specify); the existence of a revolutionary party; and the presence of a "serious ally of the proletariat (for instance, the peasantry)." If these were the only preconditions of revolution, the implication was clear that proletarian revolution could succeed in less developed countries. The Marxian model of socioeconomic maturity and a high level of development clearly did not fit non-Western societies.[38] Indeed, Lenin now argued the opposite: backwardness, far from being an obstacle, was a crucial cause of change. "In Leninism backward nations as such become the underdogs of imperialism, who will build new and better societies. Backwardness can turn into a blessing."[39]

This opened the door to an important new classification. When Marx had spoken of the exploited as the chosen people, he had social classes in mind. Lenin now added the category of nations, prefiguring his later call for an alliance of victims—oppressed classes with oppressed nations. If class struggle tended to become identified with the West, national liberation tended to be equated with the "colonial and semi-colonial" world of the East. And when, in the early 1920s, all the expectations of proletarian revolutions in the West had been bitterly disappointed, Lenin in his last reassertion

of faith in the new revolutionary era of mankind (which the
Russian revolution was presumed to have ushered in) pointed
precisely to the "East." Russia, India, and China made up the
majority of mankind which "has been drawn into the stuggle
for emancipation with extraordinary rapidity." Hence "there
cannot be the slightest doubt what the final outcome of
the world struggle will be."[40]

Yet these too were after all second thoughts, seeking one
more time to explain why history moved in such inscrutable
ways even under the prism of "scientific socialism." If the
lightning had not struck in Europe, perhaps it would strike in
Asia: nothing was any longer impossible.

Lenin, on at least two occasions, sought to define what a
"revolutionary   situation"   was—formulations   which   are
reiterated *ad nauseam* in communist publications. He would
have been the first to recognize that there is less to his formula
than meets the eye. Some of it is vague; some is tautological.
In essence, according to Lenin, a revolutionary situation is
characterized by three features:

(1) When it is impossible for the ruling classes to maintain their
rule without any change, when there is a crisis among the "upper
classes" . . . leading to a fissure through which the discontent and
indignation of the oppressed classes burst forth. For a revolution
to take place, it is usually insufficient for "the lower classes not
to want" to live in the old way; it is also necessary that the upper
classes "should be unable" to live in the old way.

(2) When the suffering and the want of the oppressed classes
have grown more acute than usual.

(3) When as a consequence of the above there is a considerable
increase in the activity of the masses, who . . . are drawn both by
all the circumstances of the crisis and by the "upper classes"
themselves into independent historical action.[41]

Such formulations did not help Lenin or his associates to
read correctly the prospects of revolutionary action abroad.

In their own takeover the analysis of the situation was of a more pragmatic sort. Power lay in the streets, and they picked it up.

While Lenin declared that a peaceful accession to power would of course be preferable, he dismissed such a prospect as implausible. Only for a short time in the summer of 1917 did he seem to have considered a peaceful takeover possible in Petrograd. More characteristically he remarked on another occasion, "The substitution of a proletarian for a capitalist state is impossible without violent revolution."[42] His approach to and rhetoric regarding revolution had a remarkably military cast. He spoke repeatedly of correlations of forces, tactical superiority, the importance of surprise and morale, fronts, campaigns, allies, strategy and tactics. Neither Lenin nor his successors apparently made any fundamental distinction between political and military forms of struggle.[43]

Insofar as the formal notions of revolution were concerned, Leninism did indeed mark a significant new departure. As Alfred Meyer aptly sums it up, in the Leninist view

a high level of industrialization no longer leads directly to internal revolution, nor does the existence of a numerically strong working class. Instead, these factors are now seen to lead to revolution somewhere else. Revolution in the leading imperialist countries will come only as they decline. In addition, the revolution itself will have aims that were not outlined in the original Marxist theories. . . . With the new Leninist theory, the aim of the proletarian revolution is not to destroy capitalist industry, not to seize it, but to create adequate means of production in those areas of the world which lacked them. . . . [Hence] political action determines economic development; consciousness is stronger than social relations; causes turn into effects, and effects into causes.[44]

The Stalin Era

The Russian revolution was a success by the one criterion that had prevailed: the communists gained a monopoly of political power. Henceforth, and to this day, the Soviet contention has been that the October Revolution opened the era of proletarian revolutions. By its success it contributed to revolutionary processes abroad, or so the Soviet leaders claimed. They waited impatiently for revolutions abroad to occur—above all, in Germany—so as to bail out the embattled, weak, and anomalous Soviet Russian regime. But wherever it was attempted revolution failed. Soon the perspective changed: instead of depending on foreign revolutions, Moscow, under the dictates of "international proletarian solidarity," assumed its role of helper, guide, and sponsor of revolutions and revolutionary movements abroad.

But the Communist International found itself unable to stimulate or direct any foreign proletarian revolution to victory. Little by little the realization sank in that the Russian revolution survived alone in a hostile world; the seizure of power in Petrograd had failed to spark other revolutions. As world revolution failed to occur, the high priests found it necessary to reinterpret the oracular expectations. Here was another retreat from optimism. At first Zinoviev could argue that the predictions remained valid but would merely take more time to come true: what had happened was an "optical illusion." Then more complex explanations followed. Stalin and the Comintern in the 1920s accepted the notion of a temporary stabilization of capitalism—temporary because it was axiomatic that in the long run it was doomed. Soviet observers correctly foresaw new economic and political crises in the West. They incorrectly predicted that they would lead to revolutionary successes: the Great Depression witnessed no proletarian revolutions.

Even if some of the upbeat predictions of revolutions abroad were no doubt dished up as convenient and effective propaganda arguments, there can be little doubt that initially —say, during the first decade of Soviet rule—Soviet policymakers believed these analyses. Yet as Marxism-Leninism became a state religion and the sacred axioms could no longer be questioned, it became necessary to find scapegoats and explanations for the lay masses and for the outside world. The result was a redefinition of doctrine that amounted to a loosening and stretching of categories, definitions, time spans, and the limits of the possible—all to explain why the future had been deferred. Lenin had after all pointed the way by, for example, substituting "Party" for "proletariat," and "toilers" for "workingmen." In the era of Stalinist manipulation and doublethink the process was easily pushed a lot further.

Originally the socialist revolution had been thought of as a sudden, "geological" shift. Now it was extended over time: the transition from capitalism to socialism filled an entire historical epoch.[45] The historical showdown between the forces of progress and reaction, it was now argued, would take place in a series of successive rounds. The first round had seen the emergence of the Soviet Russian state. A second round, and perhaps subsequent ones, would witness successful takeovers elsewhere.

Anticipating later Soviet comments, one point to the argument was invoked explicitly from 1949 on: the first round, sparked by World War I, had led to the Russian revolution; World War II had launched the second round, which brought about the emergence of a number of communist regimes in Eastern Europe and the Far East; no doubt a third round would sometime in the future complete the process. Was it bound to be tied to another world war?

Stalin repeatedly pointed to World War I as having "accelerated and facilitated the revolutionary battles of the proletariat." As he put it to the Seventeenth Congress of the Communist Parties of the Soviet Union (CPSU) in 1934, a new imperialist war "will surely turn loose revolutions and place in jeopardy the very existence of capitalism in a number of countries, as happened in the first imperialist war."[46]

He was, to be sure, prepared to contemplate the possibility of ultimately winning without the use of force. "Of course in the distant future, if the proletariat wins in the most important capitalist countries and if the present capitalist encirclement is replaced by a socialist encirclement, a 'peaceful' path of development is fully possible for some capitalist countries, whose capitalists in view of the 'unfavorable' international situation will consider it expedient to make serious concessions to the proletariat 'voluntarily.'" But this last was a most remote prospect which presupposed the possession of vastly superior forces by the "socialist camp."[47]

After World War II Stalin and others could indeed point with pride to the dozen or so countries which had been torn loose from the capitalist system, seemingly proving that communism was in tune with history. Stalin would sanction the prognosis during his final years—and Peking would repeat it later—that World War III would mark the end of the capitalist world system altogether.[48]

There had been communists who in the 1930s and 40s raised the question, somewhat obliquely, whether in fact war was a necessary precondition of proletarian revolution (something that was never doctrinally sanctified but was evidently accepted as a fact of life). But under Stalin such efforts to sever the linkage were bound to be dismissed as, at best, petty-bourgeois pacifist illusions. Only after Stalin did Moscow come around to the view that (in the words of the 1961 CPSU Program) socialist revolution is not necessaily connected with war: "Although both world wars, which were started by the imperialists, culminated in socialist revolutions, revolutions are entirely feasible without war."[49] Such a stand followed from Khrushchev's abandonment in 1956 of the doctrine of the inevitability of war: since revolutions continued to be deemed inevitable, Moscow had to subscribe to the possibility of peaceful transition to power. In fact, some (but not all) Soviet commentators spoke of a new third round that had ostensibly begun in 1955 without the concomitant of international conflict, a characterization which the Maoists were vehemently to deny.

Though "untheoretical" by inclination, Stalin was periodically called upon to pronounce on the nature of revolutions. Usually his pronouncement amounted to a gloss on Leninist verities. He would stress as a precondition a "nationwide crisis," affecting exploiters and exploited alike.[50] In the words of one student of Stalin's writings, "To sum up, Stalin's necessary 'objective' conditions for revolution are: bourgeoisie isolated and disorganized, proletariat aroused to revolt and supported by the masses, and a favorable balance of proletarian, as against bourgeois, aid from outside the country."[51] This of course amounted to stacking the deck; when the edge was not quite so obvious, Stalin preferred to leave open alternative prospects. As for "subjective" conditions, Stalin characteristically stressed the role of political organization, communist leadership, and the "monolithic unity" of the party. He repeatedly returned to the need for authoritative direction—a "general staff"—for converting a revolutionary situation into revolutionary actuality.[52]

To be sure, the Comintern and Soviet spokesmen went into considerable detail discussing different strategies and tactics for various categories of states.[53] But, while such "advice" was taken seriously by the target communist parties, for Stalin the discussions of revolutionary prospects and processes seemed to be increasingly ideological abstractions without relevance to political behavior. Stalin radically revised the approach to proletarian revolutions: revolutions would be carried out "from above," by the extension of Soviet power, or at the very least with crucial Soviet assistance. The fate of the revolution was equated with the power of the Soviet state.

There are repeated references in Stalin's statements—more candid in the early years than later—to the function of the USSR as a base for revolutions abroad. In 1924 he spoke of the use of "dictatorship of the proletariat in one country . . . for the overthrow of imperialism in all countries." Even more explicit was his comment that

the very development of world revolution . . . will be more rapid and more thorough, the more thoroughly socialism fortifies itself in the first victorious country, the faster this country is transformed into a base for the further unfolding of world revolution, into a lever for the further disintegration of imperialism.[54]

By 1927 Stalin had already revised the definition of a

revolutionary to agree with this still incipient approach:

> A revolutionary is one who is ready to protect, to defend the
> USSR without reservation, without qualification . . . for the
> USSR is the first proletarian, revolutionary state in the world,
> a state which is building socialism.[55]

What was good for the Soviet Union was good for world revolution: the notion was to be revived by Khrushchev, who would insist a generation later that the best service the USSR could render international communism was to develop itself to the utmost—a posture from which by 1960 the Maoists would vehemently dissent.

If diplomacy and revolution can be described as the two arms of Soviet strategy towards the outside world, under Stalin the revolutionary arm clearly withered, becoming dependent on state power. It was at the point of the Red Army bayonets that revolution was carried abroad—unsuccessfully to Poland in 1920; successfully to Mongolia and Central Asia in the following years; to the Baltic States and other adjacent areas in 1939–41; and across Eastern Europe and North Korea in 1944–45. "Revolution" had now acquired a very different meaning: it stood for the transformation of polity, society, and economy under communist auspices thanks to the presence (or threat) of overwhelming Soviet military or police power. Nobody worried any longer about socioeconomic preconditions or levels of maturity or even the strength and support of the local communist party. As one commentator remarks, "Certainly no one could seriously maintain that a revolutionary situation existed in Khiva and Bokhara or in Mongolia. Soviet *raison d'état* became the substitute for it."[56]

In Stalin's operational assumptions, then, revolution became tantamount to the extension of Soviet control. Thus it became a function of the two-camp struggle. Stalin appears to have foreseen such a development as early as 1920:

> Most probably in the course of the development of the world

revolution, side by side with the centers of imperialism in individual countries and the system of these countries throughout the world, centers of socialism will be created in individual soviet countries and a system of these centers throughout the world, and the struggle between these two systems will fill the history of the development of world revolution.[57]

Stalin's pessimistic view of man contrasted sharply with the positive approach of the classics of Marxism. It has often been remarked that Stalin did not trust anyone or anything he could not control. His comments about the prospects of revolution in Germany and China support such a view: he did not believe that communists abroad could succeed without his help and advice (as Yugoslavs in effect told him). No wonder, then, that in the view of some foreign comrades Moscow "let them down." Whether in China, or in the Spanish civil war, or in Greece at the end of World War II, the question was not whether Stalin supported the revolutionaries but why he did not do more for them. In effect he claimed a monopoly on paternity: the Soviet Union had to be present at the creation of any revolutionary regime. The sacrifice of this or that revolutionary opportunity could easily be justified by reference to a higher calculus of worldwide Soviet strategy.[58] (As Radek had once remarked, the clerks need not understand the revolutionary algebra of the masters.)

By the mid-1930s Stalin had come to make righteous public denials of Soviet interest in promoting world revolution. In the famous interview with Roy Howard he piously dismissed the export of revolution abroad as a tragicomical misunderstanding. Indeed, the term "world revolution" soon dropped out of official Soviet usage. The same public posture was of course exemplified in the dissolution of the International in 1943.

With some—but not much—oversimplification, one may assert that by the end of his life Stalin, as the supreme architect of law and order, had little time for revolutions. If there were to be any, he would make them. All others smacked of spontaneity and chaos, of unplanned destabilization and surprise: they were just not on his agenda.

After Stalin

The Khrushchev era witnessed a brief period of revitalization and revivalism which tallied with the general atmosphere of a new momentum and cautious hope that came with the passing of the Stalin era. Just as in domestic affairs Khrushchev erred in his overoptimism, so his outlook abroad seemed to be colored by a sense of euphoria—a new sense of expectancy that revived a faith in the prospect of communist victories abroad. Such an outlook was reinforced by a turn from voluntarism to determinism—perhaps more instinctive than articulate—and a growing acceptance of the gradualism that goes with it. Revolutionary successes, then, came (and have continued) to mean communist accessions to power—not necessarily by revolution and not necessarily by themselves.

Khrushchev repeatedly made gratuitous pronouncements that someday Britain, America, Germany, and Japan would turn communist. He liked to say, "We can already see our ultimate goal appearing on the horizon—the victory of the working class throughout the world, the victory of the ideas of communism."[59] But such professions of faith were essentially noncommittal.

In practice, what he seemed to hope for was a natural gravitation to the left of the countries involved in shaking off colonialism, aligning them with the socialist camp and—if not immediately, then later—leading them to transformations that could be characterized as socialist. Whereas Stalin had dismissed decolonization as a sham, Khrushchev correctly foresaw the collapse of the Western overseas empires. "In the second stage of the general crisis of capitalism the colonial and dependent countries are the weakest link in the system of imperialism."[60] To be sure, antiimperialist revolutions and antifeudal movements were a far cry from communism, but (Soviet observers seemed to believe) there was now at least the possibility of a smooth and gradual evolution from the first to the second stage of revolution. Of course, Soviet analysts recognized that not all countries which succeeded in their struggle for national liberation would turn to communism. Both possibilities were recognized as real: the revolution would become socialist "where the struggle is led by communist or workers' parties."

By a route too circuitous to trace here, Moscow came to accept a new category—the "noncapitalist path" of underdeveloped countries freed from colonialism. There could be no assurance that a national liberation movement would head in this direction; nor was there any certainty that, once on this path (or rather, identified as being on this path by Moscow), the country would proceed to a socialist revolution (the label "proletarian revolution" was tacitly dropped as manifestly too inappropriate); but the possibility was there.

Would such a gradual transformation amount to a revolution? And what were its prospects in any event? While the prognosis must have been comforting to Soviet observers, there was nothing to show for it as time went on. Time after time local communist parties were sacrificed by Moscow for the sake of a closer entente with ruling nationalist regimes, as, for example, in Algeria and Egypt. Time after time the leaders Khrushchev banked on—Sukarno, Qassim, Nasser, Ben Bella, Touré, Nkrumah, Lumumba—failed to come through: either they turned away from a pro-Soviet orientation, or else they were toppled from power. In the end Khrushchev's optimism regarding an early and widespread "painless revolution"—the ripe fruit of decolonization falling into his eager hands—fizzled as one more miscalculation.

To be sure, Soviet academics who rediscovered the "East" in the post-Stalin years began by applying the time-honored clichés of class analysis to the political scene of Asia, Africa, and Latin America. But, whether from pragmatic observation or in response to signals from policymakers, some of the doctrinal prescriptions were tacitly jettisoned (and sometimes not so tacitly, as debates among Soviet orientalists began to revive). By the 1960s (and the tendency continued after Khrushchev's ouster) references to the valiant class struggle of the Bantu proletariat or to the *comprador* bourgeoisie in

Uruguay disappeared from Soviet journals; articles appeared recognizing the tenacity of racial and religious identities and even suggesting ways of allying these with the cause of revolution. There was in Moscow a general decline in reliance on indigenous communist source materials and interpretations.[61]

By the mid-1960s Soviet expectations of benign revolutionary change in the East were substantially toned down. There were no victories to point to, other than the unexpected and at times embarrassing conversion of Fidel Castro. Soviet aid and influence had increased significantly in many areas of the non-Western world, but there seemed to be virtually no revolutionary situations to detect or anticipate. What remained was the lengthening list of labels and categories of friends and allies, fellow travelers to revolution: New Democracy, People's Democracy, National Democracy; national-revolutionary, mass-democratic, antiimperialist, antimonopolist, peace, and noncapitalist paths and alliances. The roster swelled as the prospects shrank.

A somewhat similar process took place with regard to the Western capitalist countries, though here neither the optimism nor therefore the disappointment was as great. In the 1960s authoritative Soviet statements, such as *Fundamentals of Marxism-Leninism*, acknowledged that there was no basis for expecting early socialist revolutions in the West. To be sure, there were conditions that could make for a revolutionary situation. But what these conditions could point to was not "proletarian revolution" but "democratic mass movements."[62] In the view of (admittedly doctrinaire) Soviet analysts, the most realistic among the hoped-for scenarios seemed to be an "antimonopolist people's revolution," which would remove the big monopolies from influence and transfer power into the hands of a "coalition of democratic forces," isolating and perhaps overthrowing the "reactionaries" in the first stage of the revolution. Nationalization would produce a vast state-owned sector of the economy, thus laying the foundations for a later shift to socialism. In some instances (the Soviet contention went) the transition to a socialist revolution might ensue promptly; in others, it would come later, step by step; in still other cases, the process would become stalled and arrested at an early stage.[63]

The options for the future are thus considerably widened. To be sure, the more theoretical discussions retain the traditional formulations. A recent Soviet dictionary of "scientific communism" still defines "revolutionary situation" as "objective circumstances characterizing the maturity of socioeconomic conditions for revolution and assuring the possibility of conquering power for the progressive class." But even this version introduces some new flexibility: "The timing of the appearance of a revolutionary situation, its forms and tempos of development depend on the condition of the state machine, on the forces of the revolutionary class, on its ties with other classes, on the prior accumulation of political experience. In brief, they depend on the complex system of sociopolitical class relations." A revolutionary situation is assumed to go through a number of stages; and the more advanced the stage, the more decisive the subjective (rather than the objective) factors in determining its outcome. But there is a characteristic irrelevance to the argument, suggested in the final remark: present conditions "create the possibility of an offensive of the working class against important foci of power of monopoly capitalism, even in the absence of revolutionary situations."[64]

Over the past twenty years, the possibility of "peaceful transition" has come to be accepted as a matter of course: the replacement of capitalism by socialism—i.e., the substitution of proletarian for bourgeois dictatorship—may occur by either peaceful or violent means. After 1956 Soviet writers and spokesmen went to great lengths to show that Marx and even Lenin allowed the possibility of peaceful accession to power, citing Marx's Amsterdam speech of 1872, Lenin's tactics until July 1917, and even the "socialist takeovers" in Eastern Europe in 1944–48.

At the same time, Soviet analysts have been careful to emphasize the possibility of a "violent revolutionary struggle" —especially where the bourgeoisie maintains control of a powerful military-police apparatus. Still, the "parliamentary path" has continued to receive consistent recognition. In the words of the 1961 CPSU Program, a communist majority in parliament, won at the polls, would serve to "transform it from a tool serving the class interests of the bourgeoisie into an instrument serving the working people, launch a broad mass struggle outside parliament, smash the resistance of reactionary forces, and provide the necessary conditions for a peaceful socialist revolution."[65] Anyone challenging the new regime would, in other words, be engaging in counter-revolutionary defiance of a legitimate regime.

Despite the frequent reaffirmation of the ritual rhetoric, the post-Khrushchev years have seen a growth of realism in Soviet perception of prospects abroad. This has involved a distinct decrease in the saliency of "revolution" as an operational political category. Some old habits seem to have disappeared at last—for example, the assumption of the compelling precedent of Soviet experience, which led to projections of past Russian experiences onto events abroad, since history was supposed to follow a unilinear path.[66] Soviet scholars have reexamined the characteristics of "modern" capitalism; Soviet policy towards the Common Market has undergone significant changes. Arms-control agreements and "mutually beneficial" commercial, technological, scientific, and political accords with the main representatives of imperialism and monopoly capitalism are part and parcel of a general mood of postrevolutionary conservatism at home, an attitude increasingly discomfited by the prospect of systemic change. The reaction to Chinese charges and attacks has not been an effort to "out-Mao Mao" but to hold the line. There is in Moscow less certainty of standard solutions, less dynamism in attacking problems, less direction and hope. Moscow has had its share of troubles with "fraternal" communist parties abroad, and given the years of effort it takes even to convene a conference of all the comrades (or at least the loyal ones), any expectations of successful revolution that remain must rely more on the failures of the adversary than on the skill and achievements of one's comrades and allies, and surely not on the automatism of history.

The primacy of Soviet state interests has remained intact since Stalin's days. Though ambiguities remain, especially regarding Asia and Africa, in the nuclear age this has come to mean essentially a foreign-policy posture of worldwide presence and frequent pressure but low risk-taking.

In 1968 the French communists, with Moscow's approval, emerged as the party of law and order which helped doom the revolt of the students and the New Left. Six years later the communist *L'Humanité* hinted not very subtly that Soviet behavior had been responsible for torpedoing the electoral campaign of the communists in alliance with the socialists on behalf of François Mitterand. If this was indeed so, Moscow may well have reasoned that the experiences of coalition governments in which communists have participated as minority contingents in recent years—in Finland, Iceland, Sri Lanka, Chile, and Portugal—have scarcely been encouraging examples of a new road to revolution: communists either have lost popular support, sharing the onus for the failings of the government, or have been ousted forcibly or even driven underground.[67] Moreover, if international stabilization is at least an instrumental goal of Soviet policy, communist takeovers might well conjure up complications which would put Moscow on the spot, as it would have to choose between committing itself to the risky rescue of friends and allowing them to go down while the Soviets, in a most awkward posture, looked on. In the end, *sacro egoismo* prevails. To a "good revolutionary" somewhere on the fringes of civilization, Moscow as well as Peking must now look like a traitor to his cause.

There have been and no doubt continue to be serious disagreements in Moscow over the prospects of revolution, over alternative strategies and different roads to power (such as the Chilean road). Even if not in terms of classical revolution, Moscow insists on providing advice to other parties. Some Soviet analysts and writers still take the whole business of ideological categories relating to the "content and regularities of the world revolutionary process" with depressingly tedious seriousness.[68] At the same time Soviet commentators have been forced on the defensive by two simultaneous tendencies—criticism of the Soviet position not only by the Chinese but by the New Left, and recent Western interest in the phenomenon of revolution. After some hesitation Moscow has responded with considerable concern, defensiveness, vigor, and venom.[69]

Reaffirmation of doctrine has scarcely improved doctrine. Here and there new formulations do break through. But who takes them seriously?[70] As far as Soviet policymakers are concerned, there is no evidence that they seriously consider revolutionary prospects as a controlling input in policy decisions. For them the ideological reformulations may be in the nature of sermons ignored in day-to-day living, or a case of *sauter pour mieux reculer*. Robert Tucker has made a strong case that a fervent reassertion of an old faith typically precedes "deradicalization."[71]

What the thrust of reformulations and redefinitions amounts to in practice is a persistent widening of options; it brings the substitution of vaguer, weaker, broader terms and categories, the elimination of compelling cause-and-effect relationships, and a withering of the fundamental optimism about the future which animated the movement at the start. "The world revolutionary process becomes ever more complex and multiform," declares a recent Soviet study of the problem.[72] In substance, the belief system now sanctions the view that anything is possible. Any one thing may or may not occur; revolutions may or may not take place; force may or may not be needed; communists may or may not be in control of "bourgeois" or "mass-democratic" movements; non-Western countries may or may not opt for a noncapitalist path, which in turn may or may not lead to socialist revolution. The multiplicity of labels, options, forms, alliances, and combinations continues to grow.

Given such a broad range, which foresees and justifies in advance all success and all failure, Soviet doctrine (which thus cannot be falsified) becomes useless as an analytical or predictive tool. It is rather a distorted reflection of a political system trying to come to terms with the present without betraying its past.[73]

Ex Oriente Lux!

Just as the characteristics of Leninism can in large measure be explained by reference to the conditions of political struggle in Russia before 1917, so the specifics of Chinese history and revolutionary experience are critical for an understanding of Maoism.[74] In particular, what is called the Yenan syndrome, or the guerrilla heritage, is an essential formative part of the Maoist tradition.[75]

At its peak in the 1960s, Maoism (a somewhat unstable commodity) expressed its outlook on revolution in several interlocking concepts, which may be summarized as the role of the peasantry and the role of violence—"people's war"—within a given country, as well as its analogue in international affairs, with the developing countries as the storm center of revolution.

Mao's reliance on the rural hinterland in rebuilding the communist movement, after its decimation in the urban, "proletarian" centers in 1927, is common knowledge. The peasantry inevitably became the main source of support and the object of sympathetic concern of the Chinese communists. This familiar but fundamental point may be taken for granted, with only this brief illustration of how Chinese experience has been projected abroad: throughout the Third World,

> as in China, the peasant problem is exceptionally important. . . . The peasant represents the main force in the national democratic revolution against the imperialists and their lackeys. . . . The rural areas, and only these, provide the vast spaces in which the revolutionaries can mount their advance toward final victory.[76]

Formally, to be sure, the Maoists consider themselves carriers of a proletarian revolution—no Marxist-Leninist could do otherwise—but the "proletarian" label amounts to little more than ritual.

The Chinese communists take it as an axiom that the road to power means armed struggle. Violence, they declare, is "a

universal law of proletarian revolution." Mac has argued that
the enemy is by nature aggressive, hence his victims must
take up arms: the only way to eliminate war is "to oppose
war by war." If "political power grows out of the barrel of a
gun," as the Chairman has proclaimed, then the revolutionaries
must use guns to smash the old state machine, suppress the
class enemies, and gain political power. This is true as much
within any one country as it is in the struggle of the colonial
and formerly dependent countries against the imperialists,
for "the imperialists will never lay down their butcher knives;
they will never become Buddhas, till their doom."[77]

War, to the Maoists, is the highest form and the ultimate
climax of the struggle. In the 1960s it was doctrinally refined
in the form of "people's war"—by definition, a just war.
Chalmers Johnson stated:

> The essence of "people's war" is that the communists, in the
> guise of anti-imperialists, should promote the mobilization and
> organization of peasants in lands subject to imperialist interference,
> leading to guerrilla warfare and finally to regular warfare against
> the forces of imperialism and their local allies.[78]

The distinction between "people's war" and "revolutionary
struggle" became virtually obliterated. Apparently no other
forms of revolutionary victory could be conceived.

The logical corollary was a bitter attack on the advocates
of peaceful transition to power. The Chinese reminded the
Soviet leaders in one of their broadsides in 1964, quoting
amply from Lenin and Stalin to support the point, and
quoting Mao's earlier pronouncement, that "the seizure of
power by armed force, the settlement of the issue by war, is
the central task and the highest form of revolution. This
Marxist-Leninist principle of revolution holds good universally,
for China and for all other countries. . . . Only with guns can
the whole world be transformed."[79]

While the chance of nonviolent transformation was theoretically granted, Peking reiterated in a variety of ways that
the entire revolutionary experience to date showed that

nowhere had the communists come to power by peaceful or parliamentary means. Neither in Russia in 1917 nor in Hungary in 1919 was the seizure of power bloodless; World War II was the precondition of victory in Eastern Europe, as it was in China, Korea, and Vietnam. Hence the Chinese' verbal blast against the advocates of "parliamentary cretinism" and their international equivalents, the Soviet "revisionists," who made peaceful coexistence the "general line" and thereby subordinated revolution to Soviet state interests.[80]

The virtual obliteration of the distinction between domestic and international conflict is characteristic of the Maoist perspective, in which imperialism looms as the principle enemy (or did, before the Soviet Union was elevated to enemy number one). The international prescription (as American observers remarked even before Chinese leaders made this point explicit) amounts to an extension of the domestic strategy of using the countryside as the base of the revolution against the enemy cities. That is, the world village —the underdeveloped world—must unite to encircle the Western, capitalist cities: the locus of the exploited is Asia, Africa, Latin America—the "East."

In 1957, even before the break with Moscow, Mao proclaimed that "the East Wind is prevailing over the West Wind. That is to say, the forces of socialism have become overwhelmingly superior to the forces of imperialism." This statement, often reiterated and elaborated, is remarkable not only for its optimistic assessment of the balance of power but also for its frank equation of socialism with the East: a total reversal of the original Marxist perspective. Before long Peking was to spell out that the "East" stood for the "antiimperialist forces" of Asia, Africa, and Latin America, and not the communists alone. Here, the Chinese proclaimed in the *Proposal Concerning the General Line* (14 June 1963), was the key to world revolution: "The various types of contradictions in the contemporary world are concentrated in the vast areas of Asia, Africa, and Latin America: these are the most vulnerable areas under imperialist rule and the storm centers of world revolution. . . . In a sense, therefore, the whole cause of the international proletarian revolution hinges on the outcome of the revolutionary struggle of the people of these areas, who constitute the overwhelming majority of the world's population."[81] Hence, as a student of Chinese policy put it, "the primary responsibility for bringing about world revolution has shifted away from the working class movement of the industrialized countries in the West to the national liberation movements of the backward areas of the Third World."[82]

The Chinese model thus became mandatory for the entire "East." As early as 1949 Liu Shao-ch'i hinted (without as yet taking on the Russians) that the Maoist pattern applied to all of Asia. By the 1960s this had become explicit doctrine: "The Russian October Socialist Revolution served as an example for revolution in the oppressor nations, that is, for revolution in the imperialist countries, while the Chinese revolution is an example for revolution in the oppressed nations, that is, the colonial and semi-colonial countries."[83]

Chinese spokesmen also specified several necessary conditions for revolutionary war, such as leadership by the communist party; reliance on the peasantry and establishment of rural bases; creation of a communist-led army; and the use of a broad national "united front," led by an alliance of workers and peasants and supported by the bourgeoisie.

But it is remarkable how little attention in this general formula—concerned as it is primarily with the first stage of revolution—is paid to the class struggle, in conventional Marxist terms. The emphasis instead is on the national, anti-imperialist struggle. The revolution, to be successful, must "capture the national movement," forge an antiimperialist alliance. Thus Peking predicts a two-stage revolution where the strategy succeeds: its first stage is a national-democratic revolution; if it is led by communists (as in China), it will move on to the second, socialist stage; if it is led by bourgeois nationalists, it will still mark a step forward by struggling against feudal and colonialist privileges (as, for example, in Algeria).

Chinese statements have frequently invoked the "New Democracy" as a model for others to emulate as a way "to link up the national-democratic with the socialist revolution":

> Comrade Mao Tse-tung has pointed out that, in the epoch since the October Revolution, anti-imperialist revolution in any colonial or semi-colonial country is no longer part of the old bourgeois or capitalist world revolution, but is part of the new world revolution, the proletarian socialist world revolution. Comrade Mao Tse-tung has formulated a complete theory of the new-democratic revolution . . . against imperialism, feudalism and bureaucrat-capitalism, waged by the broad masses of the people under the leadership of the proletariat. . . . The revolution embraces in its ranks not only workers, peasants, and the urban petty bourgeoisie, but also the national bourgeoisie, and other patriotic and anti-imperialist democrats. . . . This new-democratic revolution leads to socialism, not capitalism.[84]

Thus somehow the antifeudal revolution manages to become part of the proletarian revolution as well. Given the vacuity of the latter concept, the trick is not surprising.

In the years since China's emergence after the Cultural Revolution, public expression of such views has been toned down, but they have not been taken back. On the whole—and it may be impossible to prove the point—revolutionary doctrine does seem to matter more for Chinese policymakers than it does currently for the Soviets, even though in China, too, elite conflicts have in recent years injected elements of irrationality into the crystallization of official positions, and tactics legitimately deviate from principled orientations. In general, in China revolution (a generation younger than in Russia) is still very much "in." Even in his "Report on the Work of the Government" to the National People's Congress on 13 January 1975, Premier Chou En-lai restated the Maoist perspective in these terms:

> On the one hand, the trend of revolution by the people of the world is actively developing: countries want independence, nations want liberation, and the people want revolution—this

has become an irresistible historical current. On the other hand
. . . the two superpowers . . . are the source of a new world war.
Their fierce contention is bound to lead to world war some day.
. . . At present the factors for both revolution and war are increasing. Whether war gives rise to revolution or revolution
prevents war, in either case the international situation will develop
in a direction favorable to the people and the future of the
world will be bright.

He added that "the third world is the main force in combating
colonialism, imperialism and hegemonism. China is a developing socialist country belonging to the third world. We should
enhance our unity with the countries and people of Asia,
Africa and Latin America and resolutely support them in
their struggle."[85] Vice-Premier Teng Hsiao-p'ing found it appropriate to reiterate almost the same terms in his toast
greeting President Ford in Peking on 1 December 1975.[86]

But in this instance too, practical, operational neglect
and manipulation of ideological categories must be recognized.
This was true even before the Cultural Revolution. A careful
study examining which countries Peking had identified as
potential targets for revolution in 1965, for instance, showed
that the selection was not based on "objective," socioeconomic conditions or even on the actual "antiimperialism"
of a given state. "The primary factor in Peking's decision is
the nature of the policy pursued by the government of a particular country with respect to the People's Republic of
China."[87] Even then, the author found, "Communist China
had developed at least a limited stake in the existing [inter-
national] system, and it was this stake in the status quo that
tempered Chinese support for foreign revolutions. . . . Thus
Mao's revolutionary strategy, in a different way, was as closely
related to state interests as Stalin's."[88]

The tendency to ignore or manipulate "pure" doctrine
has been strengthened substantially since the Cultural Revolution. The Sino-Soviet split has increased Chinese dependence on other, noncommunist states. China's rapproche-
ment with the United States and its appeals to other capitalist

countries (such as Japan and the nations of Western Europe) imply tactical requirements of temperance. The actual failure of the whole strategy of "people's war" outside of China—to the surprise of communists and noncommunists alike—has been a source of real disappointment in Peking.[89] Internal difficulties and disputes have further chastened the Chinese leadership. In practice, their optimistic, voluntarist, highly unorthodox orientation has been put in limbo. Can the revolution be institutionalized without losing its soul? All the precedents argue against it. A visitor to China reported that Teng Hsiao-p'ing conveyed to his guests "a change in the model that China is presenting to the rest of the world. It is no longer the model of revolution and class struggle of the Cultural Revolution, but of economic self-sufficiency through agriculture, hardly a revolutionary approach."[90] How much of this is tactics and facade, how much is irreversible change, it may yet be impossible to tell. In its own fashion, then, China too seems to be following in the footsteps of its "older brother," even while fighting and denouncing him.

Prospects and Prophecies

If the general trend sketched in the preceding pages is correct, it suggests a curious paradox. Would it not appear that Marxists were most optimistic about the prospects of revolution when they were least successful, and least optimistic when at the peak of their power? Actually, several processes—distinct but related—seem to have been at work and help explain the suggested retreat from optimism.

In the works of Marx and Engels themselves we can observe the effects of experience—a learning process during which, willy-nilly, their earlier hypotheses were tested by reality. As Engels wrote in his 1895 introduction to Marx's "Class Struggles in France," with the benefit of half a century of hindsight it was clear that Marx and Engels had been in error in 1848: "History has proved us, and all who thought like us, wrong." The results, on this and on so many later occasions, included, first, a heightened perception of the complexity of the real world, including the revolutionary process, and, second, some gnawing doubts about the inevitability of historical processes and the controlling role of "objective conditions."

The retreat from optimism, then, was in the first place a realistic response to empirical data. Marx and Engels did not witness any of the revolutions they had prophesied. Similarly, of course, none of the revolutions abroad forecast by the Soviet leaders, from Lenin on, or by their Chinese comrades have in fact come about—except for those imposed from the outside. And the revolutions that have actually taken place were either not foreseen in Moscow and Peking or else have pursued courses widely divergent from the Marxist models, even in their Soviet or Chinese reinterpretations.

It was well for Marx to say, "Je ne suis pas Marxiste." Not so his self-styled disciples in the East, for whom Marxism became first an ideology and later a state religion. One of the functions ideology serves is to explain everything, justify everything, rationalize everything as consistent with the single Truth and allowing of no accidents. To demonstrate the unfailing congruence of the real world with the words of the masters required more and more verbal and logical acrobatics. The heady brew was watered down; the formulae lost meaning.

At the same time, the characteristic response to the delay or slowness of the "historical process" and the insistence on meeting drawn-out "preconditions" was one of impatience and activism. The temptation is great to react by twisting the arm of the bitch-goddess of history: man is the master of his destiny. Superstructure takes over for base; politics has priority over economics; subjective forces prevail over objective ones; will takes the place of fate; organization wins over spontaneity; the strong triumphs over the community.

Then, there is the logic of the exercise of power. Once state power is seized, in the crucial encounter of beliefs and images with the actual world, realism becomes crucial for survival and success. Henceforth difficulties, complexities, and ambiguities may be ignored only at the system's peril. Effectiveness dictates adaptation; politics is the art of the possible. Whatever fanaticism or blindness have been attributed to communist regimes, once firmly established they have all displayed a remarkable will (and skill) to survive. To suggest that sustained success—beyond luck and short of hubris—goes hand in hand with realism is not at all to ignore the blind spots in perception, nor the sudden swings in policy toward senseless daring, nor momentary returns to adventurous overoptimism. Nor is it to argue that the exercise of state power is a necessary condition for such a retreat: we saw Marx and Engels themselves—far from holding power—pointing the way to revisionism and reconsideration.

But it is also true of official Marxism that nothing fails like success. What was a welcome challenge to the hopeful and young revolutionaries of yesteryear—there were no mountains too high to climb, no fortresses too strong to capture—becomes an inordinately demanding task to the bureaucrats and managers and the technicians of power, a generation or two later. The humanist ethos yields to production plans. To the accounting mind which fears spontaneity, to the upwardly mobile beneficiary of the new order, revolution suggests a chaotic disturbance: it is no longer true that we have nothing to lose but our chains. Yesterday's revolutionary is part of today's establishment. As a caustic philosopher could recently remark, "Marxisms now exist only . . . in their degenerate forms of state monopolies of mass ideology and linger as apologetics tolerated by bureaucracy . . . as false consciousness of apparatuses about the new class society of monopoly socialism."[91] As for revolution abroad, more and more of original Marxism has become irrelevant and the label usurped.

The revolution Marx anticipated in the industrially most advanced communities is heralded in the most backward economic systems. The revolution that Marx had forseen manifesting itself without violence in England, the United States and Holland is now understood to ride in behind fullscale regular or irregular military operations. . . . Literally all of what could legitimately pass as Marxist theory, the partially formulated economic theory of *Kapital* and its entailments—the labor theory of value, the theory of value, the theory of surplus value and the average rate of profit, the conception of the secular decline in profit, the increasing severity of economic crises, the interstitial development of socialism within the integument of the advanced industrial system of the West, the polarization of social elements into a "vast majority" of proletarians and exiguous number of capitalists who had concentrated economic power in their hands—became largely irrelevant to 20th-century Marxists and were unobtrusively jettisoned.[92]

It is only natural, after all, that belief systems made into rituals and sermons should lose their operational relevance as guides to action in a rapidly changing world that the classics of Marxism could not possibly have foreseen. This is particularly true of systems in which the use of the creed has become increasingly manipulative and symbolic.

In the Soviet case, cumulative experience does indeed leave little room for optimism regarding genuine, grass-roots revolutions which Moscow could claim as its own. Whatever the headlines, the notion of a Marxist Angola is ludicrous. And Moscow would scarcely welcome "deviant" revolutions even if they appropriate the label of communism; the prospect of a Maoist India, for instance, would give Soviet observers nightmares.

To be sure, Soviet optimism regarding the international "correlation of forces" may well rise: this is optimism not in regard to revolution but in regard to Soviet state power; faith based on might, not on creed. And here Moscow has indeed ground for optimism.

Tensions do remain in the Soviet approach (and, similarly, in that of other Marxist-Leninist elites). The tension between state and revolution, between stabilization and disruption, between computers and barricades, between welfare and warfare is genuine. It is also not new: George Kennan pointed to the simultaneity in the 1920s of the impulse to destroy and the impulse to enjoy.

Similarly, the tension has persisted between the temptation to stretch analytical categories to reconcile the unexpected with the faith, and the fear thereby to dilute the faith, to become a victim of circumstances or of temporary allies, in another twist of the ubiquitous *kto kovo.*

And from time to time there has been a tension among different Soviet observers and policy advocates regarding the noncommunist world. Virtually echoing the earlier hopes regarding the coming "crisis of capitalism"—so often promised and so often postponed—the leftists in 1974-75 once again seized upon the observed economic and political instability in the West, implying that here were unique opportunities which must not be allowed to slip by. Typically such arguments have been put forth by men—like Ponomarev, Zarodov, and Sobolev—once associated with the Communist International. And just as typically, their special pleading and their new optimism regarding the prospects of revolutionary developments in Western Europe once again do not prevail against the priorities of the power brokers in the Kremlin who talk five-year plans, technology transfer, ICBMs, grain purchases, and space shuttles.

Still, Moscow's or Peking's optimism regarding particular situations may wax and wane from time to time. To the extent that the retreat from optimism was engendered by a sound reading of absent opportunities abroad, it is reversible. But beyond such tactical ups and downs, the general secularization of the faith and the concomitant retreat from optimism about the inevitable revolution are irreversible trends. This was but underscored by the failure of Khrushchev's efforts to revitalize them.

It remains true, of course, that those who have chosen to call themselves Marxists have by no means been alone in mispredicting revolutions. And, in spite of it, they have been prominent among those who have successfully challenged the old order. It would go beyond the framework of this essay to examine the conditions under which Marxist revolutions have in fact succeeded, as against those under which they have grievously failed. But it may be suggested that the successes have required considerable adaptation to reality and departure from the doctrine of their mentors. The successes have not been due to any unique insights provided by these beliefs. There are in fact good objective reasons for a Marxist's retreat from optimism.

Peter Lange is an assistant professor of government at Harvard University. A student of the behavior of communist movements, Professor Lange is primarily interested in the strategy and organization of the Italian Communist Party. His publications include "PCI at the Local Level: A Study of Strategic Performances" in Communism in Italy and France, *edited by Donald Blackmer and Sidney Tarrow, and "What Is To Be Done—About Italian Communism?" which appeared in a recent issue of* Foreign Policy.

158

4
The French and Italian Communist Parties: Postwar Strategy and Domestic Society
Peter Lange

The 1960s were a decade of optimism for those hoping for stable liberal democratic regimes in Western Europe. After the uncertainties of reconstruction and the confrontation of the Cold War, it seemed that economic, social, and political change had made possible the liberal ideal of societies which were both pluralist democracies and socially just. Although all economic and social differences had not faded away and could not be expected to, the gross systematic intergenerational inequalities of the past appeared to have no part in the advanced industrial and even postindustrial society of the future.[1]

I owe a special debt to Donald L. M. Blackmer and Sidney Tarrow, whose work on the PCF and the PCI has made an important contribution to my thinking. I also want to thank the following for the lucid and helpful comments they made on an earlier draft of this paper: Suzanne Berger, Stanley Hoffmann, John Keeler, Gianfranco Pasquino, Ron Rogowski, and the participants in the workshop on radicalism of the Research Institute on International Change, Columbia University, 2 April 1975.

Ideological politics as expressed through the class-based and denominational political parties also seemed on the wane. Socialist and religion-based parties throughout Western Europe appeared to have abandoned their ideologically based strategies and to have become what Kirchheimer aptly dubbed "catch-all" parties, concerned with relatively narrow policy questions, seeking to build broad electoral coalitions and political alliances, willing to compromise and make trade-offs, and far more attentive to voters than members.[2]

Communist parties, including those in France (PCF) and Italy (PCI), were not considered immune to this process of change. Despite lags due to ideological traditions and to continued links to the Soviet Union, the communists also appeared to be becoming more moderate. The PCF and PCI were not yet catch-all parties, but they were adapting and slowly becoming "integrated" into their societies.[3]

Today much of the optimism of the 1960s has disappeared under an avalanche of economic and social discontent and often highly ideological political clashes at the fringes of the traditional party system. Many of the old sources and issues of conflict, seemingly buried by the sustained growth of the previous twenty years, have risen from the grave in both traditional and new guises. The socially just, politically stable and consensual pluralist democratic advanced industrial society foreseen in the 1960s has emerged in the 1970s riven by multiple discontents, with almost no unifying social and political vision and even less political leadership from the elites who have dominated the postwar period.

But what of the communists? In both France and Italy they are today closer to sharing actively in national power than at any time since the immediate postwar years. How do their strategies, tactics, and organizations relate to the societies of which they are a part, and especially to the conflicts and problems which have recently emerged with such force? With a few notable exceptions,[4] recent research agrees that the PCI and the PCF have in fact adapted to postwar changes. No longer totalitarian parties (if they ever were in the postwar period), but not yet catch-all parties wholly integrated into what may be a disintegrating society, the PCF and the PCI have adjusted their traditions to conditions in France and Italy, becoming something other than either "organizational weapons" or social-democratic echoes of welfare state politics.

If the communist parties are neither totalitarian destroyers of contemporary Western society nor wholly integrated into the political and socioeconomic status quo, then the task becomes to describe their current strategies, tactics, and organizations, and to examine the relationship between these and the current crisis. It is to these problems that this paper is addressed. I will first describe what I see to be the contemporary strategy, similar in its general outline, of the French and Italian parties, and then turn to an analysis of some of the important differences in the ways the parties implement this strategy. Finally, I will seek briefly to speculate as to how the contemporary strategic enterprises of the two parties relate to some of the more fundamental tensions which confront French and Italian society.

General Strategic Perspective

Looking at the behavior of the French and Italian communist parties in recent years, one is immediately impressed with the general similarities. Doctrinally, both parties have moved away from some of the traditional Marxist-Leninist dogma, adopting stances which more accurately reflect the development of capitalist society in the last fifty years. Both have with increasing frequency and openness criticized not only Soviet behavior, but also the applicability of the Soviet economic and political model for the West. Furthermore, the two have participated actively in national and local political institutions, developed concrete and detailed positions on pressing issues of national policy, energetically pursued alliances, and been willing to make both doctrinal and substantive political compromises to achieve them. Finally, to a somewhat lesser extent, they have made their organizations more open to internal debate, while at the same time loosening their hold over "mass organizations" such as the trade unions.[5]

These similarities are more than superficial. They reflect an underlying coincidence of basic assumptions about the strategic perspective appropriate to the international and national contexts in which the parties operate.[6] Certain international factors and domestic conditions common to postwar France and Italy have made a classical Leninist approach unviable, and have created strong incentives for adopting a strategy of alliance-building within the institutional confines of postwar French and Italian society. The specific ways in which these contextual factors have impinged on more traditional patterns of PCF and PCI behavior has varied, as has the timing of particular behavioral changes. By the 1970s, however, a general strategic perspective common to both parties had emerged.

The preeminent international factor bearing on the strategic options available to the French and Italian parties throughout the postwar period has been the division of Europe into spheres of American and Soviet influence. Soviet restraint in Greece immediately after World War II as well as the United States' hands-off policy towards Soviet interventions in Eastern Europe provided an unmistakable lesson: if the communist parties were to come to power, they would have to do it on their own, and with no expectation of Soviet aid should the United States decide to intervene.

Two distinct implications for Party strategy follow from this lesson, and have been increasingly manifest in the behavior of both parties in the years since 1956. First, any successful attempt to reach national power would have to be made within the rules of the democratic political system. Even such a course might not avoid American intervention, but any other would assure it. Furthermore, the character of the postwar French and Italian social and political systems has meant that playing within the democratic rules has necessitated seeking broad political and social alliances. Second, the hegemony of the United States and of the societal model which it symbolizes has confronted the parties with the constant need to make a trade-off between the sense of identity and commitment among Party members which results from adherence to the principle of "proletarian internationalism" and loyalty to the USSR, and the possibility of building alliances with other political parties and of extending communist influence in the general populace. The balance between these two has shifted increasingly towards the latter as Soviet prestige has declined, Party membership has increasingly been filled with post-1956 recruits, and alliance opportunities have flourished. But, since the parties' ability to develop fruitful alliances depends significantly on their political and social dynamism and since this, in turn, is largely a function of their organizational strength and level of member activism, no total break with the USSR is conceivable. Even though the fulcrum between the two pressures has been moving steadily in the direction of greater autonomy from the Soviets, this does not mean that a precipitous move in that direction would yield the parties greater domestic fruits.[7]

Communist strategy is constrained not only by the threat of direct American intervention; international economic relationships are of considerable importance as well. The freedom of international currency flows, the interdependence of the capitalist economies and the heavy dependence, particularly in key domestic industries, on foreign trade serve to moderate communist economic policy prescriptions and to encourage the building of the broadest possible national consensus around party programs. Only in this manner can the communist parties hope to avoid or reduce the potentially devastating economic effects of a flight of capital and a partial international economic boycott which could result from a probable or actual communist accession to power. Further, should such a broad programmatic alliance fail to impede a sharp economic downturn, it might at least permit the communists and their coalition partners to shift some of the political costs of that decline onto their political opponents.[8]

On the other hand, however, détente between the U.S. and the USSR, as well as the growth of the European Economic Community (EEC) and the increasing legitimacy of the concept of a somewhat independent Europe, have in recent years opened new options for the parties. Détente has increased the

credibility of the communists' claim to be legitimate com-
petitors for national political power. It has also made it more
difficult for the communist parties' traditional opponents to
justify complete closure to the communists on the grounds
that they are subversive agents of Soviet foreign policy or
that a communist accession to power would provoke an immediate and decisive American response.

At its initiation, the EEC extended and deepened American
penetration of Western Europe and facilitated the flow of
capital across borders. It thus contributed to the constraints
already cited. The rising economic strength of the European
nations and the weakening of American hegemony, however,
have created the opportunity for the communists to press for
an international policy option free of the inhibiting logic of
the spheres of influence. First the PCI, and more recently the
PCF, have sought to exploit this opportunity by calling for a
strengthening and democratization of European institutions
and for international agreements which would support more
autonomous Eastern and Western European entities and
eventually pan-European structures independent of both the
United States and the USSR. Through their participation in
the European Parliament, their acceptance of the EEC, and
their admission that even NATO cannot immediately be
scrapped, the Italian Party and, in a significantly more limited
way, the French Party, have both begun to use international
developments in order to expand their strategic options and
to increase their legitimacy within their respective nations.[9]
Europe and its institutions have become less of a constraint
on strategy and more of a strategic opportunity.

In addition to these international factors, there have also
been two domestic factors, common to both societies and to
advanced capitalism in general, which have had an important
bearing on the development of communist strategy. The
first of these has been the class structure of advanced capitalist society. As the postwar period has progressed, the PCF
and PCI have come to accept what was evident to some
socialist thinkers much earlier: that a strategy premised on
the wholly dominant role of the industrial working class is

doomed to failure.[10] The need to build a political majority and the numerical decline of the industrial working class relative to other, often new, social groups has meant that the parties, in seeking national power, have had to develop strategies which would appeal to an extremely complex set of social strata and groups, and organizational structures and mechanisms capable of incorporating them. The common impact of the social structure of advanced capitalism has been to force the development of strategic perspectives incorporating target constituencies significantly different from those of communist tradition.[11]

Second, a major general influence on the formation of French and Italian communist strategy in the postwar period has been the role of the state. Differences between the French and Italian state have had a considerable influence on the way that strategy has been implemented in the two countries. But beneath these differences has been the common fact that the scope of activity and the instruments available to the state in both countries have markedly increased. In the 1950s the economic role of the state was confined to macroeconomic policy and to the salvage of weak economic sectors or industries. By the 1970s, however, both the French and Italian state were playing an active and visible part in shaping economic policy: determining investment goals for both the public and private sectors, utilizing the vastly expanded public sector as an instrument in determining social policy goals, and seeking continually to impose public values on the private sector. The French government's sponsorship of "national champions" and the Italian government's theoretically rigid guidelines for industrial investment in the *Mezzogiorno* are simply two of the better known examples of this development.[12]

This expanded role of the state has further reinforced the view that a revolutionary strategy would be fruitless. Gradually the parties have come to recognize that the ultimate total collapse of capitalism might be postponed almost indefinitely. This, in turn, has led them to acknowledge the moderating role played by the state in the capitalist economic cycle and the need, therefore, to seek to exploit politically the effects of cyclical downturns by proposing counter-cyclical policy alternatives different from those of the ruling political parties, rather than simply standing by and denouncing the decline as a phase in total economic collapse.[13]

Furthermore, the potential tension between the parties' desire to socialize the economy and the necessity to operate within the basic institutional structures and rules of contemporary France and Italy has been markedly reduced. The French and, to a far greater extent, the Italian parties have come to base their programs and strategies on the idea that the path to socialism could come through existing structures rather than over them. This, in turn, has meant that the parties could far more easily establish a meeting ground with potential political and social allies.[14]

The international and domestic factors discussed in the preceding pages create contextual constraints and opportunities which have led the PCF and PCI to adopt a common strategic perspective. The basic contours of that perspective should be evident, and I will outline them only briefly.[15]

I. Assumptions

A. The policy goal remains socialism, but a transitional period of "advanced democracy" will be necessary before sufficient national consensus for socialist measures can be attained. In this transitional phase a series of measures, which the Italians refer to as "structural reforms," will begin to introduce socialism while at the same time weakening the bases of strength of monopoly capital.[16]

B. The political goal is national power. Such power will have to be shared with other political parties, some of them with a Marxist perspective and others of them perhaps not. The bond binding together the ruling coalition will be programmatic.[17]

C. Power must be achieved within the existing democratic institutions and those institutions will, with possible changes which do not disrupt their democratic character, be maintained after coming to power. Both parties have committed themselves to a pluralism of parties, full respect for civil liberties, free elections, and alternation of power, though the credibility of the PCI's long-term commitment to these values is somewhat greater than that of the PCF.[18]

II. Strategy

A. At the center of the strategy is the need to build real and enduring alliances based on programmatic agreements reached through compromise. Such alliances will be both political and social.[19]

1. Political alliances refer to agreements based on common programs reached with other political parties.

2. Social alliances refer to agreements reached with the organized representatives of various social strata and groups, and to the extension of Party influence, and hopefully hegemony, into sectors of the populace other than those already committed to the communist party. Such social alliances can potentially be very extensive, including not only the peasantry and agricultural working class but also a large part of the middle classes. The reason for this potential is the character of monopoly capitalism.[20] The achievement of such social alliances is indispensible if the balance of political power is to be shifted sufficiently to create the conditions for a winning and adequately coherent political coalition. In order for the social alliances to have the desired effect they must not only operate at the electoral level but also provide the Party with the means to mobilize a diverse social coalition in favor of various programmatic principles and goals.

III. Action consequences

A. The Party must be "present" and active in as many areas of political and social life as is necessary in order to achieve the political goals. These areas include: (1) national political institutions; (2) non-national governmental institutions such as local government; and (3) social, cultural, and interest group activities at all levels of society.

B. Electoral politics assumes a great importance both as a means of increasing the Party's voting strength and thereby contributing to its ability to develop political alliances, and as a measure of the Party's success in building social alliances.[21]

C. The development of concrete programmatic stances on the major issues confronting the nation is of absolute necessity, both as groundwork for building political and social alliances, and as a way of expressing the Party's governmental vocation and competence. The stress on concrete policy positions must be evident in all arenas of political life.[22]

D. In light of the above, the strength of the Party organization is critical. Only by having a powerful, active organization with a considerable number of members can the Party hope to pursue all the facets of its strategic perspective, while at the same time maintaining a coherence of purpose and a capacity to direct the multiple elements of its action towards the achievement of strategic goals. The many arenas in which the strategy requires the Party to take positive, concrete initiatives, and the high level of interaction with an extremely heterogeneous set of political and social groups which it calls for, necessitates a strong Party organization capable of coordinating and integrating what is potentially an unmanageable set of alliances. Further, the willingness of other political and social forces to compromise over a specific program of reforms acceptable to the communists is primarily a function of the Party's organizational capacities and its resultant ability to assume a leadership role for important strata of the mass public.

Diversity in Strategic Implementation

Thus far I have argued that the PCF and PCI have come to share a common strategic perspective. Anyone familiar with the literature on the French and Italian communist parties, however, will be aware that comparative discussions tend to stress the differences between them.

The image of the PCF which emerges from the literature is of a party sectarian in ideology, rigid, dogmatic, and generally unwilling to reach policy compromises in political institutions, distrustful and rather formal in attempts to develop alliances, and tightly organized and disciplined.[23] The PCI, in contrast, is seen as doctrinally flexible, anxious to reach policy compromises and willing to pay short-run political costs to do so, open and informal in pursuit of alliances, and a mass party with a relatively (for a communist party) loose structure in which a surprising amount of debate occurs.[24]

I do not intend to argue that this image is false; in fact, I will present evidence indicating that it is descriptively rather accurate. But I am arguing, on the one hand, that this image of diversity masks a common strategic perspective and, on the other hand, that the differences between the two parties in their approach to organization and to building political and social alliances are a product of the interaction of that common strategic perspective and particular features of the postwar French and Italian political and social systems.[25]

Political Alliances

Throughout the postwar period the political alliances sought by the PCF have been narrower in scope than those of the PCI. With the exception of the immediate postwar years, the predominant political alliance targets for French communists have been the various political parties representing what can broadly be considered French socialism; they have rarely sought to go beyond this sphere to seek allies more in the center as well. During the periods when the socialists have not been part of a political coalition premised on isolation of the PCF (as they often were during the Fourth Republic) and when the communists have sought coalitions of any sort, the socialist party (or socialist parties) has been the object of their attentions. The clearest expression of this approach has been the PCF campaign since 1962 to build an enduring alliance with the Section française de l'Internationale ouvrière (SFIO) and then with the socialist party, an effort which achieved a degree of success with the agreement on the *Programme Commun* and the electoral cooperation of recent years.[26]

The PCI policy towards political alliances has been markedly different. From the "antifascist unity coalition" of communists, socialists, and Christian Democrats (DC) of

1945–47, to the appeals to the "left" DC factions in the 1960s, to the calls for a "historic compromise" or coalition of national emergency of today, Italian communist political initiatives have consistently sought to include the Italian socialists (PSI) but at the same time to reach beyond them to the Christian Democrats.[27]

Even from this brief sketch it should be evident why PCF political alliance behavior makes the PCF seem more sectarian than the PCI. The place to begin an explanation of this contrast is the party system of the two countries. In France, a coalition between the communists and the parties of the noncommunist left has consistently appeared to be the best and/or the most likely way for the PCF to share in national power. In the Fourth Republic such a coalition would have had a majority in the elections of 1946, 1951, and 1956 and would have fallen below 50 percent for the first time in the special election, dominated by the looming presence of de Gaulle, in 1958.[28] Since then the combined total vote for the parties has never recovered its Fourth Republic level, averaging 42 percent until 1973, but during this period the logic of polarization inherent in the Fifth Republic's political institutions encouraged a coalition on the left despite the decline in the electoral fortunes of the parties.[29]

The hope of the communists and socialists that through coalition they might reverse the electoral slide has been borne out in recent elections; the alliance may today command the support of a majority of French voters. This hope, however, should not be treated as justified only by hindsight.[30] The postwar fluctuations of significant sectors of the French electorate could well give the parties hope that their electoral erosion, which seemed clearly linked to the prestige of de Gaulle and the tradition he represented, might be rapidly reversed once the General disappeared from the scene. The electoral shifts in the Fifth Republic might well represent not a major realignment but simply a temporary change in voters' affections.[31] Thus the nature of the postwar party system, combined with the electoral laws of the Fifth Republic and the character of the French electorate, has created powerful incentives for the PCF to look to French socialism for allies. Electoral alignments have suggested the communists could thus build a minimal winning coalition; and, given the Party's programmatic concerns, it is not surprising that it has not actively sought to extend ties, and of necessity make compromises, with parties further towards the center.

The case for the PCI is totally different. If in France the party system and character of the electorate have encouraged the PCF to stay close to its ideological home, in Italy these same factors have obliged the PCI to go beyond the socialist party in search of political alliance partners. First, postwar elections have consistently indicated that a communist-socialist coalition had little hope of winning a parliamentary majority. Nineteen seventy-six was the first year in which the combined votes of the two parties exceeded 40 percent, and increases in communist vote percentages have generally been matched by relatively equal declines in the socialist vote.[32] A left coalition, therefore, has not seemed a promising route to power. This has been reinforced by the inflexibility of the Italian electorate's voting preferences throughout most of the postwar period. Despite massive changes in the economy, with their resultant effects on social life and demography, the strength of the major Italian parties has, until very recently, remained remarkably consistent from election to election. Even the 1976 elections, which marked major gains for the left, were also noteworthy for the continued electoral strength of the Christian Democrats, who had been expected by many to suffer a major setback.[33]

From this analysis it is evident why the communists in Italy had to seek political allies beyond the socialist party if they were to come to power. But why the DC? A lengthy answer to this question will not be developed here, but one extremely important factor further illuminates the differences between France and Italy. Since the Fifth Republic, and especially since Pompidou forsook the social vocation of Gaullism, the political and social characteristics of the governing coalition and principal opposition to the communists have been decidedly conservative. In France today there is no political force in the center with sufficient strength to make it a worthwhile target of the communists' alliance efforts.[34] In contrast, the principal governing party in Italy, the DC, has been a party of the center, which seeks to appeal to both reform-oriented and conservative sectors of the population and is open to alliances with and pressures from political parties on both its right and its left.[35] The social basis of the Christian Democrats reflects this centrist charac-ter. The party draws mass support from strata, such as the industrial working class, which would clearly benefit from a reformist policy. These strata are represented by factions within the party. At the same time, other strata providing mass support, who would clearly be the losers if broad social reforms were to be undertaken, are also represented by party factions. The overall balance of power in the DC has favored the conservative forces, as is evidenced by the failure of postwar governments—even after the entrance of the PSI into the coalition in 1963—to institute a consistent and thoroughgoing reformist policy. Nevertheless, the reform-oriented factions have remained loyal.[36]

The political dominance of the DC, combined with its centrist and "interclass" character and its seemingly un-breakable unity, make it a necessary target of the com-munists' attempts to extend their political alliances. With-out some DC cooperation the PCI is unlikely to come to power. Furthermore, even if it did, a left government's capacity to institute the policies essential to its success would probably be crippled by the opposition which the DC would be able to generate. Awareness of this latter point has been a major factor in the PCI's development and pursuit of the "historic compromise" line and of other tactics designed to force the Catholic party to cooperate with it.[37] And the political and social character of the DC gives support to the hope that at some point the balance of power within the party might shift sufficiently to the left to allow the formation of a grand coalition. Nothing in the recent electoral shifts in Italy has altered this basic PCI perspective.

The greater scope of political alliances sought by the PCI as compared to the PCF, then, is primarily a function of the strategic imperative to develop an electoral and parliamentary majority, combined with specific characteristics of the French and Italian political systems. The need for a broader set of alliances is at the root of the PCI's greater openness in political alliance efforts, its greater programmatic flexibility, and its greater willingness to tolerate tension and ambiguity in its relations with potential allies. A brief examination of recent political alliance behavior of the two parties can illustrate this point as well as provide some insights into the dynamics of contemporary party relationships on the left in the two countries.

In the last five years both the PCF and the PCI have made gains in their efforts to form their desired political alliances. In the case of the French, the alliance has in fact been achieved in the form of the *Programme Commun* and electoral cooperation between the PCF and socialist party (PS). In Italy, programmatic and informal, but not direct, governmental cooperation between the PCI, PSI, and DC are further developed than at any time since the immediate postwar period.[38] Somewhat paradoxically, however, the PCF, which would seem in the stronger position, has been far more cautious and defensive in its behavior towards its secured ally than has the PCI towards its potential allies. While the Italians have persisted in seeking cooperation with the DC despite the latter's rejection of any alliance or formal agreement,[39] the PCF has maintained a generally cautious and distrustful stance towards their socialist "partners."[40] Why should this be the case? Once more the causes would seem to lie in the logic of the party and electoral systems and the dynamics of the electorate.

The PCF's relationship to the socialists can be best understood through an analysis of the polemic which the communists carried on against the PS in 1974–75. That campaign, which at times reached levels of rhetoric reminiscent of previous eras, seemed to challenge the view that the PCF truly sought an alliance with the socialists, but a closer analysis reveals that this was not the case. Rather, it appears that the attacks on the PS were likely to cost the communists little in terms of their overall strategic design, while yielding considerable organizational and tactical benefits. The PCF could expect to suffer if its criticism of the socialists resulted in a loss of votes or, far more importantly, if the PS were to react to the communist attacks by breaking the alliance. But neither of these two alternatives was likely. There were no national elections scheduled for more than two years, and thus any electoral effects of the debate could probably be offset in the intervening period. Also, the socialists had nowhere else to go, since the polarization induced by the Gaullist electoral reforms has, for the proximate future, largely destroyed the centrist alternative. In the present party system, abandonment of the unity of the left would probably condemn the PS and, of course, the PCF as well, to hopeless opposition, particularly since precisely such a split would remove all incentives for the conservative bloc of parties to reach a meaningful compromise with the socialists. And the internal damage to the PS caused by a split would likely be great, since its organizational rebuilding of the last five years has been heavily dependent on its ability to hold out the prospect of power. This is what has kept the various factions of the party together, has attracted new members, and has led other splinter socialist formations to unify with the party.[41] Further, one can argue that the increased electoral strength of the PS, some of which has probably come at the communists' expense, would decline should the left coalition be broken.[42] These constraints on the PS have given the PCF considerable freedom to criticize its coalition partner.[43]

But of course the communists would not have made such criticisms unless they thought there was something to be gained from such behavior, for in pursuing their tactic towards the PS they did run some risks.[44] What then were the advantages of this tactic? First, the polemic between the parties enabled the PCF to reassert its special identity and role within the coalition, which had become blurred when common candidates ran on the second ballot in the 1973 legislative elections and when a socialist, François Mitterand, was presented as sole candidate for the united left in the 1974 presidential election.[45] Second, the polemic with the PS may have helped to appease those in the PCF who opposed elements of the alliance strategy and who pointed to the PCF's declining electoral position relative to the PS as a sign that the coalition had not served PCF interests. It was probably no accident that the communist attacks began shortly after some electoral losses in the 1974 reelections, and that their main theme was the PS's alleged intention to try to "realign" the coalition in a way which would make the PCF the weak partner.[46] Since in the past the communist leadership has argued that the common front would help both partners equally, the electoral losses were particularly stinging. Third, the attacks allowed the PCF to voice its discontent with the socialists' advocacy of policies, such as "autogestion," which the PCF disliked and which were not integral to the *Programme Commun.*[47]

It is apparent, therefore, that the PCF's polemic against the PS must be understood in light of the specific conjuncture of political conditions at the time.[48] The situation permitted the PCF to pursue a short-run policy which would reinforce it internally without greatly endangering its broader strategic goals. Today the political rewards of closer cooperation between the partners are more immediate. As a result, the communists have undertaken a revision of their ideological identity which may reduce some of the internal tensions to which they responded two years ago. Thus a return to the earlier level of tension seems unlikely in the immediate future. Nonetheless, the basic structure of the French party system remains constant and the relationship between the PCF and the socialists seems certain to remain a volatile one.

The PCI is constrained to adopt a rather different stance in its pursuit of allies. The same factors which oblige the Party to seek broader alliances also require a flexible and open approach to potential alliance partners. This is not to suggest that the PCI is not critical of the PSI and DC. For its alliance

strategy to succeed, the communists must point out the
weaknesses and contradictions of the positions of these two
parties, thereby highlighting the need for PCI participation in
the government. But the communists' criticisms must be carefully articulated and restrained, pointing not only to contemporary failures but also to the possibility of future improvements in policy direction. It is not difficult to understand
why such care is necessary. In Italy neither the DC nor the
PSI needs direct communist participation in order to form a
government. The PCI, therefore, must seek through its
criticisms and through the policy alternatives it represents to
force the DC and the socialists to recognize the communists
not only as a threat but also as a legitimate political force and
indispensible element in any attempt to overcome Italy's
crisis.[49]

It is in this light that the communist pursuit of a "historic
compromise" or other broad coalition including both the
PSI and *all* of the DC must be evaluated. Italy is today going
through an unprecedentedly long economic and social crisis—
a crisis from which few think the country can emerge without strong political direction. The DC is at a postwar ebb in
its prestige and political support, and has had to absorb the
votes of the small conservative parties in order to maintain
its electoral plurality. The left, with the communists in the
lead, has made major gains, winning more than 45 percent
of the votes in the 1976 elections and controlling the governments of almost all the major cities and a large percentage of
the smaller ones.

One might expect the PCI to seek to exploit these conditions by calling for a left alliance, as some have urged, or by
actively courting the progressive factions within the DC. But
to do either of these would leave at the center of the political system a large and still powerful political force capable
at some later time of drawing the PSI, and/or the left Catholic
factions, out of a coalition with the communists and back to
the center. Furthermore, the presence of a political opposition which could itself continue to claim popular roots and a
reformist avocation would weaken a left government's ability

to carry out the policies on which its success depends. In such a situation, the PCI could well fear being the eventual loser—alone paying the electoral and organizational costs which would inevitably accompany any attempt to steer Italy beyond the current economic turmoil, and quite possibly being thrust back into political isolation after such an effort. Thus the need to include the DC in any coalition. A historic compromise or grand coalition would assure that the costs of resolving the crisis would be borne by all major parties, thereby reducing the possibility that the communists could be abandoned once conditions improved. At the same time, it would make effective obstructionist actions by conservative forces more difficult.[50]

Despite the seeming astuteness of the PCI's present course, however, it must be noted that it is both a relatively risky and a conservative course of action.[51] The risk arises from the fact that the compromise is intended to bring the party into "the area of governance" within the relatively near future. This, in turn, means that the PCI will not only have to meet its promises of structural reform, but will have to do so while at the same time seeking to resolve the current Italian economic and social crisis. Therefore, the risks of sharing governmental responsibility in the immediate future are real and large for the PCI.[52]

Communist policy represents a conservative course of action because it is predicated on the stability of those contextual factors which have constrained and guided the party's political alliance effort throughout the postwar period. Most importantly, it foresees a continuing major role in national government for the DC, rejecting policy options which might split the Catholic party or force it into the opposition. Thus the PCI denies the possibility of governing with "51 percent" and conjures up the Chilean debacle whenever such proposals are advanced.[53] This stance is no doubt both prudent and, in the immediate situation, most likely to increase the Party's influence. At the same time, however, it reflects an unbending allegiance to the same strategic principles which the Party has pursued for more than thirty years. Thus, as with the PCF, contemporary PCI political allegiance policy is only the immediate manifestation of the longer-term interaction between a relatively constant strategy and the specific characteristics of the political system.

Social Alliances

For both the French and the Italian communists the building of social alliances—that is, extending the parties' influence and organized presence in social groups and strata in which their legitimacy has traditionally been low and their sway negligible—is of critical import, particularly because the relative weight of the social strata from which the communists have in the past received their strongest support is diminishing. The development of social alliances and the mobilization of this social support on the basis of shared policy positions are intended to advance the parties' political prospects in two principle ways: first, by creating electoral and other pressures on the communists' political alliance targets to establish, maintain, and develop their links with the communist parties; and second, by increasing the communists' legitimacy in society at large and enhancing their acceptability as potential government partners. Thus, the social alliance strategy is perceived as the motor which can move the political axis in the direction desired by the communists.[54]

It is difficult to compare the ways in which the PCF and the PCI carry out their respective social alliance strategies, because far more research on Party operations in this area has been done on the PCI than the PCF. Nonetheless, the limited data available once more suggest a picture of greater sectarianism in the French Party during the postwar period than in the Italian. Sidney Tarrow has recently argued that the "essence" of the PCI's strategic model in the postwar period lies in the concept of "presence"—that is, in the Party's drive to play an active and constructive role in all sectors of the society.[55] At the grass roots level the Party has made great efforts to establish mass organizations and to seek political allies directly.[56] Furthermore, at least in the last decade the PCI has been willing to give a relatively free rein to some of the mass organizations in which it has a prominent influence.[57] The picture of the PCF, on the other hand, is of a party which is not highly active in society at large (with the exception, perhaps, of the factory), which is often dogmatic and uncompromising in its dealings with organized social groups, and which has sought to exercise strong control over the mass organizations in which it has strong influence.[58]

The PCI has since the war consistently sought to develop a platform and mass organizations which would attract members of the petty bourgeoisie (artisans, shopkeepers, etc.). As early as 1946 Togliatti exhorted the PCI organizations to direct their attention to these strata, pointing out their importance to the Party's overall strategic design and to its self-image as a "national" party.[59] At the same time the PCI developed mass organizations of artisans, shopkeepers, and the like, which were intended to advance the interests of these groups while also expanding communist influence within them.[60] In contrast, Jean Ranger has pointed out that not until the early years of the Fifth Republic did the PCF even *begin* to abandon the view that petty bourgeois strata were doomed to fall into the proletariat and therefore required little special attention from Party organizations.[61] Similarly, peasant mass organizations inspired and/or dominated by the PCI have been conspicuous in most of the postwar peasant struggles in both northern and southern Italy, and land and agricultural reform have been an extremely prominent part of the Party's program since the war.[62] The first really successful effort among peasants inspired by the PCF, on the other hand, is the MODEF (mouvement de défense des exploitants familiaux), which first appeared in the late 1950s and gained little strength until the 1960s.[63]

The Italian communists have also apparently been more willing to allow freedom of action to the CGIL (Confederazione Generale Italiana del Lavoro, the trade union federation which they dominate), and to make sacrifices in order to encourage trade union unity, than has the PCF in its relations with its trade union affiliate, the Confédération Générale du Travail (CGT).[64] During the 1950s the notion that trade unions were mere "transmission belts" predominated in both parties. Since 1956, however, significant differences have appeared. These differences were conspicuous in the contrasting ways the PCF used the CGT during the crisis of May 1968 and the PCI dealt with the CGIL during the "hot autumn" in 1968–69. George Ross, in a fascinating study, has shown that during the crisis of May 1968 the PCF apparently exercised control over CGT behavior, seeking to assure that the actions undertaken by the union worked to advance the Party's tactical goals. Consequently, the CGT did not cooperate with other unions in pressing those issues in the strike which went beyond wages and benefits, but acted instead as a restraint on the militancy of the working class in a number of factories.[65] During the "hot autumn," in contrast, the PCI, while sometimes publicly disagreeing with stances adopted by the CGIL, allowed the union to pursue a policy developed in common with the Catholic and Social-Democratic unions. This stance was consistent with the postwar PCI policy of encouraging unification of the trade union movement.

The PCI's stress on unification, it should be noted, has not been without cost to the Party. It has meant that the union movement has taken some unified positions on economic questions which, because of their societal impact, have sometimes been openly opposed by the Party. There have been organizational costs as well. Part of the price for advances towards union unification has been that union officials can no longer hold Party posts or sit in Parliament. As a result, the linkages between union and Party have been weakened both institutionally and in policy, and the PCI probably could no longer exercise the leverage which it once had in the union even if it wanted to.[66]

These examples serve to indicate the differences between the PCF and PCI in their attitude and approach towards social alliances. While these differences have somewhat diminished in recent years as the PCF has become more open and flexible, important distinctions remain. The general difference in the way the two parties have sought to build social alliances seems to be primarily the result of two basic differences in the character of the contexts which the parties face.

The most fundamental of these characteristics is the nature of the social cleavage system and its relationship to politics. It would clearly be incorrect to argue that society in France is fundamentally divided in terms of class or social strata and that other sources of social cleavage, such as religion or region, do not exist and cut across class lines. People's attitudes concerning the issue of the role of the church in French society, for instance, are undoubtedly still an important predictor of political preference. Yet in postwar French society, cleavages other than class have been poorly institutionalized and specific partisan voting preferences have been only loosely tied to social position.[67] Furthermore, despite disagreements among scholars about the degree to which French society is permeated by a network of social organizations structuring the social life of the populace, it is certainly the case that the organizations which do exist only rarely have strong linkages with the party system. In fact, French society retains great autonomy from partisan politics and provides few instruments for the communication of specific partisan values (an obvious exception to this general rule is the CGT). As a result, the French citizen tends to face the political system as an individual rather than as a member of one or more partisan societal groups.[68]

The social cleavage system in Italy is markedly different. While it is true that much of the populace belongs to no party or other political organization, the percentage of those who are in social and economic organizations is probably higher than in France. Furthermore, the social system is crosscut by two major cleavages, one based on religion and the other on class, and the cleavage system is heavily institutionalized.[69] In the almost hundred years of their existence, the Catholic and the Marxist subcultures have developed a panoply of institutions which structure much of the life of the citizens caught up in them, and which include almost all

Italian economic and social voluntary associations. In sharp contrast to France, the Italian subcultures have been highly politicized and partisan throughout their history. The postwar period in Italy has been marked by a highly politicized and partisan institutionalized social and economic life, in which citizens desiring to be socially or economically active have had little choice but to participate through the organizations of one of the two partisan subcultures.[70]

The second contextual factor explaining the differences in implementation of social alliance strategy is the character and role of the state. The French state is highly centralized, with few important decisions being made outside Paris.[71] Furthermore, under the Fifth Republic most decision-making power has fallen to the executive and the bureaucracy, the role of Parliament having been weakened by Gaullist constitutional reforms.[72] The bureaucracy itself is, in Huntington's terms, highly institutionalized,[73] affording effective access primarily to those groups which the bureaucrats themselves choose to privilege. Such groups have traditionally been proponents of conservative interests, in part because bureaucratic posts have been filled on the basis of "meritocratic" criteria which, in practice, favor those of upper-middle-class background. Under the Fifth Republic the prolonged dominance of governmental institutions by the Gaullist party has also led, according to Ezra Suleiman, to a privileged position in the bureaucratic process for groups favorable to Gaullist interests.[74] The implications of these bureaucratic practices for mass politics have been described at length by Michel Crozier: they tend to encourage either public apathy or intense but fleeting forms of interest group mobilization. Except for those groups and interests which can expect to gain access to the bureaucracy, the more mundane forms of pressure group activity hold out little likelihood of success.[75]

The Italian state provides a sharp contrast with this picture. Though centralized in theory, it has in fact been somewhat decentralized throughout the postwar period, and has become even more so in recent years with the creation of functioning regional governments. Albeit against great resistance, these regional governments have increasingly been able to take responsibility for and control over the provision of a large number of social services formerly handled by the central government.[76] Furthermore, scholars have noted a trend at both the national and the regional levels for legislative bodies to increase, rather than decrease, in power.[77]

These contrasts with France are striking, but perhaps even more notable is the degree to which the Italian bureaucracy at both the national and non-national levels is politicized. While Suleiman's research suggests that the French bureaucracy is more partisan than has traditionally been assumed, the image which emerges from the study is that of a bureaucratic structure and process which is only rarely concerned or involved with petty politics and with the day-to-day concerns of the Gaullist or any other political party.[78] In Italy the case is wholly different. Whether it be the provision of state resources for the reinforcement of political clienteles, the allocation of the funds from state programs in a manner designed to strengthen party ties in certain sectors of the populace, or the filling of bureaucratic posts with party loyalists,[79] the postwar Italian state at all levels has been a major instrument for the advancement of the political interests of the parties in power, above all of the DC. Thus, whereas the French state is still only weakly linked to partisan politics, the Italian state is permeated by it.

The differences in the character of the cleavage systems and state structure in France and Italy affect social alliance strategies in two ways. First, the cleavage system in Italy creates a far greater need for the PCI to pursue social allies aggressively than does the cleavage system in France. Second, the character of the Italian state creates far greater incentives, relative to costs, for the persistent pursuit of such allies than does the character of the French state.

In Italy, the traditional presence of two powerful subcultures, each linked to political parties, has a two-pronged effect. On the one hand, it creates an unavoidable "logic of expansion" for both the PCI and the DC. The presence of a powerful and active Catholic subculture means that the communist party's chief rival (and potential ally), the DC, always has the institutional capacity to expand and encapsulate its bases of support. If the PCI wishes even to hold its own, therefore, it must develop a countervailing set of institutions capable of competing for new recruits on an equal footing with the Catholic ones; if it wishes to expand as well, its social alliance activity must be greater and more effective than that of its opponent. Since the same logic holds for the other side, both are faced with the constant need to expand the level of their social alliance activity.[80]

The second effect of the character of the Italian cleavage system is closely related to the first. The ultimate goal of social alliance activity of the communists is to shift the political balance of forces in their favor. In Italy the presence of a powerful Catholic subculture which organizes significant portions of what the Party considers its "natural" constituencies (for example, the working class) and delivers them to the DC means that the task of changing the political balance requires an intensive social alliance effort. The PCI must establish as broad a "social presence" as possible, and it must attempt constantly to bridge the religious cleavage with propaganda about specific Party programs and with efforts to organize people on the basis of concrete issues and demands which do not arouse religious sentiments. It is no accident, for instance, that the PCI, throughout the postwar period, has sought to avoid confrontations on religious questions (for instance, the inclusion of the Lateran Pacts in the constitution in 1947, and the divorce question in recent years[81]). Only by avoiding such issues could the Party hope to create the mass pressure which might induce the DC or elements of it to make a political alliance with the communists.

The different logic working on the PCF should be clear. The weak institutionalization of the social cleavages means that the barriers to new supporters faced by the French Party are much lower than for the Italians. The general weakness of subcultures and the poverty of linkages between social organization and the party system means that the PCF is not caught up in a "logic of expansion." Since its political rivals possess few direct means of expanding and encapsulating their support, the PCF has no powerful incentive for doing so. Far more than the PCI, the French Party can rely on propaganda initiatives on a grand scale, such as the *Programme Commun*, to win new support.[82] And it need not devote as much time and effort to the development of the kind of social presence which is so critical to the PCI.

To say that the PCF is not faced with the same necessity to develop intensive social alliance activity is not, however, to explain why the French Party does not do it. After all, would it not gain a considerable amount of support from such an effort? The answer would seem to be that the character of the French state, combined with the cultural tendency of the French to avoid associational life, makes adequate returns for the effort unlikely. The centralization and relatively great autonomy of the French state make it likely that there will be little payoff from the creation of mass organizations intended to advance the interests of specific social groups (and thereby increase the Party's support among them). Since major decisions are made in Paris by bureaucrats who are largely insensitive to social pressure—particularly if it comes from the left—the probability that the PCF could actually deliver on the policy goals that it used to develop the organization is rather low. Moreover, the resistance to organization typical of the French means that for the PCF to build a large number of mass organizations would require an enormous undertaking.[83] It is, therefore, not surprising that the Party only rarely attempts to develop new mass organizations.

In Italy the structure of the state works in the other direction. Its relative decentralization (which the PCI has continually sought to encourage),[84] and its greater permeability to social pressure, open the possibility of real gains in organizing groups to advance their specific interests. This both encourages and facilitates the pursuit of an aggressive social alliance strategy. Thus, in Italy the combination of institutionalized subcultures and a particular kind of state structure induces the PCI to implement its strategic need for social alliances through an active, widespread, and multifaceted attempt to reach a large number of diverse social groups. In France, the combination of a low level of cleavage institutionalization in the society and a centralized and relatively impermeable state leads to a policy in the pursuit of social allies which is selective in its targets and moderate in its initiatives, and which tends to stress propaganda over organization and central initiatives over local ones. The image of the French Party which results is far more sectarian than that of the Italian Party, but the explanation of the differences lies not in basic strategic design but rather in the interaction between a common strategy and two rather different contexts.

Organization

Despite their abandonment of much classical Leninist strategy, the contemporary PCF and PCI retain a strong drive to develop powerful and autonomous organizations to serve as instruments for the implementation of their strategic interests. This should be no surprise. Not only is it explicable by the force of tradition, but it is also a direct function of the nature of the postwar strategy itself. Although the parties differ in the ways they pursue political and social alliances, their common strategy requires that they construct organizations powerful enough to carry out a broad range of activities. But there are, of course, significant differences in the characteristics of the two parties' organizations, reflecting the differences in strategic implementation.

Throughout the postwar period, with the possible exception of the worst years of the Cold War,[85] the PCI has consistently sought to develop a more open and flexible organizational structure and set of operating practices than has the PCF. The need for the Italian Party to seek a wider set of political and social alliances, to develop a more extensive social presence in the society, and hence to accept greater ambiguity and instability in its relations with its environment, has had its analogues in the Party's relationship to its own members. Far more than the PCF, the PCI has had to develop an organization which would avoid the dangers of sectarian behavior so common to the experience of the communist parties of Europe. While the PCF remains a hybrid cadre party,[86] the PCI has been, since 1945, a communist mass party.

Perhaps the most revealing organizational difference between the PCF and the PCI is in their approach to three related issues: how many members they should have, who these members should be, and where they should come from. The PCI has consistently striven for a larger, more socially and territorially diverse membership than the PCF. Throughout most of the postwar period the Italian Party has had a membership about four or five times as large as that of the French Party. Immediately after the war, in the wake of the enthusiasm generated by the role played by the parties in the French and Italian Resistance, both parties expanded their membership dramatically from the prewar years. Though the figures are somewhat unreliable, the PCF seems to have attained a membership of almost a million, and the PCI of well over 2 million. Both parties had mass organizations, which varied considerably in the degree of commitment and level of activity of their members. With the coming of the Cold War, however, a significant difference between the two organizations developed. While the PCF lost more than half its membership, the PCI appears to have continued to grow, reaching its peak only in 1954. Since that time the membership of the PCF, according to Kriegel, has varied from about 250,000 to 400,000, that of the PCI from about 1,500,000 to 1,650,000. The data available indicate that both parties suffered some membership decline in the 1960s but appear to have reversed this trend in recent years.[87]

It might legitimately be asked whether these numerical differences actually tell us anything about the membership policies of the two parties. Could it not be that the PCF is smaller because, as we have seen before, it has no subculture like that of the PCI to lean on and because of the general distaste of the French for organizational participation? These factors undoubtedly do contribute to the difference, but the PCF has also shown greater selectivity in recruitment and greater hesitancy in seeking members beyond its traditional bases of support. The first of these points can be illustrated by an example drawn from the immediate postwar period.

Both the PCF and the PCI enjoyed a massive influx of members at the end of World War II. The available data indicate that both parties accepted these new members fairly easily. In the PCI, in fact, it appears that the traditional screening of recruits by the provincial level of Party organization (the "federation") before admission to a cell and section was abandoned on the direct orders of Togliatti.[88] It is very unlikely that the PCF ever went so far in opening its ranks to newcomers, but Kriegel suggests that at first the party was quite open.[89] With the coming of the Cold War, however, the practice in the two organizations diverged sharply. In 1947 and 1948 the French Party's leadership engaged in a wholesale purge of the membership, throwing out not only the "Trotskyists" and "Titoists" but also many of those who had joined in the immediate postwar period and who, because of their recent and perhaps incomplete commitment to the Party, might not be reliable under the new conditions.[90] In the PCI no extensive purge of members appears to have occurred. While Party leaders engaged in much the same defamation of Tito as their French comrades, their speeches at Party congresses and other occasions continued to stress the PCI's avocation to be a mass party and to press the Party activists to seek new recruits.[91] Significantly, the organizational theme, launched in 1944 and incorporated in the Party statutes, that a member need not believe in Marxism and that he could in fact be a practicing Catholic as long as he accepted the PCI's program, was not dropped with the polarization of the domestic environment and the jettisoning of the communists from the government. Rather, the theme was reasserted.[92] Using the Party's own organization as a bridge to the Catholic masses was not to be abandoned simply because the church and the DC had undertaken a campaign of vilification against the Party.[93]

The pattern established in these years remains today. While the PCF still appears to exercise considerable discretion over the selection of new members (the data on this are extremely poor, but there is no evidence to the contrary), the PCI has a very open and permeable membership. My own research on Party sections in the province of Milan indicated that almost anyone who applied for a membership card would be admitted, and that there was almost no supervision of section recruitment by the federation.[94]

The differences in membership practices of the two parties are also evident in the cautiousness of the PCF's attempts to extend its membership strength beyond its traditional bases of support; for the most part, its areas of strength are the same today as they were during the prewar Third Republic.[95] The PCI, on the other hand, has devoted much of its postwar organizational effort to developing membership strength in areas where it had traditionally been weak. This difference between the two parties has been reflected in their contrasting approaches to recruiting members both from social classes other than the working class[96] and from cultural groups with a different philosophical outlook, such as the aforementioned openness of the PCI to Catholics. It is perhaps the most clearly shown, however, in territorial terms.

Emerging from the war, the PCF received its most intense support in the "red belt" around Paris: it is probable that more than half the members came from the Paris region. Thirty years later the Paris area remains the center of Party strength, and while accurate figures are not available, all accounts indicate that a very high percentage of members still come from this region.[97] It appears that the Party has made no concerted attempts to extend its bases of strength into other regions of the country, and certainly not into those where it has traditionally had no major organizational support.

The case is decidedly different for the PCI. While it too has a "red belt" (the regions of Emilia-Romagna, Tuscany, and Umbria) in which more than 40 percent of its membership is located,[98] it has sought throughout the postwar years to develop membership in other areas of the country, especially in those where it had little or no organizational presence. The most clearcut illustration of these efforts is the PCI's massive campaign in southern Italy right after the war. To that campaign the Party committed a great deal of the organizational talent and resources which could otherwise have been used to consolidate its position in its northern strongholds, or applied to those areas—such as the major industrial cities of Milan and Turin—where it lost strength in the 1950s.[99] Its choice to go to the south, where it had never had any organized strength and where there was no Resistance-linked mobilization to draw upon, attests to the Party's commitment to expand its organizational base and to create a national, rather than merely local, Party presence.[100] In recent years, the PCI has once again sought to increase its organized strength in those regions, particularly the south, where massive migration to the north threatened to rob it of the organized presence it had developed in the 1950s.[101]

Other examples of the large differences in organizational practice of the PCF and PCI include Party structure (the PCF has retained the cell as the principle organizational unit, while in contrast the PCI has shifted to the section—a larger, more socially heterogeneous and territorially defined unit) and the nature of internal operations and procedures (both parties retain democratic centralist procedures, but the PCI appears to allow, and even encourage, far more internal debate).[102] The cases already cited, however, attest to the greater openness, flexibility, and expansiveness of the PCI's organization.

The link between these organizational differences and the ways the parties have implemented their commonly shared strategic perspectives should be clear. The PCI's organizational approach reflects the Party's desire to build broad political and social alliances going beyond the limits of the socialist subculture and, more generally, to develop a presence in all arenas of social and political life and among all social strata. To do this the Party has determined that it must have a mass organization capable of drawing in anyone willing to adhere to the Party's program and to undertake, even if only on rare occasions, the role of propagandist for the Party. Further, the Party has decided that it cannot leave any area of the country or any social stratum out of its membership. Similarly, if the Party is to be able to build social alliances with Catholics and with other social groups and strata in which it has traditionally been weak, it must have members of these target groups affiliated with it. If the Party is not willing to tolerate Catholics in its ranks, can it expect Catholics to ally with it even on programmatic issues? The Party's answer has clearly been no. The kind of implementation of the PCI strategy necessitated by Italian political and social conditions has had the secondary effect of making the Party abandon some of the traditional aspects of communist organization.

This organizational policy has not been without cost to the Italian communists. As I have discussed at greater length elsewhere,[103] the style of organization adopted by the PCI in the postwar period and especially after 1956 has led to a lower level of activism among Party members than the leadership would like, and has created an organization in which many members know little of the details of the Party's strategy or program.[104] This in turn has meant that there is greater dissidence at the base than is probably the case in the PCF, and that Party leaders must spend an inordinate amount of time just trying to keep the massive Party structure functioning. Further, it creates the distinct possibility that the coherence of the Party's overall strategic design will break down, as different sectors of the organization pursue diverse social and political alliance targets. While incidents of this type have been rare, the question remains whether the PCI has truly established "hegemony" in building its social and political alliances, or whether it has simply "caught" all its allies. If the latter, then the Party may very well lose or have to abandon many of them once it is forced to make the hard decisions which will come with governance.

The organizational philosophy of the PCF mirrors its more restrained pursuit of social allies. A cautious alliance policy has meant that the PCF could continue to operate as a cadre party, maintaining a high degree of organizational autonomy and internal cohesion and discipline. By the same token, however, the PCF's organizational practices have rendered it less effective than the PCI in forging linkages with the broader society and in enhancing its legitimacy among the general populace. For both parties, then, organization is a further product of the specific social and political characteristics of the societies in which they operate.

Before leaving the subject of organization, one final consideration is necessary. In examining the relationship between strategy and organization I have treated the latter as the dependent variable: the parties have maintained or developed organizational structures and processes which best allowed them to pursue their particular approaches to building political and social alliances. But the inverse may also be of considerable importance: existing patterns of organization, and the member attitudes which they structure, can condition and constrain strategic choice and behavior. I will not dwell at length on this point here, although it seems a subject which has received too little attention. But I do want, however, to indicate one way the cadre structure of the PCF and the mass structure of the PCI may affect the parties' pursuit of allies.

Party organization is one of the primary mechanisms through which people are induced to participate in Party affairs. The rewards (or incentives) to individuals which the Party offers in exchange for activity are generally communicated through and by its organization. People who become active expect that the incentives which initially induced them to participate will continue, and when this fails to be the case, members can be expected to reduce their activity or (if we assume that Party leaders are loathe to accept such a decline in participation) the members' expectations can become a constraint on leadership behavior. The nature of that constraint, however, will depend on the content of individual members' expectations and on the profile of such expectations in the membership as a whole. Differing organizational structures, therefore, could be expected to create different degrees and types of constraints.[105]

When we look at the organizational structures of the PCF

and PCI in light of this general argument, clearcut differences emerge. The PCF throughout the postwar period has stressed doctrine and ideological orthodoxy and has been slow to revise traditional Marxist-Leninist concepts. The Party has therefore sought to assure that members would be doctrinally trained and trustworthy. These goals, in the classical Leninist view, can best be achieved by linking membership to intense participation and by a cell structure. Such a structure, of course, creates strong incentives for ideological conformity and Party discipline; but it can also be expected to produce members whose reward for intense participation is, in large part, the sense of uniqueness, the distinctive self-identification which Party membership confers:[106] to be a PCF member is something very special, setting one apart from (and, in the Party's view, above) one's fellow citizens. Such Party members are likely to resist any actions of the leadership which appear to compromise that sense of uniqueness or to weaken the social bonds among members with which it is intimately bound up. Such resistence might, in Albert Hirschman's terms, take the form of either "exit" or "voice,"[107] but in either case it would reduce the operational effectiveness of the organization as an instrument of strategy.

The PCI has concentrated far less on doctrine and ortho-doxy and has instead stressed the development of program-matic goals and the formulation of specific "structural reform" proposals as well as applying itself "constructively" to the immediate problems of the Italian economy and society.[108] The relationship of members to the Party is obviously affected by this pattern of organization. The significance of membership is far less all-encompassing, and members are active in Party affairs both with greatly differing intensities and for markedly different reasons.[109] Member-ship in the PCI does convey a special sense of identity to the adherent, for there is little question that the communist member is generally different from militants in other parties and that the PCI constantly seeks to emphasize the Party's unique character within the Italian political system. Unlike the PCF, however, the sense of special identity is not necessarily linked to being part of an organization which is the bearer of communist doctrine and revolutionary tradition. Rather, it comes from belonging to a party which, in the Italian context, stands out because of its programmatic emphasis, its stress on immediate reforms benefiting the working strata, its administrative efficiency, and its lack of corruption.[110] The fact that members of the PCI may be attracted to the Party for a wide variety of reasons ranging from doctrine to short-run policy goals means that they can be expected to react in differing ways to leadership policies which seem to represent either a move away from or towards greater doctrinal purity, or which alter the Party's programmatic emphases. Some may respond by reducing their level of participation or by voicing their complaints, but others may find the changes a stimulus to greater activism.

These differences in members' expectations have evident consequences for leadership flexibility in the pursuit of allies. If we assume (as does most of the literature on organizations) that Party leaders will be reluctant to take actions which risk producing declines in participation, then the leadership of the PCF will be far more constrained in its alliance-seeking behavior than that of the Italian Party. Whereas PCI members' attachments to their Party are, to varying extents, premised on the desire to attain policy goals which are understood to require compromise with other political and social forces, PCF members are more sensitive to actions which appear to compromise the Party's unique identity and can be expected to be less tolerant of such agreements. They are likely to accept them, but only to the extent that they are understood in a "tactical" sense—as limited compromises which do not fundamentally affect the Party's basic identification with the goal of socialism (traditionally understood) or its underlying commitment to the doctrinally correct path. It is not necessarily compromise which the PCF member rejects, although he is undoubtedly distrustful of it; rather, he fears that compromise will alter the Party's basic identity.

The second and closely related reason why leadership of the French Party is more constrained than that of the Italian derives from the fact that the large majority of PCF members are activists and fairly uniform in their views about how the Party should behave, while a smaller percentage of PCI members are highly active and there is considerable diversity in their expectations about Party behavior. If the leadership of the PCF takes an action out of tune with member expectations, it can expect an overall decline in participation. Since most members are active and for largely the same reasons, actions which disappoint the members will evoke a relatively similar response throughout the membership. In the PCI, in contrast, there is much more slack. Leaders can take actions which run counter to the expectations of some members but which appeal to others; a decline in participation in some sectors will be compensated for by a rise of activity elsewhere.[111] Organizational constraints on strategic behavior in the PCF and PCI thus tend to reinforce the patterns of strategic behavior examined earlier: the interactions between strategic perspective, domestic society, and type of organizational structure (itself a product of the strategy-society relationship) combine to make the PCF a considerably more closed, less flexible, and, in many senses, more "sectarian" party than the PCI.

Conclusion

To conclude this discussion of the strategy of the French and Italian communist parties and of the way they have sought to implement that strategy, a speculative question needs to be raised. We have seen how both the PCF and PCI, beginning from commonly shared assumptions and imperatives about the actions to be pursued in order to attain power in the postwar world, adjusted their specific activities in response to the domestic contexts in which they operate, becoming distinctive in the way they pursue political and social allies and in the way they organize their own members.

This adjustment has led to considerable success in the 1970s. Both parties are today closer to power than at any time since 1947. Their success, it can be argued, is primarily the result of the ripening of the political and social tensions which the parties have cultivated for years. It is reflected in the increasingly likely achievement of political and social alliances which the parties have sought for at least a decade. Both the alliance of the left in France and the "historic compromise" (*compromesso storico*) in Italy are the direct outgrowths of strategic paths embarked on no later than the early 1960s and, in the case of the PCI, long before.

But the recent successes of the communists have also resulted in part from a breakdown of stable patterns of political alignment and the emergence of newly mobilized political, social, and economic forces. There are an increasing number of groups, ranging from women and students to farmers and shopkeepers to civil servants and factory workers, who have broken out of traditional patterns of representation and now seek to press their demands on the state and the party system, using methods and channels outside the institutions and rules of the game which have characterized the period of postwar stability. This phenomenon raises an interesting problem, for it would seem that the increase in social mobilization and a profusion in the number of mobilized interests could be a double-edged sword for the communists. On the one hand, the changes clearly suggest that the conditions which have supported the rule of the anticommunist forces since shortly after World War II are disappearing and that the possibilities of building a new ruling bloc in which the communist parties will be a major partner have improved. On the other hand, the disparate character of the mobilized interests, and the fact that they operate outside the "rules" which the PCF and PCI have themselves accepted and sought to turn to their benefit, mean that the task of either incorporating these interests into a new ruling bloc or encapsulating them in a stable and tractable opposition may be difficult. We need to ask, therefore, how the strategic adaptations of the PCF and PCI affect the parties' ability to relate to these new forces and to resolve the dilemma which they potentially represent.

The problem can be divided into two parts: the ability of the parties to draw these forces into their sphere of influence during the period before power is attained, and the effect of the emergence of these new forces on the parties' prospects once they are in power.

The contrasting alliance strategies and organizational structures of the two parties strongly suggest that it will be much easier for the PCI than the PCF to adjust its strategic design to accommodate these newly mobilized forces and thus to turn them to its advantage during the period of opposition. First, the greater openness and tolerance for ambiguity in the PCI's approach to political allies means that it will be more willing than the French Party to incorporate into its network of alliances political parties or party factions which may come to represent one or more of these mobilized interests. More importantly, the PCI's emphasis on "presence" and on a broad scope of social alliances, as contrasted with the relative reluctance of the PCF to expand its social base, means that the Italian Party can be expected to absorb or to reach accommodation with many of these groups far more easily. Finally, the mass structure of the PCI, as contrasted with the cadre structure of the PCF, means that it is likely to be more sensitive to newly organized demands, and that the Party will be better able to accommodate within its ranks members who also participate in such new movements or groups, thereby reciprocally influencing and being influenced by them. Further, the differences in organizational structure make it easier for the PCI to reach compromises with new political and social movements without creating strains within its own organization that might restrict such behavior. In sum, the PCI is far more likely than the PCF to be able to draw newly mobilized interests into its sphere of influence, and thereby to reduce the possibility that these interests will augment the strength of other political parties. In the case of the PCF, the probabilities are far greater that many of these interests will ally themselves either with the socialists, thus weakening the Party's position within the alliance, or with political parties opposed to the left coalition.

The different capacities of the PCF and PCI to accommodate and absorb mobilized interests should also affect the parties' prospects once they gain power. Compared with the PCI, the PCF should find it easier to pursue the basic policy directions called for in its program. Having maintained greater autonomy from social forces, it may be under less pressure to undertake policies which, while satisfying narrow interests, destroy the coherence of the Party's overall policy vision. There is, however, a reverse side to this coin. The French Party's comparative lack of presence, its greater autonomy, may mean that it will be faced with a situation in which a large number of mobilized interests, whose demands it is unable to satisfy or who cannot otherwise be accommodated, will join an effort to end communist rule or will throw their weight to the PCF's socialist partner. In the former case, the Party might well decide to turn to more repressive means of control. In the latter situation, it might choose to break up the alliance with the PS and to return to an opposition stance from which it would feel better able to preserve its internal organizational strength and its identity.

Because of its far greater capacity to accommodate and/or absorb mobilized social interests, the PCI should be better able to avoid the kinds of tensions and conflicts which might threaten the PCF. But precisely these same qualities may be the source of a different difficulty for the Party: the impossibility of maintaining the coherence of its programmatic initiatives without alienating significant elements of the coalition on which its ability to rule is based. This problem is inherent in the Party's approach to the implementation of its strategic perspective. The permeability and presence which make it possible to accommodate and absorb a multiplicity of social forces necessarily are accompanied by the danger that the Party will lose its sense of direction as it becomes captured by, rather than capturing, various social interests. The problem becomes more acute as the number of mobilized interests grows, for an increasingly diverse coalition also means increasingly divergent pressures on the Party once it is in power. Should it be unable to respond satisfactorily to these pressures, it may find its coalition rapidly disintegrating. The looser organizational structure of the PCI may make it less able than the PCF to take decisive action under such circumstances. If, on the other hand, the Party simply attempts to satisfy, at least to some degree, all of the demands being made upon it, it may destroy the coherence of its basic reform program. Instead of bringing major changes, the rise to power of the PCI in this case would do little to alter the basic structures of Italian political, social, and economic life. The third route, and the one the PCI feels it can follow, is to establish hegemony over its coalition, relying upon the Party's program and organization to create the possibilities for mediating between the various interests. To achieve this the Party must retain its close contacts with as many of the mobilized interests as possible, while at the same time maintaining a capacity for autonomous action. Whether or not the PCI will be able to accomplish this feat—something which no other communist party has been able to achieve—is a question that cannot possibly be answered. It would seem, however, that the interactions between the Party's strategic perspective and the characteristics of Italian domestic society have created a communist party which seems much more capable than the French of escaping the alternatives of ineffectual sectarian opposition or monolithic Party rule which have been the hallmark of communism in Europe.

Massimo Teodori is a professor of contemporary history in the Faculty of Political Science at the University of Perugia, Italy. Included in Professor Teodori's works on the New Left in Europe are The New Left: A Documentary History, Storia delle nuove sinistre in Europa (1956-1976), *and* Per l'alternativa, *which he edited. Professor Teodori has served as editor for the quarterly* La Prova Radicale *(The Radical Experiment) (1971-73) and has been a visiting scholar at Berkeley (1967-68) and Harvard (1974) universities.*

5

The New Lefts in Europe
Massimo Teodori

It is impossible to draw a neat diagram of the New Left in Europe, since we are not dealing with one organization or even with one homgeneous movement. Given the clear lack of ideological and political unity, it would in fact be more correct to speak of several new lefts. Differing themes, movements, struggles, or ideological positions, which at moments either seemed united or were in fact united, have been grouped together under a "New Left" label. Only a posteriori is it possible to establish common denominators, either on the level of political-ideological concepts or in terms of tactics and strategies. The problem of the New Left in Europe might therefore be best approached by taking its phenomenology and history as the point of departure.[1]

On this basis, I propose to approach the problem in three steps. I shall begin by tracing briefly the history of the new lefts; then I shall look at the key analytical and strategic concepts which have emerged from New Left action during the last fifteen years; and, lastly, I shall evaluate the vitality of the New Left position on the European scene today and its dialectical interaction with the political system.

Notes for a History of the New Lefts

The series of themes and actions which today are thought of as the New Left really date back to the mid-fifties, more specifically to a series of events—international as well as domestic, political as well as ideological—which occurred in the years around 1956. Since then the New Left and its subsequent configurations have passed through three clearly identifiable phases. The first, 1956–66, represents the long, often silent, emergence of elements traceable to the New Left; the second phase, which lasted two years, 1967–69, has as its central episode the May 1968 uprising in Paris, with the explosion of social mass movements; and the third phase, from 1969 onwards, has the New Left heritage flowing in three directions: dwindling into sects, influencing the party system, and spreading out into the reality of social struggles and movements.

The Emergence of the New Lefts: 1956–66

The Suez crisis, the Hungarian revolution, and the Twentieth Congress of the Communist Party of the Soviet Union. These outstanding events of 1956 began to draw the classical left, entrenched in the two political and ideological systems of West and East, into a state of crisis. The first warnings of the disintegration of post-Yalta Cold War bloc politics also marked the beginnings of dissent within the left. The communism of both the Soviet Union and of the communist parties of Western Europe was losing its credibility and attractiveness for the liberal and radical intelligentsia, at first because of Khrushchev's revelations about Stalinism and later because of Stalinist methods in Budapest. At the same time, the social democracy of Guy Mollet in France was at least partly tainted by the Suez invasion and by its own colonialist policies in Algeria and other African countries such as Madagascar.[2] These developments constituted a serious blow to the hopes of the traditional communist and social democratic parties for radical change in the status quo. Many intellectuals deserted the communist parties of France and Italy, the two countries where communist forces represented the majority of the working class.[3] The French Social Democratic Party (SFIO), which together with the other non-communist moderate left forces had won the 1956 elections, lost its appeal as a possible promoter of radical change in the country and lined up with the moderate conservatives who, in turn, emerged in 1958 in a coalition supporting General de Gaulle.

Opposition to atomic weapons. Another factor generating dissent within the left was the military (later the atomic) problem. In the two-year period 1954-56, the leading item on the political agenda in the German Federal Republic was rearmament, followed by atomic armament (1957-58). Inside as well as outside the Social Democratic Party (SPD), opposition to rearmament was bringing together elements from the Social Democrats, trade unionists, churches, and intelligentsia.[4] For the first time in Germany, there seemed to be an extraparliamentary force which brought pressure to bear on both the SPD and the country. In England the Campaign for Nuclear Disarmament (CND) and subsequently the more militant Committee of a Hundred, led by Bertrand Russell, appeared on the scene.[5] Opposition to the bomb brought together, for the first time since the war, not only the traditional labor and trade union left, but also the masses of young people who discovered in the Aldermaston marches a new form of political participation. From 1958, the year of the first Aldermaston march, until 1966, springtime in England was marked by these celebrations of the new politics, which went beyond mere opposition to atomic armament to become a symbol of protest against the affluent society and everything it entailed.

The theoretical contributions. An ideological dimension, arising also from varied vantage points, was interwoven with and imposed itself upon the political dimension. In France, the *Socialisme ou Barbarie* group[6] from its underground quarters developed theories on Soviet bureaucracy as an exploiting ruling class, and hence introduced the notion of the contradiction between ruler and executor instead of the traditional one of owner and exploited. Alongside the Trotskyist-oriented *Socialisme ou Barbarie* flourished a series of groups and reviews such as Sartre's *Le Temps Moderne*, Edgar Morin's *Arguments,* and *France-Observateur,* all extraneous to the *embourgeoisant* social democracy as well as to orthodox Soviet-type communism. All over Europe heterodox Marxist currents, previously repressed by Stalinism and by the Cold War communist conformity, reappeared. Authors such as Rosa Luxemburg, Karl Korsch, and Georg Lukacs were reprinted in fuller editions and reached a wider reading public. In 1960 militant university groups in Germany broke with their SPD parent organization and began to take as their point of reference the newly formed Frankfurt School of Horkheimer, Adorno, and Habermas. A few years later the "Critical Theory" of the Frankfurt School nurtured the German extraparliamentary movement both inside and outside the universities.

The secession from the consumer society. Another root of the new lefts is what Edgar Morin called the "secession from the consumer society." The fifties saw the advanced industrialized society reach a peak in all the industrialized European countries, with a vast increase in consumer goods and a search for a new and stable consensus.[7] In this period the theoretical vanguards, followed by the social and existentialist groups, initiated the "critique of everyday life." In 1957 the *International Situationist* was formed to analyze the modern world from the point of view of daily life;[8] a decade later it was to play an important role in paving the way for the May uprising at the universities of Strasbourg and Nanterre.[9] In England the countercultural revolution spawned groups of juvenile bands which later found unity in rock, pop, and folk music, and in new myths such as the Beatles,[10] while in France the Jalicite appeared as a symptom of the same revolt against modern society. A few years later the Provos and then the Kabouters surfaced in Holland,[11] representing more advanced expressions of juvenile revolt inspired by

libertarian principles and aiming at the realization of a concrete utopia. It is against this background—of the appearance
throughout Europe of new contradictions in everyday life,
and the existential rejection of aspects of modern society—
that the influence of Herbert Marcuse in the late 1960s can
best be understood. In his analysis and theoretical con-
ceptualization, the German-American philosopher expressed
an approach to the modern world which had instinctively
been felt and lived by increasingly larger numbers of young
people. Marcuse was, quite autonomously, an interpreter of
the new reality rather than the inspirer of the revolt of the
new lefts, as has sometimes been suggested.

The new groupings. It was from these multiple points of departure—some of a political nature, some sparked by new social
conflicts, others of ideological origin, and still others of an existential character—that what are defined as the new lefts originated in the decade 1956-66. In Germany there was the So-
zialistischer Deutscher Studentenbund (SDS), especially in the
universities and intelligentsia circles such as the famous Republican Club in Berlin. In England there were the New Left clubs,
the CND, and the Committee of a Hundred in 1960–63, and
the *New Left Review.* In France the process began with autonomous networks such as the Jeanson, which supported the
Algerians and grouped together militant elements outside the
communist and socialist parties, giving rise to the Parti Socialist Unifié (PSU) in 1961 and finally the autonomous action of
the Union of University Students (UNEF); there also appeared
the first dissident Marxist groups such as the Ulm circle at the
Sorbonne, inspired by Althusser. In Italy, the question of the
nature and role of the working class was reevaluated by such
magazines as *Quaderni Rossi, Classe Operaia,* and *Quaderni
Piacentini*; and the appearance in 1964 of the Socialist Party
of Proletarian Unity (PSIUP) marked the creation of a socialist left which did not accept collaboration with the moderate
Christian Democratic (DC) Party in a center-left government.
All these different manifestations, still part of the same
picture, developed up to 1966, when the new lefts entered
their second phase, the phase of the masses.

The Mass Revolt: The French Uprising of 1968

Vietnam. During 1966-69, mass movements broke out all
over Europe, representing the fusion of diverse political and
ideological currents, and ultimately giving way to spontaneous
collective movements. Among the factors which contributed
to these movements we can distinguish two types—the exogenous and the endogenous. The major exogenous factor was
Vietnam, which became a great catalyst of Western youth
revolt during 1966-67.[12] It is not by chance that in England
after the fading away of the antibomb CND, the great mass
protests were organized by the Vietnam Solidarity Campaign
(VSC). It is true that the campaign was controlled and animated by Trotskyists, but the VSC was the spontaneous
expression of the collective New Left, an interpretation of
that state of mind, widespread in Great Britain, which in
previous years had been underground or in the counterculture.
From 1961 to 1965 the SDS in Germany had been actively
engaged in theoretical reappraisal within the universities; now
it left the academic sphere in order to foster mass extraparliamentary protests over Vietnam in the cities. In France
too the Comité National Vietnam (CNV) and the Comité
Vietnam de Base (CVB) amalgamated different extraparty
components which had not cooperated since the Algerian war.
    The university crisis. The most important endogenous
factor underlying the deflagration of the great revolts in
1967-68 was the increase in the number of students and the
resulting university crisis. In the fifties the universities,
especially in France and Italy (less so in England and Germany), which had maintained a tradition of transmitting
knowledge to a relatively restricted elite, became universities
for the masses. In England students at the London School of
Economics began to stage protests in the spring of 1966[13]
and continued to do so until the following year; then Hornsey,
Essex, and Warwick were occupied. In Germany the alternative "Critical" or "Red" University was attempted after a
series of university confrontations.[14] In Italy the student
movement paralyzed all the universities during the events of

autumn 1967 and at the same time reignited the fighting spirit of the workers' movement: roused by external New Left groups, the workers overrode the discipline of the trade union organizations with the spontaneous initiative of the rank and file.[15]

The May 1968 uprising in Paris. The peak of the explosion of the collective movement came in May 1968 in Paris. It began with the revolts at Nanterre University, and its intellectual framework and impetus were conditioned to an important extent by the situationists and the angry young men in Strasbourg. The May movement has yet to be put into its historical perspective—but, whatever the interpretations, there is no doubt that in it a series of themes and methods of action of the New Left reached their maximum qualitative and quantitative points of expression.[16] The Paris revolt showed itself to be an antistructural movement par excellence: there were no hypotheses for a future order, nor did any particular class or social group fight for specific interests. Protest—or *contestation,* meaning challenge—invaded every social area, and every institution was questioned in order to be reassessed and recreated so that a cell of the antisociety could be tested against reality. Everywhere there was a generalized application of *autogestion* (literally, "self-management") conceived more as an instinctive *idée-force* than as a specific economic theory, and with it a rejection of specialized social roles based on the division of labor. In contradistinction to some of its Marxist-, Leninist-, or Trotskyist-type components, the general tone of the May movement was libertarian, as embodied in the symbol of Daniel Cohn-Bendit and his March 22 movement.[17] The claims were never programmatic but arose continually from the here and now. "Change the way of living" was the password long before "change the world we live in." In May the traditional trade unions and political forces, especially the French Communist Party (CPF), were extraneous to the movement. The CPF, in fact, stood for the stabilization of the system against a possible change or overthrow. For the first time in the West the student—or more generally the youth—movement, followed by the repercussion of the

workers' occupation movement, represented a force outside
the political system, one with such vigor that it managed to
embrace in a stranglehold and break down those elements
of the party and trade union system with which it came face
to face. The methods of action, too, were absolutely new in
their large-scale application: direct democracy, action committees, and direct action. The May movement contained a
condensation of the entire New Left message as well as of the
contradictions inherent in its attempt both to be a utopia and
to build one simultaneously.

After 1968: Three New Patterns for the New Left

The third phase of the new lefts followed the great hopes
and great disappointments of the Paris uprising in May 1968
and parallel movements in other European countries. At the
time when French events were reaching a climax, both the
German antiauthoritarian movement, with its campaign
against Springer and the emergency laws, and the Italian
university movement were on the decline.

The May movement in France highlighted the intrinsic
limitations of a spontaneous collective movement dedicated
to revolutionary change. The ensuing crisis presented yet
again to the French and other European new lefts the problems of organization-movement relationships, of utopian
proposals and their institutional realization and translation
into new balances of power.

After 1968, therefore, the three lines along which the new
lefts emerged were the following: (1) the proliferation of
highly ideologized "groupuscules" which tried to reconstruct
the "real" revolutionary vanguard party; (2) influence on the
political system, with repercussions on political and trade
union forces; and (3) social movements and ad hoc campaigns.

The proliferation of groupuscules. Delusions about the
possibility of obtaining short-term revolutionary change
brought up yet again the problem of organizing the revolutionary force. The groupuscules grew out of the dissolving
collective spontaneous mass movements and took the tenets
of their revolutionary organization from ideologies. The

Trotskyists, Marxist-Leninists, and worker-oriented groups organized their minuscule parties in France, Germany, Italy, and England in the conviction that they would be able to supplant or compete with traditional working-class or labor organizations. In France the Union des Jeunes Communistes Révolutionnaires appeared, followed by the Marxist-Leninist-oriented Gauche Proletarienne and the Ligue Communiste led by Alain Krivine, parallel with the two other Trotskyist groups, Alliance des Jeunes pour le Socialisme and Lutte Ouvrière. In Germany the Spartakus group appeared, along with various small Marxist-Leninist parties such as the KPD-AO and the DKP-ML (Kommunistische Partei Deutschlands-Aufbau Organization and Kommunistische Deutsche Partei-Marxistisch-Leninistisch). There was also an extremist current, inspired by Latin American guerrilla warfare, which generated the "Red Army fraction" with its well-known terrorist episodes of the Baader-Meinhof group. In Italy there emerged various Marxist-Leninist groups such as the Italian Marxist-Leninist Communist Party, worker-oriented groups such as Potere Operaio and later the more anarcho-syndicalist-oriented Lotta Continua, the Leninist worker-oriented Avanguardia Operaia, and il Manifesto, the first group to break away from the Italian Communist Party with an outstanding number of communist leaders and a high-level theoretical apparatus. In England the first New Left groups, which defined themselves in the *New Left Review* and in the May Day Manifesto in 1968, were overshadowed by the Trotskyist International Socialism and other worker-oriented and Marxist-Leninist groupuscules.[18]

Even though they acknowledge varied ideological inspirations and play different roles within their respective national and political contexts, all these groups share certain characteristics which distinguish them from the New Left and qualify them to be labeled traditional heretics from the old lefts. They are strongly ideological: all Marxist-oriented, they tend towards the sectarianism of closed organizations rather than forms of open action as practiced by the mass movements of 1967–69. They believe in the need to construct the "revolutionary party" with Leninist vanguard functions. In reality they manage to organize with a high degree of militancy only a few hundred, at most a few thousand, high school or university students. These groupuscules are much more the descendants of the old dissident communist and socialist currents than expressions of a new analysis of contemporary social reality or a political interpretation of its contradictions.

The impact of the new lefts on the political system. The post-1968 mass movements also had an impact on the traditional political system, which was quite permeable in some countries. In Germany a part of the membership of the dissolving SDS joined the SDP youth organization, the Jung Sozialisten (Jusos).[19] In the years following 1970 the Jusos were partly responsible for shifting the Social Democratic Party towards the left, especially in some local situations. The Jusos linked social democracy to the extraparliamentary movement of the previous years by developing a "double strategy," described thus by one of their spokesmen, Karsten Voigt: "To change the present system we must work on two levels; with reforms which update the system from within and political mobilization through direct action from the outside."[20] Thus the Jusos attempted to overcome the historical dilemma of the European left by referring to the large organized reformist-type forces working within the institutions and by pursuing radical change by action outside. The activism and militancy of these young people acting within and without the political system had a considerable impact on both the SPD and the country as a whole in the early seventies. In 1972 they contributed to Chancellor Willy Brandt's victory and also to the reinforcement of the social democratic left, even though the 1974 shift inverted the process. An analogous process of political radicalization appeared in the same years among the younger members of the German liberal party (FDP) with the Jungdemocraten, who helped take the party into the coalition with the SPD from 1969 onwards.

The case of the new Socialist Party in France. In France,

more than elsewhere, one could see how elements within the political system were affected and even transformed by forces outside the system. Without the new ideas of the sixties, without May 1968, which revealed to the whole nation the possibility of immediate change, without the development of movements in society outside of the party system, the renovation and growth of the Socialist Party would certainly never have occurred. Between 1969 and 1971 the SFIO was radically transformed—in terms of numbers, of cadres, of leadership, of program, of ideology, and of sociological composition—into the new Socialist Party of François Mitterrand.[21] In 1969 the party numbered only 10,000 members; four years later there were 140,000, the new members being mostly young people, women, workers, and Christian and leftist militants (the case of Regis Debray is significant here). *Autogestion*, antiauthoritarianism, internationalism, and quality of life became the central themes of the new French socialism, a development which has contributed to recent conflicts with the French Communist Party. The Confédération Française Démocratique du Travail (CFDT) is linked to, though autonomous of, the new French Socialist Party, and with its libertarian ideology and its support for *autogestion*, it represents the mass organization of workers more directly linked to New Left themes and methods. The CFDT now has almost one million members; and together with the Socialist Party, which in 1974 absorbed a large part of the Parti Socialiste Unifié (PSU) and other forces outside it such as trade unionists and intellectuals, exceeds the 30 percent threshold of electoral support and represents a new phenomenon in the postwar European left.[22] It is new because of its ideological search and its links with ideas originating from the New Left; it is new also because for the first time an organized socialist force has managed to attain the dominant position in an alliance with the communists, with whom it shares a common strategy for the union of the lefts; finally, it is new because it is still developing and has an energy which embraces the liveliest forces of the French left.

Social movements and ad hoc campaigns. A third line of
post-1968 New Left development is represented by a series
of social movements and ad hoc campaigns, most of which
have a high level of autonomy in comparison with both the
traditional and the new political forces. In the space of ten
years the new lefts have increased social militancy by giving
expression to the new contradictions of social life and institutions in advanced industrial society. In fact, the new lefts
have expressed themselves mainly by giving form to what
politically could not be expressed by or contained in the
traditional left ideologies and policies. The result, to a greater
or lesser degree throughout Europe, has been a widening gap
between social movements and the political system.

Movements of this type emerged as a reaction to forms of
oppression, alienation, and exploitation different from those
on which the traditional lefts were based. The Women's
Liberation Movement made its appearance in all the European
countries, concentrating especially on the issue of abortion,
which is particularly crucial in the Catholic countries such as
France and Italy. The victory for divorce in Italy resulted
from an ad hoc extraparliamentary campaign which exerted
pressure on the left and liberal parties, obliging them to vote
in Parliament for the change in legislation. The movement for
housing and for a different type of urban settlement had
episodes of particular activism, notably the squatters in
England and the occupation movement in Germany and Italy.
The health assistance issue has sparked the creation of
alternative health-care systems in France, including the
Groupe Information Santé and similar organizations. Total
institutions such as psychiatric hospitals and prisons have
given rise to movements and revolts on the part of present and
former inmates. In Germany networks of antiauthoritarian
kindergartens have been established, and there has also been a
reassessment of education with a view to its removal from
public bureaucratic management. Movements for youth
liberation and for gay liberation have acquired substance in
France, Italy, and Germany under different names. In the
armed forces there has been protest in an effort to acquire

certain civil rights. Civil rights movements have been particularly active in England, and alternative information groups in the armed forces have experimented outside institutional channels, first with underground journals and later with alternative radio and television broadcasts. Regional minorities have organized to promote their ethnic-cultural identity—the Bretons, Occitans, and Basques in France, the Scot and Welsh movements in Great Britain. The dissident Catholic movement in Italy has not only an ecclesiastic and religious but also a political dimension, as reflected in the creation of numerous Christian communities committed to social activism.

This is merely a brief outline of the ways in which the tendencies and aspirations of the New Left are embodied in today's reality. There is particular emphasis on widespread, varied, militant social action. This is novel when compared to the traditional postwar European left. In fact, most of the traditional left parties, communist as well as social democratic, have lost the ability to encompass the new social movements and struggles arising from the conditions of advanced industrial society. These tend, therefore, to arise and develop in a spontaneous fashion, fully autonomous both of the institutional left forces and of the leftist groupuscules which gained ground in the second half of the sixties. It is above all in this new militant mood, expressed by social movements, that a New Left position and inspiration can be traced into the mid-seventies.

The Strategies of the New Left

Around 1968 the explosion of the spontaneous, collective mass movements, known as *contestation*, embodied theories and analyses which in previous years had appeared only in fragmentary form with the new lefts and *goscism*. The theme of revolutionary change, which had disappeared from the horizon of the European lefts with the onset of the Cold War in 1948, now reemerged as a possible political hypothesis. Within two years, however, those who in 1968 had begun to believe in revolution as a prospect almost within reach were obliged to change strategy. After 1968, the antiauthoritarian movement in Germany veered towards collapse without provoking the chain reactions which had progressively involved various institutions in the previous two years. After May 1968, the Gaullist regime in France regained its cohesion and reinforced its electoral base. The spontaneous workers' movement in Italy, which had arisen in the autumn of 1969, was reabsorbed by the trade unions. The old strategy, which aimed at producing a crisis in the system and short-term revolutionary possibilities, was therefore abandoned even by those groups and forces which had most fervently embraced it.

If the post-1968 years have not led to the development of a revolutionary strategy of the new lefts, they have nevertheless seen the introduction of the *idea* of revolutionary change into the debate and theoretical horizon of the radical forces. One can no longer speak of a strategy of the New Left in Europe, now that the revolutionary hypothesis has faded as a political possibility. As has already been pointed out, there is no one single New Left movement: only fragments, elements, and tensions which can be traced back to phenomena of various origins. There is no doubt, however, that several political concepts or *idées-forces*, as well as several forms of political action, have continued to manifest themselves on the West European political scene and constitute the theoretical and practical heritage of the New Left. For purposes of analysis, the New Left can be divided into two spiritual families: the Marxist New Left and the libertarian New Left.

The Marxist New Left includes all those who still believe in the revolutionary seizure of power by a historical-sociological agent organized as a vanguard party. This is, in short, the reproposal of a revolutionary Leninist version of Marxism, opposed to any revisionism, and is the line of the official communist parties. In this view, the agent of revolutionary change is the working class, and/or some kind of new working-class and/or other strata of the proletariat. The function of a vanguard, either external or internal to the class, always receives heavy theoretical emphasis. This group includes the Trotskyist current, which has regained vigor especially in France, in groups organized along the lines of Krivine's Ligue Communiste;[23] the Marxist-Leninist groups; groupings such as the Italian Manifesto (now Proletarian Unity Party for Communism, or PDUP$_{pc}$), which combines Leninist and workers council viewpoints; and the communist lefts.[24]

The libertarian New Left comprises all those who refute the Leninist conception of the party and emphasize the spontaneity of social movements and struggles, and who stress antistate and anticentralist issues. This family includes different varieties of neo-anarchists, the Christian socialists, the radical antiauthoritarians, and the libertarian socialists. These groups all share a negative attitude towards state planning and intervention as well as an emphasis on direct political expression: direct action, direct or participatory democracy, and mass movements. They also tend to share an attitude of opposition to representative institutions, and to view the communist tradition itself as a form of bureaucratic oppression. While the Marxist new lefts still consider the division between structure and superstructure as pivotal to their analysis, the libertarian new lefts tend to extend the discussion of contradictions in advanced industrial society from the point of view of production to include the variety of contradictions in every social area and institution. At times a distinct Freudian-Marxist influence can be discerned, with an emphasis on the psychological, individual, and collective aspects of everyday life. When a strategy arises from specific struggles, it is seen as a "long march through institutions" aimed at transforming every aspect and relationship of life, not just that of man as worker and producer. The basic *idée-force* of this branch of the New Left is generalized *autogestion* taken as a process and not as the final organization of the socialist society. By far the largest organization of this line is the CFDT, the French union, of Christian origin and now socialist in orientation, which has a membership of 800,000 workers.[25]

A variant within this group is represented by those who

propose a strategy of social movements as a permanent counterforce to political institutions. Without expecting any revolutionary process to change the distribution of power, this strategy, which takes as its point of departure the ossification and obsolescence of the political system, sees revolutionary action in the very existence of autonomous social movements whose permanent role lies in a dialectical opposition to all institutionalized political forces, even those of the left.

Three New Lefts and the Political System

Just as the politico-ideological influence of the New Left can be explained through the reappearance of a series of *idées-forces*, so the politico-practical influence must be measured against the political party system. In no European country has the party system been modified by the appearance of the new lefts. In spite of the general crises through which the left has gone in Germany, France, and Italy, the left in these countries is still represented by its historical components. No new parties of the New Left have been created: in France, the party organization closest to the New Left, the PSU, has gradually declined in weight and influence; in Italy, the PDUP$_{pc}$ has come into existence, but it is really a small party consisting of splinters from old parties (communists from the Manifesto, plus left-wing socialists, plus Catholic dissidents of the Movimento Politico dei Lavoratori), rather than a new formation.

One conclusion that emerges, therefore, from a decade of New Left actions is that it is impossible to construct new party channels capable of paralleling or replacing those of the historic left. The persistent hegemony within the left of traditional social democratic parties (in Germany and England), communist parties (in France and Italy), and socialist parties (in France and to a lesser degree in Italy) not only attests to the persistence of organizational weights and traditional political roots, but also reflects the relationship of these parties to the organization of the working class through the traditional unions.

In the last few years, however, the new lefts have represented the main channel for whatever is new either in theory or in practice. In ideological debate, concepts such as *autogestion* and the diversification of sources and forms of exploitation, oppression, and alienation have been reintroduced. In action, a series of social movements have dynamically expressed new contradictions through new forms, means, and methods of political struggle, sometimes capable of imposing changes which the political system, badly functioning almost everywhere, does not manage to express.

Having considered the immutability of the forces of the left within the political system and of the New Left which is often expressed outside of it, one must assess the impact of the latter on the former. In France, Germany, and Italy the effect of the new lefts on the party system has been to reinforce rather than to replace the historic lefts and to transform them where they have shown permeability and flexibility. In France after 1968 there was a renewal of the Socialist Party and hence the *Programme Commun* of the left coalition, which in 1973 obtained 49.1 percent of the vote for the Mitterrand candidacy, thus coming close to winning for the left the first presidential majority since the war. In Germany, Willy Brandt entered the government in 1969. In Italy, the traditional lefts, the PCI and PSI and the institutionalized unions, consistently increased their strength from 1968 onwards.

A second conclusion to be drawn is that the socialist and social democratic components of the historic left have gained more from the stimulus of the new lefts than have the classical communists. Where the socialists operated with more initiative and dynamism, as in France and to a lesser degree in Germany, the new lefts disappeared as autonomous organizations; where, however, the Socialist Party has remained ideologically unchanged, as in Italy, there is political space for a New Left party such as the PDUP$_{pc}$ and other New Left groups. In any case, socialist political organizations have been more influenced by New Left movements than have the French and Italian communist parties, solidly anchored as they are to traditional positions and politically better organized in the social base.

To sum up, one may conclude that the vitality of the new lefts in Europe lies primarily in their dialectical relationship to, and their impact on, the traditional left forces of the political system, and secondarily in their representation of the new unstructured social movements in society.

Alfred Stepan is a professor of political science at Yale University. A specialist on the politics of Latin America, Professor Stepan has focused on various aspects of modernization and political development. Included in his major works are The Military in Politics: Changing Patterns in Brazil, *"Political Development Theory: The Latin American Experience" (Journal of International Affairs),* Authoritarian Brazil: Origins, Policies, and Failures *(editor), and* Military Force and American Society *(co-editor).*

6
Inclusionary and Exclusionary Military Responses to Radicalism: With Special Attention to Peru
Alfred Stepan

Introduction

In the twentieth century, military establishments are situational more than class elites. That is, the military's corporate and individual power, status, and material well-being depend upon its relationship to a strong and relatively stable state structure.[1] This is useful to bear in mind when approaching the question of the relationship of the military to radicalism. Such a theoretical perspective helps direct attention to the nature of the state, the character of the threats to the state, and the military's perception of the actions required to build or maintain a strong stable state and thus protect its position as a situational elite.

This perspective also prevents us from assuming that the military's relationship to radicalism is necessarily that of conservative reaction. Conservative reaction is a frequent military

This article draws in part upon my forthcoming The State and Society: Peru in Comparative Perspective *(Princeton University Press), whose permission to utilize this material is acknowledged gratefully.*

response to radicalism, but the full range of military involvement with radicalism is much broader, and we want to be
able to analyze atypical responses as well as more typical ones.
The bulk of this paper will in fact be devoted to placing the
apparently atypical response of the Peruvian military in a
framework that makes such a response more comprehensible
and—under special conditions I discuss—to some extent even
predictable. After analyzing the origins of this "radical"
military response to radicalism in Peru (and briefly contrasting
it with the rightist responses of the Brazilian and Chilean
military to radicalism) I will identify the major problems
facing the Peruvian military regime as it attempts to impose
its own brand of radical changes from above.

First, however, let me briefly indicate the variety of relationships the military can have to different types of states,
and the variety of ways the military can perceive the institutional threats it faces.

In communist revolutionary regimes created by guerrilla
armies the question is extremely complex. In China that
part of the central governing elite represented by Mao perceived that a major danger to the revolutionary character of
the Chinese state came from the deadening effect of the
behavior of the party bureaucrats. The party soldiers thus
were encouraged by Mao to play a vanguard role in radicalizing the revolution during the opening phases of the Cultural Revolution. Once this process appeared to threaten
the integrity of the state, elements of the military shifted to
a restraining, consolidationist position. In Cuba in the late
1960s, party soldiers served as the force for radicalizing the
revolution, while party civilians wanted to constrain the
mobilizational features so as to focus on the bureaucratic
tasks of rational planning.[2]

If we look at a liberal state, the United States, where
the principle of civilian control is reasonably well established,
our concern for military responses to radicalism leads us not
so much to ask the classic civil-military relations question
"How can it be ensured that the military will obey?," but
rather, "What types of orders do the civilian political elite

give?" There was an expanding domestic role for the military in the United States as a response to radicalism in the late 1960s, but this expansion came as a direct response to orders by civilians. For example, in 1968 the army was put under orders to be prepared to send as many as 10,000 men simultaneously to each of twenty-five cities in the event of major riots. A great expansion of domestic military intelligence activity grew out of the new mission and a number of the best army combat units spent much of their training time in the late 1960s preparing for domestic missions.[3] These examples demonstrate the need to examine the state elite and not just the military if we want to analyze how the military will respond to radicalism.

But what of the Third World situation, and more specifically Latin America, where the legitimacy of the state structure is often more actively challenged than it is in either communist or liberal states, and where political control of the military is usually much more tenuous? In this situation, if there are minor challenges to the functioning of the political system, or specific challenges to the military as a corporate unit, the military will often seize political power. In most instances the military normally merely performs a "moderator" or systems-maintenance role, and does not attempt either to change the character of the state or attempt to restructure the political or social system. However, if the radical challenge to the system is perceived by the military to be very strong, and beyond the capability and/or desire of the political leaders to resolve, there is a strong tendency for the military to expand its role beyond the narrow parameters characteristic of the moderator model of military involvement in politics.[4]

Brazil since 1964 and Peru since 1968 are two clear cases where the military, in response to growing societal radicalization, rejected its previous moderator role. Instead, in both cases the military has (1) assumed control of the state apparatus; (2) attempted to expand the regulatory capacity and scope of the state apparatus; and (3) attempted to use the new state apparatus to alter the political and economic system.

As in Chile in 1973 and Argentina in 1966, the military perceived that there was a growing crisis of participation and control, and in all four cases it seized power and endeavored to use the power of the state apparatus to forge a new state-society equilibrium.

In all four instances, moreover, the resulting military regimes were marked by a number of institutional and normative characteristics which, taken together, make a strong case for labeling them "neocorporatist" in initial intent. In terms of institutional structures, they all have (or had, in the case of Argentina) strong corporatist features in their preferred patterns of interest representation. In such instances the state often charters or even creates interest groups, often attempts to restrict their number, and gives them the appearance of a quasi-representational monopoly. In return for this monopoly, the state claims the right to monitor representational groups by a variety of mechanisms, so as to discourage the aggregation of "narrow" class-based conflictual demands.[5] In terms of normative orientation, all four regimes are corporatist in that they reject liberal-pluralist competitive politics and Marxist class-conflictual politics in favor of a state-forged organic unity of a functionally integrated society.

Beyond these important similarities, however, the various military regimes have acted in very different ways; thus, for instance, most observers would characterize the Peruvian military regime as left authoritarian, and the Brazilian military regime as right authoritarian.[6]

What explains these two different military responses to radicalism? To answer this question, one might explore the historical and institutional legacies of the two military establishments. However, in the specific cases of Brazil and Peru this does not get us very far, because if anything the Brazilian military—at least up to the late 1950s—had performed its moderator role with somewhat more attention to nationalistic and reform issues than the Peruvian military had. Even if this were not the case, moreover, the institutional legacy approach by itself has serious analytic weaknesses because it focuses too much attention on the military as an isolated institution and not enough on the dynamic interactions between the nature of the radical demands, the nature of the crises of the state, and military perceptions both of the nature of the institutional threats it faces and of the necessary corrective actions it must take.

Systemic Crises and Inclusionary and Exclusionary Military Responses

My basic explanation for the differences between the Peruvian and the Brazilian military's responses to radicalism can be divided into two parts. First, the pressures and the resultant state crises in Peru in the years leading up to 1968 were quite different from those in Brazil in the years before 1964 (and from the somewhat similar crises in Chile in 1973 and Argentina in 1966). Second, these differences produced contrasting military solutions to the problems of political participation and control.

I have labeled these contrasting solutions the "inclusionary" and "exclusionary" variants of corporatism. Thus, Peru is an example of *inclusionary* corporatism, in that a central aspect of the military's attempt to forge a new equilibrium has been the use of controlled inclusionary policies aimed at incorporating actual or potential radical groups into the economic and political model the military seeks to create. By way of contrast, Brazil, Chile, and Argentina are examples of *exclusionary* corporatism, in that a central feature of the attempt to forge a new order is a series of policies designed to remove or confine a broad range of practices (predominantly demand-making) and groups (usually working-class or radical) so as to contain sharply the capacity of autonomous organizations in civil society to challenge the new politico-economic design.[7]

What types of systemic crises tend to correlate with each subtype and what are the coalitional patterns characteristic of each subtype?[8]

Inclusionary attempts are most likely where the oligarchical order is beginning to erode under the pressures of early modernization, where political mobilization, while growing, is still relatively low and undifferentiated, and where the industrialization process is still at an early stage. Under such circumstances public and private industrial managers, under the leadership of the state elite, can forge alliances with the working classes against the old order of the rural and *comprador* oligarchy. Under some conditions this cross-class alliance of the emerging industrial sector can also take the form of a nationalist attack against the presence of foreign capital in such traditional investment areas as extractive industry or utilities.[9]

An exclusionary attempt, however, is most likely under either one of the two following conditions, and frequently a combination of the two.

1. Political mobilization is more intense and ideologically differentiated than that which precedes inclusionary attempts. The elite that assumes control of the state apparatus, fearing a crisis of intense internal conflict, attempts to impose a new order on the political system. The state elite attempts to exclude from the political arena a variety of relatively autonomous, largely working-class-based, institutional structures capable of resisting the elite's political design, and then seeks to reintegrate the excluded groups into associational organizations designed and controlled by the state.

2. The industrialization process is more advanced, but has begun to stagnate. In this crisis of industrial development, the elites who assume control of the state apparatus (and normally their private-sector allies) believe that further national development requires major increases in the levels of capital investment and, correspondingly, a heavy stress on effective public and private investment planning. These, in turn, require the initial exclusion and subsequent controlled reintegration of working-class and radical groups, so as to lower their capacity to make demands and impede the implementation of the state's politico-economic development design. In addition, under the conditions of more advanced industrialization, the high investment requirements of the state planners often entail a coalitional shift by the state elites towards an alliance of convenience with the modern multinational industrial sector, which is seen as a source of

scarce financial, technological, and organizational resources.[10]

In sum, the nature of the military's response to perceived systemic crisis is strongly conditioned by the level and pace of industrialization and the intensity and differentiation of political mobilization. In the specific context of Latin America, inclusionary corporatism is thus more likely in the earlier stages of import-substitution industrialization, where modern elites and modern masses perceive significant room for populist cross-class coalitions. Exclusionary corporatism, on the other hand, is more likely to be attempted if, after the import-substitution phase, the pattern of industrial development begins to stagnate, the politico-economic struggle intensifies, and politics is increasingly perceived in zero-sum terms.

To illustrate the point, let us now turn to an analysis of the interactions between growing demands and the crisis of the state in Peru.

The Nature of the Crisis in Peru
Compared to Brazil, Argentina, and Chile

It is clear that Peru, in the period before the military assumed power, had been undergoing a process of growing societal crisis. But how should we characterize this crisis, and why did it lead to an inclusionary rather than exclusionary form of corporatism? Perhaps the best way to answer the question is to identify the major dimensions of the crisis, and contrast them with the crises in Brazil, Argentina, and Chile.

One distinctive characteristic of the crisis in Peru was the main locus of conflict and tension. Whereas in the other three cases tension was centered in the modern industrial sector, the crisis in Peru had its origins in a process of rural radicalization and mobilization that one observer has called "unquestionably one of the largest peasant movements in Latin American history."[11] In terms of the number of peasants involved and the number of land seizures recorded, it was probably larger than any other such phenomenon in the Third World at the time. A report by an international organization estimates that no less than 300,000 peasants were involved.[12] Another study reported more than 150 land invasions in the Pasco, Junín, and Cuzco areas alone in the last half of 1963, and estimated that the "total number of invasions may well have been between 350 and 400" on a nationwide basis.[13] These invasions affected a wide variety of properties, from foreign-owned grazing land to traditional haciendas. Land seizures occurred throughout much of Peru, involving almost all the departments of the sierra. Moreover, these rural invasions were beginning to have an urban analogue. In 1955 Lima had a squatter population of only 120,000. By 1970 this population had soared to over 750,000.

The distinctive character of Peru's crisis was also reflected in differences in such "stress indicators" as inflation, strikes, and external indebtedness. Inflation can be taken as a partial measure of intensity of demands on the government, and we see that the average rates of inflation for the five-year period prior to the exclusionary attempts in Brazil, Chile, and Argentina were far higher than in the five-year period preceding the inclusionary attempt in Peru. Argentina experienced an average inflation rate of 29.1 percent, Brazil 60.5 percent, and Chile 102.5 percent. The comparable figure for Peru is 13.1 percent.[14]

Labor mobilization had been growing in Peru; from 1957 to 1962 the average number of strikes per year was 269. For the next six-year period immediately preceding the assumption of power by the military the figure rose to 398 per year.[15] Nonetheless, Peru in the 1965–67 period averaged only 11.4 strikers per thousand inhabitants.[16] This is much lower than Chile, which recorded 74.1 strikers per thousand inhabitants in 1970—and this even before the figure soared in the years immediately preceding the 1973 coup.[17]

The external financial dimensions of Peru's crisis were substantial, but both different from and much less severe than those that preceded the exclusionary attempts. It is true that, after having long prided themselves on their relatively stable currency, Peruvians were shocked by the 44 percent devaluation of the sol in 1967. The devaluation was widely interpreted as both a sign of the political bankruptcy of the Belaúnde government and of the intrinsic limitations of the model of economic development then being pursued.[18] Moreover, the devaluation was a symptom of the fact that Peru had been undergoing stress in its trading and balance-of-payments position. An important indicator of this stress was the fact that, despite generally favorable export prices, Peru's ratio of external public debt service to value of exports had climbed from an annual average of 7.4 percent in the period 1960–64 to 11.1 percent in the period 1965–69. Nevertheless, these figures are significantly lower than the ratios found in the other three countries. Brazil's average annual ratio for the period 1960–64 was 31.5 percent, Argentina's was 20.5 percent for the period 1961–65, and Chile had reached a ratio of 20.5 percent by 1971.[19]

In sum, the crisis of the state in Peru differed from those in Brazil, Chile, and Argentina in its main locus of conflict, in its levels of inflation and strikes, and in its external financial dimensions. These variations, in turn, were reflections of a central and underlying difference in the level and pace of industrialization and modernization. Brazil, Chile, and Argentina were experiencing crisis and stagnation at advanced levels of modernization before their exclusionary attempts, whereas Peru was just beginning its industrialization process. Peru's average annual gross domestic product growth rate for 1961–67 was a healthy 6 percent, which placed it sixth among the twenty Latin American countries in this period.[20] The crisis in Peru therefore was not so much how to exclude and contain the modern industrial labor force, but rather how to include and integrate the marginal rural and urban masses, so as to lay the groundwork for incipient modernization and industrialization. However, the crisis was no less real, because if the state elite could not clear away the obstacles to such modernization, explosive disintegration of the oligarchical order seemed a possibility, as the peasant land invasions indicated.

It should be clear, then, that inclusionary and exclusionary corporatism have corresponded to different types of

crises in civil society and to different types of state policies
aimed at surmounting these crises. In Peru, tension was concentrated in the traditional sector and found expression in
peasant-landlord conflicts and, to a lesser extent, the squatter
settlements of the urban marginals; this, in part, explains the
dominance of inclusionary policies by the Peruvian military
once in power. This contrasts sharply with the locus of conflict that preceded the exclusionary attempts in Chile,
Brazil, and Argentina. These countries, with their relatively
advanced industrial economies, experienced what might be
called a "structural crisis of transition." Conflict was centered in the modern industrial sector, and expressed itself
through such "stress indicators" as high strike and inflation
levels, and growing external indebtedness.

Thus, independent of the ideologies of the military establishments in Peru on the one hand, and in Argentina,
Chile, and Brazil on the other, the crisis in civil society in
the former country was more consistent with an inclusionary
policy response, and in the latter countries with an exclusionary policy response.

The Peruvian Military's Institutional and
Ideological Response to Growing Threats

How did the military actually respond to the crisis and
radicalization of the state in Peru? Did it in fact feel
threatened as an institution? If so, what actions did it feel
were necessary to reduce this threat? Did it undergo ideological and institutional change of the sort that disposed it to
carry out inclusionary policies?

To explore these questions I made a content analysis of
the articles published in Peruvian military journals in the
fifteen years before the military assumed power.[21] I supplemented this analysis with extensive interviews with former
faculty members and students of the military schooling system, and with visits to the Center of Higher Military Studies
(CAEM) in 1972 and 1974. I looked for two things: first,
shifts from the classical "old professional" military focus
on conventional territorial warfare to a "new professional"

concern for questions dealing with the nexus between internal security and national development.[22] Second, I wanted to ascertain the programmatic content of the new professional articles.

To what extent did a "new professionalism" exist in Peru before the military assumed power in 1968? In 1954 the General Staff School founded a new journal, *Revista de la Escuela Superior de Guerra.* I coded all the available articles appearing in this journal from its inception up through 1967, the year before the formation of the new military regime. (The methodology and classification system has been discussed elsewhere. Very briefly, articles that discussed military education, equipment, tactics, and strategy from the perspective of combating external enemies were classified under the category of "Old Professionalism of Conventional Territorial Warfare." Articles with titles like "Internal War and Engineering Social Change," or "Domestic Socio-Political Analysis" were classified under the category of "New Professionalism of Internal Security and National Development.") Figure 1 shows how new professional articles rose from only 1.7

Figure 1
Ratios of New Professional to Old Professional Articles in Revista de la Escuela Superior de Guerra, *1954–57, 1958–62, 1963–67*

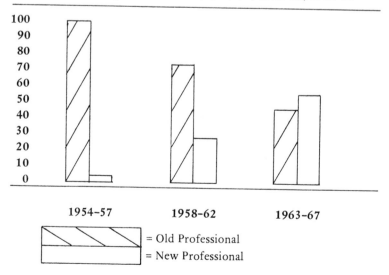

percent of the universe in the 1954–57 period—before the
Algerian war, Cuban revolution, and the beginning of peasant
land invasions in Peru—to 53 percent of the universe in the
1963–67 period, immediately before the military seized
power and began using the power of the state apparatus to
restructure Peruvian society.[23] Clearly, questions of internal
war and sociopolitical analyses of national development had
become a major concern of the Peruvian military well before
it assumed power.

Let us now turn to the specific content of the articles and
related material. The evidence is strong that the army elite
perceived the country to be in a severe crisis.[24] The first
article to raise the theme of growing crisis was by a young
lieutenant colonel recently returned from military schooling
in France.[25] He argued that the communist revolutionary
strategy represented a new form of warfare; that such revolutionary warfare had already started in Peru; and that the old
military tactics were irrelevant for the new challenge. He also
stressed that the openness of workers and *campesinos* to communist appeals was directly related to their living standards.[26]
By 1964 the General Staff School, after a study of strikes,
land invasions, and the proliferation of revolutionary parties,
concluded in one lesson plan that "we now are in the stage of
revolutionary war." Even after a guerrilla campaign was
defeated by the army in 1965, the official army report
emphasized that Peru remained in a state of "latent in-
surgency."[27] In an important article published in 1967
General Edgardo Mercado Jarrín listed a series of structural
problems in Peru, such as great income inequality and explosive land tenure problems, that contributed to the dangerous disequilibrium of the country. He argued that the
guerrillas would reappear unless reforms and structural
changes were accelerated.[28]

In numerous interviews—or more normally during informal conversations with Peruvian officers in four field
trips since 1972—a common theme emerged explicitly that
is only implicit in the articles. The army supported the
candidacy of Belaúnde in 1963 because it saw him as the last

hope to bring about changes democratically. By the mid-1960s, however, the army felt that party conflicts and the internal and external pressures stemming from Peru's economic dependency had eroded the possibility of parliamentarily induced basic changes. The military's own studies at CAEM and in its intelligence schools indicated that more peasant and guerilla insurrections would inevitably (and a number of officers stressed "justifiably" and "necessarily") develop. The specific institutional dilemma this presented for the army was that, should no structural reforms be undertaken, the military would have to continue acting as the "watchdog" of the oligarchy by repressing demands for change, because there would inevitably be other revolutionary movements that would have to be put down.[29] Some officers also strongly implied that, should a revolution be successful, the military, as the coercive force of the oligarchy, could suffer institutional dissolution and even the firing squad. Such had been the fate of the Cuban regular army. What was the way out of the dilemma? The military's answer was to seize power itself, and to use the power of the state to impose change and eliminate the structural disequilibrium impeding Peru's internal stability and national power. Part of the institutional cohesion of the Peruvian military during the period of sweeping change it imposed when it came to power derived precisely from the fact that these changes were perceived as having such a strong relationship to the survival imperatives of the military as a corporate unit and as a situational elite.

The Achievements and Problems
of the Peruvian Military "Radicals" in Power

In a very schematic fashion let me indicate some of the Peruvian military regime's major policy measures and ideological positions that warrant, despite its original features, labeling the regime's dominant policy orientation "inclusionary" and its dominant ideological orientation an "organic-statist" variety of corporatism. Notwithstanding the structural changes the regime has introduced, these terms seem more appropriate than the term "radical."[30]

Major Policy Measures

The regime has already carried out a number of structural reforms which have had strong inclusionary features, in that a major aim of the reforms was to integrate previously marginal groups into the new economic and political structures the regime is creating.

Agrarian reform has been sweeping. A study concluded just before the military assumed power asserted that "the oligarchy today consists of a central nucleus made up of the sugar and cotton growers of the coast."[31] In a 1974 revision of his classic neo-Marxist study of the elites of Peru, Carlos Malpica, in many ways one of the more stringent critics of the military government, acknowledged:

> As a consequence of the Agrarian Reform Law . . . all the agricultural enterprises with any economic significance have been expropriated or are in the process of expropriation. The most important, that is to say, the sugar producers, were the first to be transformed into agro-industrial cooperatives. Practically speaking, the agrarian [elite] has disappeared as a power group.[32]

For the poor urban migrants living in squatter settlements, who constitute almost a third of Peru's urban population, the military government has initiated a program of granting property title and of infrastructure support that is unprecedented in Latin America.

For workers in industry the government has initiated an "industrial community" reform that provides for the workers gradually to increase their ownership to as much as 50 percent of the enterprise and in theory to exercise managerial control commensurate with their equity.

Significant changes in areas such as education, health care, and communications have been initiated and the state has assumed control of significant sectors of oil, mining, and fishing.

To be sure, each of these reform policies has its share of problems and critics. Nonetheless it is clear that, leaving aside the Cuban revolution, the Peruvian military has already carried out a more sweeping program of structural change than any other regime in modern Latin American history. However, the Peruvian regime is quite different in its philosophy and structure from that in Cuba. One of the central concerns of the military elite in charge of the Peruvian state is not so much to eliminate the principle of private ownership of the means of production as to lessen class conflict and to increase the functional integration of the masses.

In agriculture, an attempt has been made to remove the owners of larger estates, giving ownership, normally in collective form, to the laborers who have worked the property. Because the old oligarchy no longer owns the land, the regime has also abolished the National Agrarian Society—once a major symbol of oligarchical organizational power and the most important interest group representing the oligarchy.

Concerning the industrial structure, the state elite has attempted to forge what it sees as a more organic unity by reducing the ownership of capital and by giving both equity and managerial participation to labor. The hope was that, over time, these actions would transform the capitalist mentality of owners and the class-conflictual attitudes of labor. In particular, the state elite viewed trade unions as the logical response of labor to situations where capital owned all the means of production. The elite hoped, therefore, that trade unions would wither away as the structural changes introduced by the state made workers both owners and participating managers.[33]

To underscore the fact that old associational forms based on "capitalist interest" were not preferred under the new regime, the government made the National Industrial Society take workers on to its Directorate. Later the society lost the right to call itself "national," and finally its president was prevented from returning to the country following his outspoken opposition to the regime's policies.[34]

As is characteristic of inclusionary attempts, the government also embarked upon a program to incorporate the population—especially those lower-class groups such as peasants, squatters, and industrial workers seen by the regime as the major beneficiaries of the structural reforms—into new state-chartered associational groups. The initial state agency

charged with this task was SINAMOS. The basic law creating
SINAMOS said the agency should "promote the organization
of the population into dynamic functional and territorial
units of communal and cooperative nature" and "foment
and stimulate the dialogue between the government and the
national population in order to orient the conscious participation of the people in the basic decisions that affect
their environment, their interests and their communal objectives," as well as "foment the systematic linkage between
the coordinated actions and services of the government and
those of the organized population."[35]

The state apparatus, working through SINAMOS and relevant ministries, had by 1974 organized the agricultural sector
into local and provincial organizations and finally into a
National Agrarian Confederation. Its industrial counterpart is
the National Confederation of Industrial Communities. The
emerging organizational model is one that emphasizes the
vertical integration of functional groups.[36]

The dominant policies of the regime have thus been inclusionary in that there have been significant distributive and
symbolic acts in favor of lower-class groups aimed at integrating these groups into the emerging economic and political systems which are being constructed by the state elite,
and that the state has linked these distributive acts with a
major effort to incorporate the beneficiaries into new state-
chartered associational structures.

Ideology

Ideologically, in its "organic-statist" variety of corporatism,
the regime explicitly rejects both the liberal idea of the
individual and the Marxist idea of class as an organizational
principle of society. The vision is "organic" in that the
goal is the nonconflictual, functional unity of civil society.
The regime is "statist" in that the elite perceives that this
functional unity will not occur spontaneously but rather
requires power, rational choices and decisions, and, where
necessary, fundamental restructuring of civil society by the
state elite. Organic unity of civil society is thus to be brought

about by the architectonic action of public authorities.

Innovations

The Peruvian regime is innovative in two separate but related areas: it is experimenting with new forms of worker participation and with new forms of ownership patterns. Both raise crucial theoretical questions for social scientists and practical problems for Peruvian politics.

In the area of participation the Peruvian regime has created more complex and elaborate structures for worker participation and functional schemes of representation than any other regime of this sort. Most observers have simply called attention to laws and formal structures. However, since other regimes will undoubtedly borrow from the Peruvian experiment, it is important that scholars and policymakers now look beyond formal structures and explore the actual problems and achievements of this experience in as great detail as possible.

The other major area of policy innovation concerns new property patterns. The regime is systematically more nationalistic than any previous inclusionary or exclusionary case. With the Andean Pact, the Industrial Community, and other experiments, the Peruvian military originally attempted to curb multinationals and to make them conform to the regime's overall philosophical and economic development goals. However, the extremely ambitious plans for rapid development required considerable sums of outside capital. As a result, by 1976 the Peruvian government's program in this area was under intense external and internal pressure, which tested severely its capacity to attract resources from the international arena without compromising its goals of worker participation and nationalism.

Questions for the Future

Two additional areas of the Peruvian experience of military change from above require close observation. First, to what extent will the extremely strong institutional base of the state in the army become an impediment in the political institutionalization of the regime? (In Mexico, for example, Cárdenas did not have a new professional army to constrain his political institution-building.) In Peru the corporate and bureaucratic existence of a new professional army was a resource for the state in its initial confrontation with the traditional roadblocks to structural change. But we need to explore the long-term constraints this new professional army base of the state may present for the political options available to the regime. Potential constraints seem most real in the area of participation. How can the government reconcile its proclaimed aspirations to build a political structure of increasing functional representation with the reality of its institutional base in a new professional army? Since 1975 the military as institution has been putting increasing checks on the military as government that have reduced the government's capacity—and increasingly its commitment—to forge new popular political institutions.

Finally, there are the questions raised by the fact that the original Peruvian military elite had a more encompassing program to restructure civil society by imposed state policies than any previous regime built on inclusionary or exclusionary policies. While the military regime espoused pluralism within the context of the new economic and political structure, the military elite in charge of the state appeared to have ambitions to penetrate and transform—without the aid of a political party—almost all sectors of civil society. At the end of eight years of rule the regime has arrived at an unusual stage. The state initially achieved substantial freedom of action in the national sphere. Some even argued it had autonomy. But because all organizations that predated the regime were threatened with penetration and transformation, there has been organizational resistance from the right, left, and center. Despite the inclusionary policies, the regime has yet to generate active organized support of the type Cárdenas and Perón generated. Also, despite the fact that the regime is more progressive than the Brazilian regime, the latter has an active constituency while the Peruvian has not yet created one. There are center-right groups in Brazil that feel the military regime protects their established interests and organizations. In Peru, however, the architectonic "organic-statist" vision of the military elite called for the restructuring of virtually all existing political, economic, and social organizations. Whether the regime can go beyond passive support for its reforms and achieve active support for its new institutions is one of the major—and increasingly pressing—questions facing the Peruvian military elite. There has been much talk in the literature about the relative autonomy of the state. This concept needs to be broadened. The other side of the coin of complete state autonomy may well be isolation, fragility, and lack of any organized constituency.

Charles S. Maier, formerly of Harvard University, is currently an assistant professor of history at Duke University. Co-editor of The Thirteenth of May: The Advent of de Gaulle's Republic, *Professor Maier has been nominated for a National Book Award for his excellent study,* Recasting Bourgeois Europe. *His most recent essay, concerning the interrelationship of science and politics in the Eisenhower era, appears as the introduction to the diary of George Kistiakowsky (special assistant for science and technology 1959-60), which was published by Harvard University Press in 1976.*

7
Beyond Revolution?
Resistance and Vulnerability to Radicalism
in Advanced Western Societies
Charles S. Maier

Only one result of our survey need be emphasized: the very great and perhaps even increasing stability of our social relationships. For the foreseeable future there is an overwhelming majority available against any extremist course from whatever side it comes . . . In no sense, in no area, in no direction is there likely to be a decisive change, rapid movement, or catastrophes. A terrible situation for those with an incandescent will to shape events—but perhaps no sorry condition for accomplishments of another sort.

Joseph Schumpeter offered this reassuring prognosis for the Weimar Republic in 1929. It followed quite logically from his valuable analysis of social and political conditions in Germany.[1] Happily the salaries and stature of social scientists remain independent of their success in predictions but are keyed to the elegance and verve of their post mortems. I shall plead for the same privilege and with good reason. No matter how scientific the description of social trends, no matter how resilient or refractory a political system appears, an element of unpredictability lies within. The deference and subordination that seem freely given or easily purchased can quickly crumble; authority can decompose almost instantaneously, not merely when assailed by mass discontent or patient revolutionaries over decades, but almost from some inner demoralization: witness May 1968, or the sudden collapse of the Greek colonels, or the fall of Caetano in Portugal.

Every witness of university turmoil in the late 1960s, every reader who reviews prerevolutionary crises—whether Louis XVI's decision to bring troops to Versailles, the "two shots in Berlin" in 1848, the daily violence in Spain during the summer of 1936, the abortive coup of General Spinola in March 1975—must realize how political upheaval is nourished by what appear to be chance events. Revolutionary polarization feeds on itself; heads banged by police deliver a social order to upheaval and put power up for grabs in unpredictable yet decisive ways.

Still, to a large degree, the concept of chance merely covers our imperfect foresight, our limitations in perceiving the deeper and progressive decay of social or political systems. Not that a universal and comprehensive social science is possible; but any analysis must push beyond the mere narration of contingencies to examine the tensions ready to explode. "It is not chance that rules the world," wrote one of the profoundest social scientists. "And if the chance of one battle —that is, a particular cause—has brought a state to ruin, some general cause made it necessary for that state to perish from a single battle. In a word, the main trend draws with it all particular accidents."[2]

Restating this Enlightenment credo serves to point up what this essay can and cannot do. My assignment is to weigh those forces in contemporary Western society that make radical upheaval likely. So that we do not fall into a wearying conflict over labels, I will use the term "radical" or "revolutionary" change to suggest a transformation that departs from legal procedures, involves a major substitution of elites, or promises a major change in the principles according to which honor and goods are distributed. Not all upheavals are so comprehensive, although a true revolution entails them all. These definitions narrow our focus; I am not going to examine the social flux and decomposition that attend family life and loyalties, law and order, religious beliefs—all spheres of profound transformation. In part, a question of tempo is at stake. Society is constantly altering, but spread over a generation or a century such great change does not seem to rip the civic fabric.

Even if one stresses the resilience of Western society, I shall not wager that radical change will not occur. For each damper that modern society puts on radical tendencies, it imposes new strains on itself, which become clear only after subsequent crises. Still, modern Western society does impose powerful structural inhibitions upon revolutionary outcomes.

These restraining mechanisms seem all the more impressive insofar as the persisting inequalities of the social order present more of a challenge to explanation than its levelling tendencies. Western society, it is true, has steamrollered old aristocracies and steadily reduced inequalities of education, wealth, and manners. For some historians this secular change has proved transfixing and one that dwarfs all counter-tendencies in its importance. But while aristocracies perish aristocrats survive, new elites are generated, and hierarchy persists. Even if the West, as Tocqueville claimed, has been moving towards the destruction of elites,[3] the pace is sufficiently slow and irregular that discontent should be serious. The issue posed here, then, is why societies that have provided such differential rewards for their members can continue to maintain such great degrees of loyalty or acquiescence. Notions of relative deprivation and limited reference groups suggest only partial answers; they leave unresolved the question of why reference groups sometimes remain circumscribed, and sometimes suddenly expand to bring hitherto unresented reservoirs of privilege under critical scrutiny.[4] In short: why do so many take so much (or so little) from so few for so long? Admittedly the question is one-sided, but it points up the fact that social organization is a contrivance as well as a natural collectivity. It must be discussed as a matrix of transactions in which rewards or constraints secure consensus. I am less interested in the use of right-wing coercion (whether imposed preemptively or as a counter-revolution) than in the structure of bargaining and voluntary transactions. Fascism remains an important subject of inquiry; but today's advanced societies frustrate revolutionary challenges to the distribution of power and wealth without recourse to fascism.[5] In the mid-1890s Friedrich Engels wrote that the working classes could rely on the ballot to win power, whereas the right, fearing that "legality shall kill us," would resort to violence.[6] Engels was correct, but only for a transitional period. Why that period may have ended—unless there ensues a prolonged economic crisis—must be part of the discussion.

I.

Stability has usually seemed less of a problem to be explained than have change and instability. To be sure, historians of Byzantium, traditional China, or Tokugawa Japan have been compelled to assess why their chosen societies endured for so long with such little apparent change. But analysts of the restless West have devoted major effort to the breakdowns of social order and the generation of new institutions. Barricades, demonstrations, street-fighting, empassioned constituent assemblies, bitter electoral conflicts are too dramatic to be resisted. Again there are notable exceptions, especially among writers who have compared British developments with those on the continent. Elie Halévy structured his massive exposition of English history in the nineteenth century around the factors that forestalled revolution, above all the influence of religious currents.[7] More recently, J.H. Plumb and Barrington Moore, Jr., have readdressed the question of relative British stability—but with a new twist. They have argued that the stability of the eighteenth and nineteenth centuries depended upon prior revolutionary change; for Moore the violent transformations wrought during the Civil War; for Plumb the regrouping of elites in the wake of the Glorious Revolution and the

Hanoverian succession.[8] For both writers, though, British stability is no "organic" growth, but the consequence of quick change instituted by decisive men on the make. (Those interested in contemporary Soviet society—apparently now one of the most refractory and resistant in the world—should find these analyses of an earlier England useful and relevant.)

Even as historians have come to emphasize the dependence of stability upon prior radical change, they have also rediscovered the sources of radical protest within traditionalist society. Rioting and crowd action have come under extensive historical and social-scientific scrutiny—in part (but only in part) the result of the uprisings in the United States during the late 1960s. Historians who have examined the role of popular agitation and demonstrations before and during the American revolution, during the French revolution, in the British countryside or in London, and continuing through the labor unrest of the last 150 years have now come to stress the sobriety and respectability of such movements. Their participants have been neither *Lumpenproletariat* nor even always proletariat, but have included artisans, men of middling rank, and (at least in the preindustrial era) solid community leaders. Their goals have been less revolutionary in intent than restorative: efforts to reinstate a "moral economy" or a "constitution" they felt was being abandoned.[9]

Of course, even if a movement's goals are restorative, the upshot of its agitation can be truly revolutionary. To demand restoration of an ancient constitutional order during an era of centralization can be explosive, resulting either in a newer and more democratic system, or at least a new settlement among contending elites and sometimes renewed and harsher centralization, depending upon the mix among social groups that patronize or resist the movement. To demand a vanishing "moral economy" during an era of burgeoning capitalism usually just helps clear the ground for a quicker conquest by the economically powerful. Radical results are compatible with restorative imagery. Marxist theory, to be sure, has resisted ideological archaism ever since the Manifesto's denunciation of feudal and petit-bourgeois socialism. Still, when Marxism has come to animate mass movements, restorative imagery had permeated their aspirations. The point is that radical movements germinate in the soil of a crumbling *traditional* order (were not the universities the last institutions to resist the encroachment of the marketplace?), while stability is wrested from change and revolution. Those who would serve as the strategists of stabilization as well as those who would be the colonels of the revolution should remember the dialectical interplay of their respective goals. For the student of change or stability it is absolutely essential to confront both phenomena together.

If we pass in review theorists of change and stability several explanatory paradigms emerge. Although classification must do violence to much subtlety I will label the theorists conservative, liberal, and Marxist. For the conservative, social order is a good in itself; social change is profoundly unsettling, whether it be centralization from above or democratization from below. He is not likely to believe that sudden and radical change can advance collective values such as equality or liberty or meaningful participation. Any equality produced will be that of despotism; liberty will usually be even further constricted under any new regime; participation will become sham ritual. The motives of revolutionaries are reduced to mere conspiracies for power, a drive, after all, that allegedly remains a constant of human nature. Ideologies become mere rationalizations. Burke and Taine's perspectives on the French revolution provide classic statements of this line of thought, as does Pareto's demystification of the socialist movement, which he viewed as merely the latest contender among groups of ambitious men seeking to become a new ruling group.[10] For the conservative the deepest cause of the revolution is not the grievances inherent in the old regime, but the ruling class's failure of nerve. Without self-doubt, or a misplaced patrician reformism, there would be no revolution. If the cry of abandon ship were never sounded, the vessel would remain afloat.

For the conservative the parameters of revolution and stability are thus individual characteristics: on the part of the challengers these include rancor and ambition; on the part of the incumbents, fortitude or irresolution will make the difference. The strength or weakness of institutions plays a role only insofar as institutions seem appropriately constructed in light of human frailty. For both the liberal and the Marxist, on the other hand, the problem of institutions becomes central in its own right. Institutional stability in turn depends upon the proper relationship of the sphere of political and legal obligation—the state—to the network of interests, associations, and economic arrangements that compose so-called civil society.[11]

For the liberal not all social order has an equal claim to preservation, and he is willing to incur transitory upheaval and extralegal action to move from a traditionalist society to one that gives free play to individual energies. The criteria of a decent polity comprise, first, the universal application of the law, and second, restriction of the state enough to allow civil society and individual energies to nurture growth, welfare, and liberty. This restriction is usually formulated as a problem of "balance of powers" or of curbing the executive's power. But the balance-of-power problem is only an instrumental one. The primary aim remains limitation of the state as a whole in respect to the realm of interests and personal rights. Once the good liberal polity is achieved, once the realm of civil society is buttressed against mystical claims to authority, radical movements and revolutions lose their purpose and sense. Social unrest should then logically cease and direct action be dismantled.

The liberal, therefore, perceives social turmoil as arising from the discordance of state and civil society. Stability is a consequence of "congruence"[12] between the principles that govern the two: preferably, voluntary association and pluralist competition. Without this congruence deformation results. These deformations are of several types. One is that of stagnation, in which a dynamic state coexists with a "stalemated society" and leads to bureaucratization and backwardness punctuated by dramaturgic revolts and uprisings.[13] This is the theory that observers of France have favored. A second failure of congruence is seen to lead to the breakdown of parliamentarism and dictatorship when civil society remains less open and democratic than political institutions—when for example, a landed aristocracy of birth retains a reservoir of social power even if it has consented to equality before the law. Schumpeter and Veblen, for instance, analyzed German imperialism as a form of archaism in this manner.[14] Finally, a third type of incongruity is seen to arise during the process of modernization when advanced economic sectors or sudden mass political mobilization overtake traditionalist values, low literacy, clientelism, and generally "backward" political institutions. For Samuel Huntington, to take the most sophisticated analysis in these terms, instability results not from any absolute level of backwardness or advancement, but from the discordant "ratios" of unequal modernization: if political participation outruns institutional development, only turmoil and authoritarian solutions can result. The result is "praetorianism," a raw and unmediated intervention by the dominant forces of civil society (whether the military, agrarians, clergy, students, unions, etc.) which displaces a weak and hypotrophic state. Praetorianism can be radical or reactionary; in either case it is a further symbol of the tension between the political and social spheres.[15] In general, the theories all suggest that right-wing dictatorship threatens when the principles of political choice become more liberal-democratic than underlying traditionalist forces can accept, while leftist military adventures or peasant revolution seems to follow when the modernization of civil society outruns the corsetting political framework.

Modernization theory, Schumpeterian "lags," and diagnoses of stalemate *cum* crisis are all variant modes of explanation that express the great liberal theoretical constructs, which since the seventeenth century have separated those sub-political associations and enterprises men operate from interest from those they endow with coercive power. For the conservative, the distinction between the two types never emerged as a theoretical problem. For the British and French liberals the development of a vital and complex society represented both the fruit of radical upheaval (or for the German liberal, the result of a Protestant monarch) and the guarantee of welfare and liberty. Marxism, too, is an extension of such dialectical analysis, but one hoping to overcome the very separation between state and civil society which is the basis of the liberals' ideal commonwealth. For the Marxist the discordance between state and civil society must grow more acute under capitalism, since this discordance reflects the distinction between the economic forces of production and the legally reified and constraining relations of production. Thus for the conservative, revolution is simply a revolt against constituted authority and an effort to seize it illegitimately. For the liberal, revolution is the once necessary, then anachronistic, effort to limit authority. For the Marxist further revolution will become necessary to close the gap that the bourgeois world has opened between a state that consecrates accumulation and a civil society that multiplies all the claims upon economic resources.

Nonetheless, in the interim between liberal and proletarian revolutions both the state and civil society take on ambiguous explanatory power for the Marxists. In the long run, to be sure, the complexities and contradictions of civil society guarantee eventual revolution, since its contradictions cannot be resolved under private ownership. In the meantime, however, this very complexity—especially the high levels of productivity and the capacity for cooptation—may help to forestall revolution. This realization keynoted Engels' caution on revolution during his last years, and was elegantly expressed by Antonio Gramsci when he suggested that not even economic crisis might overturn the bourgeois order. Comparing political rivalry to recent trends in warfare, he wrote:

The same reduction [of warfare to wars of position] must occur in the art and the science of politics, at least in so far as regards the most advanced states where "Civil Society" has become a structure that is very complex and resistant to catastrophic "eruptions" from the immediate economic environment (crises, depressions, etc.): the superstructures of civil society are like the system of trenches in modern warfare. As in the latter, it happened that a fierce artillery barrage seemed to have destroyed the foe's entire defensive system but in fact had only destroyed the exposed surface such that at the moment of an attack and advance the assailants found themselves confronting a line of defense that was still in operation. Similar developments take place in politics during the great economic crises. . . . Thus one must study "profoundly" those elements of civil society that correspond to the system of defense in a war of position.[16]

But if civil society became more complex, interlaced with trenches, harder to storm, so the state, too, has changed character for the Marxist. As many commentators have explained, Marx and Engels had to take more serious account of an entrenched state power after the dashing of their early revolutionary hopes in 1848. More recently, Marxist theorists had to come to terms with what the dissident German communist August Thalheimer termed the *Verselbständigung des Staates* when he sought to move beyond the disastrous concepts of fascism that Stalin had encouraged before 1935. As Thalheimer discerned, fascism was more than capitalism unveiled. Rather, the very precariousness of the elites and their own inner divisions had led them to cede power to the state. As a result, the state developed its own sense of autonomy and strategy. The fascist state might borrow its striking force from the *petite bourgeoisie*, but it sought to straddle class interests and resolve them through superior force.[17] And if in the interwar period fascism compelled non-Russian Marxists to recognize the independent role of the state, post-1945 welfare politics also spurred a renewed Western Marxist interest in the state. According to the Marxian analysis of contemporary capitalism, the state has centralized the tasks of allocating investment funds and spending for social welfare, and has in general assumed the "externalities" of production while leaving the profits to be distributed privately—like some great cow to be pastured on the common but milked by the squire alone. The inherent contradictions of capitalism thus express themselves, so this analytical current suggests, as crises of the state and preeminently of an overtaxed budget. The claims of welfare clients, hard-pressed municipalities, bankrupt corporations, a massive military establishment, and costly medical and educational sectors overload the state's mediating capacity.[18] Thus the Marxian analyses of the state have evolved: from executive committee of the bourgeoisie to Bonapartism; from Bonapartism to brokerage; and now from brokerage to bankruptcy. In each case, however, the focus has shifted from an unmediated class struggle to group conflict centralized through the state. The breakdown of stability, therefore, shall not result from any differential rates of modernization, but from the inability of capitalism's ruling groups to square all the claims of different sectors within states already modernized. As it did for the great empires of history and for the *ancien régime*, fiscal crisis signifies the downfall of both a political apparatus and a social order.

But is breakdown really in the cards, or shall capitalism in the West be able to rescue itself through gains by its technological inventiveness (a factor that a labor theory of value may not really credit sufficiently[19])? If long-term growth can resume sufficiently to assuage the harsh demands upon social product, then the competition that the Marxists see as burdening the capitalist state can be rechanneled into the marketplace rivalries of civil society. The state is not called upon to allocate the losses or to enforce them unevenly by constraint. The Marxist prediction remains once again neither to be definitively excluded nor accepted, but rather adjourned sine die.

II.

The three models of instability and breakdown—conservative, liberal, and Marxist—rely upon different key processes: individual corruption for the first; differential rates of modernization for the second; a crisis of those legal relationships which precludes satisfying the totality of social claims, according to the third. Keeping in view the dual analysis of state and society that underlies both liberal and Marxist analysis, we can now examine not a total explanation of social upheaval, but several partial and eclectic approaches to a theory of stability. The major variables of such a theory consist of the changing scope of Western politics, the new nature of the state, and finally the evolving sense of class allegiances. Let us consider these in turn.

The Changing Scope of Western Politics

Although recent inflation and unemployment—accompanied as it was at least for a year by the first decline in real national income since the Depression—may embitter politics, over the long haul party rivalry in the West has become increasingly routinized and channeled. To understand this, recent political disputes must be viewed in a perspective that reaches back a century and takes into account the successive issues Western nations have had to resolve. The classic political polarity of the nineteenth century, that between liberals and conservatives, expressed the basic choice of whether to modernize or not. Liberals and conservatives spoke not merely for ideological alternatives but for differing development options as well: before the conservative hovered the images of a static manorial society embodying the values of hierarchy and subordination, largesse and loyal service, that bound together the differing levels of society.[20] Before the liberal gleamed a vision of progress in which middle classes and enlightened bureaucrats would inaugurate a humming economy, commercial growth, civil liberties, and the emancipation of man as rational producer and consumer. This profound alternative was decided largely in favor of the liberals, and European societies resolved upon the option of industrial development.

Once a manorial alternative was foreclosed, however, the terms of dispute changed. Only reactionaries contested the progress and desirability of economic development (although agrarians waged last stands over tariffs and industrial development).[21] Henceforth the scope of conflict concerned the new division of income and power within societies that had developed major industrial sectors. By the new century, the railroads were largely complete; urban populations within city limits (not metropolitan areas) were reaching their peak; workers were being organized into large-scale production units and trade unions; modern forms of corporate organization had become the dominant cadres for capital. But what shares of the new earnings of the industrial state would flow to capitalists or to workers or to farmers remained an open question, as did the control of the new commonwealth.

Given these issues—the distribution of power and wealth in a mature industrialized society—the terms of political dispute evolved, replacing the contest between liberalism and conservatism with a new paradigm conflict, between social democracy and its opponents. The stages of politics also changed as growth levelled off and national output oscillated violently from 1914 through 1945. A "mature," even stagnant economy forced a harsher zero-sum political game, in which socialist ideology clearly suggested a reappropriation of finite resources in favor of the working class. In an era of mass suffrage traditional conservative ideologies could no longer serve to organize those who resisted socialist claims. Especially in the wake of world war and later the depression, how could one persuade a mass electorate of the inherent capacities of traditional elites? Instead, the socialist demand for a radical redistribution "downward" of power and wealth helped evoke new doctrines in opposition. These called not only for the reinforcement of traditional privilege but for strengthening the authority and power and territory of the nation as a whole. The confining zero-sum frame of conflict could be transformed by arguing that working class and bourgeoisie together would profit from imperial expansion. At home, an authoritarian resolution of class conflict, so nationalists and fascists suggested, would adjourn the disputes between the working class and its opponents. A strong state which eliminated parasitic parties, bureaucrats, and politicians could enroll all workers in a community of production.[22] Old liberals and old conservatives found their respective doctrines outflanked and irrelevant as Europe left an era of continuing development for a trying age of conflict over distribution.

With the advent of sustained economic growth after World

War II, a less Darwinian contest could resume. With growth presupposed, political dispute no longer contested a supposedly finite social product. What remained in play was rather the increment of growth: conservatives and Christian Democrats generally recommended that first priority be given to plough-back, reinvestment, and monetary stability, so that the productive base of modern society be kept expanding. The dividends for the working classes, they suggested, would follow automatically. Social Democrats stressed the need for collective consumption and social transfers for welfare purposes. In short, Christian Democrats and conservatives emphasized growth, Social Democrats stressed equity and welfare. What was at stake in either case was not the basic principles of distribution, but how best to utilize the dividend of growth. Not surprisingly, such lesser disputes were easily mediated within a parliamentary framework. Conservatives and socialists either governed in coalition or peacefully alternated power. The politics of growth thus became a contest at the margin. So long as Western society can generate growth, moreover, this devenoming of political party rivalries seems likely to continue. Thus much of the case for stability depends upon present economic difficulties turning out to be transitory ailments deriving from resource shortages artificially imposed. If growth continues to falter, the sharpened claims of labor and entrepreneurs will rekindle ugly distributional battles. If growth resumes, party politics can again become an incremental game.

Nonetheless, to note the long-term transition from the divisions between nineteenth-century liberals and conservatives, through the violent combats between fascists and Marxists, to the less troubled argument of the last two decades, is not to exhaust the new political trends. Working-class parties no longer provoke mass counterrevolutionary opponents, and may no longer offer revolutionary alternatives. But new strains are placed upon the political systems which the given party structures (whether left or right) were not designed to confront with any coherence. If, as the Marxists point out, the state once again has become the central arena of social conflict, then the relationship of citizens to state and to party changes.

The Changing Nature of the State

Liberal and Marxist theories, we have suggested, attributed instability to a discrepancy between state and social forces, between political institutions and contending interests. In this perspective, the modern state apparatus should seem initially less vulnerable to challenge. For the modern state has interpenetrated with civil society to an unprecedented degree. The state has become simultaneously more extensive and weaker or less sovereign—more extensive because it coordinates areas of activity that earlier eras left to private resolution. There is no need to dwell on the regulatory, welfare, investment, educational, research, and other functions that have fallen under state auspices. Perhaps the most revealing statistic consists of the share of national income that passes through the public sector. In 1914 the advanced European nations collected and spent perhaps 10 percent of their respective societies' GNP; by 1925, the pensions and reconstruction costs left by the war and the beginnings of social insurance had perhaps doubled this tithe. In contemporary Western society 33 to 50 percent or so must pass through the hands of the state.[23]

This suggests an enormous centralizing function even for capitalist polities. At the same time, however, the nature of political decision-making has evolved during the past half-century. The liberal image of politics as reflected in countless civics texts suggested parliamentary control with periodic aggregation of individual preferences through elections. In the contemporary polity, however, consensus must embrace less individuals than social groups. It involves less periodic consultation than day-to-day bargaining to pacify each important organized interest, for each organized group can threaten to disrupt the ongoing functioning of the administrative or production system. It is tempting to seek political consensus through the continuing reconciliation of all major organized producer groups, since any one can seek to enforce its demands with unpleasant costs.[24] Edward Heath lost the Tories their majority because his showdown with the coal miners seemed unproductive; the German government violated its antiinflation wage guidelines in early 1974 when government officials threatened an unprecedented strike. A French regime almost fell when its university students withheld their class attendance. Of course not all strikes work: in the winter of 1975 the Glasgow trashmen capitulated to their Labour Party City Council once it called upon the army. Nor is it fair to charge private interests with unlimited appetite. When crisis is perceived groups can rally even at the cost of short-term sacrifice: witness the Trade Union Congress' acceptance of a £6 per week ceiling on wage settlements in September 1975. Still, it is remarkable and significant that the range of groups who can exert unacceptable damage, and can thus compel serious (if not always successful) bargaining with the central power, has broadly expanded over half a century. The First World War's premium on uninterrupted production of materiel first forced the Western polities to accept organized labor as a "social partner" that had to be conciliated by a systematic integration into the certified elites of the political system.[25] Many of those concessions wrested by virtue of the war were reversed during the subsequent era, to be regained only in the 1930s and 40s. Today, however, not merely industrial labor, but doctors, civil servants, teachers, students, and others wield sufficient clout to compel bargaining and concessions. The threat of praetorianism—the direct intervention of the organized social forces of a community—has come to afflict the advanced as well as the developing world.

Thus the problem of governance has changed from finding pluralities among masses of individual voters consulted periodically. It has become one of constant assuaging of organized interests, powerful because of their leverage in a production or even cultural system. At the same time, this has meant changes in the locus of decision-making. From the parliamentary hemicycle decision-making has moved to the bureaus where interests are reconciled. Sometimes these are new departments or ministries: the armaments ministries of World

War I, the ministries of economics and commerce and labor in the interwar period, the agencies of industrial development and social welfare after World War II, have all emerged as successive loci of power. New bureaucratic agencies are supplemented by either the committees of legislatures or party caucus mechanisms. In each case, the result has been to transfer the focus of effective decision-making from the legislature strictly speaking to direct party mediation or to divisions of the national executive.

Nonetheless, this development has not produced any one-way centralization of power or simple transcendence of liberalism. For even as executive agencies proliferate and legislatures pale, the new structure of decision-making involves an osmotic flow of power between public and private sectors. Old-fashioned *pantoufflage*—the interchange of personnel between business and its regulating agencies—is only the most obvious aspect. The absorption of enterprises into a state network of subsidies and loans (if not outright takeovers) forms another aspect, as does the creation of new layers of semi-private enterprise to execute public policies and developments: Comsat, the coming U.S. national health insurance, the aerospace industries in Europe, the price and wage boards involved in war production since 1914 and more recently in administering price controls. All such ventures point up the muddying of the concept of sovereignty. Just as concepts of representation and parliamentary liberalism have profoundly altered, so too the old liberal idea of the separation of state and civil society has eroded. Public and private sectors have lost their distinctness and retain meaning only as heuristically contrasted end-points of one continuum of publicly guaranteed activity. Consequently, the state has become more extensive in its supervisory role yet less pure in its conceptual distinctiveness: weaker in its separateness vis-à-vis private interests even as it is more indispensable. In short, it is "spongier" than ever before.

This trend is hardly new. As the examples chosen above suggest, it has developed since at least World War I, when it emerged as a natural result of warfare's insatiable requirements for the continuous flow of materiel, men, and the smoothest possible allocation of resources. Lacking the bureaucratic ability to ordain such results from above, each Western government devolved public powers and functions on those interests capable of policing their respective members. Between the wars the new challenges posed by renewed and more difficult international economic competition in the 1920s, then by the Depression of the 1930s, precluded totally dismantling the new regulatory arrangements. World War II and its aftermath confirmed the interpenetration of state and economy, as did the proliferation of welfare and investment needs in political systems which assumed full-employment obligations after 1945.

But surely, it might be objected, this new permeation of private and public sectors (elsewhere I have termed it a corporate pluralism, or even a new corporatism[26]) should be even more vulnerable to breakdown and instability and changes thrust from the left than the old-fashioned nineteenth-century liberal state. Is not the "spongy" state which is hostage to each major interest group so fine-tuned, so judged by criteria of price and employment stability that it is likely to lose legitimacy overnight? Indeed, the Marxist analysis of the new state suggests just this fragility.

I do not think that this is necessarily the case. For the new state or political economy has become enormously cooptive at the very moment it divests itself of an abstract authority that meant little in practice. Even as it becomes hostage to interest-group demands, it yokes these groups into a structure of bargaining that makes revolutionary stances all the more difficult. It is not by chance that as today's conservatives lament the weakness of the state, today's revolutionaries wrestle with cooptation as a major peril for their aspiration. Just as Lenin bitterly attacked a workers' aristocracy that had been suborned into the imperialist system, so André Gorz has struggled with the difficult problem of finding concrete goals whose very achievement would not lull a portion of the working class into acquiescence.[27] Western society shall have to face the demands of many new interest groups in

unpleasant confrontations, but may thereby preempt formation of a wide, revolutionary coalition. To use an unpleasant
metaphor, it may have traded civil war for ritualized social
muggings. Is the prospect attractive? No. Is the prospect
revolutionary? Not necessarily.

Nonetheless, it would be wrong to seek the sources of
radical demands only in the producer interests whose demands are the very stuff of domestic politics. Today's state
may well be evolving into a system of adjustment, flux, and
bargaining between poles of public power and poles of private
output. In so doing, however, it creates new sources of systemic opposition that may be more truly revolutionary or
destabilizing than the praetorian interest groups whose
everyday demands are clearly visible, but also subject to
bargaining. These new sources of systemic opposition are
of at least two sorts: first, the reaction by intellectuals—
and especially students—against the tendency of the modern
state to impose bureaucratic solutions on social conflicts;
and second, the vulnerability and deprivation of those who
do not or cannot organize as producers, in a system fashioned
to respond to the interests of organized corporate groups.

The first may already have crested and ebbed. In any case
it is abstract, perhaps too diffuse to mobilize. It is almost a
cultural and spiritual reaction. Each stage in the development of Western polities in the twentieth century has tended
to impose bureaucratic solutions upon class or distributional
conflict. Each of the contending parties (say labor and
industry) is endowed with public status and appeased as a
new para-agent of the central power. Conflicts over resources,
income, or power are neutralized by integrating the claimants
into new administrative agencies. Indeed, the government of
man does give way—as in the Saint-Simonian and Marxian
visions alike—to the administration of things, but with the
twist that man becomes one of the things to be administered.
The reduction of human aspirations to a "processable" input
in the modern political economy of the West may, however,
produce a certain reaction. Much of the university ferment of
the late 1960s can be interpreted in this light. As the supposed

guardians of humanist ends not reducible to bureaucratic mediation, the universities were almost predestined to become the centers of resistance for those unhappy with the administrative mode of resolving social conflict in the West. Thus aside from their marginal economic role, their awkward post-adolescent age range, and all the social-class disaffiliation that we associate with intellectuals, students may form a revolutionary nucleus by virtue of their antiadministrative commitments to liberal learning. Their humanism gives them the status of hand-loom weavers, a picturesque and doomed remnant consigned to misery, hopeless revolt, or migration. In fact, under new economic pressures, students are abandoning this antiquated stance voluntarily for preprofessional training. For the moment, perhaps forever, the hand-loom weavers of the university have now trooped off to the textile mills.

The second source of resistance is more substantial. It originates in the fact that while the modern societies of the West have developed a political framework for negotiating with producer interests, they have often done so increasingly at the expense of those not organized as producers. The problem of inflation is the tangible expression of this expropriation of the unorganized. It is to be recalled that half the period since 1914 has consisted of years of rising prices: 1913–21/24, 1936–53, 1967–75. Especially during wartime and its aftermath this inflation has facilitated (and in turn arisen from) wage-price spirals that have purchased the high output of industry and labor at the cost of the real income of less organized groups. This does not mean labor or industrialists always win in absolute terms; in periods of slowing or declining GNP the producer interests may merely protect their income shares from attrition with more efficacy than the middle strata. This means at least a relative gain at the expense of the professions, rentiers, the aged, etc. What is more, in contemporary Western political economies where corporate bargaining is continual, inflationary trends will be endemic. Inflation becomes the mode of a long and sustained income redistribution which purchases social order.

Obviously if there is real economic expansion then inflationary redistribution may merely allocate the dividends of growth to cohesive bargaining groups without having to amputate others' real incomes. But in a period of stagnation or decline, redistribution involves real, and not merely relative, sacrifice and deprivation.[28]

How is the plight of the exposed and vulnerable to be redressed? With intelligence and sympathy and planning a liberal-democratic system can tie pensions to cost-of-living indices, impose controls if necessary, funnel money into home mortgages, etc. Since the 1960s, social security has become virtually such a pegged pension. But if liberal legislators are not prepared to undertake such interventions, no social group is more ripe for exploitation by demagogic leadership, especially by radical-right spokesmen. The radical-right crusade represents an effort to reimpose political control over the corporate pluralist marketplace. Hence it couples calls for authority with hostility towards "big business" and organized labor as well as contempt for supposedly corrupt and uncaring political incumbents. As Franz Neumann suggested, pseudo-socialist movements focus on the role of finance, not ownership.[29] Thus the nostrums of the radical right will often include simplistic monetary remedies, such as bimetallism, social credit, and ending the power of remote banks. The radical right's stress on monetary remedies suggests an incomplete analysis of its own plight, but is nonetheless logical. For radical-right coalitions are forged under the duress of inflation, or just as directly, stabilization and deflation—as in the late nineteenth century, Germany after 1924, and France in the early 1950s. Consequently the political system that buys off its producers with inflation does face countervailing dangers.

This is especially the case since the political parties in the West are ill prepared to provide coherent antiinflationary policies: the major parties originated as formations of interests and voters who faced each other across national, religious, or social-class divisions.[30] Inflation, on the other hand, unites interests on both sides of the old class divisions; and each party—especially the liberal swing groups of the center—contains both the inflation-vulnerable and the inflation-sheltered. In part this explains the poor record of coping with inflation in the polities of the West.

Peter Lange has suggested that the problem of inflation was just one instance of a situation in which client relationships were actually becoming more important and pressing than producer rivalries.[31] Let me elaborate this helpful notion. Inflation victims, like welfare mothers or those dispossessed by new production techniques or those caught in backward regions, represent not traditional class affiliations but a growing number of distressed individuals who were created by the modern state as it encouraged the more productive sectors of society. And just as the given parties of the West—those of the left (like the communists) or those of the center and conservative right—have found inflation hard to confront, so they face comparable difficulty in designing policies for these distress cases. In their embarrassment lies a major danger for stability. For even if political mediation has been removed from the classical parliamentary chamber, it has not been taken out of the hands of political parties as centers of brokerage and staffers of administrative agencies. But precisely the growth of distressed sectors and cases (rather than merely aggrieved classes) may thrust an overwhelming burden upon these systems. Nonetheless, once again there are countertrends at work that modulate this danger. To understand these, however, we must consider the final element of our analysis.

The Changing Nature of Class Affiliation

In his last brief reflections on the nature of class, Max Weber noted that class hierarchies could be envisaged under two points of view. One principle of class stratification depended upon professional and occupational criteria; it grouped men and women in the world of work (*Erwerbsklassen*) according to their training, ownership of the means of production, or other access to given occupational positions.

The other concept of class (*Besitzklassen*) divided the same men and women according to their income, wealth, and the enjoyment of goods they could command. It ranked them as consumers (or savers), not as workers.[32]

This twofold ranking of economic inequality is instructive, for the social divisions that have political consequences appear to have changed from occupational classes to consumptive classes. Increasingly the orientation points for men and women in modern Western society seem to have become less styles of work than styles of life. But any stress upon consumptive classes will yield more catholic and less divisive rankings than an emphasis on occupation. The professor and the auto worker have divided work experiences. But they may both watch "Colombo" or the Boston Patriots; they purchase their televisions at Korvettes or Sears; they fill their children at McDonald's.[33]

This does not mean class divisions do not remain refractory. But it may alter the political consequences of class. The major source of radicalism, Marxist doctrines, have from their origin stressed the class divisions of the world of work more than those in the world of consumption. For Marx, man was a producer; his class position was determined by his control over capital or surplus labor; the good society would ultimately end the division of labor and restore a wholeness and integrity to work. For a world in which work was the overwhelming role for individual men and the salient point of identity, Marxism spoke to an authentic self-perception. Can this continue to be the case when labor fades in centrality? In their effort to revive Marxist radicalism from the somewhat mechanistic and overly optimistic emphases of the Second International, Marxists at the end of World War I sought to reassert the centrality of work by their stress on factory councils. Gramsci, Max Adler, Karl Korsch, and others attempted to define a radicalism through the workplace.[34] In part, they did so because they borrowed the vehicle of political transformation in Russia (the soviet) as a model for economic transformation in the West. In part, their stress represented a somewhat desperate search for the revolutionary constituency. The same may hold for the revival of workers' control and *autogestion* doctrines in contemporary Europe. Without deprecating the need for autonomy in the workplace, one must ask whether the workplace is still so important an orientation for the working class.

The changing focus of class identity was noted earlier by the right than by the left, and by none so acutely as those "neosocialists" who embraced quasi-fascistic doctrines in the 1920s and 30s, especially Hendrik De Man and Robert Michels.[35] For these theorists (and conservatives who followed later) the concept of class became less relevant than that of "the masses." The masses were no longer oriented towards the workplace; even more fundamental, they were not an assembly of rational actors but a quasi-mob (Le Bon's crowd) prey to murky and instinctual behavior and subject to demagogic appeals. In this respect, claimed the neosocialists, the nationalists and fascists of the right were more realistic, for they appealed to the collective urges of the masses, whereas Marxist orthodoxy was mired in an obsolete stress on labor and afflicted with bureaucratized organizations. The orthodox socialists of the old International—the Hilferdings, Kautskys, Turatis—were tiresome and shallow: socialist Settembrinis.

Indeed, the fascists did exploit the new possibilities inherent in class orientation based outside the workplace. This was ironic, for originally fascism claimed it would overcome the empty liberal abstractions of man as rational citizen to deal with man in his syndical group: *Homo faber.* In fact, even as fascists organized supposed syndical and corporative structures they treated man as audience-participant and not as maker. The mass rally, the gymnastic display, the speech from the Piazza Venezia, the exploitation of radio, the organization of leisure-time activities to win over workers, were predominantly fascist innovations. The radical right and not the socialist left sensed the political potency and bonds to be exploited in stressing the new nonworkshop orientations of "mass man."[36]

Sine the 1920s socialists, too, have learned to address man

in the marketplace as well as the workplace; by the mid-1930s the French Popular Front effectively wove together rallies, sport, and the like. Nonetheless, throughout the radical critique of contemporary capitalism there has persisted a puritanical and querulous anticonsumption tendency which fears the false consciousness of a mass society. In the late 1950s it characterized the British Labour Party; in the 1960s it found its way into the Marcusian theme of a suffocating liberal society in which man as consumer was manipulated and denatured. In sum, a deep ambivalence towards consumer orientation persists in socialist thinking.

Ultimately this reticence to confront class division as a stratification of consumers must limit the potency of radical recruitment. The grievances of the workplace are likely to prompt radicalism only among a restricted group, or only during those periods when economic distress otherwise radicalizes workers. What is the relevance of workplace control, or even *autogestion* of entire plants, in a complex economy where industries cannot exist alone? The failure of the workers' takeover to salvage the Lip watch-making operation in France is a sobering instance.

On the other hand, what radical movement lies at hand to exploit the discontents of consumer classes? Certainly not the so-called consumer movements, which tend to be elitist in composition and which usually renounce any aspirations of democratizing economic power. It has been suggested that the divisive geography of the modern city helps to define classes outside of their workplace in terms of their community. Between the downtown citadels of corporate power and the middle-class suburban dormitories a new proletariat is forged in the crucible of its own living space. The working-class community represents a unifying interface with the capitalist market as well as the real arena of what Marxists term the reproduction of the system, i.e., its continuing functioning through time.[37] Nonetheless, even Marxists agree that the urban community is a problematic nexus of class action. Its economic role is increasingly marginal; the bitter issue of race and education fragments it internally, and thus its politics are often tenaciously conservative. And insofar as a genuine community consciousness can be created, what will guarantee that it does not content itself with issues of local control that leave national structures of power unchallenged? Community action may beckon to radicals as workplace organization falters; but from the viewpoint of the left one may come perilously close to the Brook Farm or other utopianism that has traditionally been the fall-back position of an exhausted American reform effort.

The upshot of these developments is self-contradictory. On the one hand, Western society faces sources of radical discontent in its "cases," not classes—that is, in the groups aggrieved by regional backwardness, age-specific deprivation (pensioners), or vulnerability to inflation. New strains are thus put on the contemporary state, which is called upon to support these ad hoc unfortunates so private entrepreneurship can survive less burdened. Its party systems conceal conflicting interests that make coherent policy difficult; in short, it appears to face debilitating crisis. Nonetheless, at the same time no radical movement or voice seems capable of rallying the discontent in a cohesive way because most radical heirs have riveted their focus upon men's roles in the world of work during an era when these roles have become less encompassing.

What, then, is the prospect for stability or for radical transformation? Much, we have suggested, depends upon growth: that growth (from 1950 to 1973) which prevented social and political rivalry from becoming bitterly divisive, which made relative deprivation tolerable within a framework of absolute gain. Growth served as the great conservative idea for a generation, conservative in that it forestalled claims for redistribution on the left or an authoritarian search for power on the part of the right. Another buttress of stability consists of the rich elaboration of civil society, such that cooptation and involvement of once disaffected groups into an ongoing bargaining system reduces polarization. In this respect, the evolution of the state and its interpenetration with civil society also reduces the chances for conflicts between the principles that govern politics and those of the economic order. Nevertheless, this new political economy, so dependent upon inflation for the reconciliation of conflicting claims, must create its own losers. These are no longer the proletariat, but the congeries of cases and clients, who still (like Marx's peasantry: potatoes in a sack) do not form a fully organized class. But if modern society generates its own displaced persons—the shipwrecked of the corporate economy—it also undermines the appeals of traditional radicalism and leaves the organizing principles of a new revolutionary doctrine uncertain. Even if in difficulties itself, capitalism thus administers euthanasia to its adversaries. Certainly social change must continue, elites become displaced, authority erode, but perhaps at a continuing *andante* pace. Meanwhile give the last word to one of the most perceptive of the challengers, a half-century back: "The crisis consists precisely in the fact that the old is dying and the new cannot be born."[38]

Samuel P. Huntington is Frank G. Thomson Professor of Government and a member of the Executive Committee at Harvard University. Author of the seminal study Political Order in Changing Societies *and "The Change to Change: Modernization, Development, and Politics," Professor Huntington has written extensively on political change and the modernization process. Among his other works are* Political Power: USA/USSR *(co-author),* The Common Defense: Strategic Programs in National Politics, *and* Authoritarian Politics in Modern Society: The Dynamics of Established One-Party Systems *(co-editor).*

8
Remarks on the Meanings of Stability in the Modern Era
Samuel P. Huntington

I have been asked to discuss the meaning of stability in the modern era. My remarks will be in the nature of informal comments rather than a more formally structured essay. They are intended as a postscript and a counterpoint to the preceding discussion of various aspects of radicalism.

Social Science and Stability

My starting point is some of the recent published writings on stability produced by social scientists. Looking over the literature of those scholars who have tried to define stability, however, led me very quickly to make a small but not insignificant change in the title which was assigned to me, from "The Meaning of Stability" to "The Meanings of Stability," since recent literature on this question has defined stability in an almost infinite variety of ways.

There are, nonetheless, a few themes which do recur. Some analysts define stability in a relatively simple and direct way. In a 1974 article, Ted Gurr argued that a stable political system is "one whose authority patterns remain similar over a long period of time."[1] That clearly is a straightforward definition which gets at the idea of longevity, duration, and persistence. Other themes are those which stress absence of violence and disorder, that is, civic peace within a society; those which stress legitimacy of the established order; and those which to some degree speak about the performance of the system—its capabilities and effectiveness. In addition, the ideas of democracy, constitutionalism, adaptability, Harry Eckstein's "congruence," and a variety of other ideas have been advanced as useful in interpreting the concept of stability. In one recent article, Leon Hurwitz tried to sum up this literature in five concepts.[2] He identified the key meanings of stability as (1) the absence of violence; (2) governmental duration or longevity; (3) the existence of a legitimate constitutional regime; (4) the absence of structural change; and (5) the presence of a variety of multiple social attributes. This last catch-all concept includes almost everything and raises the basic question as to whether stability can be defined in terms of a single characteristic or whether it has to be thought of in terms of a multiplicity of attributes, the last being Professor Hurwitz's conclusion. If this is so, then the concept, indeed, remains elusive. It remains elusive because so many of the attributes, as his statistics demonstrate, just do not add up; they do not correlate with each other. Societies which are stable in one dimension are not stable in another.

There is also in the literature a somewhat different approach to stability, which focuses not on the components or the inherent characteristics of stable systems, but rather on what may be considered the conditions of stability. This approach covers a broad front, and it is somewhat hard at times to be sure whether people are talking about what characterizes stability or what causes stability. In this literature, a wide variety of factors has been associated with stability, including consensus, cross-cutting cleavages, social equality, habit, deference, political culture, democracy, and many others. In addition, there are those who look at the causes or conditions of stability in terms not of individual variables but of some sort of ratio or relationship among variables. There is, for instance, one work which sees political stability as the outcome of the relationship between political institutionalization and political participation. There are a variety of other works which look at it largely in terms of people's expectations and the ways in which their expectations and the actual course of developments relate to each other.[3] This can be a rather fruitful line of analysis: stability exists so long as a political system performs in a way that the prevailing opinion wants and/or expects it to perform. Francis Castles, for instance, has argued that political stability depends upon the relation between "the nature of social, economic, and political organization and the expectations held by political actors of the appropriate nature of social, economic, and political action (the latter variable will be termed *images of society*)."[4] It is this latter variable (and the emphasis is his) which he sees as the critical one. In a similar vein, André Beteille has pointed to the gap between the prevailing views on the desirability of equality and the extent of equality in society as the key factor in distinguishing harmonic (and hence stable) societies from those which are disharmonic (and hence unstable).[5]

This line of analysis clearly makes a major contribution in bringing both "subjective" and "objective" considerations into focus in connection with the conditions of political stability. It can, however, lead to some conclusions which go against common sense as to what is stable and what is unstable. If the prevailing expectations are for some form of violence and institutional breakdown, that is, for revolution or upheaval, then the failure of those expectations and the absence of revolution becomes evidence of instability. This is a difficulty in which much of the literature employing this kind of analysis gets entangled. Morrison and Stevenson, for instance, argue that political instability occurs when "the institutionalized patterns of authority break down and the *expected* compliance to political authorities is replaced by violence[emphasis added]."[6] In effect, then, if political compliance is not expected, instability does not occur. This problem is also manifested in the comments people continually make about a society like Italy, for example, which seems to be stably on the brink of instability and remains there because that is precisely where people expect it to be; no one has other expectations for it and consequently, in this sense, a stable situation exists.

Sources of Instability

By and large, when one speaks about stability, one is talking about relations between two or more things—about relationships among variables, among groups, among institutions. The concept of stability implies the idea of a system of recurring or continuing relationships. The idea of a system, however, implies boundaries, and boundaries imply the existence of a different, less regular, less intense set of relationships between that which is in the system and that which is outside. The forces making for the stability or instability of the system may, hence, be inside or outside the system. Whether they are conceived as being inside or outside obviously depends upon the definition applied to the term "system." One can, for instance, talk about the political system of a society apart from social, economic, and cultural dimensions of the society; or one can also think of a national system encompassing all these aspects of the society. The way in which one defines a system is a function of one's interests and purposes.

However defined, a system has boundaries, and it is, consequently, possible to distinguish between *intrinsic* factors promoting the stability or instability of the system which stem from the inherent workings of the system itself and *extrinsic* factors promoting the stability or instability of the system which come from outside the system. Many will argue that it is impossible or even undesirable to make such a sharp distinction. In reality this is true of course. Furthermore, any theoretical distinction is useful only for some purposes and not for others. Nevertheless, in trying to think about how one can usefully conceive of and give meaning to stability, the distinction between extrinsic and intrinsic causes of instability may be useful at least for some interesting purposes.

What may be thought of as the extrinsic sources of instability for the political system? Quite clearly, there is a wide variety of possibilities. A large number of these can be grouped under three general headings. *Social and economic change* encompasses industrialization, modernization, and a variety of other social and economic processes which may or may not operate autonomously from the political system, but which obviously have effects on political stability. A substantial literature exists which analyzes the impact of various types of economic development and social mobilization on political stability.[7] A second extrinsic source of instability is to be found in the relationship of communal groups to each other within a society, the degree of *communal cleavage* which exists, and the impact which this has on the political system. (By communal groups, I mean ethnic or nationality groups, racial groups, and religious groups.) Not only are communal cleavages a source of very considerable instability in many of the developing countries, but they also affect even the more economically advanced societies and may well affect even the Soviet Union.[8] Thirdly, there is the question of sources of instability coming from outside the national system, from the *international environment*. Defeat in war is almost always destabilizing. Victory in war is often destabilizing also. Some countries are much more subject than others to forces in the international environment, either for geographical reasons or simply for reasons of size or the nature of their resources, and consequently are much more vulnerable to threats of this nature. One of the peculiar characteristics of American historical development is that, by and large, the United States has not had to worry, at least until fairly recently, about international threats to its stability.

It is difficult to make global generalizations about the relative importance of these three extrinsic sources of political instability. Nonetheless, it might be useful to put forward one such generalization, one that may be applicable to developing countries, Western capitalist democracies, and communist countries alike. As a source of political instability, social and economic change is becoming of less significance; communal nationality cleavages have at least temporarily become more significant, but the most important challenges to the stability of political systems in the future will largely come from the international environment. The extent to which the world is becoming interdependent in many ways means, in terms of preserving the stability of political systems— whether communist or authoritarian or democratic—that the primary capability required will be the ability to deal effectively with the challenges which come from abroad. And this, it would appear, has some significant implications as to the directions in which the governments of nation-states are likely to evolve.

This becomes quite manifest if one simply thinks of the logical ways in which governments or political systems may attempt to cope with extrinsic threats to their stability. One way, of course, is the attempt to eliminate the source of the threat by controlling the processes of social change, suppressing communal differences, or removing threats from the international environment by war or conquest. A second way is to accommodate to the threats and challenges. A third way is to attempt to insulate the political system from the threats. The difficulties and costs of eliminating international challenges to the stability of a political system are in most cases prohibitive. Accommodation to such challenges may be possible in some cases, but it also requires levels of political insight, skill, and authority which are beyond the capacity of most governing elites. Consequently, the most probable governmental response to perceived threats to stability from the international environment is likely to be efforts to insulate the society from these challenges. Here communist states have a tremendous advantage because they are, by their very nature, much more able to do that than are other types of states. This is one major reason why communist states are by and large relatively stable and appear likely to remain so in the foreseeable future. Other governments and other types of political systems will also move in this direction. For example, this is obviously the case with governments in less developed countries which, perceiving multinational corporations as sources of external interference in the domestic economy, are asserting their control over their own resources. I think this will become increasingly true among the highly developed capitalist states as well, with an increased tendency towards what may be referred to as protectionism in the broad sense, of not simply raising tariffs but of trying to insulate the society more generally against threats to its stability from economic and political developments outside the system.

In this respect, one should not assume, as Professor Gurr does, that simple repression or state action to prevent change and to insulate the system from change is necessarily not going to be successful.[9] He suggests in his article that a key characteristic of stability is adaptability, which he defines in terms of a system changing itself in response to changes on the outside. I would suggest that there may well be a certain amount of resistant nonadaptability left in the governments of nation-states, which may preserve their stability for some time by insulation rather than accommodation.

With respect to intrinsic sources of instability, the relationships among the relevant variables can take various forms. There may be, for instance, some sort of equilibrium relationship or a recurring tendency towards equilibrium among these variables. Or a cyclical relationship may be present in which, in effect, equilibrium exists over a period of time with a recurring sequence of phases. Cyclical phenomena have not received the attention they deserve in the study of politics, and cyclical theories are viewed as rather a primitive way of thinking about things. Yet in understanding the interrelationship among variables, cyclical theories often make sense, as indeed the economists have known for some while, and they can be based upon a very realistic psychology. Cycles may be recurrent cycles which existed before. Or they can take the form of disequilibrating cycles in which the variables interact through a sort of vicious spiral which reproduces part of the phenomena which existed before, but in which there is also a secular trend towards the end of one cycle at one point or another. Or finally, of course, one can conceive simply of an unadorned secular trend towards disequilibrium in a system.

The line of analysis which we have been pursuing here suggests that the effort to define stability in terms of certain universal relationships among variables appropriate for all societies leaves something to be desired. More useful and appropriate for most purposes is to think of stability as a historical pattern of interaction among variables that is peculiar to each society. In fact, such society-distinct historical patterns of change do exist, and a society may be thought to be stable to the extent that its particular pattern of change (1) does not generate intrinsic forces leading to its own termination, and (2) does generate the capability to deal effectively with extrinsic sources of threats to societal stability through processes of elimination, accommodation, or insulation.

Patterns of System Change

Let us illustrate the points which have been made here about stability as a historical pattern of change by reference to several quite different societies, beginning with the Soviet Union.

The Soviet Union

Each of the three extrinsic sources of instability mentioned above has been the central feature of a theory concerning the evolution of the Soviet political system. The convergence theory, in effect, argues that social and economic development leading to a more complex and affluent society will make tight party control, ideological orthodoxy, and rigid bureaucracy increasingly dysfunctional. The result will be fundamental changes in the political system: liberalization, greater freedom of expression and dissent, more open debate of policy alternatives, and greater pluralism and decentralization of decision-making in both the polity and the economy. Somewhat similar results are also predicted by a parallel theory which stresses the gradual impact of international influences on the Soviet system, flowing from Western countries directly and indirectly through the Eastern European communist countries. Détente, increased Soviet trade with the West, increased opportunity for the movement of people and ideas back and forth between the Soviet Union and other countries, all gradually chip away at the massive Soviet political monolith. Finally, it has also recently been suggested that the nationality problem may lead to a major crisis in the Soviet Union, in part simply because it exists and in part because the inherent nature of a communist system tends to stimulate nationalism. In short, these theories posit that the historical pattern of change in the Soviet Union is incapable of dealing with the challenges posed by a more complex economy, increased international involvement, and nationality conflicts. More generally, the argument has also been made that there may be intrinsic sources of instability at work in the Soviet system, long-run secular trends towards degeneration which the regime is also incapable of countering effectively without fundamentally changing its own nature.[10]

It is impossible to evaluate here the validity of these theories. To date, however, the Soviet system has certainly demonstrated the ability to contain or protect itself from extrinsic challenges. None of the challenges which are identified for the future, moreover, appear to be qualitatively different from the challenges which the Soviet system has demonstrated the ability to deal with effectively in the past. In addition, developments which may be the sign of degeneration or instability in one type of political system do not necessarily have the same import in a different type of political system. Bureaucratization, routinization, a decline in ideological commitment, a decline of the attractiveness of political as compared to other careers, some dispersion of policy initiative—all these appear more likely to be signs of the institutionalization and consolidation of the system than of its impending downfall.[11]

Developing Countries

Many different political change patterns can be found in the countries of Asia, Africa, and Latin America, which are

entering into the processes of industrialization and modernization. Generalizations are extraordinarily difficult. Social
and economic change, communal cleavages, and the international environment clearly pose major extrinsic challenges
to the political stability of most developing countries. In
addition, however, the variables within the political system
itself often seem to interact in ways conducive not to equilibrium and stability but to periodic breakdowns. Many
Third World countries, for instance, particularly in Latin
America and East Asia, have reached intermediate levels of
development where the whole complex of problems involving the full participation of the working class in politics
has become a major political issue. Such countries are often
characterized by one or another of the two "vicious circle"
patterns of political change.[12]

The *populist pattern* involves a formally democratic political
system and increasing political participation by working class
groups. This leads to an emphasis in governmental policy on the
promotion of social and economic equity through progressive
taxation, welfare programs, land reform, and public ownership of key industries. It also leads to economic nationalism in
the form of opposition to foreign capital and the nationalization of foreign-owned businesses. These policies, in turn, tend
to produce low rates of economic growth and high rates of inflation. Thus, growth stops or slows drastically at the same
time that an increasing number of people have begun to demand
their share of the pie. The result is an intensification of class
conflict and political turmoil as middle-class groups mobilize
to counter the demands of the lower classes. This, in turn, increases the power of the more extreme groups on the left,
who push governmental policies in more radical directions. The
cycle thus repeats itself. The problem in such a society, as
Salvator Allende put it in August 1973, "is to avoid both civil
war and military intervention," and his fate a month later
underlines the difficulties in avoiding one of those outcomes.
As in Chile, increasing polarization and political mobilization
is likely to lead to a military coup which breaks the vicious
circle and produces a "participation implosion."

A *technocratic pattern* of change, on the other hand, may evolve along a vicious circle in just the reverse direction. In this case, an authoritarian regime suppresses political participation, particularly by the working classes, minimizes socioeconomic equity as a goal of government policy, promotes high rates of economic growth, including foreign investment as one means of encouraging that growth, and keeps a lid on overt social conflict and political turmoil. This result is at least temporary political stability. However, the exacerbation of social and economic inequalities, plus the lack of opportunity for political participation, may lead to a buildup of resentment and eventually a "participation explosion" in which disaffected and disadvantaged social forces break loose in a revolutionary upheaval and overthrow the system. Precisely because of this possibility, the government of Brazil, whose evolution since 1964 has been very much along the lines of the technocratic model, launched in 1974 an effort at "political decompression," designed to allow a certain modest opportunity for political dissent and opposition and thus reduce the likelihood of a major political explosion. Whether the Brazilian government remains willing and able to pursue this course successfully will be some indication of whether a technocratic pattern of change can be modified so as to promote greater political stability.

The United States

Two broad theories exist concerning the intrinsic stability of democratic political systems. The optimistic theory holds that because of the opportunities they provide for political articulation, mobilization, and organization, democracies have intrinsic tendencies towards stability. Their structural characteristics enable them to respond, to adapt, to capitalize on feedback, to absorb new groups and to incorporate them into the system. The pessimistic theory, on the other hand, was perhaps most succinctly articulated by John Adams, who said, "Democracy never lasts long; it soon wastes, exhausts and murders itself. There never was a democracy yet which did not commit suicide." In somewhat more elegant form, this theme was, of course, developed by de Tocqueville and later by Schumpeter, Lippmann, and others. An "excess of democracy" (in David Donald's term) encourages an overload of demands on government and an undermining of political authority, which then lead to either the breakdown of society or the emergence of a charismatic dictator.[13]

How do these theories relate to the American experience? Political change in the United States has, I believe, taken place not in accordance with what we often think of as the usual model of relatively gradual, constant, incremental change, but rather through sporadic periods of upheaval and rapid change.[14] Within the political system, and to a certain extent in social and economic policy as well, periods of rapid change are followed by periods of very considerable stability. There is perhaps a certain analogy to earthquakes here. Stresses and strains build up along fault lines and then at some point an earthquake occurs and the geological plates get back into balance for a while and then stresses begin to build up again. It is a historical fact that the United States has had periods of great policy innovation, changes of political participation, shifts in public concerns and attitudes, realignment of political parties, shifts in the power of governmental institutions, major efforts to revamp those institutions, and challenges to the existing centers of power—efforts to reassert the ideals of liberty, equality, and justice for all, and to bring about a redemocratization of the system.

This goes to the heart of another issue—namely, whether such periods of innovation and change are best understood as destabilizing challenges to authority or as reaffirmations of traditional American values. In my opinion, both views are right. It has happened before in our history, during the revolutionary period, the Jacksonian period, and during the progressive years, and it has happened again during the past decade: an attack on authority, political and otherwise, in terms of very traditional and conservative American values. This is precisely what has made the United States, as Beteille has pointed out, the most disharmonic society in the world, that is, the society in which there is the greatest gap, in his terms, between the existential and the normative orders—the greatest gap between the political ideals and beliefs which are widely held within the society and what actually goes on in the society and in the government and the economy.[15] This gap is the principal intrinsic source of instability in the operation of the American political system. In this sense, far from being a source of stability, the consensus on basic American values is the primary source of instability. During the past decade these basic American values have been brought to the fore and used to challenge established institutions and rather drastically to overhaul and change the power of bureaucratic agencies, the presidency, and other established interests in our society. It is precisely these developments which call into question the ability of the United States to deal effectively with extrinsic sources of instability.

This, then, is the major problem which we may be confronting in terms of stability in the United States today: we are moving in the direction of reducing the intrinsic instability which comes from too large a gap between American political practice and American ideals of liberty, equality, and popular control over government. Major changes in that direction should produce greater stability and certainly should slow down the flood of dissidence in the system. But, at the same time, a real question emerges concerning the extent to which, by doing this, we may not be leaving our system vulnerable to extrinsic threats and, in particular, threats from the international environment. The reduction in the power and authority of government which is taking place could make the system extraordinarily vulnerable to challenges from both allies and enemies abroad.

One major challenge the system will inevitably be facing soon is how to react to military defeat. It may well be that many of the forces which are at work may minimize the effects of what has happened in Southeast Asia, but that would be a very optimistic view. The problem of coming to grips with what did happen there and of dealing with the consequences of the Vietnamese War is likely to be with us for a long time to come. That is one type of extrinsic challenge with which the American political system has had almost no prior experience, and the issue is whether the process of dealing with recent intrinsic challenges to political stability has left the system with the capability to deal with this and similar major extrinsic challenges.

Stability as Change

The main thrust of my remarks has been that political stability can be most meaningfully conceived of in terms of historical patterns of change peculiar to individual societies. Just as the meaning of the good life differs from individual to individual, so also the meaning of political stability differs from society to society. Attempts to measure political stability on a cross-national basis in terms of universally defined criteria and common indices are not likely to be very meaningful or useful. In assessing the meaning of political stability for any particular society, consequently, three questions must be asked and answered.

1. What is the nature of the historical pattern of political change characteristic of the society?

2. Is this pattern of political change intrinsically destabilizing or are there elements in it which tend to maintain an equilibrium among the components of the political system?

3. Does this historical pattern of political change enable the political system to eliminate, accommodate to, or insulate itself from the most probable and serious extrinsic challenges to its stability?

Notes

Notes to Chapter 1

1. The term "charter myth" refers to the popularly accepted image presented by the political and cultural elite about the founding of the existing politico-socio-economic system and the principles which underlie it. See Barrington Moore, Jr., *Political Power and Social Theory* (New York: Harper & Row, 1965), pp. 10-16.

2. I also focus on the first question because it is not discussed extensively in any other essays in this volume. Important aspects of the second and the third questions, however, are dealt with by Alexander Dallin in chap. 3.

3. The total membership of communist parties in industrialized non-communist societies is estimated at about 2,850,000. Of these, the Italian and the French communist parties alone account for 1,700,000 and 500,000 members respectively. See Richard F. Staar, ed., *Yearbook on International Communist Affairs 1976* (Stanford, Calif.: Hoover Institution Press, 1976), pp. xv-xx.

4. Transcript of the discussion of the third workshop on radicalism, Research Institute on International Change, Columbia University, 2 April 1975, p. 8 (hereafter the transcripts will be cited as Transcript 1, Transcript 2, etc.).

5. Public criticism of the Soviet past among the European communist parties is almost entirely limited to the Stalinist period; it is often very sharp and goes much beyond the Soviet attacks on Stalinism at the height of the Khrushchevian campaign. See, for example, the most recent, interesting, and quite objective histories of the Soviet Union by an Italian and a French communist: Giuseppe Boffa, *Storia dell'Unione Sovietica* (Rome: Mondatori, 1976); and Jean Elleinstein, *Histoire du phénomène Stalinien* (Paris: Grasset, 1975). While the disapprobation among the New Left concerning the Soviet past concentrates on the Stalinist period, there is notable criticism of the early periods as well in the analysis of the Bolshevik Party during the Russian revolution. See, for example, Daniel Cohn-Bendit and Gabriel Cohn-Bendit, *Obsolete Communism: The Left-Wing Alternative* (New York: McGraw-Hill Book Co., 1968), pp. 199-245.

A tendency to reach further back critically into the Soviet past can be seen lately in even some of the moderate New Left publications. It comes out clearly, for instance, when one compares the treatment of the Russian revolution and the Leninist postrevolutionary period in the issue of the *Monthly Review* devoted to the fiftieth anniversary of the Russian revolution with a recent issue in which a review article enthusiastically supports Charles Bettelheim's highly critical study *Les Luttes de classes en URSS 1917-1923* (Paris: Maspero/Seuil, 1974).

Compare, for example, Leon Huberman and Paul M. Sweezy, "Lessons of Soviet Experience," *Monthly Review* 19, no. 6 (November 1967): 9-21, with Paul M. Sweezy, "The Nature of Soviet Society," *Monthly Review* 26, no. 6 (November 1974): 1-16.

For a shrewd analysis of Bettelheim's, and incidentally *Monthly Review*'s attitudinal metamorphosis regarding the Leninist Soviet experience and its sources, see Ralph Miliband, "Bettelheim and Soviet Experience," *New Left Review* 91 (May–June 1975): 57-66.

The New Left's detestation of the Soviet system is naturally reciprocated by Soviet detestation of the New Left in industrial democracies. A typical example of Soviet invectives addressed against them is a pamphlet by V. Bogorad and R. Matveyev, with a title that leaves nothing to the imagination—*Playing into the Hands of the Monopolies* (Moscow: Novosti Publishing House, 1976).

6. One observer of West European communism remarks:

> West European communists, who had long thought that the choice facing them was simply a tactical one—whether to seek Byzantine power by electoral or revolutionary means—discovered

that the choice was rather different. They could cling to the Byzantine ideal and condemn themselves to perpetual, ineffectual opposition—or they could participate actively and effectively in political life, though at the cost of accepting the presuppositions of democracy.

(Erazim Kohak, "European Communists and European Defense," *Dissent* [Summer 1976], p. 274.)

7. John Strachey, "The Strangled Cry," *Encounter* 15, no. 5 (November 1960): 6.

8. This process is of long standing in some of the parties, especially the Italian Communist Party (PCI), and it has accelerated with the expansion of these parties' indigenous power base.

The tension within the PCI leadership, as related not simply to the question of the leaders' ideological position but to their social interests as well, was described almost two decades ago by an authority on Italian communism, as follows:

As long as the PCI was a small illegal party, unconditional adherence to the Soviets, its source of power and life, was the only objective of its leading group. Now that it was a large mass movement, its power rested also upon the roots that it had succeeded in extending into Italian social reality. Except for this reality, the Togliattis, the Longos, the Secchias, the D'Onofrios had all that the Soviet Union could give them: a bureaucratic position that was economically secure as long as they obeyed Communist discipline. A part of Italian life, they were top leaders, men politically on the international level and not obscure collaborators of exile reviews.

(Georgio Galli, *Storia del Partito communista italiano* [Milan: Schwartz, 1958], p. 261, as quoted in William E. Griffith, ed., *Communism in Europe, vol. 1* [Cambridge, Mass.: M.I.T. Press, 1964], p. 307.)

9. In this respect it may be pertinent to recall Raymond Aron's remark about Sartre's sophistry in justifying Marxism-Leninism, Stalinism, and the practices of the communist movement: "Nothing that he condemned morally rather than politically led him to break with the communist party or to deny to it the status of representing the working class and socialism." (*History and the Dialectic of Violence* [New York: Harper & Row, 1976], pp. 116-17.)

10. The term "formal democracy" remains one of the most insidious and dangerous concepts with wide currency in radical thinking and movements (left and right). Introduced initially by Marxists to describe the insufficiency, the inadequacy, and the limitations and inequalities of political freedoms in capitalist societies, the term gradually became one of total opprobrium, as if political freedoms in themselves and by themselves, and not their imperfections and limitations, were evil. A dissident Polish Marxist (the former minister of culture in the Gomulka government) makes the following observation with regard to this: "In our political life . . . 'democracy' became a sensitive, if not outright dangerous concept. Judging by some public pronouncements, one would think that democracy is a bourgeois contrivance which, to be sure, has no general utility in capitalist countries, but is, however, excellently suited to be used in the struggle against socialism." (Wladyslaw Biénkowski, *Motory i Hamulce Socjalizmu* [Paris: Instytut Literacki, 1969], p. 70.)

11. The arguments for the necessity of such an exchange are still being used in the defense of restrictions of democratic freedoms in developing nations. These arguments form the base of the justification, for instance, of Indira Gandhi's attempt at authoritarian transformation of India's democracy. The short- or middle-range efficacy of such an exchange for the achievement of specific socioeconomic goals, while debatable, is conceivable. Yet at the same time historical experience points to an immutable consequence of such a process: the political system that is established primarily to achieve social and economic goals becomes highly valued itself, thereby causing the subordination of allegedly highly desirable social and economic tasks to the preservation of that system, which then becomes frozen and sanctified in an ideological formula.

12. In *Nouvel Observateur*, 30 June 1975.

13. The radical attraction to Cuba and the disillusion with the proceeding institutionalization of the Cuban revolution in an authoritarian mold has already progressed quite far indeed. See, for example, the report on Cuba in a European New Left publication: Gunter Maschke, "Cubanischer Taschenkalendar," *Kursbuch* 30 (December 1972): 129-59; or José Yglesias, "A Cuban Poet in Trouble: The Case of Herbert Padilla," *New York Review of Books*, 3 June 1971. It is ironic that some of the most apologetic recent accounts of present-day Cuba come from American liberals rather than radicals, for example, from Frank Mankiewicz and Kirby Jones, *With Fidel: A Portrait of Castro* (Chicago:

Playboy Press, 1976); and Herbert L. Matthews, *Revolution in Cuba: An Essay in Understanding* (New York: Charles Scribner's Sons, 1976).

For a very balanced and well-documented account of Cuba, see Carmelo Mesa-Lago, *Cuba in the 1970's: Pragmatism and Institutionalization* (Albuquerque: University of New Mexico Press, 1976). If the present trend in post-Mao China towards the dominance of "bureaucrats" over "ideologues" continues, one may predict with a fair degree of certainty an accelerating radical disillusionment with the Chinese experience.

14. For a basic discussion of the primordial socialist message, its historical peregrination, the confusion accompanying it, and its contemporary relevance, see C. A. R. Crosland, *The Future of Socialism* (New York: Schocken Books, 1963), chap. 4.

15. In counterdistinction to these previous turning-point disputes, where the positions of all major participants in the debates represented to a large extent a departure from the existing orthodoxies, in the present disputes the position of one group of participants shows no change. The parties of the Soviet Union and of the East European Soviet bloc are still propounding the version of Marxism characterized, to use Kolakowski's expression, by "sclerotic religiosity."

The reactionary, petrified nature of these regimes and of those communist parties out of power that still support the societal model they created underlies Kolakowski's proposition that:

> The word *socialism* has come to have more than one meaning, and is no longer synonymous with the word *left*. And this is why a regeneration of the concept of the Left is necessary— also so that we can delimit the meaning of socialist slogans. We therefore propose the term *leftist socialism.*

(Leszek Kolakowski, *Toward a Marxist Humanism: Essays on the Left Today*, trans. Jane Zielonko Peel [New York: Grove Press, 1968], pp. 82-83.)

16. In addition to the discussion of these issues among the Western socialists, communists, and especially the New Left, some of the most important statements are coming from dissident Marxist groups or individuals in Eastern Europe, particularly though not exclusively from Yugoslavia. See the writings of the members of the neo-Marxist group in Yugoslavia which publishes the journal *Praxis* (Zagreb), which has an international edition in English, French, and German and which appears quarterly.

From Poland comes the important book by the political economist Wlodzimierz Brus, *Uspolecznienie a Ustroj Polityczny* (Uppsala: ANEKS, 1975).

The only major work from the Soviet Union of this type is the discourse by Roy A. Medvedev, *On Socialist Democracy* (New York: Alfred A. Knopf, 1975).

17. In a recent article on changes in popular beliefs in the United States, one author remarks,

> Recent American history has been marked by certain changes in popular attitudes that, though difficult to measure, may be the most significant events of our times. Old beliefs and old institutions are now more distrusted than at perhaps any time in our history. There is a significant class of persons who appear ready to accept, at least provisionally, almost every new idea, and who correspondingly tend to be at least mildly alienated from what has been regarded up to now as the mainstream of American society. The mainstream, meanwhile, appears to be getting narrower and more sluggish, the tributaries more numerous and friskier.
>
> The list of such changes could go on endlessly, but a few of the more obvious manifestations of recent intellectual iconoclasm would include the following: that America as a nation is morally soiled in its dealings with both foreign peoples and many of its own citizens; that American economic achievements are at best ambiguous, both morally and in terms of the welfare of the citizenry; that American political institutions no longer work as they should; that sexual activity apart from heterosexual marriage is morally right and should be socially respectable; that traditional family roles and family authority distort the personalities of those involved; that church membership is unimportant and belief in God perhaps irrelevant to human living; that the wisdom of the past is largely superstitious and empty; that self-gratification (without harming others) is the proper purpose of human existence; and that institutions (of whatever kind) tend inevitably to inhibit such gratification.
>
> The dynamics of public opinion—especially the process by which beliefs that seem deeply held are suddenly thrown off with little apparent regret or agony—remain largely unexplored. Since America is at least a quasi-democratic society, changes in social values have to percolate up from below, in the sense that

broad popular acceptance (not necessarily by a majority) is required for social respectability. There are no institutions (the Supreme Court perhaps comes closest) capable of simply decreeing such changes. Nonetheless, all these changes originate, in virtually every instance, with a numerically almost insignificant minority.

(James Hitchcock, "The Dynamics of Popular Intellectual Change," *The American Scholar* 45 [Autumn 1976] : 522-23.)

18. *Commentary* 62, no. 3 (September 1976): 77.

19. In January 1976 the Research Institute on International Change organized a conference titled "The Relevance of Liberalism," the proceedings of which were published in 1977 by Westview Press. In a major chapter of the book, "The Antimonies of Liberalism," Professor Edward Shils argues that in the United States the liberal community has become seriously polarized into what he has called its "autonomist" and "collectivist" variants. Although both groups still have much in common in their intellectual traditions, the divergence and tensions between them are gradually becoming more acute. This divergence manifests itself in differing attitudes towards existing institutions, towards political authority, and espcially towards control over the executive branch, as well as towards the distribution of resources and the provision of services by the central government.

In sum, there has been an evolution of liberalism from a doctrine which was critical of the authority of the state and which recommended private and voluntary action, into a set of beliefs which remains critical of authority in nearly all its forms but which at the same time supports the extremely comprehensive and penetrating extension of governmental action. This newer (and now dominant) "collectivist" liberalism is by no means homogeneous, but it is clearly different from what liberalism used to be, and may be in danger of obliterating itself through a gradual and unexamined modification of its postulates.

20. Liberalism, writes a leftist critic of the American system,

is no longer a triumphant theology. Liberalism no longer either satisfies mass needs or represents elite persuasions in an unqualified manner. Something had been missed. Liberalism itself has undergone huge changes and is faced not so much with challenge on the Right as thunder from the Left. Beyond that, liberalism's pragmatic and pluralistic character only serves to polarize further the ideological framework in American life. Liberalism, far from being the accepted foundation of all political rhetoric, has now entered a stage where it is fighting for its life, and where the majority of the people are well contented with identifying with the word *conservatism* even if they do not accept its contents.

(Irving Louis Horowitz, *Ideology and Utopia in the United States 1956-1976* [New York: Oxford University Press, 1977], p. 8.)

21. Leszek Kolakowski, "Introduction," in Leszek Kolakowski and Stuart Hampshire, eds., *The Socialist Idea: A Reappraisal* (New York: Basic Books, 1974), p. 15.

22. For a comprehensive review of the socialist left see Bogdan Denitch, "The Dilemmas and Prospects of the Socialist Left" (paper prepared for the Conference on Democratic Socialism, 7 October 1976, Research Institute on International Change, Columbia University. This paper is to be published in *Dissent* in the summer of 1977 and ultimately in a book on democratic socialism published under the auspices of the Research Institute on International Change).

23. The evolution of European social democracy is treated in a book by John Vaizey, *Revolutions of Our Time: Social Democracy* (New York: Praeger Publishers, 1972); Neil McInnes provides an interesting overview of postwar developments in "European Social Democracy since the War," *Survey* 70/71 (Winter–Spring 1969): 18-31; for a critical rejoinder to the above, see Walter Kendall, "McInnes and Social Democracy—A Rejoinder," *Survey* 72 (Summer 1969): 86-90.

24. Kolakowski and Hampshire, *The Socialist Idea*, p. 249.

25. For a good review of the critical, that is, noncommunist, radical ideas in France, see Richard Gombin, *The Origins of Modern Leftism*, trans. Michael K. Perl (Harmondsworth, England: Penguin Books, 1975); for a similar analysis concerning the development of radical thought and its relation to Marxism in the United States, see Peter Clecak, *Radical Paradoxes: Dilemmas of the American Left: 1945-1970* (New York: Harper & Row, 1973).

26. David Lowenthal, "Orwell's Political Pessimism in '1984'," *Polity* 2, no. 2 (Winter 1969): 174.

27. Willy Brandt, Bruno Kreiske, and Olaf Palme, *Briefe und Gespräche, 1972 bis 1975* (Köln: Europäische Verlagsanstalt, 1976), p. 7.

28. In the United States these writings are exemplified by such works as Michael Harrington's *The Other America: Poverty in the United*

States, rev. ed. (New York: Macmillan, 1969) and Robert Heilbroner's *An Inquiry Into the Human Prospect* (New York: W.W. Norton & Co., 1974).

29. See, for example, another rediscovery of the "real" Marx in Michael Harrington, *The Twilight of Capitalism* (New York: Simon & Schuster, 1976). In this respect Samuelson's saying, "Marxism has been the opiate of Marxists," is very appropriate.

30. Alvin Gouldner, *The Dialectic of Ideology and Technology* (New York: Seabury Press, 1976), p. 116.

31. There is a long-standing programmatic and psychological pre-disposition among the radical left to treat the desired items in the political and intellectual realm as "luxuries," in counterdistinction to the socioeconomic "necessities." Or, to use the words of the previously quoted dissident Polish Marxist, to treat the first as "consumption" and the second as "production" items. (See Biénkowski, "What is freedom intended for? Is freedom a 'consumption' good?," in *Motory i Hamulce Socjalizmu*, pp. 80-89). Such a predisposition grows partly from the tendency to treat socioeconomic items as autonomous and political items as dependent, and has one of its obvious sources in the radical left of the Marxian tradition.

32. Isaac Balbus, Transcript 4, p. 15.

33. Remarks one of the leading European Marxian sociologists:

Some writers, perhaps, would still want to contrast "bourgeois sociology" (which is conservative) with "Marxist theory" (which is radical), but this view is no longer widely held. At the present time Marxism may serve in some societies to uphold a particular *status quo* and to inhibit criticism. Elsewhere, at least in its more orthodox forms, it may be seen as having lost some of its radical thrust, because it no longer bears upon the major conflicts and problems of the age and, by ignoring certain issues, has forfeited its liberating character.

(T.B. Bottomore, *Sociology as Social Criticism* [New York: William Morrow & Co., 1976], p. 11.)

34. Gilles Martinet, "The Theory and Ideology of Socialism," in Kolakowski and Hampshire, *The Socialist Idea*, p. 245.

35. Christopher Lasch, "The Narcissist Society," *New York Review of Books*, 30 September 1976, p. 5.

36. Source: *The Economist*, 29 November 1975, p. 17.

37. In the British Labour Party's parliamentary membership, for example, the left wing is primarily represented by the "Tribune" group. At present this group accounts for about one-fourth of total Labour MPs. What is more important is the *trend* of its growing strength within Labour, as shown in the following table:

Time of Election to Parliament	*Members of the Tribune Group as % of Total Labour MPs Elected*
First elected before 1950	10
First elected 1950–63	13
First elected 1964–73	19
First elected February 1974	58
First elected October 1974	60

Source: *The Economist*, 26 April 1975.

Commenting on the vote for the new prime minister within the Labour Party after Wilson's resignation, one European publication concludes: "The final results of the election show that Jenkins (the leader of the social-democrats within the Labour Party) is no longer indispensable to the Party, since he is perceived as unacceptable to the left-wing. Michael Foote, leader of the left-wingers has become indispensable to the British Labour Party." (*Europe,* Luxembourg, Agence internationale d'information pour la presse, 23 April 1976.)

38. Norman H. Nie, Sidney Verba, and John R. Petrocik, *The Changing American Voter* (Cambridge, Mass.: Harvard University Press, 1976), p. 348.

39. Ibid., pp. 346-48.

40. The general theme "the end of American exceptionalism" is suggested and developed by Daniel Bell in an article by this title in *Public Interest* 41 (Fall 1975): 193-224.

41. For Pareto, see Vilfredo Pareto, *The Mind and Society*, 5 vols., reprint ed. (New York: Harcourt Brace, 1963), especially paragraphs 2183-86, 2190-97, 2340-41; for an interesting current evaluation of Pareto relevant to our subject, see Raymond Aron, "Pareto's Legacy,"

Encounter 47, no. 5 (November 1976): 43-53. See also the essays on Pareto in James H. Meisel, ed., *Pareto and Mosca* (Englewood Cliffs, N.J.: Prentice-Hall, 1965). For Michels, see Robert Michels, *Political Parties, A Sociological Study of the Oligarchical Tendencies of Modern Democracy*, trans. E. Paul and C. Paul (New York: Colliers Books, 1962) and *First Lectures in Political Sociology*, trans. Alfred De Gracia (New York: Harper & Row, 1965). For Schumpeter, see Joseph A. Schumpeter, *Capitalism, Socialism and Democracy*, 3rd ed. (New York: Harper & Row, 1962), especially chap. 13. For a contemporary analysis and explanation, see Helmut Schelsky, *Die Arbeit tun die anderen. Klassenkampf und Priesterherrschaft der Intellektuellen* (Opladen: Westdeutscher Verlag, 1975). For a critical and brilliant rejoinder to Schelsky, see Richard Lowenthal, "Neues Mittelalter oder anomische Kulturkrise?," *Merkur* 29, no. 9 (1975): 802-18. For a more recent article by Richard Lowenthal pursuing a similar theme (his review of Bell's *The Cultural Contradictions of Capitalism*) see *Dissent* (Fall 1976), pp. 437-48. For a most recent original attempt to specify the historical mechanisms that contribute to the radicalization of Western intellectuals, an attempt that argues these mechanisms' indispensability to contemporary revolutionary movements, see Alvin Gouldner, "Prologue to a Theory of Revolutionary Intellectuals," *Telos* 26 (1976). For a general review of the analysis of diverse points of view on the relations of intellectuals with ideologies and politics one may find very useful George B. de Huszar, ed., *The Intellectuals: A Controversial Portrait* (Glencoe, Ill.: Free Press, 1960) and the very balanced and complete analysis by Theodor Geiger, *Aufgaben und Stellung der Intelligenz in der Gesellschaft* (Stuttgart: F. Enke, 1949).

42. Peter L. Berger, "The Socialist Myth," *The Public Interest* 44 (Summer 1976).

43. Ibid., pp. 7, 9-10, 11.

44. See Daniel Bell, *The Coming of Post-Industrial Society* (New York: Basic Books, 1973), and Irving Kristol, "When Virtue Loses All Her Loveliness—Some Reflections on Capitalism and 'The Free Society'," *Public Interest* 21 (Fall 1970).

45. Quoted by Stephen Miller, "The Poverty of Socialist Thought," *Commentary* 62, no. 2 (August 1976): 37. This thought was much better expressed by G.D.H. Cole before World War II: "The will to socialism is based on a lively sense of wrongs crying for redress." (*The Simple Case for Socialism* [London: Golancz, 1935], p. 15.)

46. Charles Taylor, "Socialism and Weltanschauung," in Kolakowski and Hampshire, *The Socialist Idea*, p. 48.

47. Samuel P. Huntington, *Political Order in Changing Societies* (New Haven, Conn.: Yale University Press, 1968), p. 47.

48. Ibid., pp. 266-68.

49. Walter Dean Burnham, "American Parties in the 1970's: Beyond Party?," in Louis Massel and Paul M. Sacks, eds., *The Future of Political Parties, Sage Electoral Studies Yearbook* (Beverly Hills, Calif.: Sage Publications, 1975) 1: 258.

50. Charles Maier, *Recasting Bourgeois Europe: Stabilization in France, Germany, and Italy in the Decade After World War I* (Princeton, N.J.: Princeton University Press, 1975).

51. Antonio Gramsci, *Selections from the Prison Notebooks*, ed. and trans. Quintin Hoare and Geoffrey Nowell Smith (New York: International Publishers, 1971), p. 238.

52. Michel J. Crozier, Samuel P. Huntington, and Joji Watanuki, *The Crisis of Democracy, Report of the Governability of Democracies to the Trilateral Commission* (New York: New York University Press, 1975), pp. 162-63.

53. Ibid., pp. 188-90.

54. Charles Taylor, "Socialism and Weltanschauung," p. 54.

55. William E. Griffith, Transcript 4, p. 18.

56. A most recent strong critique of the gloomy predictions about the future of democratic societies and particularly of the Trilateral Commission's report is contained in an article by Professor Elie Kedourie, "Is Democracy Doomed?," *Commentary* 62, no. 5 (November 1976): 39-43.

57. It may be rather exaggerated to venture a *forecast*, as Stanislav Andreski does, "that it will be no mean task to prevent the United States from sliding into authoritarianism." (*Prospects of a Revolution in the U.S.A.* [New York: Harper & Row, 1973], p. 108.) One of the major premises on which his prediction is based is worth quoting. Writes Andreski:

> Every human society which has endured long enough to leave records, or to be described by travellers or ethnographers, has had elaborate customs and institutions which were effective in instilling into the young the sentiments necessary for its

perpetuation. Now for the first time in recorded history Western capitalism offers us a spectacle of a system which not only has given up altogether the task of moral education, but actually employs vast resources and the means of persuasion of unprecedented power to destroy the customs, norms and ideals indispensible for its survival; and to implant fundamentally anti-social attitudes which are incompatible with any conceivable social order. It would be miraculous if a social order which permits such massive anti-socialization could fail to destroy itself.

(Ibid.)

58. For a recent interesting and pessimistic analysis of the British situation by a prominent labor politician and author see Stephen Haseler, *The Death of British Democracy* (London: Elek, 1976).

59. Ralf Dahrendorf in Crozier, Huntington, and Watanuki, *The Crisis of Democracy*, p. 194. For the development of these ideas by the same author in a more complete and theoretical way see "Liberty and Equality—Reflections of a Sociologist on a Classical Theme of Politics," in Ralf Dahrendorf, *Essays in the Theory of Society* (Stanford, Calif.: Stanford University Press, 1968), pp. 179-214, and *Die Neue Freiheit, Uberleben und Gerechtigkeit in einer veränderten Welt* (Munich and Zurich: R. Piper Verlag, 1975).

60. See, for example, Amilcar Cabral, *Revolution in Guinea*, trans. and ed. Richard Handyside (New York: Monthly Review Press, 1969); Rudolph Dutschke, *The Student Rebellion or The New Opposition* (New York: Little, Brown and Co., 1969); Frantz Fanon, *The Wretched of the Earth* (New York: Grove Press, 1968); *A Dying Colonialism* (New York: Evergreen Books, 1965); and Ernesto Guevara, *Guerilla Warfare* (London: Cassels, 1962).

See also Tom Fawthrop, "Towards an Extra-Parliamentary Opposition"; Inti Peredo, "We Will Return to the Mountains! Victory or Death!"; Pierre Frank, "From a Student Upheaval Towards a Proletarian Socialist Revolution"; and Tariq Ali, "The Age of Permanent Revolution"; all in Tariq Ali, ed., *The New Revolutionaries: A Handbook on the International Radical Left* (New York: William Morrow & Co., 1969).

For changes and contemporary adaptations in the traditional Trotskyite approach to revolution see Ernest Mandel, ed., *50 Years of World Revolution: An International Symposium* (New York: Pathfinder Press, 1971).

For the orthodox Western communist critique of new revolutionary theories see Jack Woodis, *New Theories of Revolution* (New York: International Publishers, 1972).

61. Regis Debray, *Revolution in the Revolution?* (New York: Grove Press, 1967).

62. Transcript 1, p. 78.

63. For a useful general review of the leftist stream in present-day Marxism see Besim Ibrahimpasic, "Left Wing Heterodoxy in Contemporary Marxism," *Survey* (Sarajevo) 3, no. 1 (1976): 37-58.

For an especially important statement of the intellectual and political leftist position see Rossana Rossanda, *Il Manifesto, Analyses et thèses de la nouvelle extrême-gauche italienne* (Paris: Editions du Seuil, 1971). For an evaluation of *Il Manifesto* see Bogdan Denitch, "The Rebirth of Spontaneity: Il Manifesto and West European Communism," *Politics and Society* 1, no. 4 (August 1971): 463-77.

64. For a contemporary look at anarchism which indicates its influence on contemporary revolutionary theories and movements, see Irving L. Horowitz, ed., *The Anarchists* (New York: Dell Publishing Co., 1964). For Gramsci's influence, see Carl Boggs, Jr., "Gramsci's Prison Notebooks," *Socialist Revolution* 2 (September-October 1972): 79-118, and no. 12 (November-December 1972): 29-56; L. Colletti, "Gramsci and Revolution," *New Left Review* 65 (January-February 1971); R. Giachetti, "Antonio Gramsci: The Subjective Revolution," in Dick Howard and Karl E. Klare, eds., *The Unknown Dimension: European Marxism Since Lenin* (New York: Basic Books, 1972); A. Martinelli, "In Defense of the Dialectic: A. Gramsci's Theory of Revolution." *Berkeley Journal of Sociology* (1968); and A. R. Buzzi, *La Théorie politique d'Antonio Gramsci* (Louvain, Belgium: Editions Nauwelaerts, 1967).

For Rosa Luxemburg's influence see Dick Howard's introduction to Rosa Luxemburg's *Selected Political Writings* (New York: Monthly Review Press, 1971); Lelio Basso, *Rosa Luxemburg's Dialektik der Revolution* (Cologne: Europäische Verlagsanstalt, 1969); and Paul Frolich, *Rosa Luxemburg: Ideas in Action,* trans. Joanna Hoornweg (London: Pluto Press, 1972).

In light of the heterogeneity of input into the new revolutionary theories it would be correct to assert that revolutionary theories never die; they sometimes fade away to be rediscovered by new generations of revolutionaries.

65. On the theoretical level, I naturally refer to the concept and doctrine

of praxis, which has its direct roots in the writing of Georg Lukacs and particularly Antonio Gramsci. See Georg Lukacs, *History and Class Consciousness: Studies in Marxist Dialectics*, trans. Rodney Livingstone (Cambridge, Mass.: M.I.T. Press, 1971); Antonio Gramsci, *Philosophie der Praxis* (Frankfurt: 1967). According to the theory of praxis, it is "the reciprocal action of all aspects of human activity [which] reveals man as producing the conditions that produce him. Human ideas modify, through praxis, the very existential substratum of ideas themselves; history is the unfolding of man shaping his world." (J. Coulter, "Marxism and the Engels Paradox," *Socialist Register* [1971], p. 134.) For an elucidation of the concept and doctrine, see its leading theorist, the editor of the Yugoslav journal *Praxis*, Gajo Petrović, *Marxism in the Mid-Twentieth Century* (Garden City, N.Y.: Anchor Books, 1967). An orthodox critique of the doctrine of praxis is contained in a book by a British communist, John Hoffman, *Marxism and the Theory of Praxis, A Critique of Some New Versions of Old Fallacies* (New York: International Publishers, 1975).

66. See especially André Gorz, *Strategy for Labor* (New York: Beacon Press, 1967) and *Socialism and Revolution* (New York: Doubleday & Co., 1973), particularly chap. 4.

While Herbert Marcuse also deals in his writings primarily with industrialized democracies, I would define his broadly philosophical and sociological ideas as a political theory of revolution only with great hesitation and many reservations.

67. P.H. Partridge, "Contemporary Revolutionary Ideas," in Eugene Kamenka, ed., *A World in Revolution?* (Canberra: The Australian National University, 1970), p. 92.

68. Ibid., p. 98.

69. *Dissent* (Spring 1975), p. 153.

70. Alexander Dallin in Transcript 1, p. 70.

71. See especially Adam B. Ulam, *The Bolsheviks* (New York: Collier Books, 1965), where the term "terrible impatience" with respect to Lenin was coined (see particularly pp. 253-54).

72. Thus I consider Samuel Huntington's analysis of Leninism as applied to revolutionary activity vastly exaggerated in stressing its effectiveness and innovativeness. (See his "Leninism and Political Development" in *Political Order and Changing Societies*, pp. 334-43.) Huntington's propositions seem to fit much more closely the Maoist experience. See in this respect especially Franz Schurmann, *Ideology*

and Organization in Communist China, 2nd ed., enlarged (Berkeley: University of California Press, 1970), particularly chap. 2, pp. 105-72.

73. Debray, *Revolution in the Revolution?*, p. 20. It is also said that when Mao Tse-tung was given a manual on partisan warfare as a gift by Stalin, he presented it to Liu Shao-ch'i with the inscription "Read this carefully if you want to end up dead." (Quoted in Ali, *The New Revolutionaries*, p. 304.)

74. For the discussion of the "subculture" quality of the communist party's presence in French society see Ronald Tiersky, *French Communism, 1920-1972* (New York: Columbia University Press, 1974), pp. 310-30.

75. It is very important to note that changes in the communist party line were in the past considered as serious, long-range, or even fundamental changes not only by some outside observers but also by many of the participants, even some highly placed party members. This explains why every important switch in the communist parties' policies before and after World War II was not only associated normally with a purge directed from above but also with loss of allegiance among important groups of supporters. Those who stress the flexibility of communist party policies and the supposed freedom and ease of their leadership in switching major policy positions very often neglect to take seriously into account the heavy political costs that such switches usually entail. I will return later to this subject, obviously so crucial in evaluating the present and the future prospects of the West European communist movements.

76. Walter Laqueur, "Eurocommunism and its Friends," *Commentary* 62, no. 2 (August 1976): 27.

77. In considering the differences between the strategies of the French and Italian communist parties a very pertinent point was made by Sidney Tarrow during the discussion at the workshop. He stated that the two most successful parties in the southern tier of Europe, the Italian and the French, "are 'insertionist' parties whose idea is to create a broad presence within the structures of their societies and polities through social and political alliances, through an institutional presence, through a positive platform of social and political reforms, and through cultural activities designed to counteract the cultural activity of the bourgeoisie within capitalist society." The different approaches and prospects for success of the communist parties in the southern tier of Europe "do not relate to the nature and differences of their strategies themselves, but to the nature of the *adaptation*

between the strategies of these parties and the societies to which they are adapting." (Transcript 3, p. 113).

Signs of Soviet unhappiness and discomfort are numerous and unmistakable, ranging from the difficulties with the Conference of European Communist Parties in East Berlin in June 1976 (for a first-rate analysis of this conference see Kevin Devlin, "The Challenge of Eurocommunism," in *Problems of Communism* 26 [January–February 1977] : 1-20) to the large number of Soviet and East European speeches, articles, pamphlets, and even books which attack some policies, programmatic statements, and pronouncements of West European communist leaders, most notably the Italian and Spanish, at times in a veiled and at times in quite open fashion.

78. It is significant that in a recent book published by the Academy of Social Sciences (attached to the Central Committee of the Communist Party of the Soviet Union [CPSU]) on the subject of the relation of the communist parties with contemporary social democrats, as in many other Soviet books and articles on this subject, the critique of anonymous "right revisionists" and "opportunists" within the West European communist movement is as sharp and almost as frequent as the attacks on the policies of the socialists. See J. M. Krivoguz, ed., *Kommunisty i Sovremennaia Sotsial-Demokratia* (Moscow: Mysl, 1975).

79. The Soviet gain from successes of the coalitionist policies of the Western communist parties would be primarily the destabilization of NATO and the Atlantic Alliance. Even such a destabilization, on the face of it quite attractive to the Soviet leadership, should seem to the Soviets not without major pitfalls, drawbacks, and, most importantly, uncertainties with regard to the probable American reaction in the military area, its impact on détente, its influence on the so-important Soviet economic relations with the West, etc. If one adds to this the high probability (of which the Soviet leadership seems to be conscious) of the lack of Soviet leverage to influence significantly, let alone control, the behavior of the communist parties of the West in governmental coalition, and the potentially pernicious influence of independent communist parties in government on the aspirations of the Soviet East European clients, the tempting uncertainties of tomorrow may well in their minds be outweighed by the safer certainties of today.

There is much to be said in support of the astute observation by a leading European political analyst:

Is Eurocommunism going to be more of a problem for the

President of the United States or for the Secretary-General of the Communist Party of the Soviet Union? Clearly, the progress of Eurocommunism has so far raised much greater worries in the West than in the East; but both superpowers have shown misgivings as to the possible destabilizing effects of Eurocommunism on the "domestic" policies of the area of the world more directly controlled or influenced by each of them, as well as on the global balance of power. What displeases Brezhnev ought to please the American President, and vice versa. But things may not be that simple: Eurocommunism might be a challenge and a danger to both superpowers.

(Arrigo Levi, "Eurocommunism: A Foot in the Door or a Seat at the Table?," *Saturday Review,* 11 December 1976, p. 15.)

80. The most important programmatic change of the Italian, French, and Spanish communist parties is, of course, the abandonment of the idea of the "dictatorship of the proletariat." Equally important to the general renunciation of this basic programmatic principle is the relatively specific indication by the top spokesmen of the parties of what they mean by it in practice. (One should remember that in the 1945–47 period, the term "dictatorship of the proletariat" was also generally not used by most of the communist parties in Eastern Europe and was not reintroduced until after the Stalin-Tito break. In the 1945–47 period the term "people's democracy" was treated as a generic *counterpart* of the term "dictatorship of the proletariat"; after 1947 the term "people's democracy" was subsumed under the term "dictatorship of the proletariat" and was considered as one of its forms and manifestations, qualitatively similar to its other form, the "Soviet power." Yet at no time during the relatively brief disappearance of the term was it explained in detail what its absence suggested in practical terms for the future.)

For the basic programmatic statements of the Italian communist leadership, see Enrico Berlinguer, "Concluding Remarks to the XIV National Congress of the P.C.I." and "The Political Resolution Approved by the XIV National Congress of the P.C.I.," *The Italian Communists, Foreign Bulletin of the P.C.I.* (1975), nos. 2 and 3; Berlinguer, "Report to the Central Committee in Preparation for the XIV National Congress of the P.C.I., " *The Italian Communists* (1974), nos. 5 and 6; G. Chiaromonte, "Report to the Central Committee of the P.C.I.," *The Italian Communists* (1975), nos. 5 and 6; and Luigi Longo, "Remarks at the XIV National Congress of the P.C.I.," *The Italian Communists* (1976), nos. 2 and 3.

For a highly informative analysis of the changing position of the Italian Communist Party, see Heinz Timmerman, "Die Diskussion um den 'historichen Kompromiss'," *Berichte des Bundesinstituts für Ostwissenschaftliche und Internationale Studien* 21 (Cologne: 1975); and Timmerman, "Der 'historische Kompromiss'—Aspekte und Perspektiven," ibid., no. 45 (1975), especially chap. 5.

81. For the two best accounts of the internal power and policy dynamics of the main West European communist parties, see Neil McInnes, *The Communist Parties of Western Europe* (London: Oxford University Press 1975); and Donald L. M. Blackmer and Sidney Tarrow, *Communism in Italy and France* (Princeton, N.J.: Princeton University Press, 1975).

82. "Has the Revolution a Future?," *Encounter* 24, no. 2 (February 1965): 24.

83. It seems useful to recall that within German social democracy, before the great schism was organizationally finalized, the centrist "party leaders preached democracy without and based their power on semi-autocracy within the party, the left radicals preached social revolution without and democracy within." (Carl E. Schorske, *German Social Democracy 1905-1917, The Development of the Great Schism* [New York: Harper & Row, 1972], p. 323.)

84. Luxemburg, *Selected Political Writings*, p. 52.

85. For a discussion of revisionism and its connection with reformism in German social democracy, see Peter Gay, *The Dilemma of Democratic Socialism: Eduard Bernstein's Challenge to Marx* (New York: Collier Books, 1962).

86. For a brilliant account of this process see Schorske, *German Social Democracy*.

87. In my opinion, one quite fruitful way of approaching those indicators when analyzing the communist parties of Western Europe is suggested by Neil McInnes: to compare the programs and policies of the parties with the twenty-one conditions for admission to the Comintern (laid down at its Second Congress in 1920) which still retain their relevance. "A party," concludes McInnes, "that met none of the above conditions must be held to be no longer a communist party, even if it met the seventeenth condition—namely, that it *call* itself the communist party of such-and-such." (*Eurocommunism*, The Washington Papers, vol. 4, no. 37 [Beverly Hills, Calif., and London: Sage Publications, 1976], p. 8.)

88. Michael Parenti, "The Possibilities for Political Change," *Politics and Society* 1, no. 1 (November 1970): 87-88.

89. Robert C. Tucker, *The Marxian Revolutionary Idea* (New York: W.W. Norton & Co., 1969), pp. 185-86.

90. Ibid., pp. 186-88.

91. Luxemburg, *Selected Political Writings*, pp. 119-20.

92. In another passage of great clarity and force Rosa Luxemburg remarks:

> It is absolutely false and totally unhistorical to represent work for reforms as a drawn-out revolution, and revolution as a condensed series of reforms. A social transformation and a legislative reform do not differ according to their *duration* but according to their *essence*. The whole secret of historical transformations through the utilization of political power consists precisely in the change of quantitative modification into a new quality, or to speak more concretely, in the transition from one historical period, one social order, to another.
>
> He who pronounces himself in favor of the method of legal reforms *in place of and as opposed to* the conquest of political power and social revolution does not really choose a more tranquil, surer and slower road to the *same* goal. He chooses a *different* goal. Instead of taking a stand for the establishment of a new social order, he takes a stand for the surface modifications of the old order. Thus, the political views of revisionism lead to the same conclusion as the economic theories of revisionism: not to the realization of the *socialist* order, but to the reform of *capitalism*; not to the suppression of the wage system, but to the diminution of exploitation; in a word, to the elimination of the abuses of capitalism instead of to that of capitalism itself.

(Selected Political Writings, pp. 115-16).

93. The first view is represented typically by the following quotations from a left journal:

> [The West European communist parties] have not thrown out Marxism altogether, as the German Social Democrats did after the Second World War. In this respect their present position is more analogous to that of the SPD after the First World War; they continue to pay lip service to Marxism, but it is a thoroughly denatured Marxism which has been completely purged of its revolutionary essence. Given the fact that the prestige and

influence of Marxism are growing all around the world, there seems to be no reason why the CPs should follow the Social Democrats in totally renouncing their Marxist heritage. In its denatured form it should scare no one and might attract some. . . .

If, as we believe, the traditional Communist parties in the core capitalist countries have in fact gone the way of the Social Democrats, then it is all to the good that this should be clearly demonstrated and understood. One no longer castigates the Social Democrats for betraying Marxism—you cannot betray what is foreign to you—and it is high time the reformist/revisionist CPs were put in the same category. It should then be possible to get on with the difficult, urgent, and no doubt very lengthy task of reconstituting revolutionary Marxism on a solid foundation.

("The New Reformism," *Monthly Review* 28, no. 2 [June 1976] : 8, 10-11.) For a continuation of this theme see also "More on the New Reformism," *Monthly Review* 28, no. 6 (November 1976).

A fair example of the second view can be glimpsed from an article by James Burnham:

For years Brezhnev has wished for a summit meeting of all European Communist parties, East and West. It finally took place in East Berlin last spring. It was dismissed by Western commentators as a "setback" and "failure" for Brezhnev, because it did not explicitly declare for the unity of the Communist movement under Soviet hegemony.

This estimate was based on the assumption that Brezhnev not only would have liked but had expected such a declaration. (Cf. the media's finding that Jimmy Carter suffered a setback November 2.) The Brezhnevs of this world are not subject to the illusions that bemuse our commentators. If the East Berlin meeting was less than a triumph for Brezhnev, it gave him no reason to be discouraged. It was the first time since Comintern days that the Communist leaders of all Europe had met publicly as well as privately. They came together at Brezhnev's summons, and they met in the capital of the Communist state most closely tied to Moscow. . . .

Possibly Leonid Brezhnev is only an old man, whistling nostalgically in the dark. Still, history has many winding corridors. Brezhnev and the other Soviet leaders know there can't be a return to the old days of a centralized, monolithic Communist International. They also know that a monolithic Comintern is not necessary. Each Communist party and nation is inevitably modified by the local circumstances within which it functions. All that is required is an underlying solidarity—however engendered—that Communists (and all true believers in socialism, perhaps) can feel marks them off from the barbarians, and that can become the decisive impulse in a showdown. We Communists squabble among ourselves meanwhile? How could it be otherwise? But in the crunches, it's We or They.

("The International Party," *National Review* 27, no. 49 [24 December 1976] : 1395.)

The third view is much less explicit, is rarely expressed in a quotable quote, and represents rather a mood, a wish of the left liberal and the centrist socialist. Its main rationale, as it has been so often in the past, is not based on analysis (and knowledge) of the West European communist parties themselves, but rather on fear of and opposition to an American interventionist policy in Europe that opposes Eurocommunism.

94. There is, however, one complication that has first to be taken care of—namely, that the term "revolutionary transformation" is employed in its most general and neutral of meanings, that is, a change in the existing economic, political, and social system which, while adhering to the general outlines of the socialist prescription, is not bound by any specific model of the future society. Without this qualification, the differentiation between reformism and revolutionism is hopelessly lost again in the squabble between various radical groups over the question of who represents the *true* revolutionary vision. In this sense also one would consider as revolutionary those who subscribe to the traditional Soviet communist model as well as those who abhor this model and speak about democratic socialism.

95. The Soviet formulations and appetite in this respect have not changed much from the past, although their ability to satisfy the appetite has diminished sharply. For a typical Soviet formulation of "internationalism equals pro-Sovietism" see, for example, V. V. Zagladin, ed., *The World Communist Movement, Outline of Strategy and Tactics* (Moscow: Progress Publishers, 1973), chap. 11.

96. George Lichtheim, *Collected Essays* (New York: Viking Press, 1974), p. 271.

97. Irving Howe, "Socialists and Communists in European Politics," *Dissent* (Fall 1975), p. 385.

98. Neil McInnes, *Eurocommunism*, p. 6. In the discussion at the workshop Bogdan Denitch made a very similar point:

> What parties believe is clearly an almost theological question. The question really is to what extent can the parties make their beliefs hold vis-à-vis their memberships. If a party has been acting as a mass popular party for more than two decades, I am very dubious about the possibility of sending out a secret little missive in a little blue envelope saying that Comrades, tomorrow morning we stop playing footsie with the local priest and you hang him. I don't think it works that way. I think it is naive of a political scientist to think that maybe inside of a mass party of a million and a half members there is a hard little core which will press the right button at the right moment and the mask will fall off, and the familiar communist of the fifties will reemerge pristine pure. If that happens, I suspect that they will be on an average over sixty. Most of the people who are the activists in the CPI have joined when the activist organization of the party started being shaken up.

(Transcript 3, p. 140).

99. Transcript 3, p. 138.

100. For a highly interesting article on popular attitudes towards realignment of party alliances in Italy, see Giacomo Sani, "Mass Constraints on Political Realignments—Perceptions of Anti-System Parties in Italy," *British Journal of Political Science* 6, no. 1 (Summer 1976).

101. "The New Reformism," p. 10.

102. Schorske, *German Social Democracy*, p. 321.

103. The phrase comes from Edward Hyams, *The Millennium Postponed* (New York and Scarborough, Ontario: New American Library, 1973).

Notes to Chapter 2

1. See especially Polybius, *Histories*, vol. 3, book 4, trans. W. R. Paton (London: Heinemann, 1954), pp. 268-403; K. Von Fritz, *The Theory of the Mixed Constitution in Antiquity: A Critical Analysis of Polybius's Political Ideas* (New York: Columbia University Press, 1954), especially chap. 4; F. W. Walbank, *Polybius* (Berkeley: University of California Press, 1972), chap. 5; and Frank E. Manuel, *Shapes of Philo-*

sophical History (Stanford, Calif.: Stanford University Press, 1965), chap. 1. Plato's account of regime transformation in *Republic,* books 8 and 9, is a form of moral exegesis, not a theory of concrete historical change. Aristotle's account of the mechanics of regime transformation in *Politics,* book 5, does provide a theoretical account of concrete historical change but it is not in any way a directional account.

2. The dangers of accepting strong characterizations of historical process in social analysis are well brought out in Robert A. Nisbet, *Social Change and History: Aspects of the Western Theory of Development* (London: Oxford University Press, 1969).

3. See Filippo Buonarroti, *Conspiration pour l'égalité dite de Babeuf,* 2 vols. (Paris: Editions Sociales, 1957). The first edition was published in 1828. For recent scholarship on Babeuf see Colloque international de Stockholm, *Babeuf et les problèmes du Babouvisme* (Paris: Editions Sociales, 1963); Maurice Dommanget, *Sur Babeuf et la conjuration des égaux* (Paris: François Maspero, 1970); M. Reinhard, ed., *Correspondance de Babeuf avec l'Académie d'Arras, 1785–1788* (Paris: Presses Universitaires de France, 1961); R. B. Rose, "Tax Revolt and Popular Organization in Picardy 1789-91," *Past and Present* 43 (May 1969): 92-108; R. B. Rose, "Babeuf, Dictatorship and Democracy," *Historical Studies* (Australia) 15, no. 58 (April 1972): 223-36; and K. D. Tonnesson, "The Babouvists: From Utopian to Practical Socialism," *Past and Present* 22 (July 1962): 60-76. A full scholarly biography in English by Rose is forthcoming. For the career of Buonarroti himself and his role in establishing the tradition, see Elizabeth L. Eisenstein, *The First Professional Revolutionist: Filippo Michele Buonarroti (1761-1837)* (Cambridge, Mass.: Harvard University Press, 1959), and John M. Roberts, *The Mythology of the Secret Societies* (London: Secker and Warburg, 1972), pp. 222-37, 262-73, and 322-46.

4. George V. Taylor, "Revolutionary and Non-revolutionary Content in the *Cahiers* of 1789: An Interim Report," *French Historical Studies* 7, no. 4 (Fall 1972): 479-502. For effective recent discussions of the causation of the revolution see George V. Taylor, "Non-capitalist Wealth and the Origins of the French Revolution," *American Historical Review* 62, no. 2 (January 1967): 469-96, and Colin Lucas, "Nobles, Bourgeois and the Origins of the French Revolution," *Past and Present* 60 (August 1973): 84-126.

5. It was well understood even in the highest circles that the heads of kings could be cut off, and a number of conservative truths about the meaning of revolutionary processes were grasped by some. See, for

example, Laurence L. Bongie, *David Hume: Prophet of the Counter-revolution* (Oxford: Clarendon Press, 1965), pp. xv, 59, 66, 77, 123-24, and 126. What was not anticipated by prerevolutionary thinkers or actors was the momentum and the directional political dynamic of the revolution.

6. See especially Judith Shklar, *Men and Citizens: A Study of Rousseau's Social Theory* (Cambridge, England: Cambridge University Press, 1969). A vivid résumé of the implications of utopian thought in France in the eighteenth century, notably insensitive to the gap between classical utopianism and revolutionary practice, is J. L. Talmon, *The Origins of Totalitarian Democracy* (London: Mercury Books, 1961).

7. Morelly, *Code de la nature ou le véritable esprit de ses lois,* ed. Gilbert Chinard (Paris: Raymond Clavreuil, 1950) (my translation).

8. For Müntzer see Norman Cohn, *The Pursuit of the Millennium* (London: Mercury Books, 1962), pp. 251-71 (and see chap. 12 for his Anabaptist successors); and for a major study of the theological and historical context of Müntzer's project see George Huntston Williams, *The Radical Reformation* (London: Weidenfeld and Nicolson, 1962), especially chaps. 3 and 4. For Savonarola see Donald Weinstein, *Savonarola and Florence: Prophecy and Patriotism in the Renaissance* (Princeton, N.J.: Princeton University Press, 1970). For the Fifth Monarchists see B. E. Capp, *The Fifth Monarchy Men: A Study in Seventeenth Century English Millenarianism* (London: Faber and Faber, 1972).

9. See Pauline Gregg, *Free-Born John: A Biography of John Lilburne* (London: George G. Harrap, 1961); Joseph Frank, *The Levellers* (Cambridge, Mass.: Harvard University Press, 1955); and H. N. Brailsford, *The Levellers and the English Revolution,* ed. Christopher Hill (London: The Crosset Press, 1961).

10. John M. Roberts, *The Mythology* (chaps. 6-10), gives an excellent idea of the extent of complicity in constructing these stereotypes from across the political spectrum. The career of Nechayev gives the most chilling historical picture of the privatized imagination which can result. See Michael Confino, *Violence dans la violence: le débat Bakounine-Necaev* (Paris: François Maspero, 1973); Michael Confino, *Daughter of a Revolutionary: Natalie Herzen and the Bakunin-Nechayev Circle* (London: Alcove Press, 1974); and John Dunn, "The Private Problems of a Revolutionary," *The Listener* (B.B.C., London, 13 June 1974): 775-76.

11. The importance of this point is well emphasized by Michael

Freeman, "Review Article: Theories of Revolution," *British Journal of Political Science* 11 (1972): 339-59, at p. 359.

12. A partly convergent line of thought, directed at rescuing the category of individual moral action from an excessively appropriative philosophy of history, can be found in Leszek Kolakowski, "Conscience and Social Progress," in his *Marxism and Beyond: On Historical Understanding and Individual Responsibility* (London: Paladin, 1971), especially pp. 147-50.

13. Alasdair Macintyre, "Ideology, Social Science and Revolution," *Comparative Politics* 5, no. 3 (April 1973): 321-42.

14. Edmund Burke, *Reflections on the Revolution in France* (London: J. M. Dent and Sons, 1910), p. 83.

15. Erving Goffman, *Asylums: Essays on the Social Situation of Mental Patients and Other Inmates* (Garden City, N.Y.: Anchor Books, 1961); Michel Foucault, *Folie et Déraison: histoire de la folie à l'âge classique* (Paris: Librairie Plon, 1961); R. D. Laing, *The Divided Self* (Harmondsworth, England: Penguin Books, 1965); etc. For a useful criticism of the application of psychiatric categories to revolutionary political action see Isaac Kramnic, "Reflections on Revolution: Definition and Explanation in Recent Scholarship," *History and Theory* 11 (1972): 57-62.

16. Macintyre, "Ideology, Social Science and Revolution," pp. 340-42.

17. Paul Sainte-Claire Deville, *La Commune de l'An 11: vie et mort d'une Assemblée révolutionnaire* (Paris: Librairie Plon, 1946), pp. 305-9; Martyn Lyons, "The 9 Thermidor: motives and effects," *European Studies Review* 5, no. 2 (April 1975): 125-26.

18. For the objective force of the doubts in the case of Lenin see conveniently Roger Pethybridge, *The Social Prelude to Stalinism* (London: Macmillan, 1974), chaps. 1-3. For Lenin's own anxieties on the matter see Moshe Lewin, *Lenin's Last Struggle* (London: Wildwood House, 1973).

19. Even providentialist divine right was seen in its heyday as exhibiting only the legitimacy of the new regime, not that of the usurpers who had inaugurated it. See, for example, the position of Sir Robert Filmer in John Dunn, *The Political Thought of John Locke: An Historical Account of the Argument of the Two Treatises of Government* (Cambridge, England: Cambridge University Press, 1969), chap. 6.

20. See, for example, Nicos Poulantzas, *Political Power and Social*

Classes, trans. Timothy O'Hagan (London: New Left Books, 1973).
21. See Joseph de Maistre:

> The revolutionary current has taken successively different courses; and the most prominent revolutionary leaders have acquired the kind of power and renown appropriate to them only by following the demands of the moment. Once they attempted to oppose it or even to turn it from its predestined course, by isolating themselves and following their own bent, they disappeared from the scene. . . . In short, the more one examines the apparently more active personalities of the Revolution, the more one finds something passive and mechanical about them. It cannot be too often repeated that men do not at all guide the Revolution; it is the Revolution that uses men. It is well said that it has its own impetus.

Quoted from Jack Lively, ed. and trans., *The Works of Joseph de Maistre* (New York: Macmillan, 1964), pp. 49-50.

22. See, for example, Vladimir Kusin: "Reformed East European Socialism cannot as yet ensure its own sheer survival." "Socialism and Nationalism," in Leszek Kolakowski and Stuart Hampshire, eds., *The Socialist Idea: A Reappraisal* (London: Weidenfeld and Nicolson, 1974), p. 146.

23. Compare Abram Bergson, "Development under Two Systems: Comparative Productivity Growth since 1950," *World Politics* 23, no. 4 (July 1971): 579-617, and Bergson, *Planning and Productivity under Soviet Socialism* (New York: Columbia University Press, 1968), with Alec Nove, "Conclusion," in *An Economic History of the U.S.S.R.* (Harmondsworth, England: Penguin Books, 1972), and Maurice Dobb, *Soviet Economic Development since 1917*, 6th ed. (London: Routledge and Kegan Paul, 1966). A very helpful systematic attempt at comparison, now a little out of date, is Simon Kuznets, "A Comparative Appraisal," in Abram Bergson and Simon Kuznets, eds., *Economic Trends in the Soviet Union* (Cambridge, Mass.: Harvard University Press, 1963), pp. 333-82.

24. Cf. Nai-Ruenn Chen and Walter Galenson, *The Chinese Economy under Communism* (Edinburgh: Edinburgh University Press, 1969); E. L. Wheelwright and Bruce McFarlane, *The Chinese Road to Socialism: Economics of the Cultural Revolution* (Harmondsworth, England: Penguin Books, 1973); Dwight H. Perkins, *Agricultural*

Development in China, 1368-1968 (Edinburgh: Edinburgh University Press, 1968); Subramanian Swamy, "Economic Growth in China and India, 1952-1970: A Comparative Appraisal," *Economic Development and Cultural Change* 21, no. 4 (July 1973): 1-84 (especially pp. 82-83); and Gunnar Myrdal, *Asian Drama: An Inquiry into the Poverty of Nations* (New York: Pantheon Books, 1968), vol. 1, chap. 7, and vol. 3, pp. 1831-34.

25. See A. Ross Johnson, *The Transformation of Communist Ideology: The Yugoslav Case 1945-1953* (Cambridge, Mass.: M.I.T. Press, 1972), and Milovan Djilas, *The Unperfect Society: Beyond the New Class* (London: Allen and Unwin, 1972), pp. 157-58.

26. Deborah D. Milenkovitch, *Plan and Market in Yugoslav Economic Thought* (New Haven, Conn.: Yale University Press, 1971); Albert Meister, *Où va l'autogestion Yougoslave?* (Paris: Editions Anthropos, 1970); David S. Riddell, "Social Self-government: the Background of Theory and Practice in Yugoslav Socialism," *British Journal of Sociology* 19, no. 1 (March 1968): 47-75; Jiri T. Kolaja, *Workers' Councils: The Yugoslav Experience* (London: Tavistock Publications, 1965); Jan Vanek, *The Economics of Workers' Management: A Yugoslav Case Study* (London: Allen and Unwin, 1972); and Jaroslav Vanek, *The Participatory Economy: An Evolutionary Hypothesis and a Strategy for Development* (Ithaca, N.Y.: Cornell University Press, 1971).

27. Franz Schurmann, *Ideology and Organization in Communist China*, 2nd ed. (Berkeley: University of California Press, 1968); Mark Selden, *The Yenan Way in Revolutionary China* (Cambridge, Mass.: Harvard University Press, 1971); Barry M. Richman, *Industrial Society in Communist China* (New York: Vintage Books, 1972); Stuart R. Schram, ed., *Authority, Participation and Cultural Change in China* (Cambridge, England: Cambridge University Press, 1973), especially the chapters by Gray, Bastid, Sigurdson, and Howe: and Rensselaer W. Lee III, "The Politics of Technology in Communist China," in Chalmers Johnson, ed., *Ideology and Politics in Communist China* (Seattle: University of Washington Press, 1973), pp. 301-25.

28. David Huw Beynon, *Working for Ford* (Harmondsworth, England: Penguin Books, 1973).

29. Maurice Meisner, "Utopian Socialist Themes in Maoism," in John Wilson Lewis, ed., *Peasant Rebellion and Communist Revolution in Asia* (Stanford, Calif.: Stanford University Press, 1974), pp. 207-52.

30. Cf. A. Walicki, *The Controversy over Capitalism: Studies in the*

Social Philosophy of the Russian Populists (Oxford: Clarendon Press, 1969).

31. Jon Sigurdson, "Rural Industry and the Internal Transfer of Technology," in Schram, *Authority*, pp. 109-57; Jack Gray, "The Two Roads: Alternative Strategies of Social Change and Economic Growth in China," in ibid., pp. 199-232; Gray, "Mao Tse-tung's Strategy for the Collectivization of Chinese Agriculture: An Important Phase in the Development of Maoism," in Emmanuel de Kadt and Gavin Williams, eds., *Sociology and Development* (London: Tavistock Publications, 1974), pp. 39-65; Gray, "The Chinese Model: Some Characteristics of Maoist Policies for Social Change and Economic Growth," in Alec Nove and D. M. Nuti, eds., *Socialist Economics* (Harmondsworth, England: Penguin Books, 1972), pp. 491-510; and Ronald Frankenberg and Joyce Leeson, "The Sociology of Health Dilemmas in the Post-colonial World: Intermediate Technology and Medical Care in Zambia, Zaire and China," in de Kadt and Williams, *Sociology and Development*, pp. 255-78.

32. If one takes the revolutionary project as strictly as it is taken by Professor Kolakowski in his powerful essay "The Myth of Human Self-Identity," there are certainly grave doubts about the logical coherence of revolutionary ambitions, in addition to more vulgar doubts about their empirical plausibility. See "The Myth of Human Self-Identity: Unity of Civil and Political Society in Socialist Thought," in Kolakowski and Hampshire, *The Socialist Idea*, pp. 18-35.

33. Assessment of any such counterfactuals notoriously raises severe epistemological difficulties. Begging all the philosophical questions, the position assumed here is that politics consists in the choice between real historical possibilities. Very strong determinist assumptions would deny the conceptual reality (though not the experiential salience) of any choice at all: the history that has occurred was the sole and exclusive real historical possibility. Rejecting strong determinist assumptions does not involve denying that political choice is always choice between (probably not very clearly understood) limits; but it is likely to be based on the belief, as here, that in politics there are important choices to be made and that it is morally and intellectually desirable to recognize this. The technical problems of establishing the correctness of counterfactual arguments are severe. But assessing the correctness of counterfactual arguments is precisely what political judgment consists in. As historical actors we have no alternative but to attempt it as best we may.

The notion of one possible social state of affairs as superior to

another possible social state of affairs could hardly exclude altogether
considerations of utility. But it is intended here to be formally in-
determinate as between evaluative theories which permit the comparison
of possible social states of affairs. Any evaluative theory which precludes
the possibility of such comparison seems intellectually, morally, and
practically reckless to a degree. In the practical judgment of historical
possibilities intellectual sophistication has no privileged status before
the facts. An elegant example would be Hu Shih's epistemologically
sophisticated pragmatist arguments for the gradualist path in China
under the Kuomintang. See Jerome B. Grieder, *Hu Shih and the Chinese
Renaissance: Liberalism in the Chinese Revolution, 1917-37* (Cambridge,
Mass.: Harvard University Press, 1970), especially pp. 123-28. To be
rigorously pragmatic, Hu Shih ended up on Taiwan.

34. John Dunn, *Modern Revolutions: An Introduction to the Analysis
of a Political Phenomenon* (Cambridge, England: Cambridge University
Press, 1972), chap. 2.

35. Regis Debray, *Révolution dans la révolution* (Paris: François
Maspero, 1967). This is not, of course, to deny the rationality of the
Cuban revolution, but simply to emphasize its extreme improbability.
See Dunn, *Modern Revolutions*, chap. 8.

36. See Lenin in 1916: "Was there ever in history an example of a
great revolution occurring by itself, not tied to war? Of course not."
Cited by Pethybridge, *Social Prelude*, p. 77. See also A. J. Ryder,
*The German Revolution of 1918: A Study of German Socialism in
War and Revolt* (Cambridge, England: Cambridge University Press,
1967); F. L. Carsten, *Revolution in Central Europe, 1918-19* (London;
Maurice Temple Smith, 1972); Marc Ferro, "The Russian Soldier in
1917: Undisciplined, Patriotic and Revolutionary," *Slavic Review* 30,
no. 3 (September 1971): 483-512; Dietrich Geyer, "The Bolshevik
Insurrection in Petrograd," in Richard Pipes, ed., *Revolutionary Russia*
(Cambridge, Mass.: Harvard University Press, 1968), pp. 164-79.

37. Dunn, *Modern Revolutions*, chap. 4, especially p. 101.

38. See Chalmers A. Johnson, *Peasant Nationalism and Communist
Power: The Emergence of Revolutionary China 1937-1945* (Stanford,
Calif.: Stanford University Press, 1963); Donald G. Gillin, "'Peasant
Nationalism' in the History of Chinese Communism," *Journal of
Asian Studies* 23, no. 2 (February 1964): 269-89; and Dunn, *Modern
Revolutions*, chap. 3, especially pp. 90-94.

39. For a recent brief statement of Robinson and Gallagher's position
see Ronald Robinson, "Non-European Foundations of European

Imperialism: Sketch for a Theory of Collaboration," in Roger Owen and Robert Sutcliffe, *Studies in the Theory of Imperialism* (London: Longmans, 1972), pp. 118-42.

40. George Rudé, *The Crowd in the French Revolution* (Oxford: The Clarendon Press, 1959); Georges Lefebvre, "Foules révolutionnaires," in Lefebvre, ed., *Etudes sur la révolution française* (Paris: Presses Universitaires de France, 1954), pp. 271-87; Albert Soboul, *The Parisian Sans-Culottes and the French Revolution 1793-4* (Oxford: the Clarendon Press, 1964). But cf. Teddy J. Uldricks, "The 'Crowd' in the Russian Revolution: Towards Reassessing the Nature of Revolutionary Leadership," *Politics and Society* 4, no. 3 (1974): 397-413; and Marc Ferro, *The Russian Revolution of February 1917*, trans. J. L. Richards (London: Routledge and Kegan Paul, 1972), especially chap. 4 and Conclusion.

41. Improbable though the success of Castro's venture undoubtedly was, the consequences of his success were far from arbitrary. See Dunn, *Modern Revolutions*, chap. 8.

42. Dunn, *Modern Revolutions*, pp. 232 and 243.

43. This brief discussion is not an attempt to do justice to a literature which has plainly had many heterogeneous intellectual purposes: it is simply a report on what appears to illuminate some possibly idiosyncratic but personally troubling questions.

44. Compare Chalmers Johnson's *Revolution and the Social System* (Stanford, Calif.: Hoover Institution Press, 1964) and *Revolutionary Change* (London: University of London Press, 1968) with his *Autopsy on People's War* (Berkeley: University of California Press, 1973), p. 108: "I believe that it is time to take an entirely new tack in approaching this problem. We seem to suffer from too much reductionism and not enough attention to purposive action." (Time for whom?)

45. Of particular importance, plainly, was its enormous impact on the political and historical imagination of Karl Marx. See Jean Bruhat, "La Révolution française et la formation de la pensée de Marx," *Annales Historiques de la Révolution Française* 38, no. 184 (April-June 1966): 125-70, and George Lichtheim, *Marxism: An Historical and Critical Study* (London: Routledge and Kegan Paul, 1961), especially pp. 58 and 125.

46. For a fetching knockabout critique see Brian Barry, *Sociologists, Economists and Democracy* (London: Collier Macmillan Co., 1970), especially chaps. 3 and 8. Is the United Kingdom still a stable polity? How long can the United States be guaranteed to remain one?

47. Much insight might perhaps be drawn from a sensitively conducted comparative inquiry into the varying success of the Comintern's initiatives in different settings and at different times—comparative views from the Comintern periphery. The extensive and valuable body of writing on the Comintern has tended, for understandable reasons of academic division of labor, to be either rather central in its perspective or else somewhat regionally parochial.

48. For a vigorous and imaginative exploration of the significance of this point see Edward Friedman, *Backward Toward Revolution: The Chinese Revolutionary Party* (Berkeley: University of California Press, 1974).

49. This is the main argument of Dunn, *Modern Revolutions*, especially pp. 234-41.

50. Ted Robert Gurr, *Why Men Rebel* (Princeton, N.J.: Princeton University Press, 1970), and John Urry, *Reference Groups and the Theory of Revolution* (London: Routledge and Kegan Paul, 1973). Urry makes an attempt to set his use of reference-group theory within an account of structural contradictions in society at large; but it is not a very successful attempt. See also James C. Davies, "Towards a Theory of Revolution," *American Sociological Review* 27, no. 1 (February 1962): 5-13.

51. See especially the valuable article by Jeffrey Race, "Toward an Exchange Theory of Revolution," in Lewis, *Peasant Rebellion*, pp. 169-204. See also Nathan Leites and Charles Wolf., Jr., *Rebellion and Authority: An Analytic Essay on Insurgent Conflicts* (Chicago: Markham Publishing Co., 1970).

52. The prevalence of these agreeably relaxed criteria for explanatory success in historical writing was first emphasized by the philosopher William Dray in his *Laws and Explanation in History* (London: Oxford University Press, 1957), especially chap. 5.

53. Charles Tilly, "The Changing Place of Collective Violence," in Melvin Richter, ed., *Essays in Theory and History: An Approach to the Social Sciences* (Cambridge, Mass.: Harvard University Press, 1970), pp. 139-64; and "How Protest Modernized in France 1845-55," in Williams O. Aydelotte, Allan G. Bogue, and Robert William Fogel, eds., *The Dimensions of Quantitative Research in History* (London: Oxford University Press, 1972), pp. 192-255. And see Jeanne Favret, "Le Traditionalisme par excès de modernité," *Archives Européenes de Sociologie* 8, no. 1 (1967): 71-93.

54. Charles Tilly, "Does Modernization Breed Revolution?," *Comparative Politics* 5, no. 2 (April 1973): 425–47, and "Town and Country in Revolution," in Lewis, *Peasant Rebellion*, pp. 271-302, especially pp. 299-302.

55. In addition to previously cited treatments of the careers of Buonarroti and Nechayev, see especially the careers of Blanqui, Bakunin, the development of the Russian revolutionary tradition up to Lenin, and even briefly of Marx himself. See, for example, Samuel Bernstein, *Blanqui* (Paris: François Maspero, 1970); Arthur Lehning, "Bakunin's Conceptions of Revolutionary Organization and their Role: A Study of his 'Secret Societies'," in Chimen Abramsky and Beryl J. Williams, eds., *Essays in Honour of E. H. Carr* (London: Macmillan, 1974); Franco Venturi, *Roots of Revolution: A History of the Populist and Socialist Movements in Nineteenth Century Russia* (New York: Grosset & Dunlop, 1966); and "Address of the Central Committee to the Communist League," in Karl Marx and Frederick Engels, *Selected Works*, vol. 1 (Moscow: Foreign Languages Publishing House, 1958), especially pp. 110-13.

56. See especially the excellent article by Race in Lewis, *Peasant Rebellion*, pp. 169-204, and the editor's cautious and thoughtful introduction to the same volume, especially pp. 18-22.

57. See Leon Trotsky, *The History of the Russian Revolution*, trans. Max Eastman (London: Victor Gollancz, 1934), chap. 1; Louis Althusser, *Pour Marx* (Paris: François Maspero, 1966), especially pp. 92-116; Tom Kemp, *Theories of Imperialism* (London: Dennis Dobson, 1967); Roger Owen and Robert Sutcliffe, eds., *Studies in the Theory of Imperialism* (New York: Longman, 1975); and André Gunder Frank, *Latin America: Underdevelopment or Revolution* (New York: Monthly Review Press, 1969). Cf. George Lichtheim, *Imperialism* (London: Allen Lane, The Penguin Press, 1971); Benjamin J. Cohen, *The Question of Imperialism: The Political Economy of Dominance and Dependence* (London: Macmillan & Co., 1974); and V. G. Kiernan, *Marxism and Imperialism* (London: Edwin Arnold, 1974), especially chap. 1.

58. Helene Carrere d'Encausse and Stuart R. Schram, *Marxism and Asia: An Introduction with Readings* (London: Allen Lane, The Penguin Press, 1969), pp. 134-70.

59. See the outstanding article by Theda Skocpol, "A Critical Review of Barrington Moore's 'Social Origins of Dictatorship and Democracy'," *Politics and Society* 4, no. 1 (Fall 1973): 1-34.

60. But see Nicos Poulantzas, *Political Power and Social Classes*, trans. Timothy O'Hagan (Atlantic Highlands, N.J.: Humanities Press, 1975), and for more intellectually attractive versions of this style of Marxist analysis see Perry Anderson, *Passages from Antiquity to Feudalism* (Atlantic Highlands, N.J.: Humanities Press, 1975) and *Lineages of the Absolutist State* (London: New Left Books, 1975).

61. R. N. Berki, "On Marxian Thought and the Problem of International Relations," *World Politics* 24, no. 1 (October 1971): 80-105.

62. Macintyre, "Ideology," p. 332.

63. See Peter R. Odell, *Oil and World Power: Background to the Oil Crisis*, 3rd ed. (Harmondsworth, England: Penguin Books, 1974). To predict that such an event might well occur sooner or later, all that was necessary was elementary arithmetic and information which must have been available to tens of thousands of intelligent and responsible bureaucrats in dozens of different countries.

64. Tilly, in Lewis, *Peasant Rebellion*, p. 289.

65. Georges Lefebvre, *The Great Fear: Rural Panic in Revolutionary France*, trans. Joan White (London: New Left Books, 1973); Georges Lefebvre, *The Coming of the French Revolution*, trans. R. R. Palmer (New York: Vintage Books, 1957), especially chaps. 6-10; and Norman Hampson, *A Social History of the French Revolution* (London: Routledge and Kegan Paul, 1963), chap. 3.

66. David H. Pinkney, *The French Revolution of 1830* (Princeton, N.J.: Princeton University Press, 1972).

67. Richard Cobb, *Les Armées révolutionnaires: Instrument de la Terreur dans les départments Avril 1793-Floréal An 11*, 2 vols. (Paris: Mouton, 1961 and 1963), and Colin Lucas, *The Structure of the Terror: the Example of Javogues and the Loire* (London: Oxford University Press, 1973).

68. For relationships between the Bolsheviks and the railway workers in 1917 see Roger Pethybridge, *The Spread of the Russian Revolution: Essays on 1917* (London: Macmillan & Co., 1972), chap. 1. For a brief account of the development of Bolshevik military efforts during the civil war see David Footman, *Civil War in Russia* (London: Faber and Faber, 1961), especially chap. 3.

69. See Engels' 1895 Introduction to Karl Marx, *The Class Struggles in France 1848-1850*, in Marx and Engels, *Selected Works*, vol. 1 (Moscow ed.), pp. 130-34.

70. Bernard Brown, *Protest in France: Anatomy of a Revolt* (Morristown, N.J.: General Learning Press, 1974); Daniel Singer, *Prelude to a Revolution: France in May 1968* (London: Jonathan Cape, 1970); Richard Johnson, *The French Communist Party versus the Students* (New Haven, Conn.: Yale University Press, 1972); Phillipe Beneton and Jean Touchard, "Les Interprétations de la crise de Mai-Juin 1968," *Revue Française de Science Politique* 20, no. 3 (June 1970): 503-43.

71. See Michael Mann, *Consciousness and Action among the Western Working Class* (London: Macmillan & Co., 1973), and Anthony Giddens, *The Class Structure of the Advanced Societies* (London: Hutchinson and Co., 1973); and cf. Sidney Tarrow, "Sources of French Radicalism: Archaic Protest, Antibureaucratic Rebellion and Anticapitalist Revolt," mimeograph (paper presented at the first workshop on radicalism, Research Institute on International Change, Columbia University, 5 February 1975).

72. Urban guerrilla tactics do not yet appear to have produced the overthrow of any state power. But in Ulster they have already led to dramatic changes in the form of the regime. For the record of urban guerrilla enterprise see Robert Moss, *Urban Guerrillas* (London: Maurice Temple Smith, 1972); Martin Oppenheimer, *Urban Guerrillas* (Harmondsworth, England: Penguin Books, 1970); and Paul Wilkinson, *Political Terrorism* (London: Macmillan & Co., 1974).

73. Donald S. Zagoria, "Asian Tenancy Systems and Communist Mobilization of the Peasantry," in Lewis, *Peasant Rebellion*, pp. 29-60.

74. Eric R. Wolf, *Peasant Wars of the Twentieth Century* (New York: Harper & Row, 1969); Hamza Alavi, "Peasants and Revolution," in Ralph Miliband and John Saville, eds., *The Socialist Register 1965* (London: Merlin Press, 1965), pp. 244-77; Gerrit Huizer, *Peasant Rebellion in Latin America* (Harmondsworth, England: Penguin Books, 1973); Henry A. Landsberger, ed., *Rural Protest: Peasant Movements and Social Change* (London: Macmillan & Co., 1974); Joel S. Migdal, *Peasants, Politics and Revolution: Pressures towards Political and Social Change in the Third World* (Princeton, N.J.: Princeton University Press, 1974); and see now Henry A. Landsberger, "The Sources of Rural Radicalism," in Seweryn Bialer, *Radicalism in the Contemporary Age*, vol. 1, *Sources of Contemporary Radicalism* (Boulder, Colo.: Westview Press, 1977).

75. The cessation of growth in almost all capitalist economies, however temporary on this occasion in most cases, makes it natural for analysts to emphasize the causal weight of economic failure in revolutionary genesis, perhaps even to reassert its status as a putative necessary

condition. A priori it seems plausible enough that revolution is less likely at the peak of an economic boom and more likely at the bottom of an economic trough. But since the middle of the nineteenth century, when Marx prophesied that the next revolution was as certain as the next trade cycle slump (Karl Marx, "The Class Struggle in France: 1848-1850," in David Fernbach, ed., *Political Writings*, vol. 2, *Surveys from Exile* [London: Penguin Books, 1973], p. 131), it is difficult to point to a single revolution which appears to have been largely generated by cyclical economic crisis. Thus far the renewal of capitalist economic crisis has served more effectively to resuscitate the plausibility of one major tradition of revolutionary theory to those already strongly inclined to credit it than it has to show that we can in any sense *know* there to be a strong connection between purely economic crisis and revolution. The fact that the meaning of revolutionary conflict and change (like the meaning of most political conflict, actual or potential) must be analyzed largely in terms of class power does not imply that the genesis of revolutions can be at all adequately explained (let alone foreseen) by concentrating largely on economic factors.

Notes to Chapter 3

1. I will use the word "model" in a nontechnical, loose sense. I am not trying to cover the entire spectrum of Marxist views. In particular, I am dealing neither with the development of Western Marxism after Marx nor with such figures as Trotsky, Bukharin, Luxemburg, Lukacs, Gramsci, or their disciples. I am therefore not making any sweeping assertions applicable to all variants of Marxism. Nor am I here concerned with the uses of power for "revolutionary" transformation after the takeover.

2. See Alfred G. Meyer, *Marxism* (Ann Arbor: University of Michigan Press, 1963), pp. 76-77. There is no systematic Marxian study of revolution per se. While a number of complex variables are suggested in the context of discussions of socioeconomic and political change, their interrelation is not generalized. See also Klaus von Beyme, "Marxistische Revolutionstheorie," in Beyme, ed., *Empirische Revolutionsforschung* (Opladen: Westdeutscher Verlag, 1973), pp. 13-18.

3. Karl Marx, *Capital*, vol. 1 (Kerr, 1906), pp. 836-37, cited in Meyer, *Marxism*, p. 79. Marx writes in his "Contribution to the Critique of Political Economy": "It is not the consciousness of men that determines their existence, but, on the contrary, it is their social existence that

determines their consciousness. At a certain stage of their development the material productive forces of society come into contradiction with the existing productive relationships, or, what is but a legal expression for these, with the property relationships within which they had moved before. From forms of development of the productive forces these relationships are transformed into their fetters. Then an epoch of social revolution opens. With the change in the economic foundation the whole vast superstructure is more or less rapidly transformed." (Emile Burns, ed., *A Handbook of Marxism* [New York: International Publishers, 1935], p. 372.)

4. Robert C. Tucker, *The Marxian Revolutionary Idea* (New York: W.W. Norton & Co., 1970), pp. 15-18.

5. Shlomo Avineri, *The Social and Political Thought of Karl Marx* (Cambridge, England: Cambridge University Press, 1971), p. 144.

6. Ibid, p. 137. "Revolutionary *praxis* is an active and social epistemology; the unity of theory and practice emancipates man from the contemplative, alienated existence that was forced on him. . . . The understanding of existing reality is therefore a necessary condition for the possibility of revolutionizing it. . . . Only an understanding of the internal mechanism of capitalism makes the transition to socialism possible. Hence a theoretical analysis of the structure of the capitalist economy is undoubtedly the revolutionary *praxis par excellence.* The cycle is closed. " (Ibid., p. 149.)

7. "For Marx, . . . Kautsky, and Plekhanov, the definition of the revolutionary situation tended to be in social and economic terms. . . . Conditions for a socialist revolution could not exist unless capitalism had run its full course." (Andrew Janos, "The Communist Theory of State and Revolution," in Cyril E. Black and Thomas P. Thornton, eds., *Communism and Revolution* [Princeton, N.J.: Princeton University Press, 1964], pp. 30-31. For further discussion, see Meyer, *Marxism*, pp. 91-100.)

8. Meyer, *Marxism*, p. 80.

9. Avineri, *Thought of Karl Marx*, p. 144. For a discussion of the compatibility of action and inevitability in Marxism, and an analogy with the paradox of predestination in Christianity, see Robert V. Daniels, "Fate and Will in the Marxian Philosophy of History," *Journal of the History of Ideas* 21 (1960): 538-52.

10. George Lichtheim, *Marxism* (New York: Praeger Publishers, 1961), p. 58.

11. In suggesting a chain of revisionism, I am not implying that either the legitimacy or the magnitude of the adaptations in Marx and Engels was of the same order as, say, those of Stalin or Mao.

12. Meyer, *Marxism*, pp. 109-14.

13. Lichtheim, *Marxism*, p. 125.

14. Marx and Engels, *Werke* (Berlin, 1956–), vol. 7, p. 440, cited in Avineri, *Thought of Karl Marx*, p. 252.

15. Avineri, *Thought of Karl Marx*, p. 256. I am bypassing the special problem of Marx's attitude towards the Paris Commune.

16. Ibid., p. 147.

17. Ibid., p. 194. See also p. 257.

18. Marx and Engels, *Werke*, vol. 7, pp. 273-74, cited in Avineri, *Thought of Karl Marx*, p. 201.

19. Marx and Engels, *Werke*, vol. 18, p. 160; vol. 22, p. 234; vol. 24, p. 498.

20. Lichtheim, *Marxism*, pp. 127-29.

21. For another approach to conflicting patterns, or models, of revolution in Marx and Engels, and ambiguities in their approach, see Stanley Moore, *Three Tactics: The Background in Marx* (New York: Monthly Review Press, 1963). Moore sees three contrasting patterns, which he nicknames "the pattern of permanent revolution, the pattern of increasing misery, and the pattern of competing systems." One significant distinction between the first and second pattern is the shift from revolution by a minority, in the earlier Marx and Engels, to majority revolution, from about 1864 on.

22. Engels, "Draft for Communist Manifesto" (1847), cited in Meyer, *Marxism*, p. 113, and Tucker, *The Marxian Revolutionary Idea*, p. 130.

23. Marx to Kugelmann (1870), cited in Meyer, *Marxism*, p. 112. "Consequently everywhere" followed from the assumption that, since England dominated the world market, an English revolution was bound to spread abroad.

24. Avineri, *Thought of Karl Marx*, pp. 218-19; Lichtheim, *Marxism*, pp. 51-53. On Marx's views on Russia, see Paul W. Blackstock and Bert F. Hoselitz, eds., *The Russian Menace to Europe* (Glencoe, Ill.: Free Press, 1952).

25. *New York Daily Tribune*, 14 June 1853, cited in Avineri, *Thought of Karl Marx*, p. 254.

26. Marx to Sorge, 27 September 1877, cited in Avineri, *Thought of Karl Marx*, p. 256.

27. Eric Hobsbawm, *The Revolutionaries* (New York: Pantheon Books, 1973), p. 16.

28. Sidney Hook, *Marx and the Marxists* (Princeton, N.J.: Van Nostrand, 1955), p. 77.

29. See Jacques Ellul, *Autopsy of Revolution* (New York: Alfred A. Knopf, 1971), pp. 149-51. According to Lenin, revolutions "could be made conceivably anywhere and at any time. . . . Nothing remains of the concept that through analysis of the economic and social development of capitalism in a given country one may judge whether or not revolution is possible. Revolution has occurred widely outside that framework. In fact, the past fifty years have shown that any situation may be regarded, in one way or another as revolutionary. . . . What is important is that revolution becomes once more a matter primarily of will." See also Alfred G. Meyer, *Leninism* (Cambridge, Mass.: Harvard University Press, 1957), p. 117.

30. See Janos, "The Communist Theory," p. 34, and Moore, *Three Tactics*, p. 49ff.

31. Meyer, *Leninism*, p. 127.

32. It may well be that Lenin was here more strongly influenced by Trotsky and Parvus than he liked to admit.

33. Aleksei Petukhin, *Marksistko-leninskaia teoriia sotsialisticheskoi revoliutsii i dal'neishee ee razvitie XX s'ezdom* (Moscow: Znanie, 1958), pp. 5-6.

34. Cited in Wolfgang Leonhard, *Three Faces of Marxism* (New York: Holt, Rinehart and Winston, 1974), p. 61.

35. See also Dieter Hertz-Eichenrode, "Karl Marx über das Bauerntum und die Bündnisfrage," *International Review of Social History* 11 (1966): 382-402.

36. For the foregoing, see, for example, Meyer, *Leninism*, pp. 122-39. On the peasant question, see also David Mitrany, *Marx Against the Peasant* (Chapel Hill: University of North Carolina Press, 1951), and John W. Lewis, ed., *Peasant Rebellion and Communist Revolution in Asia* (Stanford, Calif.: Stanford University Press, 1974).

37. Lenin, "On the Slogan for a United States of Europe" (1915), cited in Robert C. Tucker, ed., *The Lenin Anthology* (New York: W. W. Norton & Co., 1975), p. 203.

38. This point was rationalized by the argument that "in the period of imperialism one must approach the analysis of objective and subjective conditions for revolution from the point of view of the maturity, not of individual countries, but of the world imperialist system as a whole."

39. Meyer, *Leninism*, pp. 259-65.

40. Lenin, "Better Fewer But Better" (1923), cited in Tucker, *Lenin Anthology*, p. 745.

41. Lenin, "The Downfall of the Second International" (1925); a short excerpt, with a slightly different translation, can be found in Tucker, *Lenin Anthology*, pp. 275-77. See also Lenin's "Left-Wing Communism—An Infantile Disease" (1920), in ibid., pp. 550-618.

42. Cited in Leonhard, *Three Faces*, p. 69.

43. See Janos, "The Communist Theory," pp. 32-33. See also Jan F. Triska, "A Model for Study of Soviet Foreign Policy," *American Political Science Review* 52, no. 1 (March 1958): 64-83.

44. Meyer, *Leninism*, pp. 271-72.

45. As Stalin stated in 1925, "The epoch of world revolution . . . is a whole strategic period, embracing a whole series of years, and, I dare say, even a number of decades. In the course of this period there can and must be ebbings and flowings." Cited in Historicus (George A. Morgan), "Stalin on Revolution," *Foreign Affairs* 27, no. 2 (January 1949); reprinted in Alexander Dallin, ed., *Soviet Conduct in World Affairs* (New York: Columbia University Press, 1960), p. 161.

46. Ibid., p. 159.

47. Ibid., p. 174.

48. See Tucker, *The Marxian Revolutionary Idea,* p. 138ff., for a good summary.

49. "The 1961 Party Program of the Communist Party of the Soviet Union," in Jan F. Triska, ed., *Soviet Communism: Programs and Rules* (San Francisco: Chandler Publishing Co., 1962), p. 50.

50. Stalin, *Ob osnovakh leninizma* (1924), cited in Historicus, "Stalin on Revolution," p. 156.

51. Ibid., p. 158.

52. See ibid., p. 162ff.

53. See, for example, Kermit E. McKenzie, *Comintern and World Revolution 1928-1943* (New York: Columbia University Press, 1964),

chap. 4; and Nikolai Tropkin, *Ob osnovakh strategii i taktiki leninizma* (Moscow, 1955).

54. Stalin, *Oktiabr'skaia revoliutsiia i taktika russkikh kommunistov* (1924), cited in Historicus, "Stalin on Revolution," pp. 167-68.

55. Speech to the Joint Plenum of the Central Committee and Central Control Commission of the CPSU(B), 1 August 1927, in Stalin, *Works*, vol. 10 (Moscow: Foreign Languages Publishing House, 1954), p. 53.

56. Thomas P. Thornton, "The Emergence of Communist Revolutionary Doctrine," in Black and Thornton, *Communism and Revolution*, pp. 56-57.

57. Stalin, *Oktiabr'skaia revoliutsiia,* cited in Historicus, "Stalin on Revolution," p. 173.

58. On this problem, see also Leonhard, *Three Faces*, pp. 114-22, and Janos, "The Communist Theory," p. 35ff. It is of course correct that those communist regimes which came to power without decisive Soviet assistance, such as Yugoslavia, Albania, and China, later quarreled with the USSR.

59. Cited in Leonhard, *Three Faces,* p. 163.

60. Petrukhin, *Marksistsko-leninskaia teoriia,* p. 25.

61. See, for example, Morton Schwartz, "The USSR and Leftist Regimes in Less-Developed Countries," *Survey*, no. 87 (1973), and sources cited therein; William Zimmerman, *Soviet Perspectives on International Relations* (Princeton, N.J.: Princeton University Press, 1969); Roger Kanet, "The Recent Soviet Reassessment of Developments in the Third World," *Russian Review* 27, no. 1 (January 1968): 27-41; and Elizabeth K. Valkenier, "New Trends in Soviet Economic Relations with the Third World," *World Politics* 22, no. 3 (April 1970): 415-32.

62. A. M. Rumiantsev, ed., *Nauchnyi kommunizm: slovar'* (Moscow: Politizdat, 1969), pp. 278-79.

63. See, for example, *Fundamentals of Marxism-Leninism* (Moscow: Foreign Languages Publishing House, 1963), chap. 20.

64. Rumiantsev, *Nauchnyi kommunizm*, pp. 278-80.

65. *Soviet Communism: Programs and Rules,* p. 51.

66. In the early years Soviet commentators would speak, for example, of Germany as being at the stage of the "July (1917) Days" or identify German politicians as the equivalents of Kornilov and Kerensky—

presumably on the assumption that if winter was there, spring could not be far behind.

It is worth noting that a similar ethnocentrism was displayed by the Chinese in the 1960s. Peking commentaries on particular African countries, for example, spoke of their not having reached (or having reached) the stage of "1911." Both Soviet and Chinese analyses of foreign situations appear to have ceased making references that imply a necessary parallelism of history.

67. On the recent experience in Portugal, see, for example, Tad Szulc, "Lisbon and Washington: Behind the Portuguese Revolution," *Foreign Policy*, no. 21 (Winter 1975-76).

68. For example, Aleksandr Kovalev, *Soderzhanie i zakonomernosti mirovogo revoliutsionnogo protsessa* (Moscow: Izdatel'stvo Moskovskogo Universiteta, 1974).

69. For example, Yuri Krasin, *Sociology of Revolution: A Marxist View* (Moscow: Progress Publishers, 1972). See also Jack Woddis, *New Theories of Revolution* (New York: International Publishers, 1972), and Klaus Mehnert, *Moscow and the New Left* (Berkeley: University of California Press, 1975).

70. Soviet university students, even if their hostility to imperialism and colonialism is genuine, seem to have little time for orthodox doctrine. One perceptive American exchange student reported: "I met no one at MGU (Moscow State University) who was losing sleep worrying over the world revolution, the coming of 'full communism,' or the withering away of the state. No one expected the workers of the world to unite. The Western proletariat, they knew, had a lot more to lose than its chains." William Taubman, *The View From Lenin Hills* (New York: Coward-McCann, 1967), p. 188.

71. Robert C. Tucker, "The Deradicalization of Marxist Movements," *American Political Science Review* 61, no. 2 (June 1967), reprinted as chap. 6 of his *The Marxian Revolutionary Idea.*

72. Kovalev, *Soderzhanie,* p. 3; see also pp. 51 and 61.

73. There is one respect, however, in which the Leninist legacy has been well heeded. In essence, this is the precedent set by the experience of 1917—not to pass up any opportunities for the seizure of power, whatever the theoretical preconditions. As Lenin remarked in defense against "pedantic" socialist critics, "revolutionary moments demand a maximum of flexibility." This stress on voluntarist flexibility implies a formula: "On s'engage—et puis on expliquera." See also Max Eastman,

Marx and Lenin: The Science of Revolution (New York: Boni, 1927), p. 116.

74. This does not imply a deterministic view of either Russian or Chinese historical development. Political alternatives did, after all, exist in both countries.

75. For a summary, see, for example, Chalmers Johnson, "Building a Communist Nation in China," in Robert A. Scalapino, ed., *Communist Revolution in Asia*, 2nd ed. (Englewood Cliffs, N.J.: Prentice-Hall, 1969), pp. 52-81; also Robert C. North, "Two Revolutionary Models," in A. Doak Barnett, ed., *Communist Strategies in Asia* (New York: Praeger Publishers, 1963), pp. 34-60.

76. Lin Piao, *Long Live the Victory of People's War!* (Peking: Foreign Languages Press, 1965). Even though Lin Piao, then Mao's heir-designate, later broke with Mao and was allegedly killed while escaping after an abortive conspiracy, his September 1965 piece stands as an effective and characteristic expression of Maoism at its peak. While Lin Piao has of course become the target of sharp attacks in Chinese media, many of his ideas expressed in this article remain common coin, even if currently somewhat toned down.

77. Mao Tse-tung, *Selected Works* (Peking: Foreign Languages Press, 1961-65), vol. 2, p. 272, and vol. 4, p. 428, and Peter Van Ness, *Revolution and Chinese Foreign Policy* (Berkeley: University of California Press, 1970), pp. 26-32.

78. Chalmers Johnson, *Autopsy on People's War* (Berkeley: University of California Press, 1973), p. 15.

79. "The Proletarian Revolution and Khrushchev's Revisionism (Eighth Comment On the Open Letter of the Central Committee of the CPSU)," 31 March 1964; reprinted in *The Polemic on the General Line of the International Communist Movement* (Peking: Foreign Languages Press, 1964), pp. 366-69.

80. The same line of reasoning led Peking to oppose communist participation in coalition governments they did not control, pointing to the disastrous experience in Algeria, Iraq, and Chile (in 1946—anticipating 1973!). See Leonhard, *Three Faces*, p. 236, and Tucker, *The Marxian Revolutionary Idea*, p. 143.

81. *The Polemic on the General Line*, p. 13.

82. Van Ness, *Revolution and Chinese Foreign Policy*, p. 28.

83. Li Ta-nien, "How to Appraise the History of Asia," *Peking Review*, no. 45, 5 November 1965.

84. Lin Piao, *Long Live the Victory of People's War!*, pp. 49-50.

85. *Peking Review*, no. 4, 24 January 1975, p. 24.

86. "Our basic view is: There is great disorder under heaven and the situation is excellent. The basic contradictions in the world are sharpening daily. The factors for both revolution and war are clearly increasing. ... In particular, the third world has emerged in strength. ... On the other hand, the contention for world hegemony is intensifying and strategically Europe is the focus of this contention. Such continued contention is bound to lead to a new world war. This is independent of man's will. ...

"The wind is blowing harder and harder, and nothing can prevent the storm. ... The outcome of a war is decided by the people, not by one or two new types of weapon. ... The people are the makers of history. Mankind always advances in storm and stress. The road is tortuous, the future is bright." (*Peking Review*, no. 49, 5 December 1975, p. 8.)

87. Van Ness, *Revolution and Chinese Foreign Policy*, p. 169. Soviet identification of countries as "progressive" has similarly been based essentially on foreign-policy criteria.

88. Ibid., pp. 186-87.

89. See Johnson, *Autopsy*, chap. 6.

90. Merle Goldman, "China's Debate Over Priorities," *New York Times* 23 December 1974.

91. Ivan Svitak, *The Dialectics of Marxisms* (Chico: California State University, 1975), p. 10.

92. A. James Gregor, *The Fascist Persuasion in Radical Politics* (Princeton, N.J.: Princeton University Press, 1974), pp. 5, 189-90.

Notes to Chapter 4

1. See, for example, Seymour M. Lipset, "The Changing Class Structure and Contemporary European Politics," in Stephen Graubard, ed., *A New Europe?* (Boston: Beacon Press, 1967), pp. 337-69; and Ralph Dahrendorf, *Class and Class Conflict in Industrial Society* (Stanford, Calif.: Stanford University Press, 1959).

2. Otto Kirchheimer, "The Transformation of the Western European Party Systems," in Joseph La Palombara and Myron Weiner, eds., *Political*

Parties and Political Development (Princeton, N.J.: Princeton University Press, 1966), pp. 184-200.

3. Ibid. pp. 191-92. Lipset also noted the trend towards change in the communist parties and the forces working to retard such change. See "The Changing Class Structure," pp. 353-59.

4. The exceptions pertain almost exclusively to the PCF. See, for example, Annie Kriegel, *The French Communists* (Chicago: Chicago University Press, 1972); her essay "The French Communist Party and the Fifth Republic," in Donald L. M. Blackmer and Sidney Tarrow, eds., *Communism in Italy and France* (Princeton, N.J.: Princeton University Press, 1975), pp. 69-86; and her "une nouvelle stratégie communiste," *Contrepoint* 17 (April 1975): 47-67. See also the discussion in "Table Ronde avec J. M. Domenach, Jacques Ozouf, Michel Winock and Georges Lavau," in *Esprit* (February 1975): 173-200. The strongest proponent of the view that the PCI was "antisystem" was Giovanni Sartori. See his "European Political Parties: The Case of Polarized Pluralism," in La Palombara and Weiner, *Political Parties,* pp. 147ff. In a recent essay Sartori seems to have somewhat altered his view. See "I communisti al governo, e dopo?" *Biblioteca della libertà* 51 (July-August 1974): 92-99.

5. These points will be covered more fully below. For discussions of the recent developments in the two parties see the essays in Blackmer and Tarrow, *Communism in Italy and France.*

6. A clear assumption behind this interpretation is that the shared strategic perspective is not primarily the result of policy guidelines imposed by a central source such as the Soviet Union. The theoretical roots of this perspective lie in the decisions reached at the Seventh Congress of the Third International in 1935 and, for the PCI, go back to the analysis of Antonio Gramsci. In more practical terms, a considerable amount of historical research suggests that the postwar origins of the perspective of the PCI, and perhaps the PCF, lie in policy developed at the end of World War II and the years immediately following. At that time the parties, although they may have retained revolutionary pretensions, had to develop tactics and/or strategies designed to protect and advance positions achieved in contexts in which revolutionary action would be detrimental to their interests. In subsequent years these contextual conditions have become permanent and, with varying degrees of continuity, so too has the strategic perspective designed to operate in those conditions.

7. This point has been developed for the case of the PCI by Donald

Blackmer. See his "Continuity and Change in Postwar Italian Communism," in Blackmer and Tarrow, *Communism in Italy and France.* See also Peter Lange, "Change and Choice in the Italian Communist Party" (Ph.D. diss., M.I.T., 1974), chap. 5.

8. The course of events in Chile is, of course, a sobering example for the communists in this respect. The PCI in particular has made some significant attempts to allay the fears of Italian capital and has indicated that, given the degree of state control of Italian industry today, little nationalization would be necessary were the Party to come to power. The PCF, though advocating a wider range of nationalizations, has also sought to define the limits on such a policy. On the PCF position towards the dangers of international economic pressure, see the interview with Phillippe Herzog in André Harris and Alain de Sedouy, *Voyage à l'intérieure du Parti communiste* (Paris: Maspero/Seuil, 1974), pp. 199-211.

9. On the foreign policies of the two parties see Donald L. M. Blackmer and Annie Kriegel, *The International Role of the Communist Parties of Italy and France* (Cambridge, Mass.: Center for International Affairs, Harvard University, 1975). An important aspect of this "Europeanization" of the parties is their behavior within international communist bodies. In this connection the role they played in the preparation of the all-European conference of communist parties and at the conference itself is of particular interest. Recent developments suggest the burgeoning of what has come to be called "Eurocommunism."

10. The PCI came to this realization considerably earlier than the PCF, perhaps because of Italy's retarded and distorted economic and social development and the Gramscian tradition, which is strongly influenced by the analysis of this development and its consequences for working class strategy. For the PCI, see Sidney Tarrow, *Peasant Communism in Southern Italy* (New Haven, Conn.: Yale University Press, 1967), chap. 5; for the PCF, see Jean Touchard, "Introduction à l'idéologie du Parti communiste français," and Frédéric Bon, "Structure de l'idéologie communiste," both in Bon et al., *Le communisme en France* (Paris: Armand Colin, 1969), pp. 83-106 and 107-40, respectively.

11. In this connection see Jean Ranger, "Le Parti communiste et les changements sociaux depuis la deuxième guerre mondiale," mimeographed (1972), and Stephen Hellman, "The Italian Communist Party's Alliance Strategy and the Case of the Middle Classes," in Blackmer and Tarrow, *Communism in Italy and France.* It should be evident that this point bears some resemblance to that advanced by those arguing for the evolution of the communist party to the catch-all type. I share their

perception that the communist parties have to reach a broad spectrum of social strata, but it does not necessarily follow that the strategy and behavior·of the parties must change in the manner predicted by the catch-all theorists. For a more developed discussion of this point see Lange, "Change and Choice," chap. 1.

12. On French and Italian developments in the relationship between state and business see Stuart Holland, "Europe's New Public Enterprises," Romano Prodi, "Italy," and Charles-Albert Michalet, "France," all in Raymond Vernon, ed., *Big Business and the State: Changing Relations in Western Europe* (Cambridge, Mass.: Harvard University Press, 1974).

13. The decline of the "economic collapse" perspective in the analysis of the PCF is discussed in Frédéric Bon, "Structure de l'idéologie communiste," pp. 109-17. See also theses 5-14 of the "Thèses adoptées par le XIX Congrès du Parti Communiste français," *Cahiers du Communisme* 46, nos. 2-3 (February-March 1970): 420-428, and "Résolution adoptée par le XX Congrès du Parti Communiste français," *Cahiers du Communisme*, 49, nos. 1-2 (Jan.-Feb. 1973): 415-18. For a recent PCI discussion see "Relazione al Comitato Centrale" of Enrico Berlinguer, announcing the basic platform for the PCI's Fourteenth Congress, in *L'Unità*, 11 December 1974, pp. 7-8. Once more the PCI is more advanced in this respect than the PCF. In the face of the current economic crisis, for instance, the Italian Party has gone much further than the French in attempting to develop concrete policy alternatives to counter the effects of the crisis and to prevent its recurrence.

14. In this connection see Georges Lavau, "The PCF, the State and the Revolution: An Analysis of Party Policies, Communications and Popular Culture," in Blackmer and Tarrow, *Communism in Italy and France*, and Sidney Tarrow's concluding essay in that volume. See also *Programme Commun de Gouvernement* (Paris: Flammarion, 1973), and Enrico Berlinguer, "Reflessioni sull'Italia dopo i fatti del Cile," *Rinascita* 30 (28 September, 5 and 12 October 1973).

15. For a synthetic statement of the basic points on which the parties agree, see the Joint Communiqué of Georges Marchais and Enrico Berlinguer after their meeting of November 1975, in *L'Unità*, 18 November 1975, p. 1.

16. For the PCF see "Thèses," no. 19, p. 433, and "Résolution," pp. 423-25. For the PCI see Berlinguer, "Relazione," section II-8. In general the PCF has stressed the imminence of the transformation from advanced democracy to socialism more than the PCI, but for a more cautious recent statement of Georges Marchais see "M. Marchais: je

constate qu'une majorité de Français veulent des changements limités,'' *Le Monde*, 19 June 1974, p. 13.

17. For the PCF the embodiment of this principle is the *Programme Commun*. See also, among others, ''Résolution,'' pp. 423-25. For the PCI a recent authoritative statement of this point is in Berlinguer, ''Relazione,'' section IV.

18. For the PCF the most recent and complete statement is the ''déclaration des libertés'' issued on 15 May 1975. For an analysis see *Le Monde*, 17 May 1975, p. 10. For the PCI see Berlinguer, ''Relazione,'' section III-3, and ''Tesi per il XII Congresso del PCI,'' PCI internal publication (Rome, 1968). See also the Joint Communiqué. There is no question that the PCF has been slower in its acceptance of these democratic guarantees than the Italian Party.

19. For the PCF see ''Thèses,'' section 4 and especially theses 32-34. For the PCI see Berlinguer, ''Relazione,'' section IV, as well as Berlinguer, ''Classe operaia e blocco sociale,'' *Rinascita* 28 (15 January 1971): 5-6. For a general discussion of the concepts of political and social alliances, see Lange, ''Change and Choice,'' chap. 5.

20. See ''Thèses,'' sections 2 and 4. For the PCI, see Berlinguer, ''Relazione,'' sections II and III; and also Palmiro Togliatti, ''Capitalismo e riforme di struttura,'' *Rinascita* 21 (11 July 1964). In general, the PCF's analysis of monopoly capitalism and its significance for party strategy has been more generic than that of the PCI. The latter has devoted a great deal of attention to an examination of the specific characteristics of monopoly capitalism in Italy and, more generally, to the distinctiveness of Italian economic and social structure.

21. To gain a sense of the importance placed on electoral politics by both parties one need only examine the character and intensity of their propaganda and activity before any electoral test and the way they interpret electoral results. In general, however, elections play a slightly different role for the two parties. The PCF, in alliance with socialist parties, actually foresees the prospect of winning power directly through the electoral process. The PCI, on the other hand, could, until recently, only expect electoral results to enhance the possibilities of building a political coalition in Parliament in light of the momentum created by electoral shifts. This point will be discussed at greater length later.

22. See ''Résolution,'' pp. 418-20, and the *Programme Commun*. See also Berlinguer, ''Relazione,'' sections II-IV. For a very early statement of this view in the PCI see Palmiro Togliatti, ''I compiti del partito

nella situazione attuale," a speech given in Florence on 3 October 1944 and reprinted in numerous places including *Togliatti: opere scelte* (Rome: Editori Riuniti, 1974), pp. 340-70.

23. See Ronald Tiersky, *French Communism 1920-1972* (New York: Columbia University Press, 1974), and his "Alliance Politics and Revolutionary Pretensions," in Blackmer and Tarrow, *Communism in Italy and France*, pp. 420-55. See also Kriegel, *The French Communists* and "The French Communist Party."

24. Among others see Sidney Tarrow, "Sociologie du communisme en Italie," in *Le communisme en Italie* (Paris: Armand Colin, 1974), and Donald Blackmer, "Continuity and Change." For more extensive treatments see Blackmer, *Unity in Diversity: Italian Communism and the Communist World* (Cambridge, Mass.: M.I.T. Press, 1968); Lange, "Change and Choice"; and Stephen Hellman, "Organization and Ideology in Four Italian Communist Federations" (Ph.D. diss., Yale University, 1973).

25. My discussion will largely ignore long-term historical factors which may contribute to the contemporary differences in party behavior. I do not wish to suggest by this omission that in an exhaustive explanation such factors would play no role. I do think, however, that the differences in the political and social systems of postwar France and Italy are of by far the greater importance in explaining the diverse ways the parties have implemented their common strategic perspective. More generally, it seems that an understanding of the behavior of any political party over any extended period of time must begin with an analysis of the party's general strategic goals and principles and of the constraints and incentives, created by the context in which the party operates, for the continuance of old patterns of behavior and for the development of new ones.

26. For discussions of this period see Tiersky, *French Communism*, chap. 7, and Kriegel, "The French Communist Party." See also Vincent Wright, "Presidentialism and the Parties in the French Fifth Republic," *Government and Opposition* 10 (Winter 1975): 37-41, and André Laurens and Thierry Pfister, *Les Nouveaux Communistes* (Paris: Stock, 1973).

27. In this connection see Blackmer, *Unity in Diversity*, chaps. 2, 7, and 8; Blackmer, "Continuity and Change"; Lange, "Change and Choice"; Tarrow, "Sociologie du communisme," and his concluding essay in Blackmer and Tarrow, *Communism in Italy and France;* and Hellman, "Organization and Ideology," pp. 104-18 and chap. 4.

28. For a recent discussion of these electoral dynamics see Wright, "Presidentialism." For more extensive and detailed discussions see Philip Williams, *French Politicians and Elections: 1951-1969* (Cambridge, England: Cambridge University Press, 1970), and Duncan MacRae, Jr., *Parliament, Parties and Society in France, 1946-1958* (New York: St. Martin's Press, 1967).

29. See among others, Wright, "Presidentialism"; Williams, *French Politicians*; and Philip Williams and Martin Harrison, *Politics and Society in de Gaulle's Republic* (London: Longman, 1971), especially part 3. For a discussion of recent elections see Jean Charlot, *Quand la gauche peut gagner* (Paris: Alain Moreau, 1973).

30. The parties, like political analysts more generally, could not escape an understanding of the importance of de Gaulle to the electoral alignments of the Fifth Republic during its first decade, nor could they fail to take cognizance of the importance of the Gaullist institutional reforms at both the electoral and government institutional levels. The former encouraged a belief that with de Gaulle's disappearance from the scene workers who had voted for his Union pour la Nouvelle République (UNR) might return to the left. The latter clearly showed the utility of building a single coalition on the left for both legislative and presidential elections.

31. For a discussion of the electorate in the Fourth Republic see MacRae, *Parliament, Parties and Society*, chap. 8. For a more general discussion of the characteristics of the French electorate see Philip Converse and Georges Dupeux, "Politicization of the Electorate in France and the United States," in Lewis Coser, ed., *Political Sociology* (New York: Harper Torchbooks, 1967), pp. 216-46. See also Charlot, *Quand la gauche peut gagner.*

32. The best study of the elections in postwar Italy is Giorgio Galli et al., *Il comportamento elettorale in Italia* (Bologna: Il Mulino, 1968), especially parts 1 and 2. See also Samuel Barnes, "Italy: Religion and Class in Electoral Behavior," in Richard Rose, ed., *Electoral Behavior: A Comparative Handbook* (New York: Free Press, 1974); Celso Ghini, *Il voto degli italiani* (Rome: Editori Riuniti, 1975); and on the most recent period, Giacomo Sani, "Recambio elettorale e identificazioni partitiche: verso una egemonia delle sinistre?," *Rivista Italiana di Scienze Politica* 5, no. 3 (1975).

33. In 1976 the DC maintained the same percentage in the elections for the Chamber of Deputies as it had in 1972—38.7 percent. That of the PCI rose from 27.1 percent to 34.4 percent and that of the PSI

remained constant at 9.6 percent. The big losers were the small parties of the right and center, especially the liberals and Social Democrats.

34. For a good discussion of this point see Wright, "Presidentialism," pp. 28-36. See also Charlot, *Quand la gauche peut gagner,* chap. 2. On the change in Gaullist politics under Pompidou see also a recent paper by Suzanne Berger, "France: Autonomy in Alliance," in David S. Landes, ed., *Western Europe: The Trials of Partnership* (Lexington, Mass.: Lexington Books, 1977), pp. 143-71.

35. For discussion of the DC see Giovanni Sartori, "European Political Parties." My view of the DC as a party of the center is to be contrasted with that put forward by Tarrow in his concluding essay in Blackmer and Tarrow, *Communism in Italy and France.* Tarrow argues that the postwar DC can be characterized as a party of the right. In my opinion both the electoral bases and membership bases of the DC, and the policies advocated by some of the important factions, make it a party of the center—with all the contradictions, in the Italian context, which that implies.

36. For discussions of the electoral and membership bases of the DC see Mattei Dogan, "Political Cleavage and Social Stratification in France and Italy," in Seymour M. Lipset and Stein Rokkan, eds., *Party Systems and Voter Alignments: Cross-National Perspectives* (New York: Free Press, 1967), pp. 129-96; Galli et al., *Il comportamento elettorale,* especially part 2, chaps. 2-4, and part 3, chap. 4; and Gianfranco Poggi et al., *L'Organizzazione partitica del PCI e della DC* (Bologna: Il Mulino, 1968), part 2, chaps. 5-11.

37. For a discussion of the "compromesso," see *Biblioteca della Libertà* 11 (July-August 1974), and Enrico Berlinguer, *La questione communista* (Rome: Editori Riuniti, 1975). There has sporadically been considerable debate within the PCI about what approach to adopt towards the DC. For an examination of this debate in the 1960s see Hellman, "Organization and Ideology," chap. 4. For a journalistic evaluation of recent disagreements on the issue see "Il Compromesso storico sono tre," *L'Espresso,* 9 March 1975. See also the precongressional debates conducted in columns in both *Rinascita* and *L'Unità.*

38. Following the 1976 elections Pietro Ingrao, a prominent leader of the PCI, was elected president of the Chamber of Deputies through an agreement with the DC and PSI, and consultations with the communists on the formation of the government have been undertaken in the open.

39. See the Italian press throughout 1975 and 1976.

40. For numerous examples of the PCF's polemic, one need simply peruse *L'Humanité* and/or *Le Monde* from October 1974 to October 1975. Two interesting analytical articles are Raymond Barillon, "Quelques questions," *Le Monde*, 16 October 1974, pp. 1 and 8, and Thierry Pfister, "Un nouvel équilibre s'est instauré au sein de la direction du parti communiste français," *Le Monde*, 21 November 1974, pp. 1 and 9. See also the previously cited "Table Ronde," and Ronald Tiersky, "French Communism in 1976," *Problems of Communism* 25, no. 1 (January–February 1976): 20-47.

41. On the rebuilding of the PS see Wright, "Presidentialism," pp. 39-41, and Wright and H. Machlin, "The French Socialist Party in 1973: Performance and Prospects," *Government and Opposition* 9 (Spring 1974): 123-45. Georges Lavau made similar points in three lectures on the PS given at the Center for European Studies, Harvard University, in the fall of 1974.

42. See Barillon, "Quelques questions." Lavau made a similar point in his lectures. The argument is essentially that there are voters who have traditionally voted for the PCF but who have seen that it is more propitious, from the viewpoint of advancing the interests of the left coalition, to vote for the PS as long as the communists and socialists are in electoral alliance. The reason for this is the belief that the legitimacy of the coalition is increased when the socialists look stronger than the communists. Should the two parties split, however, it is assumed that these "instrumental" voters would return to the communist fold.

43. Barillon, "Quelques questions."

44. Other than the possible, though unlikely, decision of the PS to break the coalition, the biggest risks for the PCF are that its behavior would reduce the legitimacy of the coalition as a whole by reviving old fears of Communist "tacticism" and/or that CP behavior would strengthen those elements in the PS which would be anxious to break with the Communists at the first opportune moment. These rather vague and long-run risks, however, probably did not hold much sway in the face of the immediate advantages which the tactic provided.

45. Barillon, "Quelques questions." See also "Les deux hypothèses du P.C.," *L'Express*, 28 October 1974, p. 33, and "Le débat Marchais-Mitterand," *L'Express*, 14 October 1974.

46. See, for instance, the statement of the Political Bureau of the PCF published in *L'Humanité*, 8 October 1974; also Barillon, "Quelques questions."

47. This position was developed even before the explicit change of line in October; see "'Ne pas donner l'impression qu'on va plus loin que le programme commun'," *Le Monde*, 14 June 1974, p. 7. See also the report presented by Marchais at the Twenty-First Congress of the PCF, 25 October 1974.

48. This distrust, of course, is mutual and has long historical roots. Its suppression in the early 1970s and reemergence in recent months is testimony to the importance of particular contextual political factors. In this connection, the release by the PCF in July 1975 of a previously unpublished report to the PCF Central Committee given by Marchais in 1972 is of special relevance. In that report, the party secretary expressed clearly the doubts which the PCF had about the PS even as he was recommending adoption of the *Programme Commun*. See Etienne Fajou, ed., *L'Union est un combat* (Paris: Editions Sociales, 1975), pp. 75-127.

49. There are numerous examples of the PCI's explicit attempts to highlight this theme. For a number of years, for instance, the Party has used the slogan "Without the PCI there can be no reform" and has been willing to assure the passage of reform legislation in Parliament by abstaining when members of the governmental coalition were expected to violate Party discipline and vote against the legislation. For a lengthy presentation of this Party position see Berlinguer, "Relazione."

50. It is also possible that weakening of the DC as a potential alliance partner is, in fact, the primary tactical goal of the "historical compromise," but there is no way of determining whether this is the case.

51. The analyses of the "compromise" which best bring out this dual character and are highly critical of it are those of the journal *Il Manifesto*, which has consistently argued that the pursuit of power in the near future by the PCI represents an "opportunistic" course for the Party which will constrain it to abandon its principles and the interests of the working class, but which is a natural outgrowth of the strategy pursued throughout the postwar period and of the conception of the DC inherent in that strategy. For examples see Antonio La Penn, "Dal blocco storico al compromesso storico," and Lucio Magri, "La natura della DC," both in *Biblioteca della Libertà* 11 (July–August 1974).

52. For a decidedly negative interpretation of these risks different from those already cited, see Sartori, "I communisti al governo, e dopo?"

53. See, for instance, Berlinguer, "Reflessioni sull'Italia dopo i fatti del Cile."

54. See Lange, "Change and Choice," chap. 5, for a detailed discussion of the functions of the social alliance component of communist strategy and for a description of the activities necessary if these functions are to be effectively carried out. A briefer discussion is found in his essay, "The PCI at the Local Level: A Study of Strategic Performance," in Blackmer and Tarrow, *Communism in Italy and France*, pp. 259-304. See also Tarrow, "Sociologie du communisme," for a similar discussion of the social alliance approach of the PCI, but with somewhat different emphases. While the concept of a social alliance dimension to Party strategy has been much more clearly delineated for the PCI, it is clearly also a part of the PCF's strategic perspective; see, for example, Ranger, "Le Parti communiste et les changements sociaux," and section 4 of the "Thèses."

55. Tarrow, "Sociologie du communisme."

56. This is the clear impression which emerges from a reading of the essays in the Blackmer and Tarrow volume. See especially those of Lange, Stern, and Hellman.

57. This change in the PCI's approach to the trade union confederation (Confederazione Generale Italiana del Lavoro) is a good example. For discussions of the Party-union relationship in the postwar period see Blackmer, *Unity in Diversity*, chap. 8, and Daniel Horowitz, *The Italian Labor Movement* (Cambridge, Mass.: Harvard University Press, 1963). For discussions of recent developments see Peter Weitz, "Labor and Politics in a Divided Movement," *Industrial and Labor Relations Review* 28 (January 1975): 226-42, and his "The CGIL and the PCI: From Subordination to Independent Political Force," in Blackmer and Tarrow, *Communism in Italy and France*, pp. 541-71.

58. See the essays on the PCF in the Blackmer and Tarrow volume. On the Confédération Générale du Travail (CGT) as an example of a mass organization, see George Ross, "The Confédération Générale du Travail: French Communism and French Politics" (Ph.D. diss., Harvard University, 1973).

59. Togliatti, "Ceto medio e Emilia Rossa," in *Togliatti: Opere scelte.*

60. For a discussion of communist policy towards these strata see Hellman, "The Italian Communist Party's Alliance Strategy."

61. See Ranger, "Le Parti communiste et les changements sociaux."

62. See Tarrow, *Peasant Communism.*

63. On the MODEF see Yves Tavernier, "Le Mouvement de défense des

exploitants familiaux," in Tavernier, ed., *L'univers politique des paysans* (Paris: A. Colin, 1972), pp. 467-96. For a point similar to that made here see Tarrow's concluding essay in the Blackmer and Tarrow volume.

64. See n. 57 of this chapter. See also George Ross, "Confédération Générale."

65. Ross, "Confédération Générale," and his "French Working Class Politics after May-June, 1968: A New Working Class?" (paper presented at the American Political Science Association Convention, 1973).

66. For a discussion of these developments see Peter Weitz, "Labor and Politics," and his "CGIL and PCI." See also Alessandro Pizzorno, "I sindacati nel sistema politico italiano: aspetti storici," *Rivista Trimestrale di Diritto Pubblico* 21 (1971): 1510-59.

67. See, for instance, Charlot, *Quand la gauche peut gagner*, and Converse and Dupeux, "The Politicization of the Electorate."

68. In this connection see, among others, Alexis de Tocqueville, *The Old Regime and the French Revolution* (New York: Anchor Books, 1955); Mark Kesselman, "Overinstitutionalization and Political Constraint: The Case of France," *Comparative Politics* 3 (October 1970): 21-44; and Michel Crozier, *The Stalled Society* (New York: Viking Press, 1973).

69. On the notion of subcultures and their importance in the explanation of Italian politics see, among others, Sartori, "European Political Parties"; Poggi et al., *L'Organizzazione partitica*; and Agopik Manoukian, ed., *La Presenza sociale del PCI e della DC* (Bologna: Il Mulino, 1969).

70. Manoukian, *La Presenza sociale*, Introduction and part 4.

71. For an argument which assigns more decision-making power to local government see Jean-Claude Thoenig, "State Bureaucracies and Local Government in France," (paper delivered at the Center for European Studies, Harvard University, March 1975). Even if this argument is correct, however, it pertains only to issues with specific local relevance; general policy comes from Paris.

72. See Crozier, *Stalled Society*. See also Wright, "Presidentialism," and almost any other account of the effects of the reforms instituted in the constitution of the Fifth Republic.

73. Samuel P. Huntington, *Political Order in Changing Societies* (New Haven, Conn.: Yale University Press, 1968), chap. 1 and especially pp. 8-32.

74. See Ezra Suleiman, *Politics, Power and Bureaucracy in France: The Administrative Elite* (Princeton, N.J.: Princeton University Press, 1974), especially chaps. 1 and 11-14.

75. See Crozier, *Stalled Society*, as well as part 4 of his *The Bureaucratic Phenomenon* (Chicago: University of Chicago Press, 1964).

76. On the process of regional reform in both Italy and France, and its greater extent and importance in the former, see Peter Gourevitch, "Reforming the Napoleonic State: The Creation of Regional Government in France and Italy," West European Studies Working Paper No. 16 (Cambridge, Mass.: Harvard University, 1973), and Sidney Tarrow, "Local Constraints on Regional Reform: A Comparison of Italy and France," *Comparative Politics* 7, no. 1 (October 1974): 1-36. See also Norman Kogan, "The Impact of the New Italian Regional Governments on the Structure of Power within the Parties," *Comparative Politics* 7, no. 3 (April 1975): 383-406.

77. See previous note. The contrast with France on this point is striking. While there was a massive increase in the power of the French executive in the Fifth Republic, in recent years there has been an overall decline in the relative power and initiative of the Italian executive in relation to Parliament and to the new regional organs of government.

78. Suleiman, *Politics, Power and Bureaucracy*.

79. The best case study of the use of state programs for partisan political gain is Tarrow's discussion of land reform in the early 1950s in *Peasant Communism*. On other aspects of state-party relations see Joseph La Palombara, *Interest Groups in Italian Politics* (Princeton, N.J.: Princeton University Press, 1964), and Percy Allum, *Italy: Republic without Government* (New York: W.W. Norton & Co., 1973), chaps. 4, 5, and 7.

80. The pervasiveness of the subcultural structures of the two parties is well described in Manoukian, *La Presenza sociale.* The importance of subcultural organizations to the effective functioning of PCI sections is described by Lange in "Change and Choice," chaps. 7 and 8.

81. For a clear exposition of the Party's position as early as 1947, see Togliatti, "Sui rapporti tra la Chiese e lo Stato," in *Togliatti: Opere scelte*, pp. 485-97. This is Togliatti's speech in Parliament in which he announced that contrary to the PCI's earlier stance and to that of the PSI, the communists would accept inclusion of the Lateran Pacts in the constitution.

82. It is, in fact, interesting to speculate what contribution the weakness

of political subcultures in France has made to the seemingly greater personalization and reliance on the media of electoral campaigns in that country than in Italy.

83. Such an undertaking would not only require a large number of organizational resources, but it would clearly also have a divisive impact on the PCF itself, since many members might be uncomfortable establishing real organizational alliances with social groups which, in dogmatic Marxist terms, are not seen as reliable allies in the class struggle. A sign of the potential for such divisive developments is the reaction of the base to the alliance with the PS. Though there is no hard data, a number of articles in the French press suggest that there has been considerable resistance within the PCF to the way the communist-socialist alliance has developed. Further, the pre–Twenty-first Congress debates published in various Party publications indicated in muted terms a sense of uneasiness about the ties made by the Party with the socialists.

84. Since 1947, the PCI has continually pressed for governmental decentralization and for giving greater power to the local communes. This appears to be part of the Party's general approach, which calls for the creation of as many arenas as possible in which it can exercise the strength which it derives from its organization, in order to build al-liances with other political parties and with social groups. In other words, the PCI not only seeks to develop its presence in existing struc-tures, but to increase the number of structures in which it can make its presence felt. In this connection, see Tarrow, "Sociologie du com-munisme," sections 1 and 2. See also n. 76 of this chapter.

85. During the height of the Cold War the PCI's organization took on a number of sectarian traits. These can be viewed as a rather natural response to the kind of political campaign being carried on against the Party by both the DC and other political parties, and by the church. The sectarianism was denounced by Togliatti as early as 1954 and was at the center of the internal critique of the Party's organization, devel-oped in 1956 by Togliatti and a number of other Party leaders. For a lengthy discussion of these developments, see Lange, "Change and Choice," chaps. 2-4. It should be noted, however, that even during this "sectarian" period the PCI's organization did not come to resemble the characteristic Party structure of the 1920s nor that of the PCF.

86. For an excellent discussion of the PCF's organization see Kriegel, *The French Communists.* For a look at the internal characteristics of the PCF today see Sedouy and Harris, *Voyage à l'intérieure.* Though

journalistic, the book offers a number of very interesting insights into the way the PCF operates in the contemporary period

87. For the data on the PCF through 1966, see Kriegel, *The French Communists*, pp. 32-33. In recent years estimates by observers of the PCF such as Kriegel and Lavau range around 400,000. For the PCI, see Poggi et al., *L'Organizzazione partitica*, pp. 309-16. For more recent data see the volumes entitled *Dati sulla organizzazione del partito*, published by the PCI in conjunction with the Party congresses in 1968 (Twelfth Congress), 1972 (Thirteenth Congress), and 1975 (Fifteenth Congress).

In the PCI the reversal is clear in the figures published by the Party, which most observers consider fairly reliable. The PCF has not published recent figures, but Marchais and others have referred to an organizational revival in the last few years.

88. A reference to the incident in which Togliatti established this policy can be found in Alessandro Natta, "La resistenza e la formazione del 'partito nuovo'," in Paulo Spriano et al., *Problemi di storia del Partito communista Italiano* (Rome: Editori Riuniti, 1971), pp. 57-84.

89. See Kriegel, *The French Communists*, pp. 41-44.

90. Kriegel, *The French Communists*, pp. 41-44, contains some general references to this policy. Tiersky, in his discussion of this period, is somewhat skeptical about an explanation resting on changes in internal Party policy, and argues instead that most of the decline was probably due to a general decline in the desire of Frenchmen to participate in political activity. See his *French Communism*, pp. 182-83.

91. See, for instance, Pietro Secchia, "Il Partito della rinascita," a report to the National Organizational Conference of the PCI, PCI internal document (Rome, 1947).

92. For a general discussion of PCI policy in this period see Giorgio Amendola, "Il PCI all'opposizione, la lotta contro lo scelbismo," in Spriano et al., *Problema di storia*, pp. 105-29. For an especially important speech directed towards the Catholics see Palmiro Togliatti, "Per un accordo tra communisti e cattolici per salvare la civiltà umana," in *Togliatti: Opere scelte*, pp. 644-59. (This speech is from 1954).

93. For a graphic view of the DC's campaign see the collection of Christian Democratic posters from this period recently published in Luca Romano and Paulo Scabello, *C'era una volta la DC* (Rome: Savelli, 1975).

94. See Lange, "Change and Choice," chaps. 7 and 8.

95. See Kriegel, *The French Communists*, chaps. 4 and 5. See also Tarrow's conclusion to the Blackmer and Tarrow volume, especially pp. 600-6. For data on areas of PCF electoral strength in the Third and Fourth Republics see François Goguel, *Géographie des élections Françaises sous la Troisième et la Quatrième Républiques* (Paris: Armand Colin, 1970), chaps. 3, 4, 6, and 7.

96. For the PCF see Kriegel, *The French Communists*, chap. 4, and Ranger, "Le Parti communiste et les changements sociaux." For the PCI see, among others, Hellman, "The Italian Communist Party's Alliance Strategy."

97. See n. 95 of this chapter.

98. See Tarrow's conclusion to the Blackmer and Tarrow volume, especially pp. 600-3. See also *Dati sulla organizzazione del partito,* PCI document (Rome, 1972).

99. See Tarrow, *Peasant Communism*, especially chaps. 10-13.

100. In this connection it should be noted that the concept of presence has at least three senses for the PCI: territorial, social class, and political/institutional.

101. The campaign to reinvigorate the Party's organization in the south followed on the heels of the disastrous events in Reggio Calabria in 1970-71 and, more generally, in the face of electoral results in 1970 and 1972 which suggested that the Party's strength was declining and that the neofascists were gaining in strength.

102. See Tarrow's conclusion to the Blackmer and Tarrow volume, pp. 606-14.

103. See Lange, "Change and Choice," chaps. 5, 7, and 8.

104. Ibid. See also Tarrow's conclusion to the Blackmer and Tarrow volume, pp. 606-14.

105. This argument, and the analysis which follows, is based on an incentive theory of organizations. For a more formal and systematic presentation of that theory see Peter B. Clark and James Q. Wilson, "Incentive Systems: A Theory of Organizations," *Administrative Science Quarterly* 6 (September 1961): 129-66, and Wilson, *Political Organizations* (New York: Basic Books, 1973), part 1. For an attempt to systematically test a variant of this approach on the PCI see Lange, "Change and Choice."

106. For an elaboration of this point see Wilson, *Political Organizations*, chaps. 3 and 6, and Lange, "Change and Choice," pp. 43-70.

107. Albert O. Hirschman, *Exit, Voice and Loyalty* (Cambridge, Mass.: Harvard University Press, 1970).

108. For a lengthy discussion of these points see Lange, "Change and Choice," chap. 4.

109. Ibid., chap. 8, presents detailed and systematic data on the character of participation in a random sample of PCI sections in the province of Milan.

110. Ibid., chap. 5.

111. Recent PCF and PCI behavior clearly illustrates the effects of these differences. As discussed earlier in this chapter (see the concluding pages of the section on political alliance behavior), the French Party's attacks on its socialist ally since October 1974 seem, to a considerable degree, motivated by member discontent with the blurring of the Party's distinctive role in the left coalition, and with an emerging confusion about the relationship between the goals of the *Programme Commun* and socialism. In particular, the leading role assumed by Mitterand in the 1974 presidential campaign, the electoral returns which suggested that the Party might no longer be the leader of the left, and PS discussions of the imminence of socialism, appear to have provoked anxiety that the Party was sacrificing its unique identity. This anxiety was evident in the debates prior to the Party's 1974 Congress. It also appears in somewhat different form in the 1972 Central Committee speech of Marchais. On these points see Barillon, "Quelques questions"; Pfister, "Un nouvel équilibre"; and the "Table Ronde." In contrast, the fact that the PCI continued to pursue the line of the historic compromise calling for a coalition with not a socialist but a Catholic party—despite the latter's complete rejection of such a partnership—is a sign of the flexibility available to the Party's leaders. There is little question that some members were in disagreement with the proposal, but such discontent was not strong enough to alter the Party position.

Notes to Chapter 5

1. For a general history of the new lefts in Europe, see Massimo Teodori, *Storia delle nuove sinistre in Europa (1956-1976)* (Bologna: Il Mulino, 1976). There are no comprehensive works in English on the European new lefts. See also Richard Gombin, *Les Origines du gauchisme* (Paris: Maspero/Seuil, 1971), and Ernst Fischer, "La nouvelle Gauche et l'ancienne," *Politique d'Aujourd'hui* (October 1969).

2. For Algerian events and the left in France, see Janine Cahen and Micheline Pouteau, *Una resistenza incompiuta. La guerra d'Algeria e gli anticolonialisti francesi 1954-1962*, 2 vols. (Milano: Il Saggiatore, 1964).

3. Michel Crouzet, "La Bataille des intellectuels français," *La Nef*, nos. 12-13 (October 1962-January 1963).

4. "Réunification ou réarmement," *Documents*, January 1955.

5. For a detailed study on CND see Christopher Driver, *The Disarmers, a Study in Protest* (London: Hoder and Stoughton, 1964).

6. The review *Socialisme ou Barbarie* was published from March 1949 to June 1965. A large reader of articles printed in the journal has been edited by Cornelius Castoriadis and published in twelve volumes under various titles by Union générale d'éditions, Paris.

7. See Jean-Michel Palmier, *Marcuse et la nouvelle gauche* (Paris: Belfond, 1973).

8. *Internationale Situationniste (1958-1969)*, reprint of the twelve issues of the magazine (Amsterdam: Van Gennep, 1972). See also Jean-Jacques Raspaud and Jean-Pierre Voyer, *L'internationale Situationniste: chronologie, bibliographie, protagonistes (avec un index des noms insultés)* (Paris: Editions Champ Libre, 1972).

9. René Vienet, *Enragés et situationnistes dans le mouvement des occupations* (Paris: Gallimard, 1969).

10. Jeff Nuttal, *Bomb Culture* (London: Paladin, 1968).

11. Bernhard de Vries, "Provo van binnenuit," in F. E. Frenkel, ed., *Provo, Kanttekeningen bij een deelverschijnsel* (Amsterdam: Polak & Van Gennep, 1966), and Reel van Duyn, *De Boodschap van een wijze Kabouter* (Amsterdam: Van Gennep, 1969).

12. For the importance of Vietnam in the youth revolt, see Mervin Jones, "Britain's New Model Army," *New Statesman*, 1 November 1968; Jean Lacouture, "L'Opinion française et la seconde guerre du Vietnam," *Le Monde*, 13 December 1966; and U. Bermann, R. Dutschke, W. Lefevre, and B. Rabehl, *Die Rebellion der Studenten oder die neue Opposition* (Frankfurt: Rowohlt, 1968).

13. Ben Brewster and Alexander Cockburn, "Revolt at the LSE," *New Left Review*, no. 43 (May-June 1967).

14. Kritische Universitat, *Documenti e programmi della contro-università degli studenti berlinesi* (Padua: Marsilio, 1968).

15. Carlo Oliva and Aloisio Rendi, *Il movimento studentesco e le sue lotte* (Milan: Feltrinelli, 1969).

16. Among the many books on May 1968 in Paris, the best critical documentation is Alan Schnapp and Pierre Vidal-Naquet, *The French Student Uprising* (Boston: Beacon Press, 1971).

17. Gabriel and Daniel Cohn-Bendit, *Le Gauchisme—Remède à la maladie sénile du communisme* (Hamburg: Rowohlt, 1968).

18. Raymond Williams, ed., *May Day Manifesto 1968* (Harmondsworth, England: Penguin Books, 1968).

19. G. Bornsen, *Innerparteiliche Opposition* (Hamburg: Rimge, 1969).

20. Karsten Voight, "Interview," in *Agenor*, no. 21. (May 1971).

21. Claude Hurtig, *De la SFIO au nouveau Parti Socialiste* (Paris: Colin, 1970); Jean Poperen, *La Gauche française*, 2 vols. (Paris: Fayard, 1972 and 1975); and Parti Socialiste, *Changer la Vie. Programme de gouvernment* (Paris: Flammarion, 1972).

22. Assises du socialisme, *Pour le Socialisme* (Paris: Stock, 1974).

23. Alain Krivine, *Questions sur la révolution* (Paris: Stock, 1973).

24. *Per il Communismo*, a special edition of *Il Manifesto* (rivista) 2, no. 9 (September 1970), and "Piattaforma per un movimento politico organizatto," in *Il Manifesto* (rivista) 3, nos. 3-4 (Spring-Summer 1971).

25. *La CFDT* (Paris: Maspero/Seuil, 1971).

Notes to Chapter 6

1. This contrasts with an aristocratic officer corps where most of the officer's power, status, and well-being derives from his class position as a member of the aristocracy.

2. For the political roles of the Chinese and Cuban military see Jonathan D. Pollack, "The Study of Chinese Military Politics: Towards a Framework for Analysis," and Jorge I. Dominguez, "The Civic Soldier in Cuba," both in Catherine M. Kelleher, ed., *Political Military Systems: Comparative Perspectives* (Beverly Hills, Calif.: Sage Publications, 1974), pp. 239-70 and 209-38, respectively.

3. For documentation and a more extensive discussion see Bruce M. Russett and Alfred Stepan, "The Military in America: New Parameters, New Problems, New Approaches," in Russett and Stepan, eds., *Military*

Force and American Society (New York: Harper & Row, 1973), pp. 3-14.

4. For a general discussion of the moderator model, and a specific analysis of how it broke down in the face of radicalization in Brazil, see my *The Military in Politics: Changing Patterns in Brazil* (Princeton N.J.: Princeton University Press, 1971), pp. 57-212.

5. For a more extensive discussion of corporatist versus pluralist approaches to interest groups see Philippe C. Schmitter, "Still the Century of Corporatism?" in Frederick B. Pike and Thomas Stritch, eds., *The New Corporatism: Social Political Structures in the Iberian World* (Notre Dame, Ind.: University of Notre Dame Press, 1974), pp. 85-132, especially pp. 93-98.

6. The Peruvian regime, for example, has initiated a sweeping agrarian reform that in its scope has only been exceeded in the hemisphere by Cuba; has nationalized numerous foreign holdings; and has begun novel experiments with new forms of property ownership patterns. Three short English-language overviews of the Peruvian regime are: Eric J. Hobsbawm, "Peru: The Peculiar Revolution," *The New York Review of Books*, 16 December 1971, pp. 29-36; Luigi R. Einaudi, "Revolution from Within?—Military Rule in Peru Since 1968," *Studies in Comparative International Development* 8, no. 1 (Spring 1973): 71-87; and Abraham F. Lowenthal, "Peru's 'Revolutionary Government of the Armed Forces': Background and Context," in Kelleher, *Political Military Systems,* pp. 147-59. I discuss the Brazilian regime in *The Military in Politics.* Also see Alfred Stepan, ed., *Authoritarian Brazil: Origins, Policies, and Future* (New Haven, Conn.: Yale University Press, 1973).

7. The distinction between policies of inclusion and those of exclusion has been well developed in the Latin American field. See, for example, Guillermo O'Donnell, *Modernization and Bureaucratic Authoritarianism: Studies in South American Politics,* Institute of International Studies, University of California, Politics of Modernization Series, no. 9 (Berkeley, 1973), pp. 53-114, and in particular his extended bibliographical footnote on pp. 55-56.

8. While I emphasize the differences between inclusionary corporatism and exclusionary corporatism, it should be underscored that *both* are subtypes of corporatism and thus share generic features concerning the control of interest groups by the state. This being said, it still remains that many characteristic policies, coalitional patterns, and symbols are so different that they merit classification as distinctive subtypes.

9. In addition to Peru, other cases that approximate this inclusionary approach to actual or potential radical groups are Mexico under General Cárdenas, Argentina under Colonel Perón, Brazil under the civil-military coalition led by Vargas, and possibly the current situation in Portugal.

10. Brazil since 1964 is a clear case where both conditions mentioned above played a role in the exclusionary attempt. In post-civil-war Spain condition 1 was dominant; in Argentina from 1966 to 1969 condition 2 was dominant. In Chile since 1973 conditions 1 and 2 are relevant, with 1 being the immediate cause of the exclusionary attempt.

11. Howard Handelman, "Struggle in the Andes: Peasant Political Mobilization in Peru" (Ph.D. diss., University of Wisconsin, Madison, 1971), p. 154.

12. Comité Interamericano de Desarrollo Agrícola, *Perú: Tenencia de la tierra y desarrollo socio-economico del sector agrícola* (Washington, D.C.: Pan American Union, 1966), p. 397.

13. Handelman, "Struggle in the Andes," pp. 130-38 and 154.

14. These inflation rates are calculated from data in *International Financial Statistics*, a publication of the International Monetary Fund (Washington, D.C.). The Chilean and Peruvian data are from volume 28, no. 1 (January 1975): 35; the Brazilian data from volume 19, no. 1 (January 1966): 33; and the Argentinian data from volume 21, no. 1 (January 1968): 33.

15. Perú, Ministerio de Trabajo, *Las huelgas en el Perù: 1967–1972* (Lima, 1973), p. II-2.

16. The absolute number of strikers is given in ibid., p. III-2.

17. Chilean data from International Labor Office *Yearbook of Labor Statistics* (Geneva).

18. The impact of the devaluation in military circles is discussed in Augusto Zimmerman Zavala, *El Plan Inca, objetivo: revolución peruana* (Lima: Empresa Editora del Diario Oficial "El Peruano," 1974), p. 3.

19. For Peru and Brazil see Inter-American Development Bank, *IDB Annual Report: 1972* (Washington, D.C.), p. 57. For Chile and Argentina, *IDB Annual Report: 1973* (Washington, D.C.), p. 77.

20. Inter-American Development Bank, *Economic and Social Progress in Latin America: Annual Report 1972* (Washington, D.C.), p. 4. This contrasts with Argentina, which had the third lowest in Latin America in this period (ibid., p. 4); with Brazil, which had a negative per capita

growth rate the year before the exclusionary attempt; and with the severe economic problems of Chile.

21. The only major military archive that is accessible to scholars is the *Centro de Estudios Histórico Militares del Perú*, located in Lima. The two most important army journals are *Revista Militar del Perú* and *Revista de la Escuela Superior de Guerra*. I read all the available articles in the latter since its foundation in 1954 and all in the former since World War II. Unfortunately approximately 10 percent of the issues were missing. More randomly, I also consulted other military publications such as *Actualidad Militar*. In all, I read somewhat over a thousand articles.

22. See my "The New Professionalism of Internal Warfare and Military Role Expansion," in Stepan, *Authoritarian Brazil*, pp. 47-68, for a more extensive discussion of new professionalism.

23. This content analysis is discussed in much greater detail in Stepan, *The State and Society*, chap. 4. In all, 396 articles were classified. Another coder, following the extensive definitions of each category, also independently classified the articles. We had a "coefficient of intercoder reliability" of 94.7 percent; that is, we independently placed 375 of the 396 articles in identical "old" or "new" professional categories.

24. The growing army perception of crisis has been discussed elsewhere, in my "The New Professionalism of Internal Warfare," and by Einaudi in Luigi R. Einaudi and Alfred Stepan, *Latin American Institutional Development: Changing Military Perspectives in Peru and Brazil* (Santa Monica, Calif.: The RAND Corporation, April 1971), especially pp. 21-31. This theme is also discussed in Victor Villanueva, *¿Nueva mentalidad militar en el Perú?* (Lima: Editorial Juan Mejia Baca, 1969); Julio Cotler, "Crises política y populismo militar," in José Matos Mar et al., *Perú: hoy* (Mexico: Siglo Veintiuno Editores, 1971), pp. 86-104; and François Bourricaud, "Los militares: por qué y para qué?" in Luis Mercier Vega et al., *Fuerzas Armadas, poder y cambio* (Caracas: Editorial Tiempo Nuevo, 1970), pp. 101-71.

25. He had attended the General Staff School of the French Army.

26. Lt. Col. Enrique Gallegos Venero, "¿Debe preocuparnos la guerra subversiva?," *Revista de la Escuela Superior de Guerra* 7 (January-March 1960): 18-20. In 1957 General Romero Pardo, the Director of CAEM, went to Algeria to observe the counterguerrilla campaign. Upon his return he gave a number of lectures at CAEM—"Charlas sobre

Argelia'' (2 and 3 January 1958)—that stressed the importance of the social and political aspects of revolutionary warfare and the necessity for fusion of civil and military powers in the army struggle against subversion.

27. Perú, Ministerio da Guerra, *Las guerrillas en el Perú y su repressión* (Lima: 1966), p. 80.

28. General Edgardo Mercado Jarrín, "La política y la estrategía militar en la guerra contrasubversiva en la América Latina," *Revista Militar del Perú*, no. 701 (1967), pp. 4-37, especially p. 17. Until his retirement in 1975 General Jarrín held central positions within the military government including foreign minister, minister of war, and prime minister. Mercado's theme—that the political and structural issues are more important in revolutionary warfare than purely military issues—was frequently sounded in the journals. For example, a lieutenant colonel recently back from attendance at the French General Staff School criticized the first phase of French strategy in Algeria for only paying attention to repression and neglecting socioeconomic action. See Lt. Col. Miguel de la Flor Valle, "La guerra en Algeria," *Revista de la Escuela Superior de Guerra* (October–December 1962), pp. 19-46. Like Mercado Jarrín, he became a ranking general and important cabinet minister under the military government. The Peruvian military's emphasis on structural change contributed to its skepticism about U.S. strategy in Vietnam. In this context it is significant that as early as 1967 the *Revista Militar del Perú* devoted great space to translating three long articles by Moshe Dayan in which he concluded that the United States would never be able to win in Vietnam because it offered no alternative plan of fundamental socioeconomic change.

29. In numerous speeches after taking power the military admitted that it had played the role of sustaining the oligarchy in the past. See, for example, a revealing interview with General Graham Hurtado in *Granma* (Havana), 17 September 1972, p. 2. Also see the first authorized account of the origins of the current regime, which says that the officer corps was "fed up with playing this role," in Zimmerman Zavala, *El Plan Inca*, p. 57.

30. I can afford to be schematic about the formal policies of the regime because there already exists an extensive literature on the subject. See, for example, the well-documented collection of essays on income distribution, agrarian reform, education, social property, and other policy questions in Abraham F. Lowenthal, ed., *The Peruvian Experiment: Continuity and Change Under Military Rule* (Princeton, N.J.: Princeton University Press, 1975).

31. Magali Sarfatti Larson and Arlene Eisen Bergman, *Social Stratification in Peru*, University of California, Institute of International Studies, Politics of Modernization Series, no. 5 (Berkeley, 1969), p. 262.

32. Carlos Malpica, *Los dueños del Perú*, 6th rev. ed. (Lima: Ediciones Peisa, 1974), p. 4.

33. As the then director-general of the labor communities of the ministry of industry, José Segovia, expressed it, "We want to create structures that do not produce confrontation. We want to reach a point where labor understands that to have a strike will be to strike against themselves. In the not too distant future I think the labor union tradition will decline but this can only happen if the managerial mentality of conflict with the workers also disappears." (Interview, 22 June 1972, Lima.) The chief of the presidential advisory office, General Graham Hurtado, made similar points. He said, "The goals of the Industrial Community are various. We want to create a sense of solidarity, to relieve tension. This will in turn create a stronger industrial base because development needs industrialization. We need both solidarity and development." (Meeting with social scientists, 14 June 1972, Lima.)

34. In bitter articles the Industrial Society complained that "in its 77 years of institutional life it never had faced so serious a problem," and that there was no "possibility of dialogue at high levels with the government." (*Industria Peruana: Una publicación de la Sociedad de Industrias*, no. 492-493 [1974], pp. 10-11, and no. 499 [1974], p. 25, respectively.)

35. Decreto Ley No. 18896, *Ley de Movilización Social*, 22 June 1971, articles 1 and 5. SINAMOS is the acronym for Sistema Nacional de Apoyo a la Movilización Social. The Spanish words "sin amos" mean "without masters." After 1975 SINAMOS came under increasing attack inside and outside the government, and underwent substantial reorganization and assumed a less prominent role than the above organizational law suggests.

36. While the government has received the official support of the Peruvian Communist Party, and from such revolutionary figures as Fidel Castro, a major attack from the intellectual sector of the left has been that the "verticalization" the state is introducing has the goal of destroying "class consciousness" and class organization among the workers, by preventing horizontal linkages within the working class. At present, the working class is fractionalized into separate, vertically organized

categories. The most important formulation of this critique is Julio Cotler, "Bases del Corporativismo en el Perú," *Sociedad y Política,* no. 2 (October 1972), pp. 3-12. A discussion of SINAMOS from the perspective of corporatism is James Malloy, "Authoritarianism, Corporatism and Mobilization in Peru," in Pike and Stritch, *The New Corporatism,* pp. 52-84.

Notes to Chapter 7

1. Joseph Schumpeter, *Aufsätze zur Soziologie* (Tübingen: J. C. B. Mohr, 1953), p. 225.

2. Montesquieu, *Considerations on the Causes of the Greatness of the Romans and their Decline,* trans. David Lowenthal (Ithaca, N.Y.: Cornell University Press, 1968), p. 169.

3. Alexis de Tocqueville, *The Old Régime and the French Revolution* (Garden City, N.Y.: Doubleday, 1955), p. xii, and Phillips Bradley, ed., *Democracy in America* (New York: Alfred A. Knopf, 1955) 1:6.

4. See W. G. Runciman, *Relative Deprivation and Social Justice* (Berkeley: University of California Press, 1966), p. 9ff, for development of these concepts and bibliography.

5. Recent Marxist theories of fascism have been far more careful in analyzing it as one among several emergency and authoritarian options of a capitalist system in crisis. See especially Nicos Poulantzas, *Fascism and Dictatorship,* trans. Judith White (Atlantic Highlands, N.J.: Humanities Press, 1975); also Anson G. Rabinbach, "Toward a Marxist Theory of Fascism and National Socialism," *New German Critique,* no. 4 (1974), pp. 127-53. This is an important refinement, although Marxist theory still implies the overlap of capitalist stability or cooptation with repression.

6. Friedrich Engels, "Introduction" (1895) to Karl Marx, *The Class Struggles in France, 1846 to 1850,* in Marx and Engels, *Selected Works* (Moscow, 1958) 1: 136.

7. Elie Halevy, *A History of the English People in the Nineteenth Century,* vol. 1, *England in 1815,* trans. E. I. Watkin and D. A. Barker (New York: Barnes & Noble, 1961), pp. 387ff.

8. J. H. Plumb, *The Origins of Political Stability: England 1675-1725* (Boston: Houghton Mifflin Co., 1967), and Barrington Moore, Jr., *Social Origins of Dictatorship and Democracy* (Boston: Beacon Press, 1966), pp. 3-40.

9. See, among others, E. P. Thompson, "The Moral Economy of the English Crowd in the Eighteenth Century," *Past and Present*, no. 50 (1971), pp. 76-136; Pauline Maier, "Popular Uprisings and Civil Authority in Eighteenth Century America," *William and Mary Quarterly*, 3rd ser. 27, no. 1 (1970): 3-35; George Rudé, *The Crowd in the French Revolution* (Oxford: Oxford University Press, 1959); Rudé, *The Crowd in History* (New York: John Wiley & Sons, 1964); E. J. Hobsbawn, *Primitive Rebels: Studies in Archaic Forms of Social Movement in the 19th and 20th Centuries* (New York: Praeger Publishers, 1959), pp. 108-25; Hobsbawm and Rudé, *Captain Swing* (London: Laurence and Wishart, 1969); Rudolf Stadelmann, *Soziale und politische Geschichte der Revolution von 1848* (Munich: Münchner Verlag, 1948), which analyzes those on the barricades; Ted R. Gurr and Hugh D. Graham, eds., *Violence in America: Historical and Comparative Perspectives* (New York: New American Library, 1969), including Charles Tilly, "Collective Violence in European Perspective," pp. 4-45; also Charles Tilly, Louise Tilly, and Richard Tilly, *The Rebellious Century, 1830–1930* (Cambridge, Mass.: Harvard University Press, 1975).

10. Edmund Burke, *Reflections on the Revolution in France* (London: J. M. Dent, 1958); Hippolyte Taine, *Les origines de la France contemporaine*, 12 vols. (Paris: Hachette, 1875–1885); and Vilfredo Pareto, *Les systèmes socialistes* (Paris: M. Giard, 1926).

11. For the development of the concept of civil society see Shlomo Avineri, *Hegel's Theory of the Modern State* (Cambridge, England: Cambridge University Press, 1974), pp. 141-54.

12. For the notion of congruent democracy, see Harry Eckstein, *A Theory of Stable Democracy* (Princeton, N.J.: Princeton University Press, 1961).

13. Michel Crozier, *The Bureaucratic Phenomenon* (Chicago: University of Chicago Press, 1967), and Stanley Hoffmann, "Paradoxes of the French Political Community," in his *In Search of France* (Cambridge, Mass.: Harvard University Press, 1963). See Sidney Tarrow's critique of these ideas at the first session of the workshop on radicalism, published as "From Cold War to Historic Compromise: Approaches to French and Italian Radicalism," in Seweryn Bialer, ed., *Radicalism in the Contemporary Age*, vol. 1, *Sources of Contemporary Radicalism* (Boulder, Colo.: Westview Press, 1977).

14. Joseph Schumpeter, "Imperialism," in his *Imperialism and Social*

Classes (New York: Meridian Books, 1955), and Thorstein Veblen, *Imperial Germany and the Industrial Revolution* (New York: Viking Press, 1939).

15. Samuel Huntington, *Political Order in Changing Societies* (New Haven, Conn.: Yale University Press, 1968), pp. 5, 78ff.

16. Antonio Gramsci, *Note sul Machiavelli* (Turin: G. Einaudi, 1952), pp. 66-67; see also Thomas R. Bates, "Gramsci and the Theory of Hegemony," *Journal of the History of Ideas* 36, no. 2 (1975): 351-66.

17. For August Thalheimer's "Über den Faschismus," of 1830, see Gruppe Arbeiterpolitik, *Der Faschismus in Deutschland. Analysen der KPD-Opposition aus den Jahren 1928-1933* (Frankfurt/Main: Eurpäische Verlagsanstalt, 1973), and Martin Kitchen, "August Thalheimer's Theory of Fascism," *Journal of the History of Ideas* 36, no. 1 (1973): 67-78.

18. For these themes see James O'Connor, *The Fiscal Crisis of the State* (New York: St. Martin, 1973).

19. On the other hand, the recently published *Grundrisse* suggest a much more elastic Marxist concept of surplus value as facilitated, if not created, by the agency of capital goods. See Karl Marx, *The Grundrisse*, ed. and trans. David McClellan (New York: Harper & Row, 1972), pp. 87-93; also the useful commentary by Martin Nicolaus, "The Unknown Marx," originally from *New Left Review* and now included in Robin Blackburn, ed., *Ideology in Social Science* (New York: Pantheon Books, 1972), pp. 306-33.

20. See René Rémond, *La droite en France de 1815 à nos jours* (Paris: Aubier, 1954), and Karl Mannheim, "Das konservative Denken," *Archiv für Sozialwissenschaft und Sozialpolitik* 57, nos. 1 and 2 (1927): 68-142, 470-95.

21. See, for example, Kenneth Barkin, *The Controversy over German Industrialization* (Chicago: University of Chicago Press, 1970); also Hans-Jürgen Puhle, *Agrarische Interessenpolitik und preussischer Konservatismus im wilhelminischen Reich (1893-1914)* (Hannover, Germany: Verlag für Literatur und Zeitgeschenen, 1967), and Eugene Golob, *The Méline Tariff* (New York: Columbia University Press, 1944).

22. Among many discussions of fascist ideology and especially the themes of efficiency and production, the most satisfying is Paolo Ungari, *Alfredo Rocco e l'ideologia giuridica del fascismo* (Brescia, Italy: Morcelliana, 1963). See also Charles Maier, "Between Taylorism

and Technocracy: European Ideologies and the Vision of Industrial Productivity in the 1920's," *Journal of Contemporary History* 5, no. 2 (1970): 27-61.

23. See the O.E.C.D. *Economic Surveys* by country for general government expenditure (including welfare payments and local taxes, but excluding nationalized industries). Cf. Secretariat for the Economic Commission for Europe, *Incomes in Postwar Europe: A Study of Policies, Growth, and Distribution* (Geneva, 1967), chap. 6.

24. For analyses suggestive of these trends, see Grant McConnell, *Private Power and American Democracy* (New York: Alfred A. Knopf, 1966); Theodore J. Lowi, *The End of Liberalism* (New York: W.W. Norton & Co., 1969); and Samuel Beer, *British Politics in the Collectivist Age* (New York: Alfred A. Knopf, 1965).

25. Gerald Feldman, *Army, Industry, and Labor in Germany, 1914-1918* (Princeton, N.J.: Princeton University Press, 1966); William Oualid and Charles Picquenard, *Salaires et tariffes, conventions collectives et grèves: la politique du Ministère de l'Armement* (Paris and New Haven, Conn.: Les Presses Universitaires de France and Yale University Press, 1928); E. M. H. Lloyd, *Experiments in State Control* (London: H. Milford, 1924); and Paul A. C. Koistinen, "The 'Industrial-Military Complex' in Historical Perspective: World War I," *Business History Review* 41, no. 4 (1967): 378-403.

26. See Charles S. Maier, "Strukturen kapitalistischer Stabilität in den zwanziger Jahren: Errungenschaften und Defekte," in H. A. Winkler, ed., *Organisierter Kapitalismus* (Göttingen, Germany, 1974), pp. 195-213; also *Recasting Bourgeois Europe: Stabilization in France, Germany and Italy in the Decade after World War I* (Princeton, N.J.: Princeton University Press, 1975).

27. André Gorz, *Strategy for Labor* (Boston: Beacon Press, 1967), pp. 8-19, 46-54.

28. I have drawn here on my paper, "The Political Contexts of Inflation," mimeographed (paper presented to the International Studies Association, February 1975, and the annual Cliometrics Conference, April 1975).

29. Franz Neumann, *Behemoth: The Structure and Practice of National Socialism* (New York: Harper & Row, 1966), p. 320.

30. See Stein Rokkan and Seymour Martin Lipset, "Cleavage Structures, Party Systems, and Voter Alignments: An Introduction," in Lipset and

Rokkan, eds., *Party Systems and Voter Alignments* (New York: Free Press, 1967), pp. 1-64.

31. See the chapter by Peter Lange in this volume.

32. Max Weber, *The Theory of Social and Economic Organization*, ed. and trans. Talcott Parsons (New York: Free Press, 1964), pp. 424-29.

33. I am not disputing here that working-class consciousness remains distinct—see John H. Goldthorpe, David Lockwood, Frank Bechhofer, and Jennifer Platt, *The Affluent Worker: Industrial Attitudes and Behaviour* (Cambridge, England: Cambridge University Press, 1968), and *The Affluent Worker: Political Attitudes and Behaviour* (Cambridge, England: Cambridge University Press, 1968)—but I do suggest that it may be less susceptible to radical arousal. See Gorz, *Strategy,* pp. 69-74, for a denial (yet also confirmation) of the worker-consumer split.

34. See Antonio Gramsci, *L'Ordine Nuovo* (Turin: Edinaudi, 1955), pp. 123-35 and 176-86; Karl Korsch, *Schriften zur Sozialisierung,* ed. Erich Gerlach (Frankfurt/Main: Europäische Verlagsanstalt, 1969); Max Adler, *Democratie et conseils ouvriers,* trans. Yves Bourdet (Paris, 1967); and recent writings collected by Ernest Mandel, *Contrôle Ouvrier, conseils ouvriers, autogestion* (Paris: François Maspero, 1970).

35. Hendrik De Man, *Zur Psychologie des Sozialismus* (Jena, Germany: E. Diederichs, 1926); Robert Michels, "Der Aufstieg des Faschismus in Italien," *Archiv für Sozialwissenschaft und Sozialpolitik* 52, no. 1 (1924); and Michels, "Psychologie der antikapitalistischen Massenbewegungen," *Grundriss der Sozialökonomie* 9/1 (Tübingen, Germany, 1926).

36. In the discussion of this paper during the workshop on radicalism this point was contested, and it was argued that church organizations and working-class parties had tried to organize all-embracing sports and cultural activities for their members from before 1914. Granted this amendment, I would still argue that in the case of these latter groups a secure sense of religious or class/political identity preceded the elaboration of a party structure. Catholic and socialist parties structured the lives of men and women who already belonged, if only because they felt the rejection of a "gentile" society. The right's activity, however, seems to have been aimed at transforming class orientations and not confirming them. The argument advanced in the paper requires refinement and more empirical research, to be sure, but still, I think, retains basic validity.

37. See Ira Katznelson, "Community Conflict and Capitalist Development," mimeographed (paper delivered at the 1975 American Political Science Association meetings).

38. Antonio Gramsci, *Passato e presente* (Turin, 1966), p. 287, cited by Bates, "Gramsci." For another skeptical assessment of the moral outcome of revolution as well as of its actual possibility (balanced, however, by an absence of illusion that the status quo will endure), see Barrington Moore, Jr., "Revolution in America?," *New York Review of Books*, 3 January 1969; now included in his *Reflections on the Causes of Human Misery and upon Certain Proposals to Eliminate Them* (Boston: Beacon Press, 1972), pp. 150-93.

Notes to Chapter 8

1. Ted Robert Gurr, "Persistence and Change in Political Systems, 1800-1971," *American Political Science Review* 68, no. 4 (December 1974): 1484.

2. Leon Hurwitz, "Contemporary Approaches to Political Stability," *Comparative Politics* 5, no. 3 (April 1973): 449-63, and "An Index of Democratic Stability: A Methodological Note," *Comparative Political Studies* 4, no. 1 (April 1971): 41-68. For the theory of congruence, see Harry Eckstein, *A Theory of Stable Democracy*, Princeton University, Center of International Studies, Research Monograph no. 10 (Princeton, N.J.: 10 April 1961).

3. See, for example, Ted Robert Gurr, *Why Men Rebel* (Princeton, N.J.: Princeton University Press, 1970); Hugh G. Graham and Ted Robert Gurr, eds., *Violence in America: Historical and Comparative Perspectives* (New York: Bantam Books, 1969); Samuel P. Huntington, *Political Order in Changing Societies* (New Haven, Conn.: Yale University Press, 1968); and Douglas A. Hibbs, Jr., *Mass Political Violence: A Cross-National Causal Analysis* (New York: John Wiley & Sons, 1973).

4. Francis G. Castles, "Political Stability and the Dominant Image of Society," *Political Studies* 22, no. 3 (September 1974): 293.

5. André Beteille, *Inequality and Social Change* (Delhi: Oxford University Press, 1972), pp. 14-16.

6. Donald G. Morrison and Hugh M. Stevenson, "Political Instability in Independent Black Africa: More Dimensions of Conflict Behavior Within Nations," *Journal of Conflict Resolution* 15, no. 3 (September 1971): 348.

7. For a brief summary, see Samuel P. Huntington and Jorge I. Dominguez, "Political Development," in Fred I. Greenstein and Nelson Polsby, eds., *Handbook of Political Science* (Reading, Penna.: Addison-Wesley Publishing Co., 1975), pp. 6-10, and also Hibbs, *Mass Political Violence*, and Robert P. Clark, Jr., *Development and Instability: Political Change in the Non-Western World* (Hinsdale, Ill.: Dryden Press, 1974).

8. See Zbigniew Brzezinski, *Soviet Politics: From the Future to the Past?* (New York: Research Institute on International Change, Columbia University, 1975), pp. 29-32.

9. Gurr, "Persistence and Change," pp. 1484-85.

10. See Zbigniew Brzezinski, "The Soviet Political System: Transformation or Degeneration?", *Problems of Communism* 15, no. 1 (January–February 1966): 1-15.

11. Samuel P. Huntington, "Social and Institutional Dynamics of One-Party Systems," in Samuel P. Huntington and Clement Henry Moore, eds., *Authoritarian Politics in Modern Societies* (New York: Basic Books, 1970), pp. 23-44.

12. See Samuel P. Huntington and Joan M. Nelson, *No Easy Choice: Political Participation in Developing Countries* (Cambridge, Mass.: Harvard University Press, 1976), chap. 3.

13. See Michel Crozier, Samuel P. Huntington, and Joji Watanuki, *The Crisis of Democracy* (New York: New York University Press, 1975), pp. 157-68 and passim.

14. This point has been cogently made by, among others, Walter Dean Burnham, *Critical Elections and the Mainsprings of American Politics* (New York: W. W. Norton & Co., 1970).

15. See Samuel P. Huntington, "Paradigms of American Politics: Beyond the One, the Two, and the Many," *Political Science Quarterly* 89, no. 1 (March 1974): 18-22.